THE PILLOW BOOK OF
SEI SHŌNAGON

IN TWO VOLUMES

Prepared for the Columbia College Program of
Translations from the Oriental Classics
WM. THEODORE DE BARY, Editor

Number LXXVII of the
Records of Civilization: Sources and Studies
Edited under the auspices of the
Department of History, Columbia University

THE
PILLOW BOOK OF
SEI SHŌNAGON

Translated and edited by

IVAN MORRIS

VOLUME II

NEW YORK

COLUMBIA UNIVERSITY PRESS

Published in Great Britain by
Oxford University Press, Ely House, London W. 1

Portions of this work were prepared under a grant from
the Carnegie Corporation and a contract with the U.S.
Office of Education for the production of texts to be used
in undergraduate education. The draft translations so
produced were available for use in the Columbia College
Oriental Humanities program and have subsequently
been revised and expanded for publication in the present
form.

UNESCO COLLECTION OF REPRESENTATIVE WORKS

This book
has been accepted
in the Japanese Series
of the Translations Collection
of the United Nations
Educational, Scientific, and Cultural Organization
(UNESCO)

ISBN 0-231-08977-5

Library of Congress Catalogue Card Number: 67-24962

PRINTED IN THE UNITED STATES OF AMERICA

9 8 7 6 5 4 3 2

CONTENTS

LIST OF ABBREVIATIONS viii

NOTES TO *THE PILLOW BOOK* I

APPENDIXES

1. Annual Observances and Other Ceremonies 197
2. Characters in *The Pillow Book* 199
3. Chinese Zodiac 204
4. Chronology 206
5. Finding List 217
6. Genealogies
   (*a*) Emperors and Minamotos 228 *and following p.* 232
   (*b*) Fujiwaras 228 *and following p.* 232
   (*c*) Kiyowaras 230, 234
   (*d*) Takashinas 230, 235
7. Government
   (*a*) Diagram of the central government 236
   (*b*) Offices and ranks *following p.* 236
8. Illustrations
   (*a*) Clothes 237, 241
   (*b*) Houses, furnishings, etc. 238, 242
   (*c*) Vehicles, etc. 238, 245
   (*d*) Miscellaneous 239, 246
9. Maps
   (*a*) Provinces of Japan 247, 251
   (*b*) Home provinces (Kinai) and neighbouring
       provinces 248, 252
   (*c*) Heian Kyō and its surroundings 248, 253
   (*d*) Heian Kyō 248, 254
   (*e*) Daidairi (Greater Imperial Palace) 249, 255
   (*f*) Dairi (Imperial Palace) 250, 256
   (*g*) Seiryō Den (Emperor's Residential Palace) 250, 257
10. Poems 258

BIBLIOGRAPHY 268

INDEX–GLOSSARY 270

LIST OF ABBREVIATIONS

Aston, *Shinto*   William Aston, *Shinto: The Way of the Gods*, London, 1905.

E.J.H.   R. K. Reischauer, *Early Japanese History*, Princeton, 1937.

Hyōshaku   Kaneko Motoomi, *Makura no Sōshi Hyōshaku*, Tokyo, 1927.

Ikeda-Kishigami   Ikeda Kikan and Kishigami Shinji, *Makura no Sōshi*, Nihon Koten Bungaku Taikei ed., Tokyo, 1958.

Notes de chevet   André Beaujard, *Les Notes de chevet de Séi Shōnagon'*, Paris, 1934.

Sansom, *History*   Sir George Sansom, *A History of Japan*, vol. i, London, 1958.

Shunshobon   *Shunsho Shōhon.*

S.S.S.T.   André Beaujard, *Séi Shōnagon': son temps et son œuvre*, Paris, 1934.

Tanaka   Tanaka Shigetarō, *Makura no Sōshi*, Nihon Koten Zensho ed., Tokyo, 1954.

W.P.B.   Arthur Waley, *The Pillow-Book of Sei Shōnagon*, London, 1928.

W.S.P.   Ivan Morris, *The World of the Shining Prince*, London, 1964.

THE
PILLOW BOOK OF
SEI SHŌNAGON

VOLUME II

NOTES

The famous opening words of *The Pillow Book* (*haru wa akebono*) (1) constitute an elliptical sentence. Their literal meaning is 'As for spring the dawn', but some predicate like 'is the most beautiful time of the day' must be understood. The same applies to the opening phrases of each of the four paragraphs in this section.

Two types of braziers are mentioned, one round (*hioke*), the other (2) square (*subitsu*). See Index-Glossary.

The 2nd, 6th, and 10th Months were associated with relatively few (3) of the annual observances (*nenjū gyōji*), which played a major part in the lives of the Heian aristocrats (App. 1); also, these months offered less in the way of aesthetic delights than the other nine.

It should always be remembered when reading *The Pillow Book* that there was a discrepancy, varying from seventeen to forty-five days, between the Japanese (lunar) calendar and the Western (Julian) calendar, the Japanese calendar being on an average about one month in advance of the Western. For example, the 20th day of the 12th Month in 989 (the date when Fujiwara no Kaneie became Prime Minister) corresponded to 19 January, 990, in the West; and the 13th day of the 6th Month in 1011 (the date of Emperor Ichijō's death) corresponded to 25 July.

The names of the months in pre-modern Japan were far more evocative than the prosaic First, Second, Third, etc. that I have used in my translation for the sake of convenience and in order to avoid the 'Honourable Lady Plum Blossom' type of exoticism. They and their conjectural meanings are as follows:

1st—Mutsuki (Social Month) or Moyotsuki (Sprouting Month),
2nd—Kisaragi (Clothes-Lining),
3rd—Yayoi (Ever-Growing, Germinal),
4th—Uzuki (U no Hana [white shrub] Month),
5th—Satsuki (Rice-Sprouting Month),
6th—Minazuki (Watery Month),
7th—Fumizuki (Poem-Composing Month, or [Rice Ears] Swelling Month),
8th—Hazuki (Leaf [i.e. leaf-turning] Month),
9th—Nagatsuki (Long [i.e. long nights] Month),

10th—Kaminazuki (Gods-Absent Month),
11th—Shimotsuki (Frost Month),
12th—Shiwasu (End of the Year).

The seasons were as follows: spring (*haru*) 1st-3rd Months, summer (*natsu*) 4th-6th Months, autumn (*aki*) 7th-9th Months, winter (*fuyu*) 10th-12th Months.

(4) New Year's Day was, and still is, an occasion for paying one's respects to the Emperor and to other superiors (*W.S.P.*, p. 156). It also marked an increase in one's own age, thus corresponding in some ways to the Western birthday. New Year's Day in the Heian calendar came at some time between 21 January and 19 February.

(5) *Wakana no Sekku* (the Festival of Young Herbs) was one of the seven national festivals listed in the code of 718 (see App. 1). Derived from Han China, it had been observed at the Japanese Court since the reign of Emperor Saga in the early ninth century. The 'seven herbs' (parsley, borage, etc.) were plucked and made into a gruel (*nanakusa no kayu*) which was supposed to ward off evil spirits and to protect one's health throughout the year. In the Palace a bowl of this gruel was ceremoniously presented to the Emperor (see *W.S.P.*, p. 157). (See App. 1.)

(6) Normally the grounds near the Palace were kept clear of plants, weeds, etc.; but at this time of the year it was possible to find 'young herbs', since they were hidden by the snow. (In this translation Palace with a capital P invariably refers to the Imperial Palace in Heian Kyō, App. 9d.)

(7) *Satobito* (lit. 'village people') were members of the aristocracy who lived in some part of Heian Kyō other than the Greater Imperial Palace (Daidairi). It should be remembered that a large proportion of the Court Nobles normally resided in the Palace, which was itself a small, self-contained town (*W.S.P.*, p. 25).

(8) *Aouma no Sechie* (the Festival of the Blue Horses) was an annual ceremony in which twenty-one horses from the Imperial stables were paraded before the Emperor in the great courtyard in front of the Ceremonial Palace. (See App. 1.) The custom, which had existed in ancient China, was imported to Japan early in the eighth century. Originally the horses were steel grey (hence the name 'blue'); but, since such horses were very rare and since white was the colour of

2

purity in Shintō ritual, they were replaced in the early tenth century
by white horses. To add to the confusion, the word used to describe
the horses was written for the character for 'white' but continued to be
pronounced 'blue' (*ao*).

Horses in general were connected with the Yang or Male principle
and were therefore regarded as auspicious; the fact that their colour
was, theoretically, *ao* also made them auspicious, since *ao* (in the
sense of 'green') was the traditional New Year and spring colour.

Naka no Mikado (the Central Gate): refers to the Taiken Mon, the (9)
main eastern gate of the Greater Imperial Palace (App. 9e). A great
wooden cross-beam (*tojikomi*) was fixed on the ground and joined the
two main pillars of the gate.

This visit must have taken place several years before Shōnagon (10)
entered Court service. 987 is a likely date, but some authorities prefer
986. (See App. 4.)

Tenjōbito (senior courtier): a gentleman of the 4th or 5th Rank who (11)
had the privilege of waiting in attendance on the Emperor in the
Senior Courtiers' Chamber (Tenjō no Ma); in certain special cases
gentlemen of the 6th Rank were also accorded this privilege (see note
156) and they too were known as senior courtiers.

For ranks and offices see App. 7b and *W.S.P.*, pp. 63–66. There
were eight numbered ranks below the Imperial orders (note 907).
Each was divided into Senior and Junior (*shō* and *jū*), and below the
3rd Rank each was further subdivided into Upper and Lower grades
(*jō* and *ge*). A Major Controller of the Left (Sadaiben), for example,
held the Junior 4th Rank, Upper Grade (*jū shi i jō*).

'Left Division' is an abbreviation of 'Outer Palace Guards, Left
Division' (Saemo), one of the Imperial Guards regiments in charge
of the outer gates of the Palace and also responsible for patrolling the
Palace grounds. Their guard-house (*jin*) was on the route of the Blue
Horse procession.

Tatejitomi (garden fence): a wooden lattice-work fence or screen, (12)
frequently placed out of doors (in gardens, etc.) to ensure privacy.
The present fence stood outside the Unmei Den, one of the buildings
in the Imperial Palace compound (App. 9f). It would be barely visible
from the Taiken Mon.

Tonomorizukasa (Office of Grounds): staffed by officials and servants (13)
in charge of the Imperial gardens, and also of water, lamps, firewood,

3

charcoal, etc. used in the Palace buildings. *Nyōkan* were women employed in the Office of Grounds and in other offices responsible for housekeeping duties in the Palace.

(14) *Kokonoe* (Nine-Fold Enclosure): a standard figure of speech suggesting the vast extent of the Greater Imperial Palace.

(15) On the 8th day of the 1st Month presents of silk and brocade were given to the Imperial consorts, and many of the Court ladies were promoted in rank. All those who had been so favoured went to present their formal thanks to the Emperor.

(16) *Mochigayu* (full-moon gruel): a special gruel eaten on the 15th day of the 1st Month (see *W.S.P.*, p. 158, and App. 1). Its name derived from the fact that the full moon in the lunar calendar was invariably on the 15th of the month. A stick of peeled elder-wood (*kayu no ki*) was used to stir the gruel, and it was believed that, if a woman was struck on the loins with such a stick, she would soon give birth to a male child. (N.B. the 15th of the 1st Month was also dedicated to Shintō deities representing the male element.) It therefore became customary on this day for women to run about the house hitting each other playfully with these sticks. The custom, which survived in rural districts until fairly modern times, possibly had phallic origins, and it may be related to the country dances in which the participants whacked each other with large wooden phalli.

(17) The young man was a *muko*, i.e. an adopted son-in-law. According to the traditional Japanese system, the husband was frequently adopted into his wife's family, especially when there was no son to ensure the continuance of the line. The bride normally remained at home, and the adopted husband would visit her at night (see *W.S.P.*, p. 219).

(18) According to some of the commentators, the woman was Shōnagon herself; the description (*ware wa to omoiyaru nyōbō*) certainly fits.

(19) *Jimoku* (period of appointments): here the word is used as an abbreviation of *agatameshi no jimoku*, the period from the 9th to the 11th of the 1st Month when appointments were made to official posts in the provinces, specifically to provincial governorships.

(20) *Mōshibumi* (official request): an official request for promotion submitted to the Imperial government. Normally provincial governorships went to men of the 5th Rank (see App. 7b), but sometimes

4

officials of the 4th Rank also applied for these lucrative posts. Any
young man who had reached a rank as high as the 4th or 5th was
almost certain to have a successful career (hence their confidence);
promotion to such rank was possible for a young man only if he had
powerful family connexions. The last part of this passage suggests the
important political influence that Court ladies exerted at this time.

This was the day known as Jōmi, which was associated with Winding (21)
Water banquets and displays of dolls (see *W.S.P.*, p. 160); it was also
called the Peach Festival (Momo no Sekku). (App. 1.)

Shōto (elder brothers): the context suggests that Shōnagon is referring (22)
either to Korechika or to Michiyori (see App. 6b and Index-Glossary:
Fujiwara). 'Empress' in this translation always refers to Fujiwara no
Sadako, Michitaka's daughter in whose Court Sei Shōnagon served
as lady-in-waiting.

For *naoshi* (Court cloak) see Index-Glossary. Colours of clothes in (23)
Heian literature frequently referred, not to single colours, but to
certain fashionable combinations produced by lining the costume with
material of a different colour from the outside. A 'cherry-coloured'
(*sakura*) cloak, for instance, was one whose outside was white and
whose lining was red or violet. The following chart shows the main
combinations (*kasane*) mentioned in *The Pillow Book*; but it should
be noted that Japanese experts do not agree about all the colours
involved:

Name	Translation	Colour of outside	Colour of lining
aokuchiba	green and withered leaf	yellowish green or green	green or yellowish green
aoyagi	(see *yanagi*)		
fuji	wistaria	violet or light blue	light green
hagi	clover	dark red	green
kareno	dried field	yellow	green
kōbai	red plum blossom	scarlet	violet
kurumi	walnut	yellowish red	white
matsu no ha	pine needle	greenish yellow	violet purple
sakura	cherry blossom	white	red or violet
shion	aster	purple	dark red or green
suō	sapanwood	white or light brown	dark red
tsutsuji	azalea	dark red	scarlet or green
ume	plum blossom	white	dark red
yamabuki	yellow rose	light yellowish brown	yellow or red
yanagi	willow	white	green

5

Idashiuchigi ('. . . cloak, from the bottom of which his under-robe emerges'): Heian style of allowing the bottom of one's robe (*uchigi*) to protrude below the outer cloak. Normally the *uchigi* was tucked into the *hakama* (see Index-Glossary), but in fine weather it was pulled out so that the full effect of the colour combination might be admired.

(24) *Matsuri* (the Festival): refers to the Kamo Festival, the main Shintō celebration of the year, which was observed in the middle of the 4th Month (see *W.S.P.*, p. 161, and App. 1).

(25) *Hototogisu*: usually translated as 'cuckoo'; but the *hototogisu* (*cuculus poliocephalus*) is a far more poetic type of bird with none of the cuckoo's cheeky associations, and I prefer to leave it in the original (cf. *uguisu*, note 230). The name, *hototogisu*, is an onomatopoeia derived from the bird's characteristic cry of *ho-to-to*; in Heian times people accordingly described the *hototogisu* as 'announcing its name' (*nanori su*).

(26) *Aokuchiba* (yellowish green), *futaai* (deep violet): see Index-Glossary. Clothes of these colours were worn during the Kamo Festival.

Hosobitsu (long boxes): long, narrow chest with legs, carried on a pole by two men. In Shōnagon's time lids were frequently used for carrying books, clothing, and other objects.

(27) Dyeing was one of the great arts of the Heian period, as well as a pastime for women of quality. It was done with particular care when the clothes were to be worn during the Kamo Festival. The three forms mentioned here are:

susogo (border shading), in which the material becomes darker towards the bottom of the garment,

murago (uneven shading), in which the material is dyed unevenly all over, and

makizome (rolled dyeing), in which the material is rolled up before being immersed in the dye.

(28) Women's language was traditionally far less influenced by Chinese and contained a much larger proportion of 'pure' Japanese words and constructions. In the *Sangenbon* texts the title of this section is: 'Cases in which people say the same thing, but sound different' (*onaji koto naredomo kikimimi koto naru mono*).

6

Popular Buddhist beliefs at the time included the following: 'If a NOTES (29) man becomes a priest, his father and mother are saved until the seventh generation' and 'When a child takes the Vows, nine of his relations are reborn in Heaven'. (*Hyōshaku*, p. 30.)

Yoshida Kenkō, the famous fourteenth-century writer and a monk, (30) refers to this passage in his *Tsurezuregusa* ('Essays in Idleness'): 'No one has a less enviable existence than a priest. Sei Shōnagon was indeed right when she wrote that people regarded him like a piece of wood.'

Because people consider that a priest should spend the night in prayer (31) and religious austerities.
    Sōjimono (maigre food) was a diet from which meat, fish, wine, and strong vegetables like onions and radishes were excluded.

In order to purify themselves spiritually, exorcists (*genza*) travelled (32) about the country visiting the many sacred Buddhist mountains. One of their most important pilgrimages was to Mt. Kimbu, also known as Mitake, the highest peak in Yoshino. The Shintō god of this mountain was regarded as the avatar of the Buddhist deity, Kongōshu. Another pilgrimage was to the three Shrines of Kumano, south of Yoshino (see App. 9b). The gods of these ancient Shintō shrines had, as a result of Ryobu Shinto eclecticism (*W.S.P.*, p. 93), come to be considered as avatars of various Buddhist deities.
    Travel in the Heian period was both uncomfortable and dangerous (*W.S.P.*, p. 35); hence the 'hardships' (*osoroshiki me*) of the exorcists.
    Concerning exorcism and related practices, see *W.S.P.*, pp. 135-9.

Daijin (Senior Steward). a 6th Rank post in the Office of the Empress's (33) Household (Chūgū Shiki), which was in charge of all matters relating to the Empresses (see App. 7b).
    Taira no Narimasa (see Index-Glossary) served as Governor of Tajima and later of Harima. He was a good Chinese scholar and had passed several official examinations, but it is obvious that Shōnagon did not take him very seriously.
    The events described in this section occurred towards the very end of the period covered by *The Pillow Book* (see App. 4). It was in the 8th Month of 999 that Empress Sadako moved from the Palace to Narimasa's house in the 3rd Ward. The move was necessitated by her pregnancy, which made her ritually unclean (see *W.S.P.*, p. 94) and therefore unable to stay under the same roof as the Emperor. The palace in the 2nd Ward, where she would normally have gone, had

burnt down and she was obliged to move into Narimasa's comparatively modest residence.

Four-pillared gates could normally be built only by men of the 2nd Rank or above (*W.S.P.*, p. 65). Because of the Empress's visit, however, Narimasa had been given special permission to add two extra pillars to his gate.

(34) *Birōge no kuruma* (palm-leaf carriage): large ox-carriage used on formal occasions and so called because it was covered with palm-leaf (*birō*). (See *W.S.P.*, p. 36, and App. 8c.)

(35) *Jige* (. . . of lower rank): a gentleman of the nobility who was not of a rank to attend the Emperor in the Senior Courtiers' Chamber (cf. *tenjōbito*, note 11).

(36) Yü Kung (Ukō) of the Former Han dynasty was so proud of his son, Ting Kuo (Teikoku), that he ordered a specially high gate to be built in front of his house; this was to permit the passage of the great retinues that he knew would one day accompany the young man. Narimasa, even though he has 'strayed along these paths' (i.e. the paths of Chinese scholarship), seems to be mixing up the name of the son and that of the father (who was not nearly so well known); Shōnagon does not take him up on the mistake—an interesting omission in view of her reputation for being learned (cf. the end of note 196). The story of Yü Kung's gate is told in the *Han shu* (*Kansho*), the history of the Former Han dynasty by Pan Ku (A.D. 32–92), and also in the popular T'ang collection of anecdotes, *Meng Ch'iu* (*Mōgyū*).

It should be borne in mind that Shōnagon and Narimasa are speaking to each other through a screen, and that they are kneeling on straw mats in the same room as the Empress but at such a distance from her that she cannot hear their conversation (*W.S.P.*, pp. 30–31).

(37) A *Shinji* (scholar), which *E.J.H.* gives as 'Bachelor of Literature', was a graduate of the Imperial University (Daigaku) who had passed certain official examinations but who had not yet been awarded the title of Doctor (Hakase).

(38) The layout of Heian rooms is difficult to suggest in translation; I have tried to make my equivalents as simple as possible, and in a few cases I have slightly abbreviated the descriptions when the details seemed unimportant.

The term *hisashi*, which is particularly intractable to smooth translation, referred to a part of the room that was covered by deep

eaves and that was situated between the main part of the room (*moya*)
and the open veranda (*sunoko*); the *hisashi* was normally divided into
four sections, designated as north, south, east, and west (in the present
passage we find *nishi no hisashi*, i.e. western *hisashi*). 'Ante-room' is
probably the best equivalent, but it must be remembered that the
hisashi was not a separate room. Latticed shutters or gratings (*shitomi*)
divided the *hisashi* from the *sunoko*; the *moya* was separated from the
hisashi by blinds or curtains or both (see App. 8b). Great importance
was attached to geographical directions both within and outside the
house (see *W.S.P.*, p. 124); the position of the boltless sliding door
is identified by no less than three directions: *higashi* (east) *no tai no*
nishi (west) *no hisashi kakete aru kita* (north) *no sōji*. Since the Heian
house faced south, *kita* (north) can conveniently be translated as
'back' (of the house, room, etc.).

Kichō (curtain of state or curtain-frame): a piece of furniture that (39)
played a most important part in Heian domestic architecture. Clearly
analogous to the Indian pardah, it was a portable frame, about six feet
high and of variable width, which supported opaque hangings (*kata-*
bira) and was mainly aimed at protecting the women of the house
from being seen by men and strangers (*W.S.P.*, p. 32, and App. 8b).
When reading *The Pillow Book*, we should remember that Shōnagon
and her companions spent a good part of their time ensconced behind
kichō.

Himemiya (Princess Imperial) refers to Princess Osako, Emperor (40)
Ichijō's eldest daughter, who was born to Sadako in 996, and who
came with the Empress to Narimasa's house in 999. (See App. 6a.)

The over-garment in question was a *kazami* (see Index-Glossary). (41)
Narimasa does not know the name and is obliged to use an absurd
circumlocution; it is much as if a man were to say 'the garment that
covers a woman's shoulders' for 'shawl'.

Instead of the normal *chiisai* ('small'), Narimasa says *chūsei*. Accord- (42)
ing to Waley (*W.P.B.*, p. 143), this is an affectation; but it sounds more
like a provincial dialect, probably from Mikasa Province near the
Inland Sea, where his father had been Assistant Governor. Anything
in the way of a provincialism was bound to amuse Shōnagon and her
companions. According to another theory, it was a type of student
dialect that Narimasa retained from his days at the University, but
this seems far-fetched.

9

Chūnagon (Middle Counsellor): one of six officials of the 3rd Rank who served in the Great Council of State, the central bureaucracy of the Heian government (App. 7a). Narimasa refers to his elder brother, Taira no Korenaka (*c.* 944-1006), who later became Assistant Governor-General of the Government Headquarters in Kyūshū. Shōnagon appears to have had more respect for Korenaka than for his younger brother, whom she clearly regarded as a figure of fun.

What impressed Korenaka, of course, was Shōnagon's neat allusion to Ting Kuo (note 36).

(44) Cats had been imported from the Continent, and there are several references to them in Heian chronicles and literature. The diary of Fujiwara no Sanesuke, for instance, contains the momentous entry (on the 19th day of the 9th Month in 999) that one of the Palace cats gave birth to a litter of kittens, that the birth-ceremony (*ubuyashinai*) was attended by no lesser dignitaries than the Ministers of the Left and of the Right, and that Uma no Myōbu was appointed nurse to the litter. Myōbu no Omoto may well have been one of the kittens born on this occasion. Readers of *The Tale of Genji* will recall the important part played by a cat in the Kashiwagi-Nyosan story. Emperor Ichijō was known to be particularly fond of cats, and there were several in his Palace; few, however, were elevated to the nobility.

Kōburi (head-dress of nobility): originally this referred to the ceremonial head-dress given by the Emperor to gentlemen of the 5th Rank and above. It was a small, round, black cap with a protuberance sticking up in the back and a wide, stiff ribbon hanging down. After the seventh century a cap was no longer actually awarded, but the word *kōburi* (or *kammuri*) was still used to designate gentlemen of these ranks.

Myōbu no Omoto (Lady Myōbu): Myōbu originally designated a lady who, either by marriage or in her own right, belonged to the 5th Rank or above; from the tenth century the term was applied to any woman of medium rank. *Omoto* was a general term for high-ranking ladies-in-waiting, especially those serving in the Imperial Palace.

(45) The following events take place in the 3rd Month of 1000 (App. 4). The scene is Ko Ichijō In (Smaller Palace of the First Ward), where the Emperor had been residing for some months owing to a fire in Seiryō Palace.

Uma no Myōbu (Lady Uma): for *Myōbu* see the previous note; *Uma* ('horse') referred, not to the lady's physical features, but to the fact that her father or some other close relation had a post in the Bureau of the Imperial Stables (Uma no Tsukasa).

The name *Okinamaro* could roughly be translated as 'Silly Old Boy', NOTES
but I prefer to leave it in the original. Numerous dogs, mostly strays, (46)
used to wander about the Palace grounds; this particular dog is
believed to have been white.

Asagarei no Ma (Imperial Dining Room): this was the room in which (47)
ceremonial meals were served to the Emperor in the mornings and
evenings; his real meals were eaten in another room. Even though the
Emperor was now residing in temporary quarters (see note 45), the
names of their rooms and their general arrangement were the same
as in Seiryō Palace (App. 9g).

Kurōdo (Chamberlain): one of the officials in the Emperor's Private (48)
Office (Kurōdodokoro), which was in charge of matters relating to the
Emperor and his Palace. This office had been established early in the
ninth century as a means of simplifying the cumbrous Chinese
administration and of concentrating power. For a time it was the most
important organ of government, relegating many of the older depart-
ments to political insignificance. In the course of the tenth century,
however, the office was in its turn displaced as the centre of effective
power by the institution of Kampaku (see Index-Glossary), another
departure from the Chinese model. For a diagram of the Emperor's
Private Office see *E.J.II.*, A. 91, and App. 7a.

Minamoto no Tadataka was a member of a minor branch of the
famous Minamoto clan, which descended from the ninth-century
Emperor, Seiwa (App. 3a). Tadataka and several of his clansmen had
been summoned to the capital some years earlier to help suppress
robbers and highwaymen. He was appointed Chamberlain in 1000;
later he became Governor of Suruga Province.

Takiguchi (Imperial Guards): a body of twenty men attached to the (49)
Emperor's Private Office and responsible for guarding the Palace.

I.e. on the occasion of the Jōmi Festival (note 21) earlier in the same (50)
month. On this day the dogs in the Palace were frequently decorated
with flowers and leaves (*kazariinu*).

Tō no Ben (Controller First Secretary): the head of the Emperor's
Private Office was an Intendant (Bettō). Under him came two First
Secretaries (Tō), normally of the 4th Rank. One of them (Tō no Ben)
was chosen from among the officials of the Controlling Boards
(Benkan), which were in charge of the work of the eight Ministries
(App. 7a); the other (Tō no Chūjō) was a Captain of the Inner Palace
Guards (Konoe Fu) (App. 7b). These two positions were very highly

regarded. The incumbent in question was Fujiwara no Yukinari (971–1027), a successful official and noted calligrapher, with whom Shōnagon was on friendly (if not intimate) terms (see App. 6b).

(51) For *Tadataka* see note 48. *Fujiwara no Sanefusa* was a Chamberlain of the 6th Rank. Unfortunately for his reputation, absolutely nothing is known about him except that he helped to flog Okinamaro. For the significance of this cruelty see *W.S.P.*, p. 122 and note.

(52) *Ukon* was a *naishi*, one of the ladies in the Palace Attendants' Office (Naishi no Tsukasa), a bureau of female officials who waited on the Emperor (see following note). Her father was Fujiwara no Suetsuna, a Minor Captain in the Inner Palace Guards, Right Division, and her name came from his official post, *Ukon*oe no Shōshō.

Almost certainly Ukon recognizes Okinamaro, but pretends that it is a different dog in order to spare him further punishment (cf. Shōnagon's own reply to Tadataka on p. 18).

(53) I.e. Minamoto no Tadataka, who was responsible for the punishment.

Daihandokoro (Table Room): a room with a large table (*daihan*), adjoining the Imperial Dining Room (note 47) and used mainly by the Emperor's ladies-in-waiting (see App. 9g).

Tadataka, of course, does not enter the Empress's room, but stands outside the blinds (*sudare*), where he cannot actually see the dog.

(54) For the names of the months see note 3.

In this section Shōnagon lists the Five Festivals (Gosekku), which in her day were as follows:

1st day of the 1st Month—New Year's Day (Chōga, Kochōhai, etc.)
3rd ,, ,, 3rd Month—Peach Festival (Momo no Sekku, Jōmi, etc.)
5th ,, ,, 5th Month—Iris Festival (Ayame no Sekku, Tango, etc.)
7th ,, ,, 7th Month—Weaver Festival (Tanabata Matsuri)
9th ,, ,, 9th Month—Chrysanthemum Festival (Kiku no Sekku, Chōyō).

(55) The Weaver Festival (Tanabata Matsuri) is derived from a Chinese legend about the love of the Weaver (Chih-nü) and the Herdsman (Ch'ien-niu), represented by the stars Vega and Altair respectively. Because of her love for the Herdsman, the Weaver neglected her work

12

on the clothes for the gods, while the Herdsman neglected his cattle.
As a punishment the Heavenly Emperor put the two stars on opposite
sides of the Milky Way, decreeing that they should be allowed to meet
only once a year, namely on the 7th day of the 7th Month, when a
company of heavenly magpies use their wings to form a bridge that
the Weaver can cross to join her lover. The magpies, however, will
not make the bridge unless it is a clear night; if it rains, the lovers must
wait until the next year. During the Tanabata Festival poems are
written in dedication to the two starry lovers, and women pray to the
Weaver for skill in weaving, sewing, music, poetry, and other arts.
The peculiar name of the month may derive from these customs.
Altars with offerings and incense were set up outside the palaces and
private houses on the night of the 7th.

Floss silk covers (*wata*) were put over the chrysanthemums on the eve (56)
of the Chrysanthemum Festival (see note 54 and *W.S.P.*, p. 164),
either to protect them from the dew or, according to another theory,
so that one might enjoy these scent-impregnated covers, which,
incidentally, were believed to protect people from old age if they
rubbed their bodies with them.

Shaku (baton): a flat stick held by officials in the right hand on occa- (57)
sions when they wore Court costume; instructions concerning details
of Court ceremony were sometimes written on the batons or on pieces
of paper pasted to them. For gentlemen of the 5th Rank and above the
batons were ivory; otherwise they were wood. Originally they may
have been one foot (*shaku*) long, but this etymology is uncertain.

Butō (ceremonial movements): a complicated series of movements (58)
performed when giving thanks to the Emperor or on other formal
occasions, and so elegant and stylized as to be equivalent to a dance,
in which the various gestures and poses are intended to express the
joy and gratitude of the performer.

Ima Dairi (Palace of Today) refers to Ko Ichijō In (note 45). This (59)
scene takes place in the 8th Month of 1000, the date on which Jōchō
became Intendant of Yamashina (App. 4). The peculiar designation
of the eastern wing as the 'northern guard-house' (*kita no jin*) can be
explained as follows. While the Court was in residence in the temporary Ko Ichijō Palace, the same names were used for the corresponding
guard-houses and other buildings even though the directions were
different—a sort of 'directional lag'. The regular Imperial residence,
Seiryō Palace (Apps. 9f, g), faced east, and the northern guard-house
was therefore to one's left if one sat in the main hall of the Palace

13

and looked out. The temporary Ko Ichijō residence, however, faced south. Consequently the guard-house to one's left, which was still designated as the 'northern guard-house', was in fact to the east of the building.

(60) *Gon Chūjō* (Provisional Middle Captain): for the hierarchy in the Inner Palace Guards (Konoe Fu) see App. 7b. Temporary or provisional posts (*gon*) carried the same salaries and perquisites as regular posts, but were usually sinecures. Such appointments were made when the regular post in question was already filled but a vacancy was required for a particular applicant. It should be noted that in Shōnagon's time the duties of Guards officers, whether or not their appointments were provisional, were almost entirely of a ceremonial, non-military nature (*W.S.P.*, p. 82).

The incumbent in this section was Minamoto no Narinobu (979–*c*. 1002), a grandson of Emperor Murakami and a son of Prince Munehira (App. 6a). Sons of Emperors and Imperial Princes were often, like Narinobu (and also Prince Genji in Murasaki's novel), affiliated to the Minamoto clan in order to limit the growth of the Imperial family and the consequent drain on the Exchequer.

Narinobu, who retired from the Guards in 1001 to become a priest, was noted for his good looks, being known as Kagayaku Chūjō ('The Shining Captain'); he was on close terms with Sei Shōnagon despite the fact that he had been adopted by his uncle, Michinaga, who belonged to the 'enemy' camp (*W.S.P.*, p. 58).

Eda-ōgi (branch-fan): commentators differ about what sort of a fan this may be; the word is possibly a corruption of *ita-ōgi* (board-fan). The Captain's remark is of course inspired by Jōchō's unusual height: a fan made from an entire tree might be appropriate for a man of his stature.

Sōzu (Bishop): 2nd in rank in the Buddhist hierarchy after Sōjō. *E.J.H.* translates Sōjō and Sōzu as 'High Priest of Buddhism' and 'Assistant High Priest of Buddhism' respectively, but these terms are rather unwieldy; 'Archbishop' and 'Bishop' are convenient equivalents, though the analogy with the Christian hierarchy must not be taken too literally.

(61) *Yamashinadera* (Yamashina Temple): the clan temple of the Fujiwara family. It was originally founded in 657 by the great Fujiwara no Kamatari near Yamashina in the village of Uji; in 710 it was moved to Nara, when the capital was established there, and it was placed in control of the Kasuga Jinja, the (Shintō) clan shrine of the Fujiwaras. It retained its original name of Yamashina, and was also known as the

Kasuga Temple and the Kōfuku Temple (Kōfuku Ji). This was the main temple of the Hossō Sect and one of the principal religious centres in Japan during the Heian period.

Bet(t)ō (Intendants): priests in charge of certain important temples (Tōdai Ji, Kōfuku Ji, etc.), where they served as the official representatives of the central government; this was one aspect of the establishment of Buddhism as the official State religion (*W.S.P.*, p. 98).

Most of the place-names mentioned by Shōnagon in this and subse- (62) quent lists (see notes 199, 274, 537, 780, 827, 879, 1015, 1022) figured in poetry, and often it was the memory of the poem, rather than of the place itself, that inspired her to include it. In other cases it was simply the name that appealed to Shōnagon: *Wasurezu*, for example, means 'No Forgetting' and *Katasari*, 'Yielding One's Place'.

In my annotations of these lists I have included the province (and district) in which the place is situated (see Apps. 9a, b); I have also given the literal meanings of the place-names when they are of interest.

The list of mountains is the longest single list in *The Pillow Book*, but the most famous of all Japanese mountains is never mentioned. This is because of Fuji's great distance from the capital and because it rarely figures in early poetry. It is significant that over half of the mountains that can be definitely identified are in the Home Provinces. It should be noted that many of these 'mountains' are in fact no more than large hills.

The following table includes all the places mentioned in sections 13-20 of *The Pillow Book*:

	Section	Place	Province (District)	Literary association	Literal meaning
1.	13	Ogura	Yamashiro (Kadono)	*Shūi Shū*	Small Storehouse
2.	„	Mikasa	Yamato (Sōno)	*Manyō Shū*	Three Sedge-Hats or Umbrellas
3.	„	Konokure	unidentified		
4.	„	Wasurezu	Rikuzen	*Rokujō*	No Forgetting
5.	„	Iritachi	? Etchū		Trespass
6.	„	Kase	Yamashiro (Sōraku)	*Kokin Shū*	Deer Back
7.	„	Iiwa	Izumo-Hōki	*Kojiki*	
8.	„	Katasari	unidentified		Yielding One's Place
9.	„	Itsuwa	Echizen	*Shin Kokin Shū*	Five Flags
10.	„	Nochise	Wakasa	*Manyō Shū*	
11.	„	Kasatori	Yamashiro (Uji)	*Kokin Shū*	Taking a Sedge-Hat (or Umbrella)

15

	Section	Place	Province (District)	Literary association	Literal meaning
12.	13	Hira	Ōmi	*Manyō Shū*	
13.	„	Toko	„	*Kokin Shū*	
14.	„	Ibuki	„	*Goshūi Shū*	
15.	„	Asakura	Chikuzen	*Rokujō*	
16.	„	Iwata	Yamashiro (Uji)	„	
17.	„	Ōhire	Settsu		Great Fin
18.	„	Tamuke	Yamato (Sōno)	*Kokin Shū*	Offerings
19.	„	Miwa	Yamato (Shiki)	*Manyō Shū*	Three Wheels
20.	„	Otowa	Yamashiro (Uji)	*Kokin Shū*	
21.	„	Machikane	Settsu	*Rokujō*	Impatient Waiting
22.	„	Tamasaka	„	*Tadami Shū*	Jewelled Slope
23.	„	Miminashi	Yamato (Shiki)	*Manyō Shū*	No Ears
24.	„	Sue no Matsu	Rikuzen or Mutsu	*Kokin Shū*	Pines of Sue
25.	„	Katsuragi	Yamato (Katsuragi)	*Kokin Shū*	
26.	„	Mino	Mino	*Ise Shū*	
27.	„	Hahaso	? Yamashiro	*Gosen Shū*	Notched Slope
28.	„	Kurai	Shinano or Hida		
29.	„	Kibi no Naka	Bichū	*saibara*	Interior of Kibi [Province]
30.	„	Arashi	Yamashiro (Kadono)	*Shūi Shū*	Storm
31.	„	Sarashina	Shinano	„	
32.	„	Obasute	„ (Sarashina)	*Kokin Shū*	Abandoned Aunt
33.	„	Oshio	Yamashiro (Otokuni)	„	Little Salt
34.	„	Asama	Shinano	*Ise Monogatari*	
35.	„	Katatame	unidentified	? *Rokujō*	
36.	„	Kaeru	Echizen	*Kokin Shū*	Return
37.	„	Imose	Yamato	*Manyō Shū* *Kokin Shū*	Two Lovers
38.	14	Yuzuruha	Settsu		Yielding
39.	„	Amida	Yamashiro (Kadono)	Fujiwara no Kintō	
40.	„	Iyataka	? Ōmi		Still Higher
41.	15	Taka	Yamato or Kawachi		Bamboo
42.	„	Mika	Yamashiro (Sōraku)	*Manyō Shū*	Jug
43.	„	Ashita	? Yamato	*Kokin Shū*	Reed Field
44.	„	Sono	Shinano	*Shin Kokin Shū*	
45.	„	Hagi	Kii		Clover
46.	„	Awazu	Ōmi	*saibara*	Millet Cove

16

Section	Place	Province (District)	Literary association	Literal meaning	NOTES
47.	15 Nashi	Yamato (Sōno)		Pear Tree	
48.	„ Unaiko	unidentified	*Rokujō*	Child (whose hair is fastened at the back of the neck)	
49.	„ Abe	Settsu			
50.	„ Shino	Ōmi or Kaga			
51.	16 Tatsu	Yamato	*Shūi Shū*	Dragon	
52.	„ Tsuba	Yamato (Shiki)	*Manyō Shū*	Camellia	
53.	„ Ofusa	Mikawa or Yamato	*Yamato Monogatari*	Small Tuft	
54.	„ Shikama	Harima			
55.	„ Asuka	Yamato (Takaichi) or Mino			
56.	17 Kashiko	unidentified		Wisdom	
57.	„ Nairiso	Kawachi		No Entry	
58.	„ Aoiro	unidentified		Yellowish Green	
59.	„ Ina	Yamato (Takaichi)		Nay	
60.	„ Kakure	unidentified		Hiding	
61.	„ Nozoki	„		Peep	
62.	„ Tama	„		Jewel	
63.	18 Biwa	Ōmi	*Shūi Shū*	Lute	
64.	„ Yosa	Tango			
65.	„ Kawaguchi	Settsu		River Mouth	
66.	„ Ise	Mikawa Shima	*suibara*		
67.	19 Shikasuga	Mikawa	Minamoto no Shitagau	Nevertheless	
68.	„ Mizuhashi	Etchū		Water Bridge	
69.	„ Korizuma	Settsu		Suma Ferry [where there is] No Learning from Experience	
70.	20 Uguisu	Kawachi or Yamato		Nightingale (see note 230)	
71.	„ Kashiwabara	Yamashiro (Kii) or Yamato		Oak Plain	
72.	„ Ame	? Yamato		Heaven	

Katasari Yama: note 62 (no. 8): Literal meaning. (63)

Toko Yama: note 62 (no. 13): Literary association. (64)

The *Kokin Shu* poem is ascribed to Emperor Shōmu (reg. 724–49), but it is actually an adaptation of an anonymous poem in the *Manyō*

17

Shū. As it appears in the *Kokin Shū*, the poem is addressed to a girl in Ōmi Province:

Inugami no	By Isaya River
Toko no Yama naru	In Mount Toko
Isaya Kawa	That stands [so high] in Inugami—
Isa to kotaete	Answer that you do not know me,
Waga na morasu na	Nor ever dare reveal my name!

The *isa* in Isaya is repeated with the sense of 'Well, I'm sure I don't know', and the purpose of the first three lines is precisely to provide these syllables which lead to lines 4-5.

(65) *Asakura Yama*: note 62 (no. 15): Literary association.

Mukashi mishi	Like Mount Asakura
Hito woba ware wa	Hidden in the distant clouds,
Yoso ni seshi	Far I find myself from her
Asakura Yama no	Whose closeness once I shared.
Kumoi haruka ni	

(66) *Ōhire Yama*: note 62 (no. 17): Literary association.

Rinji no Matsuri (Special Festivals): Shintō festivals held annually in the 11th Month at the Kamo Shrines, and in the 3rd Month at the Iwashimizu no Hachiman Shrine in the district of Tsuzuki south of the capital (App. 9c). They were called 'special' to distinguish them from the Festival (note 24) in the 4th Month. An ancient song called Ōhire ('The Great Fin') was sung during the Special Festivals and during certain other Shintō ceremonies. Also, the name of the mountain, Ōhire, probably reminds the author of the word *hire* ('fin') which designated a sort of shoulder-sash worn by Court ladies on formal occasions such as the Special Festivals.

Tsukai (envoys): Imperial messengers dispatched by the Emperor during the Kamo and Iwashimizu festivals to carry gifts to the shrines. Court ladies were sometimes sent; but usually the envoys were chosen from among the Guards officers, and no doubt their dashing appearance had made an impression on Shōnagon.

(67) *Hase* (or *Hatsuse*)*dera*: famous eighth-century temple of the Shingon sect; it was situated south of Nara (App. 9b) and dedicated to the eleven-faced Bodhisattva Avalokiteśvara, known in Japan as Kannon, the Goddess of Mercy. To have a connexion (*go-en*) with the Goddess means 'to be joined by a karma'.

Towns in Japan frequently had their origins in markets (the same character was used for 'town' and 'market'); often they were

situated near temples like Hasedera that attracted large numbers
of pilgrims.

Kashiko Fuchi: note 62 (no. 56): Literal meaning. (68)

Nairiso no Fuchi: note 62 (no. 57): Literal meaning. (69)

Aoiro no Fuchi: note 62 (no. 58): Literal meaning. (70)
   Chamberlains (note 48) were allowed to wear clothes of the same
colour as the Emperor's, that is, purple (*murasaki*) and yellowish
green (*aoiro*). *Aoiro*, the name of the pond, was probably derived from
the colour of the water.

Mizuumi (the Lake): in Shōnagon's time this invariably referred to (71)
Lake Biwa, the great lute-shaped lake north-east of the capital
(App. 9b). Sea (*umi*) in this section is used in a very general sense.

Konoe no Mi-Kado (the Gate of the Inner Palace Guards): refers to (72)
the Yōmei Mon, one of the gates at the east of the Greater Imperial
Palace (App. 9e). The headquarters of the Inner Palace Guards, Left
Division, were directly inside this gate, whence the designation. In
ancient Japan gates (*mon*, *mi-kado*) were often substantial structures
that might appropriately be described as 'buildings'.
   Nijō Ichijō (the Palaces of the Second Ward and the First Ward):
Heian Kyō had nine numbered avenues (*jō*), running parallel from
east to west, the 1st Avenue being at the level of the Imperial Palace
and the 9th Avenue at the southern extremity of the city (see App. 9d
and *W.S.P.*, pp. 22–23). The area between two avenues was also
known as *jō* (here the usual translation is 'ward') and was numbered
according to the avenue that bordered it on the north. Thus the entire
east–west rectangle between the 5th and 6th Avenues (Gojō and
Rokujō) was known as the 5th Ward (Gojō). Detached palaces and
other buildings were often named by reference to the avenues or
wards where they were situated; certain important people were given
palace names (*ingō*) that referred to the avenues or wards where they
or their families resided (e.g. the *ingō* of Fujiwara no Akiko was
Higashi Sanjō no In—the Eastern Palace of the Third Ward). The
Palace of the Second Ward was used by Emperor Murakami; the
Palace of the First Ward belonged to Fujiwara no Koretada and later
to his brother, Tamemitsu. (For the location of these and other buildings see App. 9d.)
   Somedono no Miya: belonged to Fujiwara no Yoshifusa, who left it to
his daughter, Akiko; later it became the residence of Prince Tamehira.

19

Sekai: another residence of Yoshifusa's daughter, Akiko.

Sugawara no In: residence of Sugawara no Koreyoshi and of his famous son, Michizane.

Reizei In: a palace used by abdicated Emperors since the early ninth century.

Suzaku (or *Sujaku*) *In*: named after Suzaku Ōji, the great central avenue that divided the capital into the Left and Right Cities; the palace was used by abdicated Emperors.

Tō In: probably refers to Teiji no In, the residence of Emperor Uda after his abdication.

Ono no Miya: situated by the foothills of Mt. Hiei north-east of the capital, it was the residence of Prince Koretaka in the ninth century and of the famous statesman, Fujiwara no Saneyori, in the tenth.

Kōbai: another residence used by Sugawara no Michizane prior to his exile.

Agata no Ido: also known as Ido Dono, a residence of the Tachibana family.

Tō Sanjō (the Eastern Palace of the Third Ward): another residence of Fujiwara no Yoshifusa, and later of his grandson, Tadahira.

Ko Rokujō Ko Ichijō (the Smaller Palaces of the Sixth and First Wards): the Smaller Palace of the First Ward was another of Tadahira's residences; later it was used by Fujiwara no Morotada and by Emperor Ichijō himself (notes 45 and 59).

Not a single building listed in this section has survived. We know very little about them, except their names, locations, and occupants.

(73) For the importance attached to geographical directions see note 38.

Ushitora (north-east), lit. ox-tiger, was the unlucky direction according to traditional Chinese beliefs (see *W.S.P.*, p. 124). Directions were frequently named by reference to the Chinese Zodiac (App. 3).

Seiryō Den (Seiryō Palace), lit. Pure and Fresh Palace, was the normal residence of the reigning Emperor. The Empress's room was the Kokiden no Ue no Mi-Tsubone (App. 9g); it was used by her when she came from her own palace, the Koki Den, to stay with the Emperor; the sliding screen (Araumi no Sōji, App. 9g) 'protected' this room from the northern veranda of the Palace by scaring away any evil spirits that might be lurking in the vicinity. The terrifying creatures with long arms and legs (*tenaga ashinaga*) were, of course, imaginary; they were of Chinese origin.

(74) *Dainagon Dono* (His Excellency the Major Counsellor): the Dainagon were among the top officials in the Great Council of State (App. 7a); originally there were four, but the number varied.

The present incumbent was Fujiwara no Korechika, the elder
brother of the Empress (see Index-Glossary), who received the
appointment in 992. Two years later he became Minister of the
Centre; but in 996 he was exiled from the capital, ostensibly because
of a scandal involving a former Emperor, but in fact because of the
rivalry of his uncle, Michinaga (see *W.S.P.*, p. 57). Korechika was
noted for his good looks, and many commentators have regarded him
as a (or even the) model for the Shining Prince, the hero of *The Tale
of Genji*. Korechika figures frequently in Shōnagon's book, but she
makes no overt reference to his disgrace.

This section belongs to the 3rd Month of 994 (see App. 4); the
Emperor is only thirteen, and Korechika's report to him is purely
ceremonial.

The fact that clothes frequently matched the season accounts for
the cherry-coloured cloak and jackets.

The dark-red robe came over the white under-robe and trousers (75)
(*sashinuki*) and under the cloak (*naoshi*). This was the fashion known
as *idashiginu* (see Index-Glossary).

For *karaginu* (Chinese jacket) and *kohajitomi* (small half-shutter) see (76)
Index-Glossary. Women frequently displayed their taste in colour by
allowing the sleeves or other parts of their many-layered costumes to
protrude from beneath the curtains of state, screens, etc. behind
which they sat (*W.S.P.*, pp. 204-5).

Hi no Omashi (Daytime Chamber): the main room of Seiryō Den; the (77)
hi no goza, which corresponded to a throne, was placed in this room
(App. 9g).

Nageshi (threshold): the threshold between the main part of the (78)
room (*moya*) and the *hisashi* (note 38).

Taken from the *Manyō Shū*, but with a few minor changes. The (79)
original poem is as follows:

> Tsuki mo hi mo
> Kawariyukedomo
> Hisa ni furu
> Mimoro no Yama no
> Totsumiyadokoro

Korechika omits the final line (*totsumiyadokoro*—'the place where the
Detached Palace is situated'). Mimoro, in eastern Yamato, is the site
of an ancient Shintō shrine mentioned in the *Kojiki*. The mountain is

associated with the idea of the everlasting power promised to the Japanese Imperial line by the Shintō deities. Korechika no doubt has in mind the continued prosperity of the Empress, his sister.

(80) *Naniwazu*: famous poem attributed to the Korean scholar, Wani (who is said to have introduced Chinese writing into Japan), and later to Emperor Nintoku (*c.* 400). The second attribution was made by Ki no Tsurayuki in his preface to the *Kokin Shū*: 'The Naniwazu is the first poem to have been composed by an Emperor.'

The poem is as follows:

Naniwazu ni	Ah, this flower that bloomed
Saku ya kono hana	In the port of Naniwa
Fuyugomori	And was hidden in the winter months!
Ima wo harube to	Now that spring is here
Saku ya kono hana	Once more it blossoms forth.

Naniwa is the old name of Ōsaka; the flower in question is the early-blooming plum blossom. Children in the Heian period were taught the poem for writing practice; accordingly the word *naniwa* (*zu*) was often used as an equivalent of ABC (e.g. in *The Tale of Genji*: 'She still does not know her *naniwazu* properly'); and by extension it could mean 'elementary', 'unformed' (note 739).

(81) The original poem, which is included in the *Kokin Shū*, was composed by Fujiwara no Yoshifusa while admiring some sprays of cherry blossom in a vase. It was inspired by pleasure at the success of his daughter, Akiko, who had become Emperor Montoku's principal consort (App. 6b), and the flower in his poem refers to the girl. Yoshifusa's poem is as follows:

Toshi fureba
Yowai wa oinu
Shika wa aredo
Hana wo shi mireba
Mono omoi mo nashi

By changing *hana* (flower) to *kimi* (lord), Shōnagon makes the poem refer to Emperor Ichijō.

(82) *Enyū In*: see Index-Glossary. This was the father and predecessor of Emperor Ichijō (App. 6a).

(83) *Tadaima no Kampaku Dono no Sammi no Chūjō* (His Excellency, our present Chancellor, who was then Middle Captain of the Third Rank): the Kampaku, who was invariably the head of the Northern

branch of the Fujiwara family, was the real ruler of Japan during most
of the tenth and eleventh centuries, overtopping not only the Daijō
Daijin, who headed the Chinese-type bureaucracy that had been
established in the seventh century, but, so far as real power was concerned, the Emperor himself. *E.J.II.* translated Kampaku as 'Civil
Dictator', which is somewhat misleading and hardly appropriate as a
title. Sansom gives 'Regent', but this could be confused with the post
of Sesshō. 'Maire du palais' (*S.S.S.T.*) furnishes a good idea of the
importance of the post, but the analogy with French history must not
be pressed. On the whole, 'Chancellor' seems to be the least misleading equivalent; but readers of Sansom should be warned that this
is his normal rendering of Dajō Daijin (which I translate as 'Prime
Minister'). It may be significant that even the Emperor is reported as
referring to the Kampaku as 'His Excellency' (*Dono*). Though
Michitaka and the other Fujiwara leaders were prepared to grant the
Emperor the trappings of authority, there was no doubt about the locus
of actual power. Shōnagon refers to the Kampaku as the First Man
(Ichi no Hito) and to his residence as the First Place (Ichi no Tokoro).

The incumbent in question was Fujiwara no Michitaka (953-95),
the elder brother of Michinaga and the father of Empress Sadako (see
Index-Glossary and App. 6b). He figures in *The Pillow Book* as the
leading politician of his day. The climax of his career came in 990,
when he succeeded his father, Kaneie, in the crucial post of Regent
and when his daughter was appointed Empress; in 994 he was still at
the height of his power and success; one year later he was dead. In
my translation of *The Pillow Book* 'Chancellor' invariably refers to
Michitaka.

Shio no mitsu (84)
Izumo no ura no
Itsu mo itsu mo
Kimi woba fukaku
Omou wa ya waga

The origin of this old love-poem is unknown. There is a play of words
on *Izumo* (province on the Japan Sea) and *itsu mo* (ever). *Kimi* has the
double meaning of (i) you (intimate), (ii) Lord, Emperor.

Because of its reference to having grown old. Shōnagon had now (85)
reached the ripe age of about thirty and was therefore, by Heian
standards, well into her middle years.

Kokin Shū: see Index-Glossary. (86)
   The thirty-one-syllable *uta* (*tanka*) is divided into a beginning

(*moto*) of three lines (5-7-5 syllables) and an end (*sue*) of two lines (7-7 syllables). Guessing games of this type were extremely popular.

(87) *Saishō no Kimi*: granddaughter of Fujiwara no Akitada; she was a lady-in-waiting to Empress Sadako (see App. 6b). Despite her difficulties with the *Kokin Shū*, Saishō rivalled Sei Shōnagon in readiness of wit and she appears frequently in *The Pillow Book* (see p. 129). She should not be confused with her less important namesake (note 468) who belonged to the Sugawara family and who also served the Empress. Unless otherwise specified, 'Lady Saishō' in my translation refers to the Fujiwara (not the Sugawara) lady of that name.

(88) *Murakami*: grandfather of the reigning Emperor; see Index-Glossary and App. 6a.

    Nyōgo (Imperial Lady): a consort of the Emperor or Crown Prince, ranking below the Chūgū (Second Empress) but above the Kōi (Imperial Concubines).

    Senyō Den (Senyō Palace): building in the Imperial Palace compound (App. 9f), used as a residence for Imperial Ladies.

    Hidari no Otodo (Minister of the Left): see App. 7a. The incumbent is Fujiwara no Morotada (Index-Glossary, App. 6b), who received the coveted appointment in 969 and died in the same year.

    For Smaller Palace of the First Ward see note 72.

    The woman in question was Fujiwara no Yoshiko (Index-Glossary, App. 6b), a great favourite of Emperor Murakami's; she was noted both for her poetic talents and for her beauty, especially her long hair.

(89) *Kin no on-koto* (seven-string zither): there were three kinds of *koto* (Japanese zither or harp), the six-string *wagon*, the thirteen-string *sō*, and the seven-string *kin*.

(90) *Monoimi no hi* (day of abstinence): one of the frequent inauspicious days (*mono-imi* = 'fear of things') determined by the Onyōji (Masters of Divination), when, according to current superstition, it was essential to stay indoors and, as much as possible, to abstain from all activities, including eating, sexual intercourse, and even such seemingly innocuous acts as reading a letter. Particularly strict rules applied to what the Emperor did on these days.

(91) The poems in the anthologies were usually provided with short notes or introductions (*kotobagaki*) explaining the circumstances in which they had been written. It was these that Emperor Murakami read to Yoshiko. He might, for example, have asked her to identify a poem

on the basis of the following information: 'This poem was composed by Ason, Narihira, on the last day of the Third Month; it was raining, and he plucked a sprig of wistaria to give to his companion.' (*Hyōshaku*, p. 98.) In identifying the poem, Lady Yoshiko simply recited a few words to show that she recognized it; this was regarded as far more elegant than repeating the entire poem (see *W.S.P.*, p. 182).

Go: a fascinating, complicated game, introduced from China in the (92) eighth century. It is played with black and white stones on a board with 361 intersections (19 × 19). The two players take turns in placing their stones on any suitable intersection. Once a stone has been placed, it cannot be moved to another intersection; stones that have been encircled by the enemy, however, are forfeit unless they are so placed that they themselves enclose at least two independent and viable openings or 'eyes' (*me*).

Go stones were frequently used as counters for scoring games and contests.

Esemono (people of humble station): lit. 'false people', i.e. those who (93) are not genuine or (socially) good people. The word reflects the current attitude to the plebs (*W.S.P.*, p. 85). *Hyōshaku* and Ikeda-Kishigami both suggest that the Emperor makes this remark, but in view of his age (note 74) some readers will prefer to follow Tanaka and other texts in attributing it to 'people' (*hitobito*) or 'ladies-in-waiting' (*nyōbō*).

Shōnagon refers to the poem from the *Kokin Shū* that she had quoted (94) earlier (p. 17).

Naishi (Attendant): the following three ranks of women officials (95) served in the Naishi no Tsukasa (Palace Attendants' Office): (i) two Naishi no Kami (Chief Attendants), (ii) four Naishi no Suke or Tenji (Assistant Attendants), (iii) four Naishi or Shōji (Attendants). Under them came one hundred women known as *joju* or *nyoju*. In Shōnagon's time the two top posts were occupied by concubines of the Emperor; in the present passage she refers to the third category of official.

Kandachibe or *Kandachime* (High Court Noble): a designation for all (96) gentlemen of the 3rd Rank and above, as well as for Imperial Advisers (Sangi) of the 4th Rank, but not usually applied to the Chancellor or the Regent.

Tonobara (the young men): originally referred to sons of Ministers
and other important men; later the term came to be used in a general
way to apply to young gentlemen (as opposed to young commoners).

(98) See note 66.

(99) *Gosechi*: Court dances performed in the 11th Month by young girls
of good family (App. 1). Of the four girls who participated in the
dances, three were the daughters of High Court Nobles and one (as
in the present passage) the daughter of a provincial governor. Scholars
do not agree about the origin of the element 'five' (*go*) in the word
Gosechi. Among the theories are: (i) the dances coincided with the
last of the Five Palace Festivals (*Go*sechie), (ii) when the dances were
performed at the time of an Imperial accession, there was a total of
five performers, (iii) the dances involved five basic movements, (iv)
the angels who first performed the dance in the presence of Emperor
Temmu began by shaking their feathered sleeves five times, (v) the
accompaniment was sung by five voices, (vi) the dances and related
activities usually lasted for five days.

The Gosechi performances dated from the reign of Emperor
Shōmu in the eighth century and commemorated Emperor Temmu's
vision of a group of angelic dancers (see theory iv above).

(100) These nets (*ajiro*) were designed for catching whitebait (*hio*) during
the winter; in spring-time they were useless.

(101) For red plum-blossom (*kōbai*) see note 23. Dresses of this colour could
be worn only during the 11th and 12th Months.

(102) Scholarly activities, like most other specialized occupations, tended
to run in families; and they were not considered suitable for girls (see
W.S.P., pp. 209-10).

When reading these lists, we must remember that the word *mono*
can refer to both things and people; *Depressing Things and People*
would be a more comprehensive translation of the heading.

(103) *Katatagae* (avoidance of an unlucky direction): when a Master of
Divination informed one that a certain direction (e.g. north) was
'blocked up' (*katafutagari*) by one of the invisible, moving deities that
were central to Heian superstition (*W.S.P.*, p. 125), one might
circumvent the danger by first proceeding in a different direction
(e.g. west); after stopping on the way at an intermediate place and

staying there at least until midnight, one would continue to one's
intended destination (e.g. by going north-east). People would also
leave their house for a *katatagae* because they wished to obtain release
from some future taboo, abstinence, or prohibition, even though they
had no particular desire to go anywhere at the time. By performing
such a seemingly gratuitous *katatagae*, they were freed in advance
from the baleful effect that one of the moving divinities might exert
if they remained at home or indulged in some tabooed activity like
ground-breaking. Such moves were especially common during the
Seasonal Change (*Sechibun*, *Setsubun*) that preceded the onset of the
Great Cold on the 21st of the 1st Month; though this was a festive
period, a particularly large number of inauspicious spirits was abroad:
'On the eve of the [Spring] Seasonal Change all sorts of ceremonies
took place, and feasts were held to celebrate the occasion. Moreover,
it was customary for everyone, including the Emperor, the Retired Emperor, the Empress Dowager, and the Great Ministers, to perform *katatagae*; these were known as the "*katatagae* of the Seasonal Change".
Katatagae were not limited to occasions on which people wished to
travel abroad, but also took place on those inauspicious days when they
had to be absent from their homes [because of the unlucky position
of one of the moving deities]. At such times they would go and stay
in the house of an acquaintance—for a couple of days in the case of a
short *katatagae*, for seven or even forty-nine days in the case of a long
one.' (*Kōchū Nihon Bungaku Taikei*, xxv. 211.) Thieves often took
advantage of these beliefs to enter their victims' house when they
knew that the master and his family would have to be absent because of a *katatagae*. Another way of performing *katatagae* was
to remain all night in a carriage parked at the gate of one's building;
this, however, was hardly practical when the *katatagae* was a
long one.

For a lucid and detailed discussion of this complicated subject see
Bernard Frank, *Kata-Imi et Kata-Tagae* (Tokyo, 1958). '. . . le *katatagae*', writes M. Frank (p. 55), 'n'avait pas seulement pour but . . .
de tourner l'interdiction de se déplacer. . . . Il avait également pour
but d'écarter les interdictions . . . concernant le "viol de la terre",
l'accouchement et nombre d'autres travaux ou activités sans rapport
nécessaire avec l'idée d'un déplacement.' M. Frank suggests (pp. 98–
99) that these '*katatagae* préventifs' may actually have been more
important than the '*katatagae* de déplacement', though most modern
definitions refer exclusively to the latter.

The traveller who stopped at a *tabisho* during the performance of
any *katatagae* was normally accorded a special welcome and friendly
entertainment.

Apart from official correspondence the two main types of formal letters were *musubibumi* (knotted) and *tatebumi* (twisted). Both were folded lengthwise into a narrow strip; but, whereas the *musubibumi* was knotted in the middle or at one end, sometimes with a sprig of blossoms stuck into the knot, the latter was twisted at both ends and tended to be narrower. A few thick lines of ink were drawn over the knot or fold by way of a seal.

(105) See note 17.

(106) The aim of the exorcist was to transfer the evil spirit from the afflicted person to the medium (*yorimashi*), who was usually a young girl or woman, and to force it to declare itself. He made use of various spells and incantations (*kaji*) so that the medium might be possessed by the Guardian Demon of Buddhism (*Gohō-dōji*). When he was successful, the medium would tremble, scream, have convulsions, faint, or behave as if in a hypnotic trance. The spirit would then declare itself through her mouth. The final step was to drive the spirit out of the medium. See *W.S.P.*, pp. 135–9.

(107) One watch (*toki*) was the equivalent of two hours (see App. 3).

(108) I.e. appointments to provincial governorships (note 19). Despite the low social status of provincial officials, these posts could be extremely lucrative.

(109) The aspirant visits shrines and temples to pray for success; his lick-spittles want to accompany him in the hope that, if he is appointed, they will be given posts on his staff. The eating and drinking serve as a preliminary celebration.

(110) The messengers cannot bring themselves to announce in so many words that their master has failed to obtain an appointment; instead they answer by giving his existing title, which he had hoped to shed in favour of the new one.

(111) When one received a poem, it was *de rigueur* to reply promptly by a 'return' poem (*kaeshiuta*) in which one would normally ring the changes on some central image. A failure to reply (or at least to have a friend, relation, colleague, etc. make a reply in one's place) was regarded as the height of rudeness—no less rude, Professor Kaneko points out (*Hyōshaku*, p. 126), than a failure nowadays to answer when someone says, 'How do you do?' It was socially permissible not

28

to answer love poems, but this of course signified that one was totally NOTES
uninterested in the sender.

On the 3rd, 5th, and 7th days after a child's birth it was customary (112)
for the grandparents and other members of the family to send presents
of swaddling-clothes, etc., known as *ubuyashinai*.

Presents were also given to people leaving on a journey. Originally
it was the custom for the traveller's friends to see him off personally
and, just before he left, they would turn his mount's head in the
direction for which he was bound. This is the origin of the word used
to describe the parting present: *uma no hanamuke* ('turning the horse's
nose'). Later it became customary to send a messenger with presents
of food, etc., rather than to go oneself.

Messengers were originally rewarded by having a gift of clothing (an
early form of currency) put on their shoulders; hence *kazuke* ('placed
on the shoulders'), the name for rewards given to a messenger. In later
times other forms of compensation were given (*W.S.P.*, p. 73).

Kusudama (herbal balls): during the Iris Festival in the 5th Month (113)
various kinds of herbs were bound into balls and put into round
cotton or silk bags, which were decorated with irises and other plants,
as well as with long, five-coloured cords; they were then hung on
pillars, curtains, etc. to protect the inhabitants of the house from illness and other misfortunes. They stayed there until the Chrysanthemum Festival in the 9th Month, when they were changed for balls
decorated with chrysanthemum leaves, which were left hanging until
the Iris Festival in the following year. A close Western equivalent is
the asafoetida bag, worn about the neck to ward off illness.

Uzuchi (hare-sticks): three-inch sticks with long, coloured tassels
presented at the New Year to keep away evil spirits. They were hung
on pillars in the Palace and in the houses of the nobility on the 4th day
of the month, which corresponded to the 1st Day of the Hare (App. 3).
Both the herbal balls and the hare-sticks were of Chinese origin.

That is to say, the young man has still not made his wife pregnant; (114)
the principal aim of this type of adoption, of course, was to ensure the
continuity of the family line.

There was a strong prejudice against taking naps in the day-time (115)
(*W.S.P.*, p. 287); the practice was considered especially undignified
and unaesthetic for elderly people.

Because it interfered with the many New Year's celebrations. (116)

Fasting (*sōjin*) was enjoined by the Buddhist church on the 8th, 14th, 15th, 23rd, 29th, and 30th of each month (see note 31). There were also periods of abstinence in the 1st, 5th, and 9th Months; and on certain special occasions, when people wished to expiate serious offences, they would undertake fasts lasting 100 or 1,000 days. The efficacy of the entire fast was sacrificed if one violated the restrictions for a single day.

(118) This was the Leaf-Turning Month, i.e. the beginning of autumn (note 3). A white under-robe (*shitagasane*) was normally worn only in the summer months. As a rule Shōnagon and her contemporaries strongly disapproved of anything that deviated from the seasonal or diurnal routines. The first three items in the present list belong to the same category.

(119) When a fast lasts for only a single day, one is liable to forget about restrictions, since one has not had time to accustom oneself to the routine.

(120) It was fashionable for the men and women of Shōnagon's circle to make retreats to the temples that were scattered about the environs of the capital. These were often simply excuses for trysts. A long retreat was apt to become irksome and often led to a slack performance of one's religious duties.

(121) *Kita-omote* (north side): in the current Shinden style of architecture houses invariably faced south; the north side was therefore the back part.

(122) *Kariginu* (hunting costume): men's informal outdoor costume, originally worn for hunting.

(123) *Yoroshiki* (or *yoki*) *hito* (good people): i.e. socially good (cf. *W.S.P.*, p. 66); I frequently use the translations, 'person (people) of quality' and 'gentleman'.

Shikibu no Taifu (Senior Secretary of the 5th Rank in the Ministry of Ceremonial): the Ministry of Ceremonial (App. 7a) was responsible for Court ceremonies, registration of officials, promotions, awards, education, etc. The Senior Secretary, the third-ranking official below the Minister (App. 7b), normally belonged to the 6th Rank, but in certain cases he was promoted to the 5th.

Suruga: province in the Tōkaidō corresponding to modern Shizuoka Prefecture. The Governor belonged to the 5th Rank.

The song, though evidently popular in Shōnagon's time, is no longer NOTES (124) extant. It was apparently sung by children to the accompaniment of certain conventional gestures.

Eboshi (tall, lacquered hat): black, lacquered head-dress worn by men (125) on the top of the head and secured by a mauve silk cord that was fastened under the chin; two long black pendants (*ei*) hung down from the back of the hat. The *eboshi* was a most conspicuous form of headgear and hardly suited for a clandestine visit. Originally *eboshi* were worn at Court by the nobility, but later they came into fairly general use.

Iyosu (Iyo blind): a rough type of reed blind (*sudare*) manufactured (126) in the province of Iyo on the Inland Sea.
  Mokō no su (head-blind): a more elegant type of blind whose top and edges were decorated with strips of silk. It also had thin strips of bamboo along the edges and was therefore heavier than ordinary blinds.

Sneezing was a bad omen, and it was normal to counteract its effects (127) by reciting some auspicious formula, such as wishing long life to the person who had sneezed (cf. 'Bless you!' in the West). Shōnagon does not like the sneezer himself to utter the auspicious words. For further references to sneezing see p. 182.

In the texts based on the *Shunchobon* edition this sentence comes at (128) the very end of the present section; but it seems to be misplaced, and here I have followed the order in the *Sangenbon* version (Ikeda-Kishigami, p. 71).

Owasu ('good enough to do') and *notamau* ('kindly remarked') (129) designate the actions of a superior; *haberu* (lit. 'to serve') is used to describe one's own or someone else's actions in relation to a superior. See my *Dictionary of Selected Forms in Classical Japanese Literature until* c. *1330*, App. IV. The correct use of honorific, polite, and humble locutions was of course enormously important in a strictly hierarchic society. In the present passage the sentence beginning 'No doubt . . .' is ironic.

Etiquette demanded that in the presence of the Emperor or Empress (130) one referred to oneself by one's name rather than by the first person singular. One referred to other people by their real names; if Their Majesties were not present, however, one referred to these people by their offices (e.g. Major Counsellor). On the whole, personal pronouns were avoided, and this added to the importance of correct honorific usage.

(131) *Futokorogami* (paper): elegant coloured paper that gentlemen carried in the folds of their clothes. It served for writing notes and was also used like the *hanagami* in more recent times (see *The Life of an Amorous Woman and Other Writings*, note 134). Owing to its later function it acquired an erotic significance.

(132) For Palace of Today see note 59.

(133) This must be a mistake. The Empress did not return to the Palace of Today until the 12th of the 2nd Month (in the year 1000); the music lesson probably took place on the 20th instead of the 10th (see App. 4).

(134) For Fujiwara no Takatō, the Emperor's music teacher, see index-Glossary. His post (Daini) in the Government Headquarters at Dazai came directly below that of the Governor-General (App. 7b). These headquarters, which were situated near the modern city of Fukuoka in northern Kyūshū, were particularly important because of their responsibility for defence and foreign trade.

(135) *Takasago*: well-known folk-song that starts,

Takasago no	Ah, the jewel-white camellia
Saisago no	And the jewel-like willow
Onoe ni tateru	That grow in Takasago
Shiratama-tsubaki	Upon Saisago Hill. . . .
Tama-yanagi	

(136) The original has *seri tsumishi . . . koto koso nakere* ('never picked parsley'), a curious expression meaning 'to grieve', 'to suffer unhappiness'. Its origin appears to be an old story about a man of humble station who falls in love with a well-bred young girl he happens to have seen while she was eating some wild parsley. Later he tries to console himself by picking parsley and eating it, but this only increases his forlorn love. 'To pick parsley' (*seri tsumu*) acquired the sense of 'not to have things one's own way', 'to be unhappy'. 'Parsley' is a rough but convenient equivalent of *seri* (*oenanthe stolonifera*).

(137) Suketada's father, who belonged to the Southern Branch of the Fujiwara family, was Governor of Owari; his mother appears to have come from a humble family in that region. Suketada was adopted by

a more influential branch of the Fujiwara family and managed to rise
in the hierarchy until he became Governor of Yamato.

Moku no Jō (Secretary in the Bureau of Carpentry): this was a
lowly post, corresponding to the 7th Rank, and Suketada's appointment as Chamberlain represented a great step upwards. The Moku
Ryō (Bureau of Carpentry) came under the Kunai Shō (Ministry of
the Imperial Household) and was responsible for all wood construction in the palace buildings. (See App. 7a.)

> Sau nashi no nushi   (138)
> Owari-udo no
> Tane ni zo arikeru

'Who can stand next to . . .?': lit. 'He has no one on his left or right.'
This has a double meaning: (i) no one is his match (in roughness),
(ii) no one wants to be near him (because of his rough manners).
Owari, in eastern Japan, was noted for the uncouthness of its inhabitants.

The Empress's building was further from the Chamberlains' office (139)
than Emperor Ichijō's own palace.

A literal translation of Ichijō's words would be, 'This thing (i.e.
Suketada) is not [here].'

The Kamo Festival was also known as the Hollyhock Festival (Aoi (140)
Matsuri). During the celebrations (see note 24) hollyhock was
attached to the pillars, blinds, etc. and left there until it withered and
fell off. Hollyhock was also used to decorate people's hair and head-
dresses.

To find dolls or any of the other things used during the Hiina Asobi (141)
(Display of Dolls, note 21) would be like coming across a box of old
Christmas decorations.

Futaai (deep violet): see note 26. Another reminder of the Kamo (142)
Festival. A piece of material from a costume to be worn at the Festival
turns up between the pages of a notebook, where it has been lying for
months or perhaps even years.

Tsurezure (bored): for the role of boredom in women's lives see (143)
W.S.P., pp. 211–12.

Kawahori (paper fan): a fan covered with paper on one side of the (144)
frame and used in the summer months. When open, it looked like a

bat with spread-out wings. Coming upon this fan, perhaps during the winter, Shōnagon is reminded of something that happened in the summer.

(145) In Japan, as in China, the moon traditionally evokes memories of the past. See p. 239.

(146) *Onnae* (pictures of women): possibly refers to erotic drawings, but we have no extant examples from the Heian period. See *Hyōshaku*, p. 165, and *W.S.P.*, p. 186.

(147) This is a reference to *idashiguruma* (*idashiginu*), the fashion of letting one's full array of sleeves hang outside the carriage so that passers-by might admire the colour combination.

(148) *Michinoku*: thick, white paper used for writing love letters, notes, etc. and normally carried in the breast of one's robe. It was manufactured in the district of Michinoku(ni) in the north of the main island; originally spindle-tree was used, but later mulberry.

(149) *Hagurome* (blackened teeth): the earliest mention of this curious fashion dates from the tenth century, but it is probably far older and may have its origins in the South Sea Islands (see *W.S.P.*, p. 204). At first it was practised only by women of the aristocracy, but later it spread to men and to the lower classes. In the Muromachi period girls who had reached the age of eight blackened their teeth as a sign of adulthood. In Edo times it became the mark of a married woman; courtesans blackened their teeth on the grounds that they were 'brides for one night'. The custom persisted among women in rural districts until quite recently. The usual method of producing the dye was to soak bits of iron in a solution of tea or vinegar mixed with powdered gallnut. For such readers as may be interested in practising the fashion, A. B. Mitford (Lord Redesdale) gives the prescription in detail (*Tales of Old Japan*, London, 1888, p. 374).

(150) *Chōbami* (dice) was played with the dice normally used in *sugoroku* (backgammon, see note 660). If the player threw dice of the same number, he won the turn and picked up the dice-box for another throw; if the numbers were different, his opponent picked up the box.

(151) Purification services (*suso no harae*) were performed to ward off bad luck that might otherwise ensue as the result of some enemy's curse

(*suso*); they often took place by rivers, because it was believed that the current would carry away the evil.

Ajiro: cf. *biroge no kuruma*, note 34. The *ajiro* (wickerwork carriage) (152) was a lighter, less impressive form of vehicle, covered with a reed or bamboo trellis.

I have followed Ikeda-Kishigami (p. 99) in putting the section on cats (153) after those on oxen and horses rather than after the section about page-boys (as in the *Shuncho* texts).

Lit., 'If my age were [more] appropriate, I should probably write (154) words that would expose me to such sin.' Both Waley (*W.P.B.*, p. 114) and Aston (*Japanese Literature*, p. 116) seem to have misinterpreted the passage, though in entirely different ways.

Sekkyo, which I have translated as 'preaching' or 'sermon', has the (155) literal meaning of 'expound the sutras'.

Shōnagon refers here to the relatively low-ranking members of the (156) Emperor's Private Office who were known as Higerō. During the six years of their tenure they had access to Seiryō Palace, where they attended the Emperor at his meals and performed similar duties. If at the end of their six years there was no possibility of promotion, the Higerō normally retired, or 'went down' as the expression was. It was, in other words, a case of 'up or out'. As a sort of compensation they were elevated from the 6th to the 5th Rank; they were, however, no longer allowed to attend the Emperor in the Senior Courtiers' Chamber. Such ex-Chamberlains were known as Kurōdo no Goi (5th Rank Chamberlains). They should not be confused with the Goi no Kurōdo (Chamberlains of the Fifth Rank), who had obtained the coveted promotion while still in office and who thus had a chance of climbing to the highest rungs of the administrative ladder.

Monoimi no fuda (taboo tags): a sign made of willow-wood and hung (157) outside one's house on days of abstinence (note 90) to warn possible visitors. If one was obliged to venture abroad on one of these days, one would wear such a tag on one's head-dress (men) or sleeve (women).

This probably refers to women's carriages. Ladies usually remained (158) in their carriages during the service, and the retired Chamberlains are not too pious to have a good look. According to Motoori Uchitō, however, they are actually looking at their own carriages to make sure that they have been placed in a better position than those of the other visitors. In any case their minds are far from religion.

(159) *Hakkō* (Eight Lessons): a series of eight services in which the eight volumes of the *Lotus Sutra* were expounded. Two services were held each day, one in the morning and one in the afternoon. The commentary normally took the form of a sort of catechism, in which one priest would ask questions about important sections of the sutra and another would reply.

Kyō Kuyō (Dedication of Sutras): refers to the practice of ordering copies of the sutra to be made and dedicated to some person or institution or to the Three Treasures (Sambō), the Buddha, the Law, and the Priesthood. The Chinese characters were usually written in silver or gold on heavy white or dark-blue paper. After the copy was completed, the sutra would be recited in a special service of dedication.

(160) The interpretation of this passage is disputed. According to the *Shunchobon* commentary, the final statement (*Ikaga wa*) implies that the lady in question did not attend the service. But this does not seem to fit with what comes afterwards, and I have followed the interpretation in *Hyōshaku*, p. 181.

(161) *Tsubo-sōzoku* (travelling, lit. 'jar', costume): costume worn by women for pilgrimages and other journeys; it comprised a long cloak and a large, basket-shaped hat (*ichimegasa*).

(162) *Bodai Ji* (Bodai Temple): see Index-Glossary.

Kechien no Hakkō (Eight Lessons for Confirmation): Eight Lessons (note 159) carried out in order to confirm people in the Buddhist vocation. The ceremony, which lasted from four to five days, included morning and evening services.

(163)
> Motomete mo
> Kakaru hachisu no
> Tsuyu wo okite
> Ukiyo ni mata wa
> Kaeru mono ka wa

The service of the Eight Lessons included a scattering of lotus blossoms, and Shōnagon's poem was written on a paper lotus used for this purpose. It contains a pun on *oku*—(i) to settle (of dew), (ii) to depart. I have tried to suggest its effect by the pun 'on leave'.

The story of Hsiang Chung (Sō Chū) is told in *Lieh hsien chuan*
(*Ressenden*), a collection of biographies of Taoist immortals. One
day the old man was so absorbed in his study of a Taoist text
that he did not realize that the river had flooded and he was surrounded by water; meanwhile his family waited impatiently for him
at home.

Ko Shirakawa (Smaller Shirakawa): abbreviation of Ko Shirakawa (165)
Dono (Smaller Shirakawa Palace). Shirakawa ('white river') was a
stream to the north-east of the capital; it gave its name to the entire
district. The exact site of Ko Shirakawa Dono is unknown.
   For Smaller Palace of the First Ward see notes 45, 72, etc. Shōnagon
refers to Tadahira's grandson, Fujiwara no Naritoki, who was in
charge of the Imperial Guards stationed at Ko Ichijō Palace (see
Index-Glossary). Although in his lifetime Naritoki never reached high
rank (his last post was that of Imperial Investigator in the northern
wilds of Mutsu and Dewa), his daughter was appointed Empress in
1014. To regularize the anomaly Naritoki was named Prime Minister,
this being some twenty years after his death.

Women normally remained in their carriages during the service (note (166)
158); unless they were placed fairly close, they had little chance of
hearing.
   There is again a play of words on *oku*—(i) to settle (of dew), (ii) to
get up.

In 986. The present service took place several years before Shōnagon (167)
became a lady-in-waiting and is by far the earliest datable scene in
The Pillow Book (App. 4).

Hidari Migi no Otodo (Ministers of the Left and the Right): the two (168)
highest posts (apart from Dajō Daijin) in the Chinese-type administrative hierarchy that had been introduced in the seventh century (see
App. 7a). The incumbents were Minamoto no Masanobu and Fujiwara no Kaneie (Index-Glossary).

The *Shunchobon* text gives the name of Fujiwara no Yasuchika, but (169)
Yasuchika did not become Imperial Adviser until 987. According to
other early texts, which I have followed in this instance, Shōnagon is
referring to Fujiwara no Sukemasa (Index-Glossary), who was
appointed Imperial Adviser in 978. Sukemasa, one of the Three
Great Calligraphers of his day, later became Minister of Military
Affairs.

37

Fujiwara no Sanekata and *Fujiwara no Nagaakira* (see Index-Glossary): the nephew and son, respectively, of Fujiwara no Naritoki (App. 6b); hence their familiarity with the house where the service of the Eight Lessons for Confirmation was being held. In 986 Sanekata was Assistant Captain of the Middle Palace Guards (Hyōe no Suke). In 996 he was 'banished' from the capital by being sent as governor to the northern province of Mutsu, where he died two years later; this unfortunate appointment was the result of a quarrel with the prepotent Yukinari. According to some writers, Sanekata became Shōnagon's husband after her separation from Tachibana no Norimitsu; but the evidence is unconvincing.

Though Nagaakira is generally believed to have been Naritoki's son, some authorities believe that his father was in fact Sadatoki and that accordingly Naritoki was his uncle.

Jijū (Gentleman-in-Waiting): one of eight officials in the Ministry of Central Affairs who waited on the Emperor and advised him on sundry matters. Their functions were originally important, but by Shōnagon's time they had become purely ceremonial. Later the number of Jijū was increased to twenty.

(171) When Shōnagon was writing this passage, Michitaka had risen to the top post of Kampaku; but in 986, the date of the present scene, he was Middle Captain of the Inner Palace Guards, Right Division, and held the Junior Third Rank. It appears, therefore, that Shōnagon was writing at least seven years after the events she describes.

(172) Fujiwara no Yoshichika (see Index-Glossary) rose to fairly high rank owing largely to his connexions with Emperor Kazan (his nephew). He appears to have been a man of considerable learning. In 986, only a few weeks after this service, he retired from politics to become a priest at the same time as Kazan, who secretly left the Palace and entered a mountain monastery.

(173) It was customary to refer to distinguished people by their titles and ranks, and Shōnagon feels it necessary to justify her departure from the practice. The taboo on the use of personal names, which has lasted in Japan until modern times, can result in considerable confusion, since the same titles and ranks were often held by several different people, and the same person held different ranks. This is one of the many difficulties that we encounter in historical texts, as well as in works like *The Pillow Book*.

(174) Tamemitsu (see Index-Glossary) was appointed Major Counsellor in 977.

Michitaka refers to a poem (included in the *Gosen Shū*) about a man
who was always looking for qualities and charms where they could
not reasonably be expected:

Naoki ki ni	The straightest tree
Magareru eda mo	Grows many a crooked branch:
Aru mono wo	Foolish it is to blow the hair
Ke wo fuki kizu wo	And so uncover faults.
Iu ga warinasa	

That is to say, since even the best objects and people in this world
have imperfections (*kizu*), there is no point in expecting normal things
or people to be ideal; rather we should leave well enough alone. Cf.
the well-known proverb, *tsuno wo tamete ushi wo korosu* ('straightening the horns, one kills the ox'). In this particular case Yoshichika has
expected too much from the unknown woman in the carriage: by
demanding a good poem ('straightening the branches') he has spoiled
everything ('broken the tree'). The way in which Michitaka changes
the reference to the tree imagery, while retaining the central point of
the original verse, is typical of the technique of poetic quotation in
Shōnagon's time.

Hitoegasane (set of robes): set of unlined silk robes worn by women (176)
and usually matched to produce a subtle blending of colours. The
sleeves of each dress were normally longer than those of the one over
it. When travelling in carriages, women often let the sleeves of their
various robes hang outside the blinds (note 147); this allowed Shōnagon
to see exactly what the unknown lady wore.

Seihan (see Index-Glossary): high-ranking priest of Kōfuku Ji, the (177)
Fujiwara clan temple. He was noted for his eloquent sermons.

Yoshichika is referring to a passage in the *Lotus Sutra*, the main text (178)
of that morning's service, in which the Buddha comments to his
disciple, Śāriputra (Sharihotsu), on the fact that 5,000 people in his
congregation have left while he was in the middle of preaching:
'People of such pride do well to depart.' Shōnagon picks up the
reference with her usual acumen, and implies that Yoshichika, by
using the Buddha's own words, is no less guilty of pride than the
people who left.

See note 172. Yoshichika took holy orders on the 24th day of the 6th (179)
Month.
    The *Shunchobon* text reads, 'the period of waiting for old age' (*oi*

39

wo matsu ma), but this is almost certainly a corruption of 'the period of waiting for [the dew] to settle' (*oku wo matsu ma*). In that case we have a reference to a poem by the early tenth-century writer, Minamoto no Muneyuki:

Shiratsuyu no	The *asagao* bloom
Oku wo matsu ma no	Waits but for the dew to fall
Asagao wa	Before its life is done.
Mizu zo nakanaka	Better it were by far
Arubekarikeru	That we had never seen its charms.

Unlike the short-lived *asagao* (for which see note 297), which awaits only the morning dew before dying, Yoshichika retired from the world while still at the height of his career, well before reaching the period when one might expect worldly things to end for him. As the present passage suggests, Yoshichika's interests were far from being limited to religious matters.

(180) In the Heian period rooms were not covered with straw mats (*tatami*) as became normal in later times; instead mats were spread out when and where they were needed for sleeping, sitting, etc.

(181) *Kichō* (curtains of state) were usually classified in terms of the length of the horizontal wooden bar (*te*) from which the curtains (*katabira*) were suspended. A three-foot curtain of state (*sansaku no kichō*) normally had five widths of curtain.

On a hot summer night it was advisable to place one's *kichō* in as cool a part of the room as possible, i.e. near the veranda. Besides, since the main purpose of the *kichō* was to protect women from prying eyes, it would be illogical to place it in the rear of the room where people were unlikely to be looking at one from behind. I take *oku no ushiro-metakaramu* to mean 'what can there be to worry about in the back of the room?' *Ushirometashi* means both 'worrying' and 'suspicious', and, according to some commentators, the phrase implies that people will be suspicious if the *kichō* is in the back of the room, since they will think the woman is hiding a lover; but this seems far-fetched.

(182) It was customary in Shōnagon's time to use clothes as bed-covers; also it was normal to sleep fully dressed. The two sets of clothing described in this paragraph are, respectively, the woman's bedclothes and her dress.

(183) Heian women usually let their long, thick hair hang loosely down their backs. The closer it reached the floor, the more beautiful they were

considered. For the aesthetic significance of women's hair see *W.S.P.*, NOTES
p. 203.

Mata izuko yori ni ka aramu: lit. 'again whence may [he] be . . .'. (184)

It was an essential part of Heian etiquette for the man to write a love- (185)
letter (*kinuginu no fumi*) to the lady with whom he had spent the night;
it usually included a poem and was attached to a spray of some appropriate flower (*fumitsuke*). The letter had to be sent as soon as the man
returned home or, if he was on duty, as soon as he reached his office.
The lady was of course expected to send a prompt reply. If the man
failed to send a letter, it normally meant that he had no desire to
continue the liaison.

The word *kinuginu* was a reduplicative of *kinu* ('clothes') and
derived from the fact that after spending a night together (i.e. without clothes) the man and the woman put on their clothes and parted
for the day. It referred (i) to their parting, (ii) to the morning on which
they parted.

From a *Kokin Rokujō* poem, (186)

Sakurao no	The sprouts of the cherry-flax
Ou no shitakusa	In the flax fields
Tsuyu shi araba	Are heavy now with dew
Akashite yukamu	I shall stay with you till dawn
Oya wa shiru tomo	Though your parents be aware.

The expression 'cherry-flax' (*sakurao*) is found in a similar poem in
the *Manyō Shū* and refers (i) to the fact that flax was sown at the same
time that the cherries blossomed, (ii) to the similarity in appearance
between cherry blossoms and the leaves of flax.

The gallant declares that he will stay with the girl until daylight,
though this probably means that her parents will find out about his
visit. His ostensible reason is that it is hard to make his way through
the heavy morning dew (a standard euphuism); the real motive, of
course, is his reluctance to leave the partner of his night's pleasures.
'Dew on the sprouts' (*shitakusa tsuyu*) may have a secondary erotic
implication such as one frequently finds in early Japanese love
poems.

I.e. the house of the woman with the long hair and the orange robe. (187)

If the man was sensitive to the beauty of the dew, he would want to (188)
leave at early dawn before it had disappeared. The real reason for

41

early departures, of course, was fear of discovery; but pretty conceits of this type were common.

(189) See note 131.

(190) As a rule a Heian woman of the upper class would not let herself be seen by a man unless she was actually having an affair with him— and not always then. They were usually protected by curtains of state, screens, fans, etc., and above all by the darkness of the rooms.

(191) I.e. so early; but see the end of note 186 for a possible *double entendre*.

(192) *U no hana*: a shrub with white blossoms, something like the syringa; it blossoms in the 4th Month (Uzuki, note 3) at about the time of the Kamo Festival, when *hototogisu* (note 25) were most frequently heard. *Deutzia scabra*, its Linnaean equivalent, brutally conceals the poetic connotations that the plant has in Japan, and I prefer to leave the word in the original.

(193) *Murasaki [No]*: a famous plain north of the capital, named after its violets (*murasaki*); it was the site of the Kamo Shrines (see App. 9c).

(194) In the Far East animals and plants often have traditional affinities, e.g. in China the tiger and bamboo, the lion and peonies, the phoenix and paulownias. Several early Japanese poems suggest such an affinity between the *hototogisu* and the orange tree. The following *Manyō Shū* verse is an example:

Uzuki yama	Ah, my beloved whom I met in the Rice-
Hana tachibana ni	Sprouting Month,
Hototogisu	When the *hototogisu* lurked
Kakurou toki ni	In the mountain's flowering orange tree!
Aeru kimi ka mo	

The *hototogisu* is also associated with *u no hana* flowers (note 192) and the *uguisu* has an affinity with plum trees (note 231).

(195) It was customary to attach flowers or leaves to one's letters; the choice depended on the season, the dominant mood of the letter, the imagery of the poem it contained, and the colour of the paper. See *W.S.P.*, p. 188.

(196) *Rika isshi haru no ame wo obitari* ('a spray of pear blossom in spring, covered with drops of rain'): reference to 'The Song of Everlasting Regret' (*Ch'ang hen ko, Chōgonka*), a famous poem by the great T'ang

writer, Po Chü-i (Hakurakuten), who was by far the most popular
Chinese author in Shōnagon's Japan and, as Dr. Waley points out
(*W.P.B.*, p. 151), the easiest. It tells the story of the tragic love between the Chinese Emperor and his favourite concubine, the beautiful
Yang Kuei-fei (Yōkihi), who according to one version was hanged from
a pear tree by mutinous troops in 756 owing to her alleged responsibility for the Emperor's neglect of state affairs and to the unpopularity
of her scheming family. The grief-stricken Emperor sends a Taoist
magician to look for the lost lady; but, though the messenger finds her,
he is unable to bring her back. Here Shōnagon refers to the passage in
which Yang Kuei-fei comes forth to meet the messenger:

Yü jung chi mo lei lan kan	Her face, delicate as jade, is desolate ·beneath the heavy tears,
Li hua i chih ch'un tai yü	Like a spray of pear blossoms in spring, veiled in drops of rain.

It appears, however, that Shōnagon had misunderstood the Chinese
original, in which Yang Kuei-fei's beauty is compared to that of jade
(*yü*), the pear blossom (*li hua*) being introduced only to evoke her
pallor. This is one of several instances that have led commentators to
question Shōnagon's reputed erudition in the Chinese classics.

I.e. the fabulous phoenix (*hōō*), whose appearance presaged the advent (197)
of a virtuous Emperor. This splendid, five-coloured bird was said to
dwell in paulownia trees (*kiri, paulownia imperialis*).

At the time of the Iris Festival. The *melia japonica* has small, violet (198)
flowers.

Cf. note 62. (199)

	Place	Province (District)	Literary association	Literal meaning
1.	Katsumata	Yamato (Sōnoshimo)	*Manyō Shū*	
2.	Iware	,, (Tōchi)		
3.	Nieno	Yamshiro (Sōraku)	*Kagerō Nikki*	
4.	Mizunashi	Yamato		No Water
5.	Sarusawa	,, (Sōnokami)	*Gosen Shū*	Monkey Marsh
6.	Omae	,, (Ikoma)		Divine Presence
7.	Kagami	unidentified		Mirror
8.	Sayama	Musashi (Kitatama)	*Rokujō*	
9.	Koinuma	unidentified		Love Swamp
10.	Hara	Kōzuke	popular song	
11.	Masuda	Yamato (Takechi)		

Almost all the ponds appear to have been in the Home Provinces of
Yamashiro and Yamato; few of them remain. It was probably only

from her reading of poetry that Shōnagon knew the names of the more distant ponds like Sayama.

(200) For Hase Temple see note 67. Nieno Pond figures in both *Kagerō Nikki* and *Sarashina Nikki*.

(201) *Mizunashi no Ike*: note 199 (no. 4): Literal meaning.

(202) *Uneme* (Palace Girl): these girls were usually chosen for their looks and talents from among the daughters of provincial governors and presented to the Palace to serve the Emperor. This form of recruitment was stopped in 807.

Yamato Monogatari (Index-Glossary) tells the story of a Palace Girl who served a certain Emperor in Nara. When he terminated her service (i.e. broke off relations with her), she was overcome by grief; in the middle of the night she made her way secretly to Sarusawa Pond and drowned herself. The Emperor was much moved by her deed and paid an Imperial Visit to the pond, where he ordered his gentlemen to compose suitable verses. The poem to which Shōnagon refers was by Kakinomoto no Hitomaro (Index-Glossary) and appears in the *Gosen Shū*:

Wagimoko ga	Grievous indeed to see
Nekutaregami wo	The tangled hair of my beloved
Sarusawa no	Floating like seaweed
Ike no tamamo to	On Sarusawa Pond!
Miru zo kanashiki	

(203) *Omae no Ike*: note 199 (no. 6): Literal meaning.

(204) Reference to a poem in the *Rokujō* anthology:

Musashi naru	Pull out the water-bur
Sayama ga Ike no	That grows in Sayama Pond in Musashi
Mikuri koso	And yet it will not break.
Hikeba taezare	But, oh, how broken I become
Ware ya taesuru	[When torn from him I love]!

(205) Here Shōnagon refers to a popular song from the province of Kōzuke in eastern Honshū:

Oshi takabe	The mandarin duck,
Kamo sae kiiru	The teal,
Hara no Ike no ya	And the wild duck too—
Tamamo wa	All come to Hara Pond.
Mane na kiri so ya	Do not cut the seaweed by the roots!
Oi mo tsugu ga ni ya	Oh, let it go on growing!
Oi mo tsugu ga ni	Let it go on growing!

44

This was one of the Five Festivals; it dated from the early seventh century and was known as Ayame no Sekku or Iris Festival (App. 1). (206) The 5th of the month was regarded as an inauspicious day, and many of the festival observances were aimed at warding off evil spirits. Herbal balls, decorated with irises, were hung on the houses to protect the inhabitants from illness and also attached to the sleeves of people's clothes (see note 113); the eaves were covered with iris leaves and branches of mugwort, which were also believed to have prophylactic virtues. The Emperor, wearing a garland of irises (*ayamekazura*), gave wine, in which iris root had been steeped, to his high officials; the gentlemen of the Court put irises on their head-dresses and the women wore irises in their hair. Irises were also attached to clothes and to all kinds of objects in daily use—palanquins, swords, pillows, wine-cups, etc.—and placed under the pillow (*ayame no makura*). Abstinence signs were used as a further protection. The officers of the Guards, who were responsible for supplying the various palaces with irises and mugwort for the occasion, brought the festival to an end with a ceremonial twanging of their bow-strings to scare away any evil spirits that might still be hovering in the precincts.

Lit. 'dwellings of people of whom one does not know how to speak' (207) (*iishiranu tami no sumika*).

Nuidono Ryō (Bureau of the Wardrobe): one of the bureaux under (208) the Ministry of Central Affairs (App. 7a). Among other things it was responsible for supplying clothes to the Imperial Princesses and noblewomen in the Palace.

  Chōdai (curtain-dais): a platform or dais about 2 feet high and 9 feet square, surrounded by four pillars and by curtains. Curtains of state (*kichō*) were placed on three sides of the dais, and the platform itself was covered with straw mats and cushions. The *chōdai* was used by the master of the house for sleeping and was also the place where he normally sat in the day-time. In the Imperial Palace it served as a sort of throne.

For 'uneven shading' see note 27. (209)

See the end of note 25. (210)

Soba no ki (Chinese hawthorn) literally means 'tree on the side'. The (211) Chinese hawthorn turns red at the beginning of the summer instead of in the autumn; hence its conspicuity.

Because its virtues were already well recognized, says Kaneko (*Hyōshaku*, p. 234); but such considerations have not inhibited Shōnagon elsewhere. The spindle tree (*mayumi*) was used for making bows and high-quality paper.

(213) Being dependent on the strength of other trees, the parasite's existence is precarious; hence it is *aware* ('moving', 'pitiful'). For a discussion of *aware* see *W.S.P.*, pp. 196–7.

(214) After sunset on the day of the Kamo Festival sacred Shintō dances (*kagura*) were performed in the Palace in the presence of the Emperor. The *sakaki* is the sacred tree of the Shintō religion and plays an important part in the *kagura* and other Shintoist observances. Its name means 'prosperity tree' (*sakae-ki*). The present-day *sakaki* corresponds to the cleyera, but the consensus of scholars is that it was originally an anise tree.

(215) A rather precious play of words on *odoro* (tangled, bushy) and *odoroodoroshi* (frightening).

(216) Reference to the *Rokujō* poem:

Izumi naru	One thousand branches grow
Shinoda no Mori no	Upon the camphor tree in Izumi's Shinoda
Kusu no ki no	Wood—
Chie ni wakarete	A branch for each sad care that troubles those
Mono wo koso omoe	who love.

(217) Lit. 'it is not familiar to people' (*hito chikakaranu*) because it usually grows deep in the hills. Shōnagon refers to the following old song (*saibara*):

Kono dono wa	Rich indeed has this palace grown.
Mube mo tomikeri	To three ridges, four ridges, do its roofs extend.
Sakigusa no	
Mitsuba yotsuba ni	
Tonozukuri seri	

Scholars differ about the meaning of *ba* in *mitsuba* and *yotsuba*. The most likely explanation is that it refers to the ridge (*mune*) of a roof and that each new *ba* of the palace corresponds to an additional room or hall. Cypress (*hinoki*) had been used since ancient times for constructing palaces and other important buildings.

The dew dripping from the leaves of the cypress and the wind blowing through its branches both sound like rain. Shōnagon specifies the 5th Month since that is the beginning of the rainy season.

Asuwa hinoki: large-leaved cypress or *thuya dalobrata*. Its name NOTES literally means 'tomorrow [he will be] a cypress'. (218)

Shōnagon refers to Hitomaro's poem in the *Manyō Shū*: (219)

Ashibiki no	Climbing the arduous mountain path,
Yamaji mo shirazu	I lose my way.
Shirakashi no	For the snow from the white oaks
Edamoto wo o ni	Has fallen on the craggy slope
Yuki no furereba	And clad the trail in white.

So far as we know, this has no connexion whatsoever with the Storm God (Susanoo no Mikoto, 'His Impetuous Male Augustness') or with his journey to Izumo in the west of Japan after his expulsion from the Plain of High Heaven. In Shōnagon's time, however, it was evidently believed that Hitomaro wrote this poem to commemorate the hardships that the God suffered when he was caught in a snowstorm on his way westward across the steep mountains. The accounts of Susanoo in the chronicles contain no mention of the white oak (*shirakashi*), but the God is described as having performed dances holding the branches of certain other trees.

Yuzuriha: the Linnaean equivalent is *daphniphyllum macropodum*, (220) but I prefer the Japanese word.

In Heian times the Buddhist Festival of the Spirits (Tama Matsuri) was celebrated on the last day of the year (App. 1). The spirits of the dead returned to earth at noon on this day and left at six o'clock in the morning of New Year's Day.

Among the many New Year's customs was that of tooth-hardening (*hagatame*). This was observed in the Palace on the 2nd day of the year, when the Imperial Table Office prepared certain special dishes, such as melon, radish, rice-cakes, and *ayu* fish, which were supposed to strengthen the teeth. This in fact had the same purpose as many other New Year practices, viz. the promotion of health and longevity. Aston (*Shintō*, p. 313) explains the connexion by the fact that the same Chinese character (*ch'ih*) is used for 'teeth' and 'age'. Evidently the tooth-hardening foods were served on *yuzuriha* leaves. This strikes Shōnagon as strange since the same leaves were used to serve the food for the dead.

The poem about the *yuzuriha* that Shōnagon cites in this paragraph is in the *Rokujō* anthology:

Tabibito ni	When the leaves of the sheltering *yuzuriha*
Yado Kasuga No no	On the plain of Kasuga
Yuzuriha no	Turn red—
Momiji semu yo ya	Not till then shall I forget you.
Kimi wo wasuremu	

47

'Full of promises' (*tanomoshi*) refers to this poem. The *yuzuriha* is an evergreen.

(221) *Hamori no Kami*, lit. 'the god who protects the leaves'. This god was believed to inhabit the Mongolian oak (*kashiwa*), a tree that the ancient Japanese appear to have regarded with particular awe. Cf. the following poem in *Yamato Monogatari*. The speaker is a man who is paying a secret visit to a married woman and who has mistakenly broken off the twig of an oak to give her; the 'God of Leaves' represents the cuckolded husband:

Kashiwagi ni	Not knowing what I did,
Hamori no Kami no	From the oak where dwells the God of Leaves
Mashikeru wo	I broke a twig.
Shirade zo orishi	Oh, grant that I be spared
Tatari nasaru na	The punishment for my deed!

It is not clear why the officers of the Middle Palace Guards (Hyōe no Suke Zō) were referred to as 'oaks'. Kamo no Mabuchi suggests that it is because they were held in particular respect, but from what we know of the prestige of the Guards regiments this seems dubious. Kaneko (*Hyōshaku*, p. 242) mentions that in the past an oak had grown outside the Headquarters of the Middle Palace Guards, and this would appear to be a more likely explanation.

(222) Objects 'in the Chinese style' (*karamekite*) were to be found only in the houses and gardens of the aristocracy.

(223) Parrots (*ōmu*) had been imported from Korea in earlier times as tribute, but they appear to have died out by Shōnagon's time and it is unlikely that she had ever actually seen one; hence the vagueness of this sentence.

(224) Because it sees itself in the mirror and thinks it is its mate. The copper pheasant (*yamadori*) is said to have been introduced from China. It was recommended for its beautiful voice, but on arrival at the Palace (so the story goes) it refused to sing. A certain Court lady explained that this was because the pheasant missed its mate. She ordered that a mirror be hung in the cage, and the bird immediately began singing.

Shōnagon is thinking of the following *Rokujō* poem:

NOTES
(225)

Takashima ya	In Takashima even the herons of Yurugi Wood,
Yurugi no Mori no	Where the branches quiver in the wind,
Sagi sura mo	Refuse to nest alone
Hitori wa neji to	And keenly seek a partner for the night.
Arasou mono wo	Yet . . . [I, alas, must spend the night alone].

Hakodori (box bird): the bird is mentioned in contemporary poetry (226) and also in *The Tale of Genji*; but its identity is unclear. Its name may be an onomatopoeia derived from a characteristic cry of *hayako-hayako*.

Oshi(dori) (mandarin duck): the traditional symbol of conjugal love (227) in the Far East. Cf. the *Rokujō* poem:

Ha no ue no	The mandarin ducks, the husband and his mate,
Shimo uchiharau	Brush from each other's wings the frost.
Tomo wo nami	How sad if one is left to sleep alone!
Oshi no hitorine	
Suru zo wabishiki	

Poem by Ki no Tomonori (Index-Glossary), included in the *Rokujō*: (228)

Aki kureba	Autumn is here
Sao no kawabe no	And with it comes the plover's cry—
Kawagiri ni	The plover who has lost his mate
Tomo madowaseru	On Sao River's misty banks.
Chidori naku nari	

Sedōka from the *Manyō Shū*: (229)

Saitama no	In Saitama
Osaki no Numa ni	In Osaki Marsh
Kamo zo hanekiru	The wild duck flaps its wings,
Onoka o ni	Striving to sweep away the frost
Furiokeru shimo wo	That has settled on its tail.
Harau to narashi	

Shōnagon has substituted wing (*hane*) for tail (*o*).

Uguisu: usually translated 'nightingale', but this is misleading since (230) the *uguisu* does not sing at night and is far closer to the Western bush warbler (cf. *hototogisu*, note 25).

This passage was probably written in the summer of 999, when (231)

Shōnagon was about thirty-four. It is likely that she entered the service of Empress Sadako about 990 (see note 802 and App. 4).

(232) See note 194.

(233) Perhaps Shōnagon is thinking of the following poem, which can be found in the *Shūi Shū*:

Aratama no	Since the morning of this day
Toshi tachikaeru	That ushered in the fresh New Year
Ashita yori [9]	I have waited for one sound alone—
Mataruru mono wa	The sound of the *uguisu*'s song.
Uguisu no koe	

In the traditional calendar the year began with spring.

(234) The text here is particularly laconic; I have eked it out with the help of *Hyōshaku* and other commentaries.

(235) *Urin In Chisoku In*: temples near the Kamo Shrines on Murasaki Plain north-east of the capital (App. 9c).

(236) But *kari no ko* could mean 'duckling' or (less likely) 'gosling'.

(237) Ice was stored in ice-chambers (*himuro*) and eaten during the summer (for instance in sherbets) or used to preserve perishable food. The stems and leaves of the liana (*amazura*) were used for mild sweetening; sugar was not introduced into Japan until the Ashikaga period.

(238) *Warekara* (shrimp insect): a small, shrimp-like insect that lives on water-plants, seaweed, etc. When the plants are pickled and dried, the insect's shell breaks; hence its name, lit. 'break-shell'.

(239) *Chi-chi* is the characteristic sound of the basket worm as well as the word for 'milk'. The insect in question is a *psychidae*; it was called *minomushi* ('straw-coat insect') because of the nest in which it is wrapped. This nest is made chiefly of dirt.

(240) *Nukazukimushi* (snap-beetle): lit. 'bowing insect', so called from its characteristic motion.

(241) See section 27.

(242) In ancient Japan people were often named after animals (e.g. *Semi*maro and *Mushi*maro after cicada and insect respectively). Haemaro (in

50

which *hae* means 'fly') was probably given to members of the lower
orders because of its unpleasant associations.

A rather curious passage, especially in view of Shōnagon's usual (243)
fastidiousness. According to Kaneko (*Hyōshaku*, p. 257), it implies,
not that she enjoyed the smell of sweat as such, but that she liked
familiar clothes to cover herself when sleeping (see note 82); but this
seems a quibble.

Because such beauty is wasted on *hoi polloi* and inappropriate to their (244)
gross nature.

Yakata naki kuruma (plain waggon): lit. 'carriage without a compart- (245)
ment', i.e. a carriage used to convey goods, not people.

Acorns, says *Hyōshaku* (p. 262), were for children and plums for (246)
young women.

This and the following item are not included in the *Sangenbon* texts. (247)
In the *Shunchobon* texts they come at the end of the next section
(section 48 in my numbering), where they are obviously misplaced;
I have transferred them to what seems a more suitable position and
have omitted the second reference to an open carriage in the moonlight, since this is surely a copyist's error.

Yugei (Quiver Bearers): another name for the Outer Palace Guards (248)
(Emon), one of the three Guards regiments stationed in the Greater
Imperial Palace; it patrolled the grounds and carried out police duties
in conjunction with the Kebiishi. As this passage suggests, these
guards were regarded with some trepidation. *The Tale of Genji* also
refers to the 'terrifying red clothes' of the Quiver Bearers.

Kebiishi (Imperial Police): established in the ninth century as one (249)
of the many departures from the Chinese administrative system.
Originally they were responsible for apprehending criminals, but
their functions gradually extended into the judicial field, and, as
Sansom points out (*History*, i. 208), they 'built up a body of case law
of their own'. The hierarchy consisted of a Chief (Bettō), four
Assistant Directors (Suke), four Lieutenants (Jō or Hōgan), etc.
(App. 7b). One of the Lieutenants could hold the additional post of
Chamberlain (Kurōdo) in the Emperor's Private Office; in this
capacity he had access to the Senior Courtiers' Chamber (Ue) and

was therefore known as Ue no Hōgan ('Lieutenant of the Courtiers' Chamber').

Shōnagon obviously resented these parvenu police officers who, despite their low rank, were allowed to swagger about the Palace buildings without proper regard for decorum, and who even had affairs with Court ladies of much higher rank than themselves.

(250) Most of the ladies-in-waiting occupied rooms off the long, narrow corridors (*hosodono*) on both sides of the Palace buildings and in the rear.

(251) Incense was normally used to perfume the blinds, screens, and other furnishings in upper-class houses. Often the burner itself was hidden behind a screen or in a neighbouring room so that the visitor could not tell where the smoke was originating.

Indiscreet as it may seem, it was normal for male visitors to hang their *hakama* (trouser skirts) over the curtain of state belonging to the lady they were visiting. Officers of the Outer Palace Guards wore white *hakama* of heavy, rough cloth.

(252) Shōnagon despises these low-ranking men who pride themselves on being allowed to wear the officer's *wakiake* (Index-Glossary).

(253) These weapons were used mainly for ceremonies, processions, and the like.

(254) The Controllers (Ben) were among the most important and busy officials in the government (see App. 7a). So that they could move about more freely, they were allowed trains (*shiri*) that were considerably shorter than those normally worn by people of their rank.

(255) *Shiki no Mi-Zōshi* (Empress's Office): also known as the Shiki In. This building, situated to the north-east of the Imperial Palace (see App. 9e), housed several offices of the Ministry of Central Affairs, the most important of these being the Office of the Empress's Household (Chūgū Shiki). The Emperor often lived in Shiki no Mi-Zōshi when his own Palace had burnt down; it was also frequently occupied by his consorts, especially by Empress Sadako.

(256) *Ben no Naishi*: one of Empress Sadako's ladies-in-waiting. From the context it appears that she was a mistress of the Major Controller; hence perhaps the element Ben (Controller) in her name.

There were two Major Controllers (Daiben), one of the Left (Sadaiben) and one of the Right (Udaiben) (see App. 7a). The

52

gentleman in question was either Minamoto no Yoriyoshi (Left) or
Fujiwara no Tadasuke (Right). Yukinari, being a Middle Controller
(Chūben), was his subordinate.

Kakaru koto (that business): i.e. Ben no Naishi's relations with the (257)
Major Controller.

Yukinari refers to a story in Ssu-ma Chien's *Shih chi* (*Shiki*). When (258)
Yü Jang's lord, the Earl of Chih, had been killed by Viscount Hsiang
of Chao, he promised to avenge him; for, as he said, 'A knight dies
for one who has shown him friendship. A woman [continues to] yield
to one who has taken pleasure in her. Now the Earl of Chih showed me
friendship. I will certainly avenge him and die.' Cf. the following free
translation of the same passage in Wolfgang Bauer's and Herbert
Franke's *The Golden Casket* (New York, 1964), p. 18: 'Yü Jang fled
into the mountains and cried: "Alas! A knight must die for his friend,
a woman be at the call of her lover. It is my duty to avenge the Baron
of Chih!"' Yü Jang, having failed in two attempts to kill Viscount
Hsiang, took his own life.

It is interesting that Yukinari should reverse the order of Yü Jang's
dictum: in the Heian world the warrior-lord relationship was far less
important than a woman's obligation to her lover.

The reference is to a *sedōka* in the *Munyō Shū*: (259)

Arare fuii	Oh, the willow tree
Tōtōmi no	On Ado River in Tōtōmi
Ado Kawa yanagi	Where the hail comes down!
Kareredomo	Oh, the willow on Ado River
Mata mo ou chū	Though it be felled,
Ado Kawa yanagi	It grows again, so people say

Me tatezama (her eyes were turned up): i.e. rather than being thin (260)
and narrow (*hikime*), which was the mark of the classical Heian
beauty. Women plucked their eyebrows, and, as we can gather from
'The Lady Who Loved Insects' (Arthur Waley, *The Real Tripitaka*,
p. 221), thick eyebrows were regarded as repulsive. The nose was
supposed to be small, delicate, and up-turned (*kagihana*), the chin
and neck shapely and well-rounded. See *W.S.P.*, pp. 201-4, for the
criteria of feminine beauty in Heian times.

Shōnagon deliberately echoes the advice (*Ikai*) given by Fujiwara (261)
no Morosuke to his descendants: 'In all matters, whether it be
Court costumes or carriages, take things as they are and use them

53

accordingly (*aru ni shitagaite kore wo mochiiyo*). On no account seek out new luxuries.' Shōnagon refers, not to frugality, but to the importance of adapting oneself to circumstances.

(262) Reference to the *Analects* of Confucius: 'If you are wrong, do not be afraid to correct yourself' (*kuo tse wu tan kai*).

(263) Despite the sexual licence of the period, adult women normally hid themselves from men behind screens, fans, etc., except at the most intimate moments. This concealment applied even to their fathers and brothers (cf. notes 39, 190, and *W.S.P.*, pp. 210–11).

(264) *Shikibu no Omoto* (Lady Shikibu): lady-in-waiting at Empress Sadako's Court. She appears to have been a good friend of Shōnagon's, for we find them sharing a room two years later in 1000. The present scene takes place in the 3rd Month of 998 and can be dated as follows (*Hyōshaku*, p. 277): (i) Fujiwara no Nariyuki served in the Empress's Office from 998 (2nd Month) until 999 (6th Month); (ii) Noritaka was a Chamberlain until his promotion in 999 (1st Month), and the present incident occurred while he still held that post; (iii) Shōnagon tells us that it happened at about the end of the 3rd Month; (iv) the only 3rd Month in which both Nariyuki and Noritaka would have been in the Empress's Office was in the year 998 (see App. 4).

(265) Gentlemen of the 4th Rank and above wore black over-robes (*ue no kinu*). Noritaka, who belonged to the 6th Rank, would have worn green, but in the semi-darkness this could easily have been mistaken for black.

(266) *Fujiwara no Noritaka*, the elder brother of Nobutaka (Murasaki Shikibu's husband), was at this time a Chamberlain; later he was promoted to the post of Major Controller of the Left (see Index-Glossary). The reason that the ladies do not mind being seen by Noritaka is that he belongs to the 6th Rank; Yukinari is of the 4th Rank and therefore a far more awesome figure.

(267) *Tsubone no sudare uchi-kazuki nado shitamaumeri*: lit. 'he seemed to wear the blinds of the room [on his shoulders]'. This had become a set phrase.

(268) Every night at ten o'clock there was a roll-call (*nadaimen*) of the high-ranking courtiers on duty in Seiryō Palace, followed by a muster (*monjaku*) of the Imperial Guards of the Emperor's Private Office, who, as they approached, would twang their bow-strings (*yuminarashi*)

to scare away the evil spirits. When the Officer of the Guards, kneeling on the wide balcony outside the Imperial residence, called out,
'Who is present?' they all twanged their bow-strings and then
announced their names in turn. Since the lattice windows were all
closed'at night, Shōnagon and her companions could not actually see
the roll-call and muster; as a result the impressions in this passage are
mainly auditory.

I.e. from the Kokiden no Ue no Mi-Tsubone (App. 9g). (269)

Minamoto no Masahiro, a Chamberlain and subsequently governor of (270)
Awa Province, appears in *The Pillow Book* as a gauche, ludicrous
figure, and Shōnagon obviously enjoys describing his solecisms. Here,
instead of listening to the report of the Officer of the Guards and then
retiring with silent dignity as was the custom on these occasions,
Masahiro feels that he must comment angrily on the absences, even
though in the past he went to the opposite extreme of not listening to
the report at all. In the following paragraph he commits the appalling
gaffe of leaving his shoes on the board where the Imperial meals were
served (see *omonodana* in Index-Glossary), having presumably mistaken it for a shoe-shelf. Since ancient times the Japanese have
regarded shoes as ritually unclean objects, and Masahiro's carelessness therefore calls for purgation (see *harae* in Index-Glossary).
    The probable date of this section is 996 (see App. 4). For more
about Masahiro see section 104.

Even Masahiro cannot bring himself to pronounce the name of some- (271)
thing so (ritually) unclean as shoes.

Susogo (see note 27). Because the lower part of their clothes is spattered (272)
with mud.

Various grades of attendants (*tsukaibito*) were allotted to people (273)
according to their rank. A man of the Junior Fifth Rank, for example,
received twenty official retainers known as *shijin*. This, of course,
represented an additional form of income.

The following table includes the places mentioned in sections 58–61: (274)

	Section	Place	Province (District)	Literary association	Literal meaning
1.	58	Otonashi	Kii (Muro)	*Shūi Shū*	No Sound
2.	„	Furu	Yamato (Yamabe)		
3.	„	Nachi	Kii (Higashimuro)	*Fuboku Shū*	

	Section	Place	Province (District)	Literary association	Literal meaning
4.	58	Todoroki	Rikuzen		Roaring
5.	59	Asuka	Yamato (Takechi)	*Kokin Shū*	
6.	,,	Ōi	Yamashiro (Arashiyama)		Great Dam
7.	,,	Izumi	Yamashiro (Sōraku)		Source
8.	,,	Minase	Settsu	*Kokin Shū*	Shoals Without Water
9.	,,	Mimito	Yamashiro (Heian Kyō)	*Rokujō*	Keen-Eared
10.	,,	Otonashi	Kii (Muro)	,,	No Sound
11.	,,	Hosotani	? Bitchū	*Kokin Shū*	Narrow Valley
12.	,,	Tamahoshi	Rikuzen	*Fuboku Shū*	Jewelled Star
13.	,,	Nuki	? Mino (Mushiroda)	*saibara*	
14.	,,	Sawada	Yamashiro (Sōraku)	,,	Marsh Field
15.	,,	Nanoriso	unidentified		Do Not Say It
16.	,,	Natori	Rikuzen (Natori)	*Kokin Shū*	Notoriety
17.	,,	Yoshino	Yamato (Yoshino)	*Kokin Shū*	
18.	,,	Ama no Gawa	Kawachi	*Kokin Shū*	The Milky Way
19.	,,	Asamutsu	Echizen	*saibara*	Shallow Water
20.	60	Nagara	Settsu	*Kokin Shū*	
21.	,,	Amabiko	unidentified		Echoes
22.	,,	Hamana	Tōtōmi	*Shigeyuki Shū*	
23.	,,	(hitotsubashi)	Settsu	*Rokujō*	
24.	,,	Sano	? Higo		
25.	,,	Utajime	Yamato (Nara)		
26.	,,	Todoroki	? Yamato (Nara)	? *Horikawa Hyakushu*	Roaring
27.	,,	Ogawa	? Mutsu	*Shūi Shū*	Small River
28.	,,	kakehashi	Shinano (Kiso Dōchū)	,,	
29.	,,	Seta	Ōmi (Biwa)		
30.	,,	Kisoji	Shinano (Kiso Dōchū)	*Shūi Shū*	
31.	,,	Horie	Settsu		Canal
32.	,,	Kasasagi	Yamashiro (Heian Kyō)	*Yamato Monogatari*	Magpie
33.	,,	Yukiai	unidentified	*Rokujō*	Meeting
34.	,,	Ono	unidentified		
35.	,,	Yamasuge	Shimotsuke (Nikkō)		Mountain Rushes
36.	,,	Utatane	Yamato	*Fuboku Shū*	Nap
37.	61	Ōsaka	Ōmi (Shiga)	*Gosen Shū*, etc.	Slope of Meetings
38.	,,	Nagame			Contemplation
39.	,,	Isame	Mino (Ibi)	*Rokujō*	Remonstrance

56

Section	Place	Province (District)	Literary association	Literal meaning
40.	61 Hitozuma	unidentified		(Another Man's) Wife
41.	„ Tanome	Shinano (Ine)	Fuboku Shū	Confidence
42.	„ Asakaze	Yamato		Morning Zephyr
43.	„ Yūhi	Tango		Evening Sun
44.	„ Tōchi	Yamato (Yamabe)	Shūi Shū	Ten Markets
45.	„ Fushimi	? Yamato (Sōshimo)	Kokin Shū	Furtive Glance
46.	„ Nagai	? Yamato	Fuboku Shū	Long Well
47.	„ Tsumatori	Mutsu		Wife Abduction

In Shōnagon's time only two Emperors (Uda and Kazan) had held (275) the title of Hōō (Cloistered Emperor or Priestly Retired Sovereign), and the chronicles do not mention either of them as having visited Furu Waterfall. She is probably confusing two events: (i) the visit of Emperor Kōkō (reg. 885–7) to Furu Waterfall when he was still Crown Prince, (ii) the visit of Emperor Uda (reg. 887–97) to Yoshino no Miya Waterfall.

Probably because Emperor Kazan had recently made a pilgrimage (276) to Nachi and had written about the falls. As in the previous lists of this type (cf. sections 62 and 199), many of the names are included only because of their poetic associations.

A play of words on todoroki ('roaring', 'booming'). Shōnagon had (277) almost certainly never visited this waterfall in the northern wilds of Japan.

Reference to the Kokin Shū poem: (278)

Yo no naka wa   What in this world of ours can last?
Nani ka tsune naru   In Asuka River
Asukagawa   Yesterday's deep pools
Kinō no fuchi zo   Have dwindled to the shallows of today.
Kyō wa se to naru

Since Asuka is a mountain stream, its depth changes rapidly depending on the rainfall.

Shōnagon is thinking of Ki no Tsurayuki's poem in the Rokujō: (279)

Momoshiki no   Ah, the keen-eared stream of Mimito
Ōmiya chikaki   That flows outside the Palace of the hundred
Mimitogawa   rocks—
Nagarete kimi wo   Its waters hear the voice of my beloved!
Kikiwataru ka na

57

There is a play of words on *mimito* ('ear-sharp'). Mimitogawa was a small river near the Greater Imperial Palace.

(280) *Otonashigawa*: note 274 (no. 10): Literal meaning.

(281) I.e. the two following *saibara*:

Nukigawa no sese no	As Nuki River gently flows along,
Yawara temakura	Softly she makes a pillow of her arm,
Yawaraka ni nuru	And night after night she lies awake—
Yo wo nakute	The young wife weeping for her kin.
Oya sakuru tsuma	

Sawadagawa	If you cross the stream of Sawada,
Sode tsuku bakari	The water scarcely wets your sleeve.
Asakeredo	Yet Kuni's courtiers built a lofty bridge
Kuni no miyabito	To span its shallow flow.
Takahashi watasu	

Kuni (in Yamashiro Province) was the Emperor's residence from 724 to 748.

(282) *Nanoriso*: unknown. It was presumably included for its odd name, which meant 'Do not say it' with the implication, 'Do not divulge the truth about this secret love affair' (cf. note 283).

(283) A further reference to the *Kokin Shū*:

Michinoku ni	Alas, how sad
Ari to iu naru	That the River of Natori,
Natorigawa	Which waters Michinoku's northern lands,
Ukina torite wa	Should take a name so base!
Kanashikarikeri	

Natori has the secondary sense of 'notoriety' (usually from being involved in a scandalous love affair).

(284) *Ama no Gawa* (lit. 'the river of heaven') refers to (i) the Milky Way, (ii) a river in Kawachi, south of the capital. Here Shōnagon recalls Narihira's poem in the *Kokin Shū*:

Karikurashi	After the long day's hunt
Tanabatatsume ni	We reach the Heavenly River's banks.
Yado karamu	Let us ask the Weaver maiden
Ama no kawara ni	To lodge us for the night!
Ware wa kinikeri	

For the Weaver (Tanabatatsume) see note 55. The poem was com-

posed by the famous poet-lover, Ariwara no Narihira, when he NOTES
accompanied Prince Koretaka on a hunting expedition.

Funabashi (boat bridge): boats were lined up all the way across the (285)
river and used as a bridge.

There is some confusion here, and the original text appears to be (286)
corrupt. The name Yamasuge ('Mountain Rushes') is not especially
interesting; possibly Shōnagon is thinking of the old name, 'Snake
Bridge of the Mountain Rushes' (Yamasuge no Hebibashi).

Most of the villages appear to have been included for their names (287)
rather than for their poetic associations.

Tsumatori no Sato: note 274 (no. 47): Literal meaning. (288)

See note 140. According to the chronicles, the deity Kamo no (289)
Wakiikatsuchi on the eve of his return to the Plain of High Heaven
instructed his followers to decorate themselves with hollyhock if they
wished to ensure his return to earth.

A play on words: *omodaka* (water plantain, *alisna plantago*) has the (290)
secondary meaning of 'high face', i.e. 'pompous', 'haughty'.

Shōnagon is probably thinking of the Chinese poem in *Wakan* (291)
Rōei Shū:

> Kuan shen an o li ken ts'ao   I see that this, my life,
> Is like the flower on the mountain's
> edge,
> Whose roots are far away.

The name of this plant (*itsumadegusa*) has the literal meaning of (292)
'until-when? grass', with the implication that its existence is precarious. It usually grows on old walls, crumbling houses, etc.

Kotonashigusa: lit. 'nothing-wrong herb'. Commentators have been (293)
unable to determine its identity.

Shinobugusa: a type of fern or moss (*polypodium lineare*) that grows (294)
mainly on rocks, old walls, tree stumps, etc. Its name has the literal
sense of 'the grass that endures [hardships]'; this is why Shōnagon
considers it pathetic.

For the anthologies in this section see Index-Glossary.

(295) Shōnagon prefixes the title of the *Manyō Shū* with the word *Ko* ('Old') to distinguish it from later works with similar names, e.g. the *Shinsen Manyō* ('New Selection of Myriad Leaves'), a collection of poems by members of the Sugawara family, and the *Zoku Manyō Shū* ('Continuation of the Collection of Myriad Leaves'), which was an alternative name for the *Kokin Shū*.

The other collections extant in her time were 'family collections' (*kashū*) and the *Kokin Rokujō*. The *Shūi Shū* (the third of the 'Three [Official] Anthologies') was not compiled until after *The Pillow Book*, but most of its poems were known to Shōnagon.

(296) All but two of these items (viz. the boat and the jujube tree) are subjects of poems in the *Kokin Rokujō*.

(297) *Asagao* (althea): lit. 'morning face'. In modern Japanese this word designates the convolvulus or morning glory, but in Shōnagon's time it apparently referred to (i) the shrubby althea or rose of Sharon, *hibiscus syriacus*, nowadays called *mukuge*, (ii) the campanula, a plant with broad, bell-shaped, violet blossoms (sometimes known as the 'Chinese balloon flower'), *platycodon grandiflorum*, nowadays called *kikyō*. Such changes in meaning have occurred frequently in words designating Japanese flora and fauna, and they provide one of the main difficulties in understanding these passages of *The Pillow Book*; almost anyone who nowadays reads Shōnagon's book without a commentary would assume that *asagao* referred to the morning glory.

(298) *Kamatsuka* means, literally, 'sickle handle', presumably because the wood of the amaranth plant was used for their manufacture. The word can be written with Chinese characters signifying 'wild-goose-come-flower'; for it blossomed in the autumn with the arrival of the wild geese.

(299) See note 297. *Yūgao* ('moonflower') has the literal meaning of 'evening face' and *asagao* ('althea') of 'morning face'; the flowers open in the evening and morning respectively.

(300) During a Shintō festival in Shinano Province on the 27th of the 7th Month reeds were made into pendants and hung outside shrines, etc., as offerings (*mitegura*) to the gods. Later the reeds themselves came to be known as *mitegura*.

(301) Kaneko suggests (*Hyōshaku*, p. 317) that the late autumn miscanthus

(*susuki*) may have .reminded Shōnagon of some old lady with dishevelled white hair whom she had known at Court. For *susuki* see
note 448.

There is a traditional poetic association (see note 194) between the (302)
bush-clover (*hagi*), which is represented as a beautiful girl, and her
lover, the stag, who visits her every morning.

This poem, which was probably written by Shōnagon's contemporary, (303)
Izumi Shikibu, is included in the *Goshūi Shū*:

Iwa-tsutsuji	I plucked a rhododendron
Orimote zo miru	And brought it home
Seko ga kishi	And gazed at it.
Kurenai some no	For in the blossom's crimson hue
Iro ni nitareba	I saw the robe my lover wore.

Shōbi wa . . . yūbae (after it has been raining . . . shines down on them): (304)
roses (*shōbi*) were particularly admired in China, and probably
Shōnagon is thinking of Po Chü-i's

Chieh ti ch'iang wei ju hsia k'ai	Under the steps
	The roses blossom in the summer
	sun.

Being a woman, she can never visit him in his monastery. Twelve (305)
years was a standard period for retreats (*yamagomori*) in Buddhist
centres like Hieizan.

Strawberries (*ichigo*) in Shōnagon's time were smaller than the present (306)
(Western) variety eaten in Japan; but they were far prettier in colour,
and it would be particularly 'unsettling' (*obotsukanashi*) to eat them in
the dark, when one could not admire their attractive nuances of red.

Note the *Rokujō* poem: (307)

Omowanu to	He whom I loved
Omou to futari	And that same lover when my love has gone—
Kurabureba	How can I say that both are one?
Onaji hito to ya	
Iubekarikeru	

But see p. 48 for Shōnagon's usual opinion about crows (*karasu*). (308)

Shōnagon refers to a well-known Taoist story. One day a wood- (309)
cutter, Wang Chih (Ō Shitsu), came on two sages playing a game of

61

go in a mountain cave. He began watching them and was soon absorbed in their game. They were still playing when he saw to his amazement that the handle of his axe had rotted away. When he returned to his village, he found (in Rip Van Winkle fashion) that everyone he knew had been dead for years. After this disturbing discovery Wang Chih returned to the mountain and in the end joined the ranks of Taoist immortals.

(310) *Bonnō kunō* (the bondage . . . the suffering): Buddhist terms referring, respectively, to the bondage of the flesh and to the suffering inherent in all life. Here, of course, they are used without any religious significance, rather in the way that we might say, 'What a cross to bear!' Kaneko (*Hyōshaku*, p. 326) cites this as an example of how Buddhist terminology had come to be adopted by even the lowest members of society.

(311) Being members of the lower orders, they are unaware of good or evil; the words that issue from their mouths are closer to animal grunts than to the rational comments of human beings.

(312) Shōnagon is thinking of the *Rokujō* poem,

Kokoro ni wa	He who does not speak his love,
Shita yuku mizu no	Yet feels its waters seething far below,
Wakikaeri	Loves more than he who prates his every thought.
Iwade omou zo	
Iu ni masareru	

The dismay of the attendants is all the greater for not being expressed in words.

(313) They say this in order to encourage their master to end his visit and return home.

(314) In this fashion, known as *oshidashi*, women let the bottom of their many-layered costume protrude outside their curtain of state so that visitors might admire the colour combination. Here the curtain of state has been set up underneath a set of bright green blinds.

(315) Here Shōnagon refers to one of the Special Festivals (note 66), which had been celebrated since the end of the ninth century. In the 10th Month the messengers, envoys, dancers, and singers were chosen, and a series of rehearsals was organized. The festival itself took place in the 11th Month, and two days before its opening there was a formal rehearsal (*shigaku*) of dancing and music in front of Seiryō Palace.

During the Kamo and Iwashimizu celebrations the dancers and
singers proceeded from the Palace to the respective shrines, where they
carried out their performances; they then returned to the Palace and,
depending on the occasion (see note 672), performed an encore.

Traditional song of the *fūzoku-uta* type: (316)

Arata ni ouru   Come, lads, let's pluck the rice-flowers from the
Tomikusa no hana   freshly-planted fields
Te ni tsumirete   And bear them to the Palace for our lord.
Miya e mairamu
Naka tsutae

The following two scenes probably take place in the 6th or 7th Month (317)
of 997; Kaneko (*Hyōshaku*, p. 343), however, puts them a year later
(App. 4).

The approach of a High Court Noble was heralded by prolonged cries (318)
of 'Make way!' (*ōsaki*); the cries for a senior courtier were shorter
(*kosaki*). *Konoe no mi-kado* (Gate of the Inner Palace Guards) referred
to the Yōmei Mon (App. 9e), which was directly to the east of the
southern side of Shiki no Mi-Zōshi.

Nanigashi hitokoe no aki ('So on and so forth—and the voice of (319)
autumn speaks'). the courtiers are reciting a Chinese poem by
Minamoto no Hideakira (later included in *Wakan Rōei Shū*):

Ch'ih leng shui wu san fu hsia   Fresh is the pond,
Sung kao feng yu i sheng ch'iu   Whose waters ban the summer's heat.
                                  In the wind that sways the towering
                                    pines
                                  The voice of autumn always speaks.

The early texts all have *itōshige naki mono* ('things that do not arouse (320)
pity'), but the context suggests that this is a copyist's error for
itōshige naru mono ('things that make one sorry'), the *ru* having been
mistaken for a *ki*.

Uzue (hare-wands): cf. hare-sticks (*uzuchi*), note 113. These were (321)
also associated with the New Year observances on the 1st Day of the
Hare. The wands, which were five feet long and decorated with five-
coloured tassels, were presented to the Imperial Palace by Shingon
and Tendai exorcists and also by officers from each of the six Guard
Divisions (Rokoefu); like most other appurtenances of the New Year
celebrations, they were supposed to ward off evil influences. The

63

priests and officers who presented the wands to the Emperor were especially proud of their duty. See also note 730.

(322) *Kagura no ninjō* (director of dancers . . .): see note 673.

(323) *Goryō E* (Feast of the Sacred Spirit): held annually in the capital on the 14th day of the 6th Month in honour of Susanoo, the Storm God (App. 1). Horses from the Imperial Palace were led through the streets, and there were races and sacred dances.

(324) The provinces (*kuni*) of Japan (App. 9a) were divided into four categories depending on their size, wealth, and importance: (i) *taikoku* (great provinces), (ii) *jōkoku* (superior provinces), (iii) *chūkoku* (medium provinces), (iv) *gekoku* (inferior provinces). Provinces listed in the Index-Glossary are all identified accordingly. *Daiichi no kuni* ('first-class province') refers to categories (i)–(iii).
For 'period of official appointments' see Index-Glossary.

(325) *Butsumyō* (Naming of the Buddhas): one of the last of the annual ceremonies, being celebrated in the various palaces towards the end of the 12th Month (App. 1). It dated from 774. The ceremony consisted of three services, each directed by a different Leader (*Dōshi*) on three successive nights. It was aimed at expunging the sins one had committed during the course of the year. While the ceremony was being held, painted screens depicting the horrors of hell (*jigoku-e*) were set up in Seiryō Palace to remind the participants of the need for penitence.
The present scene takes place in 993 or possibly 994 (see App. 4).

(326) *Tsurezure* (bored): see note 143.

(327) *Minamoto no Michikata* (see Index-Glossary): son of the Minister of the Left, Shigenobu, he was appointed to be one of the three Minor Counsellors in 990, promoted to the post of Minor Controller of the Left in 998, and ended his career as Provisional Middle Counsellor.
Minamoto no Narimasa: minor official, mentioned in Murasaki Shikibu's diary. He served in Mino Province and was appointed Middle Captain in 1010.
Yukinari: see Fujiwara no Yukinari in Index-Glossary.
Minamoto no Tsunefusa: son of the former Minister of the Left, Takaakira; at the time of this scene he was a mere Minor Captain of the Inner Palace Guards, Left Division, but later he rose to the posts of Imperial Adviser and Provisional Middle Counsellor; he was Governor of Ise from 995 to 996.

Sō no fue (thirteen-pipe flute): set of reeds comparable with the Pan- NOTES (328) pipe; it was used mainly for Court music. According to some of the texts, Yukinari is a mistake for (Taira no) Yukiyoshi, a well-known flautist who at the time of this scene was a Captain in the Middle Palace Guards.

Biwa no koe wa yamete monogatari semu to suru koto ososhi ('the music (329) stops, but still we sit there quiet, loath to break the silence with our talk'): quotation from Po Chü-i's famous 'Song of the Lute' (*P'i p'a hsing*) describing his exile from the capital. One evening, when he is seeing off a friend whose boat is moored on a river, he hears the sound of the *p'i p'a* (lute) from a neighbouring boat:

Hu wen shui shang p'i p'a sheng	Suddenly we hear the lute's voice
Chu jen wang kuei k'o pu fa	on the water.
Hsün sheng an wen t'an che shui	At the plucking of its strings.
P'i p'a sheng t'ing yü yü ch'ih	My host forgets to go.
	I too find it hard to leave.
	We search the darkness, wondering
	who the player is.
	The music stops, but the player
	will not speak her name.

That is, the lute-player hesitates to identify herself to the poet and his friend.

Tsumi wa osoroshi: lit. 'my guilt is fearful'. Instead of contemplating (330) the Buddhist paintings of hell, Shōnagon is enthralled by the secular activities in the Empress's apartments.

Fujiwara no Tadanobu (see Index-Glossary) was a successful official (331) who attained the posts of Chief of the Imperial Police and Major Counsellor. He was one of the 'Four Counsellors' known for their poetic talents, the others being Fujiwara no Kintō, Fujiwara no Yukinari, and Minamoto no Toshikata. Tadanobu is frequently mentioned as one of Shōnagon's chief lovers, but Waley (*W.P.B.*, pp. 154-5) believes that their affair had already finished by the time she entered the Empress's service and that his position at Court was now too elevated for her to be on terms of easy familiarity with him. The reader can draw his own conclusions from the passages that follow.

Kurodo (Black Door): door leading to the gallery at the north of (332) Seiryō Palace (App. 9g); *Kurodo* also referred to the gallery itself.

The 2nd Month of 995 (App. 4).

(333)   *On-Monoimi* (Imperial Abstinence): when the Emperor went into retreat, certain important officials like the Captain First Secretary and the Controller First Secretary secluded themselves in Seiryō Palace with him and observed the rules of abstinence (*monoimi*).

(334) *Hen* (game of parts): a popular, upper-class game that consisted in guessing the identity of partially hidden characters in Chinese poems. One of the ladies might, for instance, cover the phonetic part of the character and from the context the other ladies would try to guess the radical.

(335) *Nanigashi saburai*: these are the messenger's own words; instead of giving his name or saying who has sent him, he simply refers to himself as *nanigashi* ('a certain [person]').

(336) *Ise no monogatari* (a tale from Ise): proverbial expression referring to stories that were strange or incredible. It apparently derived from the supposed unreliability of the inhabitants of Ise, rather than from any far-fetched quality in the episodes of 'The Tales of Ise' (*Ise Monogatari*), but scholars disagree about the origins of the phrase. See Fritz Voss, *A Study of the Ise-Monogatari*, pp. 66-75.

(337) *Ranshō no hana no toki kinchō no moto*: lit. 'during the flower season under the brocade dais'. Tadanobu quotes a line from the third stanza of a poem that Po Chü-i wrote during his exile (note 329) to a friend who was still basking in the delights of the capital:

Lan sheng hua shih chin chang hsia	With you it is flower time
Lu Shan yü yeh ts'ao an chung	Where you sit in the Council Hall
	Beneath a curtain of brocade;
	Here in the mountains of Lu Shan
	The rain pours down all night
	Upon my grass-thatched hut.

Although Shōnagon knows the following line (*Rozan no ame no yoru*—'Here in the mountains . . .') perfectly well, she prefers to avoid Chinese characters, the so-called 'men's writing' (*otoko-moji*). Instead she uses the *kana* script to write the last two lines (7-7 syllables) of a Japanese poem on the same theme; in her reply she implies that, since Tadanobu is angry with her, she can expect no visitors. To understand why Shōnagon's reply (*Kusa no iori wo / Tare ka tazunemu*) was so successful we must remember that Chinese literature, even

the poetry of such a popular writer as Po Chü-i, was supposed NOTES
to be beyond women's ken. To send a Chinese poem to a woman
was most unconventional; that is why Shōnagon was at a complete loss.

Kusa no Iori (Grass Hut) would be a most inappropriate name for (338)
anyone living in the Imperial Palace.
   Tama no Utena (Jade Tower) is a further reference to Chinese
literature. The phrase (*yü t'ai*) occurs in the *Li yüeh chih* ('Treatise
on Rites and Music') in the *Han shu* (note 36). Here Shōnagon uses
it in opposition to 'grass hut', echoing the contrast between the hut
and the Council Chamber in Po Chü-i's poem.

Nusubito (lit. 'thief'): used in contemporary literature as a favourable (339)
epithet to designate an unusual or original person; 'rogue' is the
closest English equivalent.

This was one of the many forms of poetic exchange current in (340)
fashionable circles. The standard Japanese poem (*tanka*) consists of
two main parts: (i) the beginning (*moto*) having three lines of 5-7-5
syllables, (ii) the end (*sue*) having two lines of 7-7. One could
send either of these parts, inviting the recipient to provide the
other.

Suri Shiki (Office of Palace Repairs): office in charge of building and (341)
repair work in the Imperial Palace; *Suke* (Assistant Master) ranked
second among the officials in charge.
   Tachibana no Norimitsu (see Index-Glossary): government official
who rose to be Governor of Harima and later of Mutsu. He did not
obtain his post in the Office of Palace Repairs until 996, one year
after the present incident; such anachronisms are common in *The
Pillow Book*.
   Norimitsu was on such friendly terms with Shōnagon that people
referred to him as her 'elder brother' (*shōto*), a term often used to
describe a husband; he knew nothing of the all-important art of
poetry, however, and a few years after the present incident Shōnagon
broke with him (see pp. 79-80). The chronicles refer to his physical
courage (on one occasion he arrested a bandit single-handed); but
this did not count for much among 'good people' of Heian. According
to some scholars, Norimitsu was Shōnagon's husband before she
entered Court service (Nihon Bungaku Taikei ed. of *Makura no
Sōshi*, p. 10); but, considering the way in which he is described in her

67

book, this would appear unlikely. It seems more probable that Shōnagon had several lovers, including Norimitsu, but never became a principal wife (*kita no kata*).

(342) It was not obligatory to reply to a reply.

(343) *Sodegichō*: lit. 'use one's sleeve as a curtain'.

(344) I.e. the 2nd Month of 996 (App. 4).

(345) *Umetsubo*: lit. '[Palace of the] Plum-Tree Tub', also known as the Gyōke Sha. It was one of the smaller buildings north of Seiryō Palace (see App. 9f), and was usually occupied by Imperial consorts. Many of the Palace buildings, especially those used by women, were named after the flowering shrubs planted in tubs (*tsubo*) outside.

(346) *Kurama*: Shingon temple some seven miles north of the capital (App. 9c); it was founded in 797.

(347) For details about the avoidance of unlucky directions see note 103. In this case the southern direction was 'closed' by the temporary presence of one of the moving divinities (probably Nakagami or Konjin), and Tadanobu had to stop at some intermediate point south-west of Kurama before returning to the capital. It was essential to reach the intermediate point (*tabisho*) before sunset, but one could leave it and proceed to one's destination at any time after 11 p.m. 'Once the Hour of the Boar [i.e. 10-12 p.m.] has passed, one can continue one's journey; there is no need to wait until daybreak' (*Shintei Zōho Konjitsu Sōsho*, xxii. 496). Therefore Tadanobu can reasonably expect to be back in the capital before dawn.

(348) *Mi-Kushige* (Office of the Imperial Wardrobe): housed in Jōgan Palace (Index-Glossary). Its main duty (overlapping with those of the Bureau of the Wardrobe, note 208) was to provide the robes worn by the Emperor and his wives. The Office was under a Mistress of the Robes (Bettō), who was often one of the Emperor's secondary consorts. She was in charge of a number of Lady Chamberlains (Nyo-Kurōdo), low-ranking attendants who were responsible for sewing and for miscellaneous duties in the Palace. Here the incumbent is Empress Sadako's sister, the fourth daughter of Fujiwara no Michitaka.

Shōnagon was about thirty.
Aesthetic convention demanded long, straight hair that hung over (349)
the shoulders in perfect order.

For Michitaka, who had died some ten months earlier. (350)

Nishi no Kyō (West City): the section of the capital to the left (looking (351)
north) of the central north-south avenue (see note 72 and App. 9d).
It fell into an early decline, becoming overgrown with weeds and much
frequented by footpads, while the main part of Heian Kyō expanded
eastwards.
Although the temple that Tadanobu had visited lay north of the
capital, he was obliged to spend part of the night in a house to the west
in order to avoid an unlucky direction (note 347). This is why he
reached Shōnagon's house from the West City.

Minamoto no Suzushi and Fujiwara no Nakatada were characters in (352)
Utsubo Monogatari ('The Tale of the Hollow Tree'), a long, popular,
but for many modern readers ineffably dull, romance of the late tenth
century, whose authorship has variously been attributed to the father
of Murasaki Shikibu and to Minamoto no Shitagau.
Nakatada, the handsome hero, was since his early youth noted for
his musical gifts, which he displayed on a set of miraculous zithers.
He was also distinguished for his filial piety. Nakatada's father,
Toshikage, a gentleman in the Court of Emperor Suzaku (reg.
930–46), had been obliged to leave his wife; the dutiful son
looked after this unhappy woman, feeding her on fish and the fruits
of the forest, and even finding her a comfortable shelter in a hollow
tree (which had thoughtfully been abandoned by a family of bears
who were impressed by the young man's Confucian virtues). In the
course of a pilgrimage Nakatada's father eventually discovered his
wife and son and brought them back to the capital, where the hero
enjoyed a brilliant career, climaxed by betrothal to the Emperor's
daughter.
Suzushi, Nakatada's rival, was also a talented musician. His accomplishments were of course no match for the hero's, though on one
occasion when he was playing the zither at dawn he managed to charm
a heavenly maiden into descending from the sky for a short time and
dancing to his music. It is to this incident that Shōnagon refers in her
reply to the Empress, who has evidently been running down Nakatada
in favour of Suzushi.
Despite the somewhat doubtful literary merits of *Utsubo*, Shōnagon
mentions it more than any of the other *monogatari*. Until the

69

appearance of *The Tale of Genji* it was probably the most discussed work of prose fiction in Heian Kyō. The partisanship that we saw in this scene was typical of literary discussion among educated women of the time.

(353) Lit. 'how could we thus have discovered the thread that tied it all together down to the [last] seam?'

(354) An elliptical sentence; the implied ending is something like 'I should have been still more moved'.

(355) For Lady Saishō see note 87. Here she displays her erudition by referring to some nostalgic lines of Po Chü-i's from the poem that describes the desolation of the old palace of Mount Li (to the west of the Tʿang capital of Chʿang An). The poem starts, 'On lofty Mount Li stands a palace' and the lines in question are:

Tsʿui hua pu lai hsi sui yüeh chiu	How many months, how many
Chʿiang yu i hsi wa yu sung	years, have passed
Wu chün tsai wei i wu tsai	Since the Imperial banners last
Ho pu i hsing hu chʿi chung	appeared!
Hsi fang chʿü tu men chi to ti	The walls lie silent under moss
	And the tiles are choked with fern.
	His Majesty has been five years
	on the Throne.
	Why has he not once paid a visit
	here?
	It is not far from the city's
	western gate. . . .

That is, it does not take long to reach Mount Li from the western gate of the capital, yet during the five years of his reign the Emperor has not once visited the Old Palace. The words used by Lady Saisho are *kawara no matsu wa aritsu ya*; Tadanobu's reply is *nishi no kata tomon wo sareru koto, ikubaku no chi zo*. The western gate of the old Chinese capital is of course identified with the desolate West City (note 351) of Heian Kyō.

(356) When they were ill and during their *menses* ladies-in-waiting returned to their homes (*sato*) or to some other private dwelling outside the Imperial compound. This was to avoid ritual defilement in the Palace, where Shintō rules of purity were meticulously observed.

(357) In the 2nd, or possibly the 8th, Month of 999 (App. 4), these being the two months when the Sacred Readings (note 360) took place.

Seaweed (*me, hirume, kombon, nori*) has been part of the Japanese diet NOTES
since the earliest times; it is usually eaten with rice, fish, etc. (358)

Lit. 'a letter from the Outer Palace Guards Left Division' (*Saemo no* (359)
fumi). This was the Guards regiment in which Norimitsu served.

Mi-Dōkyō (Sacred Readings): a half-yearly Buddhist ceremony (360)
during which a large group of priests gathered in the Palace and took
turns in reading the 600 chapters of the Sutra of Great Wisdom
(*Mahāprajñāpāramitā Sūtra*, Jap. *Dai Hannya Kyō*). The readings,
which took place weekly in the 2nd and 8th Months, continued for
four days, the last being known as the Day of Conclusion (*Kechigan*).
The eve of this day was an occasion for Imperial Abstinence (*On-
Monoimi*).

Since it was by putting a piece of seaweed in his mouth that he had (361)
earlier managed to keep the secret. But Shōnagon's implication
('Continue to hide my whereabouts from Tadanobu!') is completely
lost on the blunt-witted Norimitsu.

I.e. unless it had some special meaning. (362)

> Kazuki suru (363)
> Ama no sumika wa
> Soko nari to
> Yume iu na to ya
> Me wo kuwasekemu

The poem is cryptic and might have confounded a more perceptive
reader than Norimitsu. In it Shōnagon compares herself to a woman
diver (*ama*) who spends most of her time in the water and has no fixed
abode. She is probably referring to a verse in the *Wakan Rōei Shū* that
establishes the idea that a woman diver has no proper home:

Shiranami no	How should I have a fixed abode
Yosuru nagisa ni	Who spend my life upon the wave-washed shore
Yo wo tsukusu	And diving in the sea?
Ama no ko nareba	
Yado mo sadamezu	

The crux of Shōnagon's own poem is a play of words on *me wo
kuwase* — (i) glance or wink meaningfully (lit. 'spread one's eye'),
(ii) cause to eat seaweed. The last line therefore has the additional
meaning, 'That must be why she [sent you] seaweed to eat'. There is
also a pun on *soko* = (i) there (where), (ii) the bottom [of the sea].
The link between seaweed (*me*) and woman divers (*ama*) was well

71

NOTES established in Japanese verse, but the particular word-plays in Shōnagon's poem are original.

(364) I.e. a poem. For the significance of Norimitsu's attitude to poetry see *W.S.P.*, p. 181.

(365)   Kuzureyoru
                           Imose no Yama no
                           Naka nareba
                           Sara ni Yoshino no
                           Kawa to dani miji

Another brain-twister for the unfortunate Norimitsu. The mountains of Imo and Se (see note 62, no. 37), standing close together in Yamato Province, are separated by Yoshino River; they had a poetic association with lovers or with husband and wife. (*Imo* means 'younger sister', *se* 'elder brother', and these words often referred to a woman and her lover; cf. *shōto* in note 341.) A well-known example of such an association is this *Kokin Shū* poem, which was no doubt in Shōnagon's mind when she wrote her own:

Nagarete wa	Between Mount Imo and Mount Se
Imose no Yama no	The River of Yoshino falls.
Naka ni otsuru	So goes this world of ours
Yoshino no Kawa no	[For those who love and cannot meet].
Yoshiya yo no naka	

In Shōnagon's poem the river represents the deep, steadfast relationship that has existed between herself and Norimitsu: once it has been broken off, she will no longer be able to recognize him even if they should meet. There is the usual play of words on *kawa* = (i) river, (ii) as for him. *Naka* has the double meaning of (i) between, (ii) relationship (of a man and woman). The poem can therefore also be understood as follows:

> Smoothly runs the river of Yoshino
> Between the woman and the one she loves.
> Yet, should their bonds be broken off,
> No longer would she know that man who used to be so near.

(366) Lit. 'things that cause people to know the pathos of the world (*mono no aware*)'. For a discussion of *mono no aware* see Hisamatsu Sen'ichi, *The Vocabulary of Japanese Aesthetics*, chap. 2; also *W.S.P.*, pp. 196-7.

(367) Heian women plucked their eyebrows and painted a thick new set about one inch above. See *W.S.P.*, pp. 203-4.

The present scene probably belongs to the autumn of 997 (App. 4). NOTES Shōnagon refers to the events of a few months earlier, described in (368) section 72 of her book (pp. 102 ff.). The opening words of the section (*Sate sono . . .*) suggest that it was intended to follow directly on section 72.

Another reference to *Utsubo Monogatari* (note 352). When Minamoto (369) no Suzushi sees that the heavenly maiden, whom he has charmed to earth by his music, is about to leave him, he vents his regret in a poem:

> Asaborake Faintly I saw her by the dawn's pale light,
> Honoka ni mireba The heavenly maiden hovering in the air.
> Akanu ka na Oh, that I could but make her stay a while!
> Naka naru otome
> Shibashi tomenamu

The expedition to the guard-house also took place very early in the morning. In her reply the Empress wonders why Shōnagon should allude to Suzushi's musical talents when previously she had taken the side of his rival, Nakatada.

Inochi mo sanagara sutete ('even if it means risking my life'): a con- (370) ventional hyperbole.

Fudan no Mi-Dokyō (Perpetual Sacred Readings), often abbreviated (371) to *Fudan Kyō* (Perpetual Readings), were held at irregular intervals in the Palace. Readings of the Sutra of Great Wisdom, the Lotus Sutra, and other scriptures would continue day and night; each priest (in a group of twelve) read for about two hours at a time.

This section probably belongs to the 12th Month of 998 (see App. 4). The reader should remember that in the Japanese lunar calendar the 1st Month marked the beginning of spring rather than (as in the Julian calendar) the height of winter: hence the lady's doubts, later in the section, about how long the snow mountain will last.

Omina no hōshi: i.e. a mendicant nun. (372)

> Yoru wa tare to ka nemu (373)
> Hitachi no Suke to nemu
> Netaru nada mo yoshi

Hitachi no Suke: Assistant Governor of Hitachi Province.

> Otoko Yama no
> Mine no momijiba
> Sazo na wa tatsu tatsu

73

Mount Otoko, the site of the famous Iwashimizu Shrine south of the capital, was noted for its red autumn foliage. The beggar-nun's song naturally has a double meaning: just as the colourful leaves have made the mountain famous, so an association with lustful women (*iro* = (i) colour, (ii) lust) makes a man notorious (*otoko* = (i) name of the mountain, (ii) man). Both these songs appear to have been popular at the time.

(374) When a courtier or other person of rank received a robe as a reward (this being a common form of payment in Heian times), he would naturally put it over his shoulders and perform a short ceremonial dance of thanks. To Shōnagon and her companions it was shocking that a beggar-woman should ape her superiors in this way.

(375) *Tare ka wa omoiidemu*: lit. 'Who would remember her?'

(376) *Mono no futa* (lids): see note 26.
Building snow mountains (*yukiyama*) was a common winter pastime for members of the leisured class. Some of the mountains reached considerable dimensions. The *Taiki* in an entry dated 1146 describes a snow mountain that was about fourteen feet square and over eighteen feet high.

(377) *Shirayama no Kannon*: Shirayama (White Mountain), situated in the northern prefecture of Kaga in the so-called Snow Country (Yuki-guni), the area formerly known as Koshi, was dedicated to the worship of the eleven-faced Kannon (note 67). The upper part of Shirayama was perpetually covered with snow, and Shōnagon naturally chooses this particular divinity when composing her prayer about the snow mountain.

(378) *Tōgū* (Eastern Palace): refers to the Crown Prince's quarters, which were in the eastern part of the Emperor's own residence, the eastern direction being associated in Chinese geometric theory with the spring season and thus the idea of growth. The Crown Prince himself was usually called by this name; he was also known as Haru no Miya (Spring Palace). In 998, the date of the present scene, the Crown Prince was Ichijō's cousin, the future Emperor Sanjō (reg. 1011–16).
Koki Den (Koki Palace) (App. 9f) was the Empress's Residential Palace. (Readers of *The Tale of Genji* will recall that the name of Genji's stepmother, the scheming Empress who helped to have him exiled, was taken from this building.) At this time it was occupied by Ichijō's consort, Fujiwara no Yoshiko.

74

Kyōgoku Dono (Kyōgoku Palace) was a Provisional Imperial Palace
in the north-east corner of the capital; its present occupant was
Michitaka's brother and political successor, Fujiwara no Michinaga.

> Koko ni nomi (379)
> Mezurashi to miru
> Yuki no yama
> Tokorodokoro ni
> Furinikeru ka na

There is the usual play on words: *furu* = (i) to snow, (ii) to be old,
trite, commonplace.

> Urayamashi (380)
> Ashi mo hikarezu
> Watatsumi no
> Ika naru ama ni
> Mono tamauramu

In her poem the first beggar-nun (Hitachi no Suke) reveals her unpleasant character by referring enviously to her crippled colleague,
who has been so generously treated by the Empress and her ladies.
Ama ('nunnish diver') has the double sense of (i) woman diver,
(ii) nun; *watatsumi* (which I have translated as 'briny depths') is a
'pillow word' or stock epithet used in conjunction with *ama* (woman
diver). It originally referred to the Shintō sea-god and later to the
sea itself.

In aristocratic circles letters were usually attached to sprays or sprigs, (381)
the colour of whose leaves or flowers matched those of the paper as
well as the season and the mood of the poem (see *W.S.P.*, p. 188).

Saiin (the High Priestess of the Kamo Shrines) was chosen at the (382)
beginning of each reign from among the virgin daughters (sometimes
granddaughters) of the new Emperor. Her household was adminis-
tered by an office under an Intendant (*Bettō*). The institution of High
Priestess of Kamo was started in 818 (several centuries after that of
High Priestess of Ise) and lasted until 1204. Waley (*The Tale of Genji*,
pp. 298–300) refers to the Saiin as the 'Vestal Virgin of Kamo', but
he points out that she was not the guardian of any sacred fire.

The present incumbent was Princess Senshi (Index-Glossary),
the daughter of Emperor Murakami. Though High Priestesses were
usually changed with each new reign, Senshi held the post through
the reigns of three Emperors, from 976 to 1031; during her last years,
however, she was a Buddhist nun.

Moya ni ataritaru mi-kōshi: i.e. the lattice on the side of the central apartment (*moya*) next to the Empress's bedroom.

(384) *Ika de ka isogiagehaberazaramu*: lit. 'How could I not hurry to give it up (i.e. to present it) [to Your Majesty]?'

(385)
> Yama toyomu
> Yoki no hibiki wo
> Tazunureba
> Iwai no tsue no
> Oto ni zo arikeru

'Festive wands' (*iwai no tsue*) refers to the auspicious hare-wands distributed at the New Year (see Index-Glossary: *uzue*). *Yoki* has the double meaning of (i) axe, (ii) good, happy (linked here to 'festive'). A confusion of sense impressions (e.g. mistaking the snow for scattering cherry blossoms or vice versa) was a common convention in classical poetry.

(386) The plum-blossom colour combination (see *ume* in note 23) was especially popular at the New Year.

(387) *Koshi*: see note 377.

(388) *Koto no yoshi wo mōse*: lit. 'tell the state of affairs', i.e. tell them who has given the orders.

(389) *Sato* (home): see note 356.

(390) *Oribitsu* (chip-basket): box with curved corners made of strips of wood.

(391) *Ito kashikoshi to namu omoitaramu*: lit. 'I really think I was very clever'. But in Japanese she does not sound quite so cock-a-hoop.

(392) *Mono no futa* (a lid): see note 26.

(393) *Kano yorikitaramu hito ni kō kikasu na*: lit. 'Do not thus inform that person who approaches.' This may refer to Shōnagon's messenger; but the phrase is as vague as the literal translation suggests.

(394) I.e. it might have lasted all the year if it had been left alone. A playful exaggeration.

Rokui no Kurōdo (Chamberlain of the Sixth Rank): also known as Higerō (see note 156). Despite their low rank, these men were allowed to enter the Emperor's residence (Seiryō Den) and even to wear the Imperial colours (note 70). At the end of six years (not three or four as Shōnagon says) they were usually obliged to retire from the Emperor's Private Office; by way of compensation they were awarded the head-dress of nobility, i.e. promoted to the 5th Rank. (For the difference between 5th Rank Chamberlains and Chamberlains of the Fifth Rank see note 156.)

The privilege of access to the Emperor was highly regarded, and even promotion to the coveted 5th Rank did not make up for having one's name removed from the list (*hidamai no fuda*) of those who were admitted to the Senior Courtiers' Chamber. This was one of the few cases in which office took precedence over rank. In order to avoid having to 'go down' (note 156), Chamberlains would sometimes decline their promotion and serve another term of six years in the 6th Rank.

Whenever a new minister was appointed to the Great Council of States (i.e. the *Daijōkan*, the supreme organ of government below the Emperor according to the old Chinese-type administrative system), the Council officials gave a special entertainment known as the Ministers' Banquet (*Daijin no Daikyō*). On the occasion of such an appointment a Chamberlain of the Sixth Rank brought the new official a gift of sweet chestnuts (*amaguri*) from the Emperor. Lower officials (*shiyō*) of the Great Council were offered a cup of wine and a special bonus.

Akekure mishi mono to mo oboezu: lit. 'it would not seem to be a thing that he saw morning and night'. The messenger, a mere 6th-ranker, receives this courteous treatment because he is a Chamberlain.

(*Monjō-*)*Hakase* (Doctor of Literature): one of two officials in the Bureau of Education (*Daigaku Ryō*) who taught Chinese literature and history and who were also responsible for composing the prayers (*gammon*) that the Emperor addressed to the gods on special occasions. Although they belonged to the 5th Rank, Shōnagon describes them as 'commoners' (*gerō*): scholars in Japan had a considerably lower status than in China and did not usually enjoy the all-important privilege of being admitted to the Senior Courtiers' Chamber.

For the purpose of reading the scriptures, the day and night were divided into six periods, each with a special Buddhist designation (*hanya*, *goya*, etc.). Lectors (*Jikyōza*) specialized in studying and reciting the Lotus Sutra.

(400) A delivery room might seem an incongruous item in this list of 'splendid things'. The delivery of a Heian empress, however, was attended by a good deal of impressive ceremonial. Religious services took place for several days in the Imperial birth chamber (*mi-ubuya*), and the birth itself was witnessed by numerous white-clad courtiers. This was followed by ceremonial bathing, after which a sword and a tiger's head were shaken in front of the infant and rice scattered about the room—all to keep evil spirits at bay. Murasaki Shikibu's diary starts with a detailed description of an Imperial birth ceremony in 1008.

(401) The installation of an empress (*miyahajime*) was another elaborate ceremony. Shōnagon was probably present when her mistress, Sadako, was installed as Empress (*Chūgū*) in 990. The new Empress would be seated in her curtain-dais, next to which were placed the statues of a leonine creature known as *shishi* and of a 'Korean' dog (*komainu*), which were believed to ward off evil influences. (These two animals were actually the same, except that the 'lion' was yellow and had an open mouth, while the dog was white and had a closed mouth; both were originally imported from Korea.) Officials from the Table Office (Naizen Shi) would bring in the Imperial Cauldron (Mihetsui), an ancient object which was always taken along when the Court moved from one palace to another. The cauldron represented the god of the hearth, and the ceremony of setting it before the Empress symbolized that she had assumed a connubial status in which she and the Emperor would share divine protection (*not*, as some commentators have suggested, that she was now assuming responsibility for the Emperor's meals).

(402) *Ichi no Hito* (First Man: see note 83). The pilgrimage took place on the 13th of the 3rd Month (App. 1).

(403) The little Prince is Atsuyasu (Index-Glossary). His uncles are Michitaka's two sons, Korechika and Takaie, who were twenty-five and twenty-one respectively when the Prince was born. Shōnagon's optimism about the child's future was misplaced: owing to the fall of the Michitaka faction, Atsuyasu never became Emperor.

(404) *Natsu no kichō*: lit. 'summer curtain of state'; plain white material was used for *kichō* in the summer months. For 'uneven shading' see note 27.

Higeko (bearded basket): basket of plaited bamboo; the protruding ends of the bamboo were entwined round the basket to give a shaggy, beard-like appearance.

Hiwarigo (cypress box): partitioned box used for carrying food and (406) other provisions; it was made of *hi*, an expensive type of cypress.

As part of the preparations for the Iris Festival in the 5th Month. (407)

Kuchikigata (pattern of decaying wood): a design used in decorating (408) material, etc., and based on the grain of rotting wood.

Natsu no mokō: lit. 'summer head-blinds'. For 'head-blind' see note (409) 126. In the summer such blinds were decorated with light material (cf. note 403).
   Ikari no o (anchor cord): a cord with the cat attached to one end and a weighted object on the other; it was intended to prevent the animal from straying too far.

For *Nyo-Kurodo* (Lady Chamberlain) see note 348; for *Satsuki no* (410) *Sechi* (Festival of the Fifth Month, i.e. Iris Festival) see note 206.

Akahimo no iro ni wa aranu hire kutai: lit. 'sashes and waistbands that (411) are not the colour of red ribbons'. *Hire* (lit. 'fin') was a light piece of material that Court ladies wore over their shoulders as a decoration (see note 66); *kutai* was a long ribbon attached to the sash round their waists. Shōnagon is reminded of the red ribbons worn by the gentlemen (the Young Noblemen of the Lesser Abstinence) who participated in the Shintō ceremony of the Lesser Abstinence (Omi) during the 11th Month (App. 1). A pair of these ribbons (*himo*) was draped on the right shoulder over a white jacket with blue designs.

Butō (ceremonial movements): see note 58. (412)

See note 99. These dances took place shortly after the ceremony (413) of the Lesser Abstinence; hence the association of ideas (see note 411).

This was exceptional. Normally the Gosechi dancers were chosen (414) from among the unmarried daughters of Court Nobles and provincial officials (see note 99). The present scene probably took place in the 11th Month of 993; but 992 is possible (see App. 4).

Miyasundokoro no hito idasu woba waroki koto ni zo suru to kiku: lit.
(415) 'I heard [people] make (*or* regard) it as a bad thing to dispatch people of Miyasundokoro'.

Miyasu(n)dokoro (lit. 'honourable resting place') referred originally to the Emperor's bedchamber, but after the ninth century came to designate the Crown Prince's consort. The lady in question is Fujiwara no Genshi (Index-Glossary), Michitaka's second daughter, who rose to the rank of Imperial Concubine (Nyōgo) in the household of the Crown Prince, Prince Okisada (later Emperor Sanjō). She resided in the Shigei Sha, one of the buildings in the Imperial Palace compound (see Index-Glossary) and was sometimes known as 'the Imperial Concubine of the Shigei S(h)a' or simply as 'Shigei S(h)a'.

(416) *Nyōin* (Empress Dowager): lit. 'woman who has taken holy orders'; refers in *The Pillow Book* to Fujiwara no Akiko (Senshi), the widow of Emperor Enyū and mother of Ichijō (see Index-Glossary). She took her vows in 991, thereafter being known as Higashi Sanjō no In.

Shigei Sha no hito ('one from the Shigei Sha') refers to one of the ladies attendant on Fujiwara no Genshi (note 415). Kaneko (*Hyōshaku*, p. 475) estimates that each of the four main Gosechi dancers had some forty ladies in attendance, making a total of about 170 participants, apart from friends, relations, etc.

(417) See App. 3. The actual performance of the Gosechi dances took place on the 2nd Day of the Dragon (in the 11th Month) (App. 1).

(418) The women's costumes on the present exceptional occasion were similar to those of the Young Noblemen of the Lesser Abstinence (note 411); hence the surprise of the Court Nobles and senior courtiers and hence their novel designation of the ladies.

(419) On the final day of the Festival of the First Fruits (Niiname no Matsuri), which was the occasion of the Gosechi dances (see App. 1 and *W.S.P.*, pp. 164-5), the blinds, screens, curtains of state, etc. were removed from the room in Jōnei Palace that was used by the dancers; this meant that the young girls were no longer protected from prying eyes.

(420)
Ashihiki no
Yamai no mizu wa
Kōreru wo
Ika naru himo no
Tokuru naruramu

Sanekata's poem is based on the double imagery of ice melting in a
mountain well and of the knot on a woman's costume coming undone.
Both refer to Lady Kohyōe's refusal to unbend ('melt') towards him.
(The untied knot is a standard image for yielding to a man; according
to some commentators, it is related to the custom of a woman's un-
tying the sash of her under-robe before giving herself to her lover.)
The pillow-word *ashihiki* ('foot-dragging'), which is linked with
'mountain', is entirely conventional and I have omitted it from my
translation. There are two plays on words: (*a*) *yamai* = (i) mountain
well, (ii) (*yamaai*) mountain sedge, the plant used to produce the
dark-blue dye of the costume worn by the women: (*b*) *himo* =
(i) the ice too, (ii) ribbon, cord; sash.

In both China and Japan snapping the fingers in someone's presence (421)
(*tsumahajiki*) was traditionally a gesture of disdain.

> Usu-kōri (422)
> Awa ni musuberu
> Himo nareba
> Kazasu hikage ni
> Yurubu bakari wo

In her reply Shōnagon preserves Sanekata's two images and brings
them closer by comparing the thin ice itself to a ribbon of foam or
bubbles (*usukōri awa ni musuberu himo nareba*). (This last idea, incidentally, may derive from the *Manyō Shū*, in which we read of a
'thread of foam'.) Again there are two plays on words: (*a*) (*kazasu*)
hikage = (i) the sunshine (against which one shades oneself), (ii) a
delicate sunshade or veil (*hikage no kazura*); (*b*) *yurubu* = (i) to melt,
(ii) to loosen, undo. *Bakari* ('only') refers (i) to the ice, which needs
only a ray of sunshine to melt away, (ii) to the ribbon, which is *only*
as strong as the delicate threads of a veil.

I.e. than on the normal occasions when the Gosechi dancers were not (423)
chosen from the Empress's own household (cf. note 414).

Fujiwara no Sukemasa: not to be confused with his distinguished (424)
namesake (note 169), who now held the post of Minister of War. The
present Sukemasa was to receive an Imperial Reprimand for his
involvement in the Korechika scandal (note 74).
   Somedono no Shikibu Kyō no Miya: lit. 'the prince who was the
Minister of Ceremonial of Somedono'. Refers to Prince Tamehira,
a son of Emperor Murakami. Shōnagon typically avoids his given

name and designates him by his office and residence. The identification of the dancer is complicated by textual discrepancies, but the likeliest pattern appears to be:

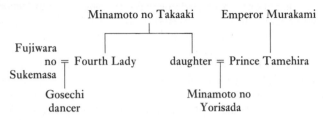

(425) I.e. to the apartments occupied by the Empress in the northern part of Seiryō Palace. The actual performance took place in Jōnei Palace (see App. 9f).

(426) The *Shunchobon* (but not the *Sangenbon*) text has the two following sentences: 'A handsome man goes by carrying a formal, narrow-bladed sword and with a flat ribbon hanging from his sword-belt—very splendid. One has written a letter on purple paper; now one folds it and attaches a long cluster of wistaria—this too is most attractive.' These sentences are almost certainly misplaced. The first sentence, and possibly the second, belong far more appropriately to section 84 (Splendid Things) than in the middle of the long passage devoted to the Gosechi dances (see Ikeda–Kishigami, p. 142).

(427) This is in fact the fourth sentence of the passage beginning 'At the time of the Gosechi dances . . .', but I have moved it back to where it makes better sense. In extant texts 'It is no wonder . . .' (*kotowari nari*) follows '. . . each woman had her own particular charm' (*samazama ni tsukete okashū nomi zo aru*).

(428) *Seiryō Den no sorihashi* (the arched bridge by Seiryō Palace): a special bridge set up during the Gosechi dances to connect the Seiryō and Shōkyō Palaces (App. 9f).

(429)   Tsukasa masare to
          Shikinami zo tatsu.

The lines are from a song and mean that one messenger appears after another, all announcing the recent promotions at Court. There is a play of words on *tatsu* = (i) (the waves) rise high, (ii) (the envoys) come forward.

On the 2nd Day of the Ox (i.e. three days before the actual per- NOTES
formance) there was a formal dress-rehearsal of the Gosechi dances (430)
in the presence of the Emperor, who was seated on his curtain-dais
(*chōdai*) in Jōnei Palace. This was known as the 'dais rehearsal'
(*chōdai no kokoromi*) (App. 1).

Warawa (girl assistants): these were the girls who dressed the dancers' (431)
hair and helped them with their costumes.

A special performance known as the 'attendants' dance' (*warawamai*) (432)
was given on the eve of the main dances (that is, on the Day of the
Hare) by the young girls who attended the Gosechi dancers (App. 1).
The Gosechi programme was as follows:

2nd Day of the Rat	.	.	rehearsal,
,,	,,	Ox .	.	.	Dais Rehearsal (note 430),
,,	,,	Tiger	.	.	banquet with songs and dances,
,,	,,	Hare	.	.	Attendants' Dance (note 432),
,,	,,	Dragon	.	.	Gosechi Dances (note 417).

This was the name of a famous lute (*biwa*) that had been kept in the (433)
Palace since ancient times; literally it means 'Nameless'. The present
incident probably dates from the 3rd Month of 996 (App. 4).
    Owing to the absence of honorifics, the subject of 'strumming'
(*kakinarashi nado su*) cannot possibly be the Emperor; 'ladies-in-
waiting' (or 'lady-in-waiting') must be supplied.

Rather than spell out the name of the instrument, the Empress hints (434)
at it by saying that it 'does not even have a name' (*na mo nashi*) (cf.
note 433).

I.e. Fujiwara no Genshi (note 415). Her father was Michitaka, who (435)
had died almost exactly one year earlier.

Refers to Ryūen (see Index-Glossary), Michitaka's fourth son and the (436)
brother of Empress Sadako and the Lady of the Shigei Sha. He took
orders at an early age, being appointed Provisional Junior Assistant
High Priest (Gon Daisōzu) in 993 when he was only fourteen. His
rapid rise in the ecclesiastical hierarchy was broken off by a rather
early death.

Inakaeji was the name of a well-known flute (*fue*) belonging to the (437)
Imperial collection. It is homonymous with the words meaning, 'No,
I will not exchange'; hence the Empress's pun.

83

Sōzu no kimi mo ('priest though he was'): clerics were expected to be more knowledgeable than ordinary people. *Tada urameshi to zo oboshitameru*: instead of enjoying the Empress's pun, he assumes that she is simply confirming the Shigei Sha's refusal to exchange instruments.

(438) Genshō = Above the Mysteries
Mokuma = Horse Pasture
Ide = Sluice
Ikyō = The Bridge of the River Wei
Mumyō = Nameless (note 433)
Kuchime = Decaying Eye
Shiogama = Salt Kiln
Futanuki = The Two Openings
Suirē = Water Dragon
Kosuirō = Small Water Dragon
Uda no Hōshi = Father (Master of the Buddhist Law) Uda
Kugiuchi = Nail Striker
Hafutatsu = Two Leaves

(439) *Giyō Den* (Giyō Palace) (see Index-Glossary): housed the Imperial treasures.

(440) *Nakaba kakushitarikemu mo*: lit. 'even [she whose face] was half hidden'. Shōnagon refers to a line in Po Chü-i's 'Song of the Lute' (note 329) about a girl whom the poet meets on a boat when he is about to leave on a journey:

Yu pao p'i p'a pan che mien   She lifts her lute, and I can see but half her face.

The girl, who has now sunk to the status of professional entertainer, tells the poet that she has known better days. Yet compared to Empress Sadako she is, of course, a 'mere commoner' (*tādoto*). The present scene probably takes place in 994 or 993 (App. 4).

(441) This section occurs only in the *Sangenbon* texts; see Ikeda-Kishigami, pp. 246-7 and 353-4, also Tanaka, p. 312. To judge from Tadanobu's title (Chūjō), the date is probably 994 (5th Month), but 995 is also possible (see App. 4).

(442) Damp weather enhanced the scent of most types of incense.

(443) *Ide no Chūjō* (Captain of Ide): commentators disagree about his identity. According to Kaneko (*Hyōshaku*, pp. 484-5), he is probably

84

the hero of an old romance that is no longer extant. Ide was the name
of a village near the capital.

Kotoba ni: although the poem was in the standard thirty-one-syllable (444)
form, the Empress had not divided it into lines.

> Akane sasu
> Hi ni mukaite mo
> Omoiide yo
> Miyako wa harenu
> Nagame suramu to

Akane sasu ('to shine crimson *or* madder red') is a pillow-word con-
ventionally linked with 'sun'. There is a standard play of words on
nagame = (i) gazing, contemplation, (ii) long rains. *Harenu nagame*
('endless rains') has the further implication of 'endless tears' and suggests that the Empress will be weeping sorrowfully after the nurse has
left. 'Facing the sun' (*hi ni mukaite*) refers to Himuka, the ancient
name for the province of Hyūga in eastern Kyūshū, the nurse's
destination (App. 9a). The capital was north-east of Hyūga, and when
the Empress speaks of facing the sun (the *rising* sun is implied) she
means that the nurse will be looking in the direction of the capital.

The two parts of the poem correspond, of course, to the two sides
of the fan. One explanation of the custom of giving fans to parting
travellers is that the word for 'fan' (*ōgi*) includes the auspicious sound
ō (*au*) = 'to meet [again]'.

Minami no In (Southern Palace): one of the detached palaces (i.e. (445)
palaces outside the Imperial Palace compound). Situated in the 3rd
Ward at the south of Tōsanjō In (see App. 9d), it was part of the residence of the Empress's father, Fujiwara no Michitaka, who died there
in 995. The present scene probably belongs to the 12th Month of 992,
but some authorities place it in the 4th Month of 995, just before
Michitaka's death (see App. 4).

The text has *hiranuki*, but this is almost certainly a misprint for (446)
hiraginu (= 'plain *or* untwilled silk').

Toku nuitaramu hito wo omou to shiramu: lit. 'I shall know she who will (447)
have sewn fast[est] loves [me]'.

Susuki: Japanese pampas grass, *miscanthus sinensis* or *eularia japonica*. (448)

Sei Shōnagon's father was a provincial governor (see Index-Glossary: (449)
Kiyowara no Motosuke).

See note 150. (450)

Archery contests (*noriyumi*) took place on the 18th of the 1st Month
as the final event of the New Year celebrations (App. 1). They were
held in the presence of the Emperor. Teams of four men each were
chosen from two divisions of the Imperial Guards. Like most events
of the kind, the contests were followed by a banquet.

(452) Here, as so often, the sex of the person (*hito*) is unclear.

(453) *Amari migurushi to mo mitsubeku wa aranu*: lit. 'they cannot have been
too unpleasant to see'. Such litotes occurs frequently in Heian
Japanese.

(454) *Satsuki no Mi-Sōji* (Abstinence of the Fifth Month): the Buddhist
church enjoined periods of abstinence (*mi-sōji*) during the 1st, 5th,
and 9th Months. These periods were marked by strict observance of
the dietary and other purifying rules that applied during certain days
of each month (note 117), and also by the recital of special prayers.
The following events probably took place in 995, but some scholars
prefer a later date (App. 4).

(455) The standard measure for rooms, halls, etc. was a *ma*, the distance
between two adjacent pillars (*hashira*) in the *shinden* mansion. A *ma*
was about 3·3 yards, and a 'two-span room' was therefore about
twenty feet long.
    Fire-proof storerooms (*nurigome*) were built in the palaces and
patrician houses to keep clothes and other valuables that were not in
the outside storehouse.

(456) *Kasasagi* ('Magpie') was the name of the bridge that the Weaver had
to cross once a year if she was to meet her Herdsman lover (note 55).
The name was 'unpleasant' (*nikuki*), not because of the sound, but
because of its sad legendary association.

(457) According to regulations in the *Engi Shiki* (tenth-century civil code),
Court ladies were not usually allowed to enter or leave their carriages
at this gate; but during the rainy season an exception was made since,
if the ladies walked all the way to one of the main gates of the Greater
Imperial Palace, they were liable to be caught in the rain and to have
their clothes ruined.

(458) Four was the normal complement of a Heian carriage.

(459) I.e. of the Kamo Festival in the previous month.

Takashina no Akinobu was governor of Harima Province and later served as Middle Controller of the Left. As will be seen from App. 6d, (460) he was Empress Sadako's maternal uncle; hence it was natural that he should give hospitality to her ladies.

Ason (Lord) became second highest of the hereditary titles established in Japan in 685. It was held by certain members of the Fujiwara family and other distinguished clans.

Kaneko (*Hyōshaku*, p. 521) emphasizes the unfamiliarity of the Court (461) ladies with rustic matters like rice plants and threshing machines. 'What I took to be rice plants' ('what I suppose were rice plants', *ine to iu mono*), however, seems almost a deliberate affectation.

Ito waroku hinabitari ('only rough, country fare'): the standard type (462) of self-deprecatory remark that a polite Japanese host makes today just as he would have done a thousand years ago.

Shōnagon objects to her host's excessive informality. It was most un- (463) conventional for ladies of quality to be served with food in public on a row of tables; usually each of them was given her meal on an individual tray or dish and she would eat in private.

Fujiwara no Kiminobu (Index-Glossary) was the first cousin of the (464) Empress and the adopted son of his own brother, Tadanobu (App. 6b). He received several good appointments at Court, including those of Imperial Adviser and Provisional Middle Counsellor. He did not become Gentleman-in-Waiting until the 9th Month of 996; it is clear that Shōnagon wrote the present section at least one year after the events it describes.

Tsuchi Mikado (Tsuchi Gate): one of the gates at the east of the (465) Greater Imperial Palace (App. 9e); also known as Jōtō Mon.

Carriages were unyoked at the main Palace gates and then pulled by (466) attendants to the veranda of the building where the passengers alighted.

> Hototogisu (467)
> Naku ni tazune ni
> Kimi yuku to
> Kikaba kokoro wo
> Soe mo shitemashi

For the sake of scansion I have used the conventional translation of *hototogisu* (note 25).

87

Saishō no Kimi (Lady Saishō): not to be confused with her colleague
(468) of the same name (note 87) who belonged to the Fujiwara family. The
present lady was the daughter of Sugawara no Sukemasa (Index-
Glossary) and a direct descendant of the famous Michizane. In
section 100 she is described as serving Fujiwara no Genshi.

(469) A facetious reference to the doctrine of *karma*, according to which all
events in this life, even the most trivial, are rigidly predetermined by
what has happened in previous incarnations.

(470) Cf. note 340. People would frequently compose one part of a *tanka*
(either the opening 5-7-5 lines or the concluding 7-7 lines) and
challenge someone else to write the other part on the spur of the
moment. This called for fluency and virtuosity of a type that Shōnagon
delighted in displaying. The Empress's lines (*Shitawarabi koso |
Koishikarikere*) imply that her ladies were more interested in the food
they were served at Akinobu's house than in the poetic song of the
hototogisu. The opening lines supplied by Shōnagon are:

> Hototogisu
> Tazunete kikishi
> Koe yori mo.

(471) Shōnagon's father, Motosuke, and her great-grandfather, Fukayabu,
were both distinguished poets; many other members of the Kiyowara
family were also known for their literary talents.

(472) *Uchi no Ōidono* (Minister of the Centre): see App. 7a. The incumbent
is the Empress's brother, Fujiwara no Korechika, who was exiled in
the following year (996).

Kōshin (Night of the Monkey): once in every sixty days, when the
Sign of the Elder Brother of Metal (Kanoe or *Kō*) coincided with the
Sign of the Monkey (Saru or *Shin*) (see App. 3), people were advised
to spend the whole night awake in order to protect themselves from
the three 'corpse worms' (*shichū*), who might otherwise penetrate the
sleeper's body and cause him great harm. This belief, which was related to Chinese Taoist superstition, had gained wide acceptance in
Heian Japan. Members of the aristocracy spent the inauspicious Kōshin
night writing poetry and playing games to keep themselves awake.

(473)
> *Empress*: Motosuke ga
> Nochi to iwaruru
> Kimi shi mo ya
> Koyoi no uta ni
> Hazurete wa oru

Shōnagon: Sono hito no
Ato to iwaruru
Mi nariseba
Koyoi no uta wa
Mazu zo yomamashi

Tsutsumu koto saburawazu wa: lit. 'if I had no [cause for] diffidence'. (474)

This is section 100 in the Ikeda-Kishigami text and section 96 in the (475) Tanaka text. It is not included in the *Shunchobon* versions. The date is either 997 or 998 (App. 4). The full moon in the 8th Month is traditionally considered the most beautiful of the year.

Tada aki no tsuki no kokoro wo mihaberu nari: lit. 'it is that I am (476) intently looking at the heart of the autumn moon'. Various Japanese poems about the autumn moon have been suggested as the source for Shōnagon's reply; but, in view of the lute music, the most likely source is this passage from Po Chü-i's 'Song of the Lute' (note 329):

. . . wu yen	Wordless we gaze into the
Wei chien chiang hsin ch'iu yüeh pai	river and the moon's white light.

Reference to a passage in the Lotus Sutra (*Hoke Kyō*): 'There is but (477) a single vehicle of the Law; there are not two, nor are there three.' Accordingly the Lotus was known as the 'Law of the Single Vehicle' (Ichijō no Nori).

A rigid rank system applied to the Heian after-life as well as to the (478) present world. There were nine ranks of rebirth in Amida's Western Paradise; the lotus seat one obtained after rebirth depended on the weight of sin or merit accumulated in one's former existences. As expounded in the 'Nine Ranks of Rebirth' (*Kubon Ōjō*) by the priest, Ryōgen (912-85), these were the Lower, Middle, and Upper Births, each being divided into the Lower, Middle, and Upper Ranks. Shōnagon makes it clear that she would accept a Lower Birth of Lower Rank (Gebon). Her Buddhist imagery is of course inspired by the joke about the 'Single Vehicle of the Law' (note 477). She implies that, when it comes to being loved by the Empress, even the lowest rank in her affections would suffice; when less distinguished people are involved, she insists on being first.

Fujiwara no Takaie, the Empress's brother (App. 6b), served as (479) Middle Counsellor from 995 to 996. The *Ōkagami* describes him as an 'intractable fellow' (*yo no saganamono*).

89

The Japanese use the same word, *hone*, for the frame of a fan and the bone or cartilage of an animal. (The English word 'frame' contains some of the same ambiguity.) Since Takaie claims that his fan has a *hone* which has never been seen (*sara ni mada minu hone*), Shōnagon comments that it must be the *hone* of a jelly-fish; for, while everyone knows fan-frames, no one has ever set eyes on the frame of a jelly-fish. Pickled jelly-fish was a popular dish among the Heian aristocracy.

(481) *Kore wa Takaie ga koto ni shitemu*: lit. 'as for this, let us make [it] a saying of Takaie's'. Kaneko's commentary (*Hyōshaku*, p. 531): 'Since this is an amusing joke, let us make it Takaie's saying.'

(482) I.e. section 92. 'Embarrassing' because it is a case of Shōnagon's blowing her own trumpet. But *The Pillow Book* is full of episodes in which the author shows off her wit and erudition, and it is not clear why she should have felt diffident on this particular occasion.

(483) Fujiwara no Nobutsune, a cousin of Murasaki Shikibu's, became Chamberlain in 995 and was appointed Secretary in the Ministry of Ceremonial in 997; later he became Governor of Echigo. The present incident probably occurred in 997 (App. 4).

(484) It appears that when Nobutsune delivered an Imperial message he usually knelt on the floor next to the cushion as a mark of respect to the Empress, rather than seating himself comfortably on it. Kaneko (*Hyōshaku*, p. 534) suggests that this was the usual custom.

(485) *Senzoku* = (i) cushion, (ii) to clean or wipe one's feet. In my translation I have made a lame attempt to suggest the nature of Shōnagon's joke. The play on words is far more effective in Japanese; also it should be remembered that the Heian tolerance for puns was considerably greater than ours. A closer translation would be: 'Do you suppose this is for the sake of wiping your feet (serving as a cushion)?'

(486) *Ōgisai no Miya* (the Great Empress): Fujiwara no Yasuko (Index-Glossary), the consort of Emperor Murakami. She enjoyed great influence as Acting Empress Dowager under Emperor Reizei and Acting Great Empress Dowager under Emperor Enyū. The incident that Shōnagon recounts here is at least thirty years old.

Enutagi was the name of one of Empress Yasuko's low-ranking women (*shimozukae*). According to *Hyōshaku*, p. 535, it had the unfortunate double sense of 'dog's vomit' (*enu = inu, tagi = taguri*); but other texts give Enudaki, which means 'holding a dog in one's arms'.

Tokikara, an obscure member of the Fujiwara family, was appointed Governor of Mino in 968 and died *en poste*. His name, which could be taken to mean 'depending on the weather' (*tokigara*), does not appear in any of the Fujiwara genealogies; some of the texts give it as Toki-kashi.

Kataki ni eritemo: lit. 'even though [they] choose her as an opponent'. (487) Kaneko's commentary (*Hyōshaku*, p. 536): 'Even though they chose her in advance as an opponent and caused her to compete with witticisms. . . .'

Nobutsune suggests that, just as it was he who put the idea of the (488) *senzoku* pun (note 485) into Shōnagon's head, so Tokikara gave Enutagi her opportunity to shine: in both cases the inspiration came from the man. This is hardly a suggestion that would endear him to Shōnagon and it may well have prompted her subsequent attack.

Or, if we follow other texts, which give *on-kaeri* instead of *on-dai wa*, (489) 'the Empress's reply [to the Emperor] was handed to him'. In this case Nobutsune uses the reply as a pretext to avoid being put to the test. According to Kaneko (*Hyōshaku*, p. 537), he never had the slightest intention of writing a poem and was simply waiting for the first opportunity to take his leave.

Tsukumodokoro (Office of Palace Works): an independent government (490) office (i.e. not attached to any of the eight Ministries). Its workshop was in the Imperial Palace compound, and it was responsible for supplying the Palace with furniture, objects of art, etc. Nobutsune became Director (*Bettō*) of this office in 996.

I.e. when she became his consort. For the Lady of the Shigei Sha see (491) note 415. The year is 995 (App. 4). *Shōyū Ki*, *Nihon Kiryaku*, and other sources give the date as the 19th (not the 10th) of the 1st Month. According to the chronicles, Fujiwara no Genshi's visit to the Empress took place on the 18th (not the 10th) of the 2nd Month. Since Yorichika was not appointed to be Director of the Imperial Storehouse until 1005 (note 514), this passage may not have been written until ten years after the events it describes, and the mistakes in the dates are hardly surprising. The scene is Tōka Palace (Index-Glossary and App. 9f).

A good example of the formality of Court life. See *W.S.P.*, (492) pp. 165-7.

I.e. the Chancellor, Fujiwara no Michitaka, the father of the Empress
(493) and of the Shigei Sha. For his principal wife, Takashina no Takako, who died in 996 about a year after her husband, see App. 6e.

(494) *Shakuzen Ji* (Shakuzen Temple): founded by Michitaka in 990; it was situated in Hōkō Palace, his father's old residence in the 2nd Ward (App. 9d). The service in question was arranged by Michitaka in 994, almost exactly one year before the present scene; it is described in section 256.

(495) Members of the aristocracy normally observed a rigid correlation between the seasons and the colour of their clothes. Red plum colour was worn from the 11th Month until the beginning of the 2nd Month. Now the time had come to change to light green or to some similar vernal colour, but the Empress had decided to defy convention.

(496) *Izariizu* ('creep out') might seem an odd form of locomotion for an empress; but it becomes clear when we remember the traditional Japanese seating position, which was a sort of squat. If one was seated and wished to move to a place near by, one would normally go on one's knees, rather than stand up and kneel down again in the new place.

(497) 'Pretty as a picture' is a more literal translation of *e ni kakitaru yō ni utsukushige*; but it would hardly be fair to Sei Shōnagon.

(498) She was now twenty years old.

(499) Shigei Sha (palace) was connected to Tōka Palace by covered galleries which passed through Senyō and Jōgan Palaces (App. 9f).

(500) For 'Chinese roof' see *karabisashi* in the Index-Glossary. The Shigei Sha's ladies-in-waiting were seated at the Tōka Palace end of the gallery joining Jōgan and Tōka Palaces. The gallery was covered by deep eaves whose ends were turned upwards in the Chinese style.

(501) *Shōshō no Kimi* (Lady Shōshō): possibly the same girl who is described in section 86 as having taken part in the Gosechi dances (note 424). Since she was eleven at the time, she would now be about fourteen. Alternatively Lady Shōshō may be the dancer's sister. Sugawara no Sukemasa was appointed to the 3rd Rank in 992; Kitano Shrine was associated with the worship of his ancestor, Michizane. Hence he was known as Kitano no Sammi (Third Rank of Kitano).

(502) Demons had straw coats (*mino*) that made them invisible.

Michitaka is alluding to the *Kokin Shū* poem:

Yamazakura	Ah, what fond memories she summons forth—
Kasumi no ma yori	She whom I dimly glimpsed
Honoka ni mo	Through the clearing in the mist
Miteshi hito koso	Of mountain cherry blooms!
Koishikarikere	

Michitaka is facetiously referring to himself and his wife. As Kaneko (504) points out (*Hyōshaku*, p. 559), the fact that the Empress and her sister were served before their father and mother shows that the State hierarchy (in which members of the Imperial family and their official consorts were ranked above all other people) took precedence over the Confucian hierarchy (where parents came before children).

I.e. Korechika and his brother Takaie (App. 3b). Matsugimi (Index- (505) Glossary), Korechika's little son, was later known as Michimasa and became Governor of the Left Division of the Capital. He was known to be Michitaka's favourite grandchild. At the time of the present scene Michitaka was 42, Korechika 20, Takaie 17, and Matsugimi 3.

Michitaka was head of the main branch of the great Fujiwara clan, (506) and it was only natural that his children should have reached the position they had. His wife, however, came from a relatively undistinguished family of Confucian scholars (note 460) and for her to be the mother of such impressive offspring must be the result of an unusually auspicious *karma* (note 469).

Fujiwara no Chikayori: see Index-Glossary. (507)

Kurushige ni mochite tachinu: lit. 'he took [clothes] in a pained- (508) seeming way and left'.

Messengers were normally paid in kind by gifts of clothes, material, etc. It is unclear why Chikayori, the present messenger, is displeased with his reward. The identity of the Middle Captain who hands him the clothes is also unclear; Takaie has already returned to his barracks, and no other Captain of the 3rd Rank has been mentioned.

I.e. given birth to a prince. (509)

... *nado notamawasuru wo ge ni nado ka ima made saru koto no to zo kokoromoto naki*: lit. 'His Excellency spoke in such a way, but I was worried, thinking, "In fact why (indeed) has there [not] until now been such a thing?"' I have tried to preserve some of this vagueness in my translation.

93

The Empress did not give birth to Prince Atsuyasu until the end of 999. Since the Fujiwaras' position at Court depended to a large extent on whether their daughter bore boy children to the reigning Emperor, Michitaka had good reason to wish that Matsugimi were Sadako's son rather than Korechika's. Emperor Ichijō was now fifteen, which was a normal age to begin siring children.

(510) Michitaka, like his brother Michinaga, was known as a heavy drinker but also had the reputation of being able to recover his sobriety at a moment's notice. Chronicles like *Ōkagami* frequently describe Michitaka's carousals. His jocularity on the present occasion, which was no doubt encouraged by a liberal consumption of *sake*, is remarkable when we recall that he was already seriously ill.

Michitaka's death from diabetes two months later was certainly aggravated by his drinking, but not caused by it. The author of *Ōkagami* (who was of course unaware of the connexion between diabetes and drinking) ascribes Michitaka's fatal illness to over-indulgence (*omiki no midaresasetamaishi*).

(511) I.e. Fujiwara no Michiyori (Index-Glossary), eldest son of Michitaka by a concubine; half-brother of Korechika, Sadako, etc. (App. 6f). In 994 he was appointed Provisional Major Counsellor; he died in the following year, about four months after the present scene, at the age of twenty-five. Yamanoi was the name of his wife's residence in the 3rd Ward.

(512) The Emperor has been enjoying a long siesta with Empress Sadako; now he gets ready to return to his own palace, Seiryō Den.

(513) Korechika was famous for his good looks. Yamanoi (Michiyori) was Michitaka's eldest son and held the same post (Dainagon) as Korechika; but his mother was of inferior birth (note 511) and so people always spoke disparagingly of him (*sechi ni iiotoshi*).

(514) Fujiwara no Yorichika (Index-Glossary): fifth son of Michitaka. He was Middle Captain of the Inner Palace Guards, Left Division, and also served as Director of the Imperial Storehouse (note 491). The Imperial Storehouse (*Uchi no Kura*) was a government office attached to the Ministry of Central Affairs (App. 7a); it was responsible for storing the property of the Imperial family.

This was the zenith of Fujiwara no Michitaka's career, and the Emperor's escort appears to have consisted entirely of Michitaka and his sons. With his death shortly afterwards, the preponderant position that he and his sons had enjoyed at Court was taken over by Michinaga and his own numerous progeny.

She and Masahiro (note 270) were the children of Minamoto no (515) Tokiakira, who served as Assistant Director of the Bureau of Imperial Stables (*Uma no Suke*), whence her name. (For Naishi no Suke and Uma see Index-Glossary.) According to the seventeenth-century commentator, Kitamura Kigin, this woman was a poet and it was she who was responsible for giving Murasaki Shikibu the embarrassing sobriquet of 'Lady Annals' (Nihongi no Tsubone). The evidence for the identification, however, seems slight, especially since the woman in Murasaki's diary was called Saemon (*not* Uma) no Naishi.

Because, according to Kaneko (*Hyōshaku*, p. 562), she wanted to take (516) advantage of this rare opportunity to talk to her parents. This in fact turned out to be her very last meeting with her father, who died two months later.

Uchihashi: a bridge that had been put up temporarily to span a gap (517) in one of the corridors. See Kitayama Keita, *Genji Monogatari Jiten*, p. 109.

This was typical of repeated efforts to put Shōnagon and the other (518) ladies-in-waiting to the test. Their success or failure in promptly producing an apt reply reflected on the prestige of the Court where they served. A bare branch from a plum tree was an unusually challenging subject, and the courtiers are much impressed by Shōnagon's quotation.

Hayaku ochinikeri: lit. 'they have fallen early'. From the (Chinese) (519) preface to a Chinese poem by the Japanese writer, Ki no Haseo (Index-Glossary), included in *Wakan Rōei Shū*:

> Ta-yü ling chih mei tsao lao   Early have they scattered—the blossoms
> Shui wen fen chuang   on the plum trees of Ta-yü peak.
> Who cares about the beauties any more?

Ta-yü peak in Kiangsi province was famous for its plum blossoms.

Probably in 999 (App. 4). This dating is based on the following points: (520) (i) Fujiwara no Sanenari (note 527) was appointed Middle Captain of the Inner Palace Guards in 998 (10th Month); (ii) Empress Sadako died in 1000 (12th Month); (iii) the present scene takes place in the 2nd Month; (iv) therefore it must be in either 999 or 1000; (v) but

95

there is a reference to the Black Door, and we know that Seiryō
Palace, where this door was situated, had been destroyed by fire in
999 (6th Month) and was not rebuilt until 1000 (10th Month); (vi)
therefore the scene takes place in 999 (2nd Month).

(521) *Kō shite saburau*: lit. 'thus I have come'.

(522) *Fujiwara no Kintō*, the noted poet, literary critic, calligrapher, and
musician (Index-Glossary), had been appointed Imperial Adviser
in 992.
   Another text gives: 'This is from Lord Kintō and from his Excellency, the Imperial Adviser and Middle Captain (Kintō no Kimi
Saishō Chūjō Dono).' The latter gentleman was Fujiwara no
Tadanobu; but I agree with Kaneko (*Hyōshaku*, p. 567) that it would
have been most peculiar to mention one writer by name and the other
only by his rank (especially when they both held the rank of Saishō).

(523)   Sukoshi haru aru
                                   Kokochi koso sure

   See note 526.

(524) Cf. note 470.

(525) *Toridokoro nakereba*: lit. 'because I would have no redeeming point'.

(526)   Sora samumi
                                   Hana ni magaete
                                   Chiru yuki ni

   The idea that snowflakes can be mistaken for scattering blossoms
is one of the hoariest conceits in the Japanese poetic vocabulary. We
must remember, however, that the use of conventional images was
far from being regarded as a weakness among Heian poetasters.

(527) Fujiwara no Sanenari (Index-Glossary), eldest son of the former
Prime Minister, Kinsue, was appointed Middle Captain of the Inner
Palace Guards in 998 (10th Month), Imperial Adviser in 1008,
Captain of the Middle Palace Guards in 1009 (3rd Month), and Pro-
visional Middle Counsellor in 1016. At the time of the present scene
Sanenari was still a Middle Captain (*Chūjō*); he did not become
Captain (*Kami*) until 1009. Shōnagon identifies him by both titles,
which would suggest that she wrote this passage ten years after the
scene it describes. See also note 520.

Minamoto no Toshikata (Index-Glossary) was appointed Imperial Adviser in 995; in 1018, helped by his family connexion with Michi- naga, he reached the apex of his career as Major Counsellor. Toshikata was a distinguished poet (he became one of the 'Four Counsellors' known for their poetic talents), and Shōnagon has good reason to value his opinion.

For *mono* ('things') see note 102. (529)

Hampi: type of waistcoat worn above the under-robe in formal attire. (530) A long braided cord (*o*) hung down from the left side of the garment.

See note 305. (531)

Minamoto no Masahiro. The incidents described in this section (532) belong to the years 995 and 996 (App. 4). See also section 52.

The reference to a one-measure jar is proverbial; but in general (533) Masahiro's remark is as meaningless in Heian Japanese as in the English translation.

The popping of peas (*mame*) in a stove was proverbially compared to (534) people who are in a great hurry (cf. the word *mamegara* for a busy person); but Masahiro's use of the expression is as peculiar as every- thing else about his speech.

Gotai ('five parts') is a Buddhist term (Sanskrit *pañcanga*) referring (535) to the knees, elbows, and head; when all are placed on the floor, it implies the utmost respect. *Gotai* can also refer to the head, hands, and feet, or to the sinews, veins, flesh, bones, and hair. Some elegant courtier has no doubt used this expression to his mistress, instead of the more commonplace 'your whole body' (*mukurogome*).

Kosōji (Little Screen): the screen in Seiryō Palace that divided the (536) Imperial Dining Room (*Asagarei no Ma*) from the Imperial Washing Room (*Go-Chōzu no Ma*) (App. 9g). It had a cat painted on one side, birds and bamboo on the other.

Barriers (*seki*) were used to keep a check on travellers, levy tolls, etc. (537) They were established at the borders of provinces and other strategic points.

The following table includes places mentioned in sections 105, 106, and 108:

Section	Place	Province (District)	Literary association	Literal meaning
1.	105	Ōsaka	Yamashiro-Ōmi	Gosen Shū, etc.	Slope of Meetings
2.	,,	Suma	Settsu (Muko)		
3.	,,	Suzuka	Ise-Ōmi (Suzuka)		
4.	,,	Kukida	Ise (Ichishi)		
5.	,,	Shirakawa	Iwashiro (Nishi Shirakawa)	Shūi Shū	White River
6.	,,	Koromo (Gawa)	Rikuchū (Iwai)	Izumi Shikibu Shū	Clothes
7.	,,	Tadagoe	? Yamato (Kawachi)	Manyō Shū	Easily Crossed
8.	,,	Habakari	Rikuzen (Shibata)	Goshūi Shū	Fear
9.	,,	Yokobashiri	Suruga (Suntō)	Kanemori Shū	Running Sideways
10.	,,	Kiyomi	Suruga (Iwara)	,, ,,	Pure Look
11.	,,	Mirume	? Ōmi		Seeing Eye
12.	,,	Yoshina-Yoshina			Futile, Futile
13.	,,	Nakoso	Iwashiro (Iwashiro)	Gosen Shū	Do Not Come
14.	,,	Ashigara	Sagami (Ashigara)-Izu	,, ,,	
15.	106	Ōaraki	Yamashiro (Otokuni)	Kokin Shū	
16.	,,	Shinobi	Kawachi or Iwashiro (Shinobu)		Secret
17.	,,	Kogoi	Izu (Takata)	Shūi Shū	
18.	,,	Kogarashi	Suruga (Abe)	Rokujō	Withered Tree
19.	,,	Shinoda	Izumi (Kita)		
20.	,,	Ikuta	Settsu (Muko)		Living Field
21.	,,	Utsuki			Hollow Tree
22.	,,	Kikuta			Chrysanthemum Field
23.	,,	Iwase	Yamato (Heguri) or Iwashiro (Iwase)	Manyō Shū or Tsurayuki Shū	
24.	,,	Tachigiki			
25.	,,	Tokiwa	? Yamashiro		
26.	,,	Kurotsuki			
27.	,,	Kannabi	Settsu (Mishima)		Godless Day
28.	,,	Utatane	Iwashiro (Nishi Shirakawa)		Nap

98

	Section	Place	Province (District)	Literary association	Literal meaning
29.	106	Ukita	Yamashiro (Kuze)		Floating Field
30.	„	Uetsuki	? Yamato	? *kagura-uta*	Planted Tsuki (Zelkova) Tree
31.	„	Iwata	Yamashiro (Uji)	*Manyō Shū*	Rock Field
32.	„	Kōdate	? Yamashiro (Otagi)		Palace of the Gods
33.	„	Koi	Iga *or* Yamashiro	*Rokujō*	Love
34.	„	Kohata	Yamashiro (Uji)	*Manyō Shū*	Small Flag
35.	108	Nanakuri	Ise (Ichishi)	*Fuboku Shū*	Seven Chestnuts
36.	„	Arima	Settsu (Arima)	*Rokujō*	
37.	„	Tamatsukuri	Rikuzen (Tamatsukuri)		Jewel Making

Because of the connotation of their names. As we have seen, the type (538) of humour that depends on the literal meanings of place-names is far more accepted in Japan than in the West. Such puns are also important in poetry (e.g. those centred on the sadness of Uji River [*ushi* = 'sad'], *W.S.P.*, p. 272, and see note 540).

So far as we can tell, it is only because of the similarity in their names (539) ('Futile [to cross]' and 'Do Not Come') that Shōnagon identifies two barriers.

Poems based on the double meaning of Ōsaka (= (i) Great Slope, (540) (ii) Slope of Trysts or [Amorous] Meetings, Lovers' Slope) are legion. For example, the following from the *Kokin Shū*:

Ōsaka no	If to its name it were but true,
Seki shi masashiki	The barrier on Lovers' Slope,
Mono naraba	Never should I let us part again,
Akazu wakaruru	And never more endure this grief.
Kimi wo todomeyo.	(*More lit.* Oh, let me keep you, whom I love insatiably and from whom I am parted.)

The actual Ōsaka Barrier (east of the capital) had gone out of use by the end of the eighth century, but poetry kept its memory alive (see notes 639–40).

I have followed Kaneko's interpretation (*Hyōshaku*, p. 578) of this very laconic sentence, which literally says, 'If reconsider even such a thing as Ōsaka, it must indeed be sad' (*Ōsaka nado wo made omoi-kaeshitaraba wabishikaramu ka shi*).

Possibly because Kōdate (*kami-tate*) means 'Palace of the Gods' and (541) was associated in Shōnagon's mind with the popular Kamo Festival.

99

The 'forest' was probably situated near the Kamo shrines in the district of Otagi. All the forests listed in this section appear to have been connected with Shintō shrines and therefore to be of a sacred character.

(542) See App. 9b.

(543) Water-oats (*komo*) were used for making rush mats.

(544) Poem chanted as an accompaniment to a *kagura* dance:

Komomakura	Ah, what sweet repose
Takase no Yodo ni	On this my sheaf of water-oats
Karu komo no	Culled from the waters of Takase Pool!
Karu tomo ware wa	To such a pillow I'll entrust my sleep
Shirade tanomamu	And care not if I drift away.

(545) In preparation for the Iris Festival two days later. The iris decorations were arranged on the 4th.

(546) Hot springs (*yu*) have been used in Japan since ancient times for their medicinal properties. Emperor Jomei (reg. 628–41) visited Arima to take the waters.

(547) *Gansan*: lit. 'triple first', being the beginning of the day, the month, and the year. In Heian times as now this was a day for paying calls; hence the sound of carriages.

(548) Because it is disagreeable to experience extreme hot or cold, but pleasant to see these conditions skilfully represented in a painting.

(549) See note 213. The cry of the deer (*shika no koe*) is the *aware* sound *par excellence*.

(550) *Mitake* (note 32) was some sixty miles from the capital, a considerable journey by Heian standards.

(551) *Mutsumashiki hito*: lit. 'the intimate person', i.e. the young man's wife or mistress.

(552) *Emon no Suke*: Assistant Captain of the Outer Palace Guards, Right Division. The basic *Shunchobon* text gives *Nobukata*. This might be Minamoto no Nobukata (Index-Glossary), son of the Minister of the Left, Shigenobu. Kaneko (*Hyōshaku*, p. 588) points

out, however, that Shōnagon does not use the honorifics that would normally accrue to a gentleman of such high rank. (When, for example, he 'returns' to the capital, the verb is an unadorned *kaerite* instead of *kaeritamaute.*) There is another Nobukata, also of the Minamoto family. He was an officer of the Guards; but he never served as Governor of Chikuzen nor was he in the *Right* Division of the Outer Palace Guards, and Shōnagon cannot be referring to him in this passage. Almost certainly there has been a copyist's error and the name should be *Nobutaka*. This would be Fujiwara no Nobutaka (Index-Glossary), the husband of Murasaki Shikibu, who was appointed Governor of Chikuzen (in northern Kyūshū) in 990 and who in 998 became Provisional Assistant Captain of the Outer Palace Guards, Right Division, and concurrently Governor of Yamashiro Province. This accords with the fact that he was the father of Takamitsu, who is mentioned as having accompanied him to Mitake.

Probably in 990, but 991 is possible (App. 4). Shōnagon appears to be (553) writing at least seven years later (note 552).

Ge ni iikemu (Sangenbon: iikeru) ni tagawazu: lit. 'it truly does not (554) differ from what he said'. Nobutaka's promotion to governorship of the large province of Chikuzen showed that the God of Mitake approved of his elegant dress.

Kokoro ni shi mo makasenu: lit. 'they certainly do not act according (555) to their hearts (feelings)'.

Hatsuka amari muyuka nanuka bakari: lit. 'on about the 26th or 27th (556) of the month'. According to the lunar calendar, the moon was theoretically bound to be in the same phase on any given day of the month.

A typical repetition (cf. p. 124), which may result either from Shōna- (557) gon's carelessness or from a copyist's error.

This is Ippon 27 in Ikeda-Kishigami and Ippon 26 in Tanaka; it is (558) not included in the *Shunchobon* texts. In the Tanaka text it is placed in the same section as the last paragraph of my section 112 (*Hyōshaku*, section 102) ('A dilapidated house . . . the wind blows gently'). The editors of Ikeda-Kishigami (p. 329) suggest that it may have been written during Shōnagon's later years, i.e. after she left Court service.

The wording is almost identical with that in Book 5 of *The Tale of Genji* (*tsukuzuku to nagamekurashite*), and the season is the same. For the double sense of *nagame* see note 444.

(560) For *Hasedera* see note 67. The date of this visit is unknown. The *Sangenbon* text gives Kiyomizu (Index-Glossary), instead of Hase, Temple. This has been the subject of much scholarly, and inconclusive, discussion. See, for example, Morimoto Shigeru in *Kokubungaku* (November 1964), pp. 42-44.

(561) A typical example of Shōnagon's shorthand style. She says that the young priests were wearing only their sashes (*obi bakari shitaru*). This would be a bizarre costume to find in a Buddhist monastery; what she actually means is that the priests were informally dressed in their under-robes and sashes without their full sacerdotal vestments (*hōe*). High clogs (*ashida*) were presumably unfamiliar to a city-dweller; hence 'things called' (*to iu mono*).

(562) *Kusha*, abbreviation of *Abidatsuma Kusha Ron* (*Abhidharma Kósa Śāstra*), a Sanskrit metaphysical treatise translated into Chinese. For ease of recitation it was divided into verses (*ju*) of four words each; the full text of the *Kusha* comprised 600 such verses.

(563) These were no doubt country folk who wore their clothes inside out to prevent them from being soiled on the way to the temple.

(564) *Hotoke no o-mae ni*: before the statue of the Buddha in the sanctuary.

(565) *Inufusegi* (dog barrier): low, latticed screens separating the inner part of the temple from the outer. They were derived from the barriers (known as *komayose*) placed at the foot of the steps leading up to private mansions in order to keep out stray dogs (which were numerous in the capital).

(566) *Mazu kokoro mo okosaru*: lit. 'first of all my feelings (also) were awakened'. I have followed *Hyōshaku*, p. 596.

(567) *Raiban* (platform of worship): special dais placed in front of a Buddhist statue or image for the use of the priest reading the sutras.
The petitions were written requests that the priests addressed to the Buddha on behalf of their patrons; they were based on the 'original vows' to help believers (see note 568).

Dan ('platform', 'altar') had the secondary meaning of 'alms', 'offer- NOTES
ing'. *Sendan* ('one thousand platforms') signified a generous offering. (568)
The *Shunchobon* text gives *sentō* ('one thousand lights'), but here the
Shōhon version seems preferable.

Members of the aristocracy frequently dispatched messengers to
Hase and other temples carrying letters and offerings. The letters
contained petitions that the priests were to convey in their prayers
after reciting the appropriate sutras; the offerings consisted of robes,
lengths of silk, and other valuables.

Normally the ends of the shoulder-sash were knotted in front of the (569)
skirt.

Shikimi (anise): branches of the Chinese anise tree (*illicium religiosum*) (570)
decorated Buddhist altars; its leaves were used for the manufacture
of incense.

'This pious gesture also delighted me' is based on the *Shunchobon*
text, which reads . . . *motekitaru nado no tōtoki mo nao okashi. Nao*
(corresponding to the modern *yahari*) is ambiguous. Waley (*W.P.B.*,
pp. 106-7) takes it to mean 'notwithstanding', 'all the same', and
gives '. . . a courtesy which though merely pious in intention was very
agreeable'. But 'merely pious' seems to contradict the tenor of this
passage, especially of the earlier sentence, 'I was overcome with
awe . . . my old feelings were aroused' (*imijiku tōtoku . . . kokoro mo
okosaru*). In my interpretation *nao okashi* ('also delighted me') refers
to the previous uses of *okashi* in this passage (viz. *okashikere* and
okashi, *Hyōshaku*, p. 593, and *mata okashi*, ibid., p. 595).

The Ikeda-Kishigami text (p. 174) has . . . *motekitaru ni ka nado
no ito tōtoki mo okashi*, in which *ka* means 'scent', reminding us that
anise was used for incense. Other texts have *kaku nado no* (*kaku* =
? *gaku* = pleasure) and *ka nado no*; some omit the phrase entirely and
give simply *motekitaru ni* (*ito*) *tōtoki mo okashi*.

It appears from the context that the man has been weeping; hence (571)
Shōnagon's sympathy.

Conch-shells (*kai*) were used in temples to announce the time. (572)

Tatebumi (Index-Glossary) containing a petition for special prayers (573)
(see notes 567-8).

Kyōge (instruction and guidance): the priests direct their prayers at (574)
the evil spirits (*mono no ke*) who cause difficult childbirth and illness.

They 'instruct' (*kyō*) the spirits by preaching the Buddhist Law; they 'guide' (*ge*) them from evil to good.

(575) *Sarasara* and *soyosoyo* both mean 'rustling'; but the latter, as its sound suggests, is softer. *The Pillow Book* is full of onomatopoeias of this kind. See Ikeda Isamu in *Kokubungaku* (November 1964), pp. 91–94, for a complete list and discussion.

(576) *Aigyōzuki ogoritaru koe* (proud, charming voice): when it came to one's tone in addressing servants (*saburai no hito*) there was obviously no contradiction between the two adjectives. Waley's 'rather spoilt and conceited we thought, judging from his voice' (*W.P.B.*, p. 111) suggests a disapproval on Shōnagon's part that I do not detect in the original.

(577) Matins (*goya*) lasted from 1 to 4 a.m.
The sutra in question is the *Avalokiteśvara* (*Kannongyō*), dedicated to the eleven-faced Kannon, the tutelary deity of Hase Temple (note 67).

(578) *Esemono to wa miezu ka shi*: lit. 'they certainly did not seem wicked'. Cf. pp. 5–6 for a similar observation.

(579) *Sakura aoyagi* (cherry blossom and willows): i.e. white robes with red (or violet) and green linings respectively (see note 23).

(580) *Keshiki wo misemashi mono wo nado iu mo okashi*: lit. 'to say such a thing as, "I wish I could show him [my] looks" is strange'. *Okashi* here seems to mean 'interesting, strange' rather than 'amusing'; but the commentaries do not agree with each other.

(581) *Minafumizuki no Umahitsuji no toki bakari* (summer afternoon): lit. 'between the hours of the Horse and the Sheep (i.e. noon to 4 p.m.) in the 6th or 7th Months' (App. 3).

(582) This is a confusing sentence, but Kaneko (*Hyōshaku*, p. 615) describes it as 'full of variety and interest' (*henka ga atte omoshiroi*). Presumably Shōnagon means that in the summer the rain would give a pleasant effect of coolness. This leads directly to the following section.

(583) This was the officer (Shōshō = Minor Captain of the Inner Palace Guards) who, seated in a special stand (*dei no za*), presided over the archery and wrestling (*sumō*) contests held in a garden of the Imperial

Palace; he was dressed in full uniform and carried arms—all extremely
hot on a summer day.

According to Kaneko (*Hyōshaku*, p. 616), Shōnagon is referring to a (584)
fat woman, whose long hair makes her look even hotter in the warm
weather.

I.e. one made of heavy cloth. (585)

Azari (Holy Teacher): distinguished title (Sanskrit: *ācārya*) given to (586)
learned monks of the Shingon and Tendai sects. The ceremony in
question (*zuhō*) was held in front of the main Buddhist image in the
temple, where the priest recited incantations and burnt incense. *Zuhō*
were normally performed by Shingon priests, who addressed prayers
to Dainichi and other deities.
    The 6th and 7th Months were of course the hottest of the year (see
note 3).

The sex of the second thief is not specified. (587)
    As Kaneko observes, the situation was amusing for the thief but
shameful for the person whom he catches in the act of pilfering.
    Petty theft was a common occurrence in the type of dormitory
atmosphere inhabited by Shōnagon and her colleagues (*Hyōshaku*,
p 620).

Certain priests (*yoi no sō*) were always on duty at night in the Imperial (588)
Palace and elsewhere, so that they could be summoned immediately in
case of illness or other emergencies. In Empress Sadako's palace the
room occupied by the priests on night duty was directly next to that
of Shōnagon and the other ladies-in-waiting. Owing to the flimsy
nature of Japanese architecture, these priests were all liable to overhear the 'shameful things' spoken by the young ladies, but a light
sleeper was particularly defenceless since he would almost certainly
be awakened by the sound of their gossip.
    The order of the sentences in this section is confused. Shōnagon's
reference to light sleepers comes at the beginning, where it makes no
sense at all. I have accordingly transferred it to what seems the proper
place. The section opens with an isolated reference to the 'inside of a
man's heart' (*otoko no kokoro no uchi*) (or, according to the *Shōhon*
text, the 'inside of an amorous man's heart'); this almost certainly
belongs with the later sentences about men's unprincipled behaviour
to women, and I have moved it accordingly.

Hazukashi ('shameful') from whose point of view? The text is ambiguous. According to Kaneko, it is the young ladies who feel shame; but he admits (*Hyōshaku*, p. 620) that, since they have already gone to sleep (*nenuru nochi mo*), this involves a contradiction. *Hazukashi* occurs three times in this particular passage: (*a*) *ito hazukashiki mono nari*, (*b*) *kokoro no uchi mo hazukashi*, (*c*) *nenuru nochi mo hazukashi*. (*a*) and (*b*) clearly refer to the priest's feelings; surely (*c*) should also be taken from his point of view. The confusion results from the ambiguity of *hazukashi* which, like most Japanese adjectives of emotion, refers both to what causes the feeling and to the person who feels it (e.g. *kanashi* = both 'it is sad' and 'I am sad').

(590) *Koto ni tanomoshiki hito mo naki miyazukae no hito*: lit. 'a person serving in the Palace who has no trustworthy person'.

(591) *Mutoku naru mono*: lit. 'virtue-less things', i.e. things that have lost their *virtue* (their inherent power or efficacy).

(592) *Sumō* (*Sumai*) wrestling tournaments normally took place in the Imperial Palace every year at the end of the 7th Month (App. 1), skilled fighters being specially recruited from the provinces. The traditional beginning of these tournaments is recorded in the chronicles in the 7th Month of the 7th year of Emperor Suinin's year (probably *c.* A.D. 260): 'Tagima Kehaya and Nomi-no-Sukune, the latter being from Izumo-no-kuni, were summoned to fight each other to see who was the stronger. [. . . Nomi-no-Sukune won by killing his opponent with terrific kicks.]' (*E.J.H.*, A. 118).

The tournaments did not in fact start until the eighth century. See *W.S.P.*, p. 163 and note.

(593) According to Kaneko (*Hyōshaku*, p. 624), he has lost his position and his reprimands are therefore ineffectual.

(594) To remove one's hat in public was a grave solecism; for an old bald-head to do so was especially unfortunate.

(595) *Komainu* (Korean Dog) (see note 401) was the name of a piece of ceremonial Court music (*gagaku*) to which a Court dance (*bugaku*) was performed. Though considerably more formal, it was similar to the Lion Dance (*Shishi Mai*) and it is to this famous piece that Shōnagon refers. The Lion Dance, originally introduced from T'ang China, was performed by two men who, covered by a real or artificial lion skin, danced about, imitating the animal's movements. It started

as a graceful performance, but often deteriorated into a noisy romp;
hence its inclusion among 'things that have lost their power'.

Butsugen Shingon: lit. 'the True Words of the Buddha's Eyes' (596)
(Buddhalocanā), Butsugen being an abbreviation of *Issai Butsugen
Daikongo Kisshō Issai Butsumoson* (the Eye of All the Buddhas, Great
Diamond, Happy Augury, Reverend Mother of All the Buddhas).
This deity, who is represented in female form, is a metamorphosis of
Dainichi Nyorai (Mahāvairocana Tathāgata), the 'Great Illuminator'
of the Shingon sect. The formula in question is a Shingon *darani*
(*dhāraṇi* or mystic incantation) designed to avert calamities and
promote longevity. Kaneko suggests (*Hyōshaku*, p. 625) that for
Shōnagon the overpowering charm (*namamekashi*) of this incantation
may come from the feminine character of the deity to whom it is
addressed.

I.e. from his visit to Iwashimizu no Hachiman Shrine at Yawata near (597)
Yodo River, some ten miles south of the capital. This was one of the
three main shrines (see note 66) dedicated to Hachiman, the God of
War. The visit took place on the 21st of the 10th Month in 995
(App. 4). Tadanobu became Imperial Adviser in the 4th Month of
996 and so Shōnagon did not describe this scene until at least half a
year after it occurred. Kaneko points out (*Hyōshaku*, pp. 630-1) that
this was the first Imperial procession that Ichijō (now aged fifteen)
had taken without his mother, the Empress Dowager; therefore it was
an especially moving occasion for everyone concerned.

Sajiki: an elaborate sort of grandstand, complete with screens,
curtains, etc., built for viewing Imperial processions and the like.
Here the spectacle is the return of the Imperial procession to the
capital.

Nijō no Ōji (the Second Avenue): one of the nine great avenues (*jō*) (598)
that ran at equal distances across the capital from east to west (App.
9d). The 2nd Avenue, being directly south of the Imperial Palace,
was the largest and most impressive of these nine streets; it was
almost sixty yards wide.

Because of the Emperor's return the streets through which the procession passed (i.e. Suzaku Ōji and Nijō Ōji) had been specially swept
and kept clear of all other traffic.

From the posts occupied by Michitaka and others in this section we (599)
can tell that this visit occurred at some time between the 4th Month of
993 and the 8th Month of 994 (App. 4). From the last words in the

section, however, we can tell that it was not written until after the Empress's death at the end of 1000.

(600) Michitaka refers to himself (cf. note 504).

(601) For the special significance of shoes see note 270.

(602) *Yamanoi*: i.e. Fujiwara no Michiyori (note 511). Shōnagon has made a mistake about his post. In 994 Michiyori succeeded his half-brother, Korechika, as Provisional Major Counsellor; when Korechika held that post, Michiyori was Middle Counsellor.

Kuroki mono wo hikichirashitaru yō ni: lit. 'as if they had scattered black things'. Gentlemen of the 4th Rank and above wore black over-robes in the Palace.

Fujitsubo: lit. 'Wistaria Tub'; also known as Higyō Sha (cf. note 345). Genji's adulterous stepmother in *The Tale of Genji* is named after this building, where she lived when she was the Emperor's official concubine.

(603) *Chūnagon no Kimi* (Lady Chūnagon): daughter of Fujiwara no Tadagimi (App. 6b); wife of Minamoto no Tokiakira (note 515); lady-in-waiting to Empress Sadako. Tadagimi's actual father was Morosuke, but he was adopted by his grandfather, Tadahira, according to a form of adoption still commonly practised in Japan.

(604) *Okonaite medetaki mi ni naramu to ka*: lit. 'performing [like that] do you [suppose] you will become [such] a splendid person?' The woman teases her colleague and suggests that she has been praying so devoutly in order to acquire spiritual merit, which in a future incarnation will give her a life as splendid as Michitaka's. Despite their banter the ladies-in-waiting are all deeply impressed by Michitaka.

(605) I.e. better than being a Chancellor.

(606) 'She would have understood . . .' (*oboshimesarenamashi*): the original is as illogical as the translation.

Michinaga's meteoric rise to undisputed political control started in 995-6 with the death of Michitaka and the disgrace of Korechika. His great days of glory, however, did not come till after Sadako's death in 1000. This passage was obviously written at least six years after the event it describes (see App. 4).

Shōnagon had the reputation of being partial to Michinaga (cf. note

60 and p. 149); this proved very damaging to her at Empress Sadako's
Court, since Michinaga was soon to emerge as his niece's chief political enemy.

Tsuyu okashikaraji to omou koso mata okashikere: lit. 'The very fact (607)
that they did not find it at all interesting was also interesting.' *Pace*
Beaujard (*Notes de chevet*, p. 159), *tsuyu* here is not *rosée*; preceding
the negative it is clearly the adverb meaning 'in the least', 'in the
slightest', etc.

I.e. for the Festival of Young Herbs in the 1st Month (note 5). (608)

Miminagusa, which literally means 'herb without ears', correspond- (609)
ing to our myosotis; both words contain the element 'ear' (*mimi* and
ōtos). The *miminagusa* is not usually included among the seven herbs.

> Tsumedo nao (610)
> Miminagusa koso
> Tsurenakere
> Amata shi areba
> Kiku mo majireri

A tissue of double meanings, which the children would certainly not
have understood. Apart from the pun on *miminagusa* (note 609), we
find *kiku* used in the double sense of (i) chrysanthemum, (ii) to hear
('hear' and 'here' in my attempt at translation) and *tsumu* meaning
both 'to pinch' and 'to pluck'. In her poem Shōnagon identifies the
children who did not answer when she first spoke to them with the
myosotis which 'have no ears'. Yet surely, she says in her last two
lines, since there are so many plants / children, there must be some
that hear / that are chrysanthemums.

Kaneko observes (*Hyōshaku*, p. 640) that pinching was evidently
one of the ways in which children were punished; in the present
instance, of course, it is used simply as a figure of speech and to provide
an extra pun.

Kōjō (the Inspection): the records of officials of the 6th Rank and (611)
below were inspected with a view to possible promotion; like most
official occasions during the Heian period, the Inspection was
followed by a banquet. This examination in fact took place on the 11th
day of the 8th Month; Shōnagon may be confusing it with Reken, a
similar examination held on the 11th day of the 2nd Month for
officials in the Ministries of Military Affairs and of Ceremonial.
Kaneko (*Hyōshaku*, p. 641) suggests as an alternative explanation for

the mistake that '2nd Month' refers to the Worship of Confucius (which Shōnagon mentions later in the section) and was removed from its correct position in the text by a careless copyist. See App. 1.

(612) *Shakuten* (Worship of Confucius): service held biannually in the 2nd and 8th Months on the 1st Day of the Younger Brother of the Fire (Apps. 1 and 3). It took place in the Bureau of Education and commemorated Confucius and the ten Sages, whose portraits were hung on the walls for the occasion. The Rector of the University read an address in honour of Confucius; afterwards there was a formal discussion of Confucian texts, and Chinese poems were composed on a given subject. On the following day a Chamberlain presented the Emperor with Offerings of Wisdom (Sōmei), specially prepared dishes, including chestnuts and rice-cakes, known as 'black-and-white' (*shirokuro*), that were associated with the official cult of Confucius.

Concerning these references to the Kōjō and Shakuten ceremonies Waley writes (*W.P.B.*, p. 128): 'I quote this passage because it illustrates the extraordinary vagueness of the women concerning purely male activities.' Shōnagon is rather vague about the paintings (*suru koto narubeshi*), whose existence she would know only at second hand, but definite about the offerings (*mairasuru wo*), since she may well have been in attendance at the Palace when they were being made.

(613) Cold, square rice-cakes (*heidan*) filled with special vegetables, goose eggs, duck, and other delicacies were presented to the Court Nobles and top-ranking officials on the day after Reken and Kōjō (see note 611). The present incident probably occurred in 995 on the day after the Reken, the 12th of the 2nd Month, but Ikeda puts it one year later (App. 4). Shōnagon again uses the phrase 'things known as' (*to iu mono*), suggesting her vagueness about this 'purely male' activity; and later she wishes there were someone there to tell her what she should do when she has received the cakes.

(614) *Kemon* (submission): official document submitted by a Bureau or provincial office to some higher authority in the capital. For 'twisted letter' (*tatebumi*) see Index-Glossary.

(615) Nari-yuki is a reversal of the two characters in the given name of Shōnagon's friend, Fujiwara no Yukinari, and the note is from him. Mimana is the name of an ancient clan descended from one of the royal families of Mimana in southern Korea. By the time of *The*

Pillow Book the Mimana family had come down in the world, its members occupying lowly posts in the 6th Rank or under. Since submissions normally came from humble officials of this sort, Yukinari playfully assumes the name of such a family.

Reference to the legend about Hitokotonushi no Kami, one of the gods (616) of Mount Kazuraki, who, when asked why he was taking so long to build the bridge between his mountain and Mount Kimbu, replied that he was too ugly to show himself during the day and therefore could work only at night. Hence the bridge was never finished, and as a punishment for his negligence he was bound by a spell in a deep valley.

Having assumed a menial role in his letter, Yukinari now compares himself to the unfortunate god who was treated like a servant.

Apart from being a distinguished poet (note 331) Yukinari was one of (617) the great calligraphers of his day. The Empress takes his letter, no doubt intending to keep it as an example of skilled penmanship.

Sadaiben (Major Controller of the Left): the post (App. 7a) was (618) occupied by Taira no Korenaka (Index-Glossary). The Major Controller took part in the Examination, and Korenaka could accordingly be expected to know all the protocol.

The reason he arranges his clothes very carefully (*ito koto uruwashüte*) is that he believes the Empress wishes to speak to him.

This could be either Ben no Naishi or Ben no Omoto, both ladies-in- (619) waiting to the Empress. Sei Shōnagon refers to herself as Shōnagon.

Pun on *heidan* ('cold square cakes') and *reitan* ('cold', 'cool', 'indif- (620) ferent'). The basic *Shunchobon* text has *reitō* ('bad behaviour') instead of *reitan*, but this would seem to remove the entire point of Shōnagon's reply; both Kaneko and Ikeda-Kishigami follow the *Kohon* text, which gives *reitan*.

Waraite yaminishi koto: lit. '[he told him] that they had ended by (621) laughing'. Tachibana no Norimitsu was known for his dislike of poetry (see note 341); Nariyasu is unidentified, but he too must have belonged to the small band of poetry-haters. In the present scene they are delighted to hear that Shōnagon has for once turned down an opportunity to answer in verse.

In Shōnagon's time this building was greatly dilapidated and parts of the wall had come to pieces. For one reason or another, either because this was the part that had crumbled first, or because of *yin-yang* directional theories, it had become traditional to take wood from the framework of the south-east corner of the mud wall in order to make batons (*shaku*) for newly appointed Chamberlains of the Sixth Rank.

(623) *Hosonaga* (long robe worn by women and children): lit. 'thin and long'.

Kazami (woman's loose coat, note 41): lit. 'sweat garment'. *Kazami* originally referred to an undergarment that was designed to absorb sweat, but later it was applied to the coats worn by Palace girls.

Shiranaga (robe with a long train worn by boys): lit. 'long train'.

Karaginu (short jacket worn by women): lit. 'Chinese robe'.

Ue no kinu (men's over-robe): lit. 'robe above'.

Ue no hakama (over-trousers, trouser-skirt worn by both men and women together with the over-robes as part of their formal Court costume): lit. 'trouser-skirt above'.

Shitagasane (man's formal under-robe, note 118): lit. 'under-suit'.

Ōguchi (wide, red trouser-skirt worn by men): lit. 'big mouth'.

Hakama (trouser-skirt or divided skirt worn by men and women): lit. 'wear train' (*haki-mo*).

Sashinuki (loose, laced, silk trousers worn by men): lit. 'insertions'.

(624) None of these derivations (*kazami*, *hakama*, etc.) is particularly obscure; but the study of etymology was not very advanced in Shōnagon's time.

(625) Cf. note 588 about these priests and what they overheard. According to an early commentator, one of the ladies is imitating the priest's voice as a joke, but this theory is rejected by Kaneko (*Hyōshaku*, p. 651) as 'reckless' (*midari*).

(626) In 995 (App. 4). Michitaka had died on the 10th of the 4th Month.

For a description of Shōnagon's relations with Tadanobu earlier in the year see section 78.

(627) There is no distinction in Japanese between defining and non-defining relative clauses. It is not clear, therefore, whether Shōnagon's remark about insensitivity to the pathos of things (*mono no aware*) applies to young people in general or whether it is intended to define these particular young people.

From a Chinese poem written by Michizane's grandson, Sugawara
no Fumitoki, for Fujiwara no Koretada as a prayer (*gammon*) in
memory of Koretada's father and mother. The quotation is especially
appropriate since the present service is in memory of the Empress's
father; note also that the season (autumn) is correct. The poem, which
is included in *Wakan Rōei Shū*, goes as follows:

Pi chin ku tsui hua chih ti	This golden valley, this earth,
Hua mei ch'un kou erh chu pu kuei	Whose perfumed flowers make
Nan lou wan yüeh chih jen	one drunk!
Yüeh yü ch'iu ch'i erh shen ho ch'ü	It's spring, and once again the
Huang ch'ung shen che szu yu shen	air is heavy with their scent;
Jung shen che wei yu shen	Yet he, their master, is no
	longer here.
	He who climbed the southern tower
	To gaze with joy upon the moon,
	Where is he now
	When moon and autumn reappear at the appointed time?
	Those deeply loved should deeply bear [these things] in mind,
	And those who are most honoured [by the world] should also be most fearful.

As usual in quotations from Chinese, Tadanobu says the words in
Japanese: *Yüeh yü ch'iu ch'i erh shen ho ch'ü* becomes *tsuki aki to ki
shite mi izuku ni ka.*

Because Shōnagon was known to be especially fond of Tadanobu.

Akekure: lit. 'day and night'. As Chief Chamberlain (Index-Glossary)
he had free access to the Empress's residence, where Shōnagon was in
attendance. But men who held this office were usually promoted to
the post of Imperial Adviser, and, according to Kaneko (*Hyōshaku*,
p. 657), this is what Tadanobu has in mind when he suggests that his
visits may have to stop (*naki ori mo araba*).

Tada obose ka shi: lit. 'Do just think [of me].' I have followed Kaneko
and Ikeda-Kishigami; but according to some of the commentaries
this means, 'Please be considerate of my feelings.'

The Japanese *norokeru*, meaning i.a. 'to speak fondly or proudly of one's wife, husband, lover, etc.', has no real equivalent in English. It is always used in a derogatory sense, and in the present passage Shōnagon, though she does not use the word itself, expresses her doubts about people who indulge in this activity. An exaggerated effort to avoid such partiality can make people seem disloyal, and this is the tenor of Tadanobu's final remark. Kaneko suggests (*Hyōshaku*, pp. 657–8) that Shōnagon's argument is a skilful pretext to avoid having an affair with Tadanobu, and he describes his last remark as 'the disappointed voice of a man whose proposal has been rejected'. There is considerable evidence, however, that Tadanobu had already been Shōnagon's lover; perhaps she is now simply trying to avoid resuming a relationship that no longer suits her.

(633) Probably in the 2nd or 3rd Month of 998 (App. 4).

(634) I.e. before 2 a.m. (App. 3).

(635) A conventional euphuism; cf. *W.S.P.*, p. 230.

(636) *Uraue ni*: 'back to front', 'reverse', 'contrary'; by referring to the rooster's crow, the letter gives the impression that he had spent the night with Shōnagon as a lover.

(637) T'ien Wen, the Lord of Meng-ch'ang (Mō Sō), was the grandson of the King of Ch'i. In 289 B.C. he was invited to the state of Ch'in, where he became a minister. The King of Ch'in grew suspicious of him and had him arrested, but T'ien Wen was able to escape one night and to reach the frontier barrier of Han-ku (Kan Koku). This barrier remained closed until dawn; a posse had set out in hot pursuit, and the prince would certainly have been captured had not one of his party, who was skilled at making bird calls, conceived the astute idea of imitating the crow of a rooster. This deluded the barrier keeper into believing that it was dawn, whereupon he opened the gate, permitting the prince and his party to escape and return to Ch'i. Shōnagon playfully suggests that Yukinari's cock-crow is as untrue as the rest of his letter in which he falsely suggests (note 636) that they have shared a night of love.

(638) Determined to show that he is familiar with Shōnagon's historical allusion, Yukinari adds a detail that is in fact incorrect. The *Shih chi* mentions that the Lord of Meng-ch'ang had 3,000 followers (*shih k'o*) in his fief at home; it certainly does not suggest that this was the

number of men who accompanied him on his escape. We can assume that Shōnagon failed to notice the error; for she would hardly have missed such an opportunity to discomfit Yukinari.

For the erotic connotations of Ōsaka (*au-saka*) see note 540.   (639)

Yo wo komete   (640)
Tori no sorane wa
Hakaru tomo
Yo ni au saka (Ōsaka) no
Seki wa yurusaji

Au saka (Ōsaka) wa
Hito koeyasuki
Seki nareba
Tori mo nakanedo
Akete matsu to ka

Far from being hard to cross as Shōnagon had suggested in her poem, the barrier of the 'slope of meetings' (note 540) is always wide open to the traveller. Yukinari alludes to Shōnagon's reputation of having many lovers. It is hardly a flattering innuendo, but she takes it in good part. This poem of Shōnagon's ('There may be some who are deceived . . .') did a great deal towards confirming her literary reputation at Court; it is included in the famous *Hyakunin Isshu* anthology.

Her postscript implies that the gate keeper at Ōsaka is far more prudent than the one who let Prince Meng Ch'ang cross the barrier; it suggests, in other words, that she will not let down her defences so easily.

Sore wa mezurashūte ima no koto no yō ni mo yorokobitamau ka na: lit. (641) 'Oh, that is uncommon and you rejoice as if it were a thing of [just] now.' *Mezurashi* can also mean 'impressive', 'superb'; Tsunefusa's speech would then start, 'How splendid! . .'.

In 999 (App. 4).   (642)

Shōnagon is thinking of the bamboo-loving Tzu-yu (Wang Hui-chih) (643) (d. A.D. 388), who referred to bamboo as 'this gentleman'. The *Chin shu* (chap. 80) has the following passage: 'Hui-chih merely whistled and hummed. Pointing to the bamboo, he said, "How could I be without this gentleman for a single day?"' 'This gentleman' (*kono kimi*) as used by Shōnagon therefore means 'bamboo'. She probably derived this particular piece of erudition from the preface to a Chinese poem by Fujiwara no Atsushige (included in *Wakan Rōei Shū*): 'Wang

115

Tzu-yu planted bamboo and called it "this gentleman". The follower of the heir-apparent of T'ang, Po Lo-t'ien [Po Chü-i], loved it and considered it "my friend".'

(644) The only identifiable member of this party is the 'new Middle Captain'. This must be either Minamoto no Yorisada, who was appointed to the rank in 998, or Fujiwara no Sanenari, who received the appointment in the same year. The 'Middle Captain' may be Minamoto no Tsunefusa. In the Sangenbon texts we find (instead of 'the Middle Captain, the new Middle Captain'): 'the Minamoto Middle Captain, [son of] Prince [Tamehira], the Minister of Ceremonial'. This can only be Minamoto no Yorisada.

(645) Since Heian Japanese, like the modern language, usually makes no distinction between singular and plural, *kono kimi* can mean both 'this gentleman' (i.e. bamboo) and 'these gentlemen' (i.e. the men who came to the Empress's residence). Though Shōnagon knew the first meaning perfectly well, and would have been horrified if anyone had doubted it, she playfully pretends to Yukinari, and later to the Empress, that she was using the phrase in its second, more conventional, sense.

(646) *Ch'eng tz u chün* (*kono kimi to shō zu*). From the prose preface by Atsushige (note 643). Because of their close link with poetry it was customary to refer to the prefaces themselves as *shi* (poems).

(647) *Tenjō nite iikishitsuru hoi mo nakute wa nado kaeritamainuru zo*: lit. 'Why have you returned without (even) accomplishing the purpose that you planned at the Palace?'

(648) *Torinashitaru*: lit. 'intervened' [on my behalf].

(649) Emperor Enyū, who died in 991, was Empress Sadako's father-in-law (App. 6a). This scene takes place in the 2nd Month of 992, when Emperor Ichijō is only twelve years old (App. 4).

(650) The poem, which appears in the *Kokin Shū*, is by the illustrious cleric Henjō (Henjō Sōjō) (Index-Glossary) and commemorates the first anniversary of the death of Emperor Nimmyō in 850:

Mina hito wa	All, once more, in flowery clothes are decked.
Hana no koromo ni	Oh, that these mossy sleeves of mine might dry!
Narinu nari	
Koke no tamoto yo	
Kawaki dani seyo	

The poet contrasts the bright clothes (*hana no koromo*) of the courtiers,
who have now discarded their mourning, with his own dark habits
(*koke no tamoto*). *Kokegoromo* ('moss clothes') is a standard epithet for
priestly robes. There is the usual sleeves-wet-with-tears imagery.

For basket worm see section 45, p. 49. Tōzammi was Morosuke's (651)
daughter, Fujiwara no Shigeko (App. 6b), who served as Imperial
Nurse to Emperor Ichijō. She was married to Fujiwara no Michikane
and, after his death in 995, to Taira no Korenaka. *Tō* is the Chinese
reading for *fuji* in *Fujiwara*; *zammi* (third rank) refers to the lady's
Court rank. Imperial Nurses (On-Menoto) were chosen from among
Court ladies of the highest birth and rank; hence Tōzammi's familiar
behaviour with the Empress later in this section.

Kanju (account of scrolls): when someone had arranged for incanta- (652)
tions, sacred texts, etc. to be read at a temple, he would receive an
'account of scrolls', a long strip of paper attached to a white stick,
stating the number of scrolls that had been recited at his request,
e.g. 'Sutra of Great Wisdom, 600 scrolls'. Here Tōzammi has arranged
for readings to be carried out on behalf of the Emperor, and she
assumes that the missive which arrived on the previous evening is a
document of this kind. She washes her hands and kneels down out of
respect for what she believes to be a sacred object; hence her annoyance
(*asamashiku netakurikeru*) when she finds out that it is a poem.

> Kore wo dani (653)
> Katami to omou ni
> Miyako ni wa
> Hagae ya shitsuru
> Shiishiba no sode

Shiishiba was a type of oak used to produce a dark dye for mourning
dress. (Dark brown was associated with Buddhist priests, death, etc.,
and the poem is written on dark-brown paper.) *Shii* also means 4th
Rank and may allude to the fact that Tōzammi, to whom the poem is
written, has recently been promoted from 4th to 3rd Rank. *Hagae*
('changed to brighter hues') literally means 'changing of leaves'.

Niwa Ji no Sōjō (the Archbishop of Niwa): Niwa (usually Ninna) Ji (654)
was a Shingon temple a few miles west of the capital (App. 9c). The
Archbishop (*Sōjō*) was Kanchō, a son of Prince Atsumi (Index-
Glossary). Note that Henjō, the author of the 'flowery clothes' poem
(note 650), was also an archbishop. Henjō's poem has obviously
influenced this one.

117

Refers to Fujiwara no Asamitsu, Naritoki, or Michinaga (see Index-Glossary).

(656) *Osoroshū iitaru monoimi*: lit. 'an abstinence that they had declared to be fearful'. During a period of strict abstinence it was dangerous to communicate with the outside world. See note 90.

(657) *Zushi*: small wooden cupboard with twin leaves, originally used for storing Sutra scrolls and Buddhist images, but later also used for books and personal effects.

    Kaneko suggests (*Hyōshaku*, p. 679) that the letter produced by the Emperor is a draft copy of the one received by Tōzammi.

(658) The child who brought the poem looked like a basket worm, and the Emperor is alluding to the legend about the insect's demon-father (note 651 and section 45). It now becomes evident that the first letter originated in his Palace but was made to look as if it came from a priest. Lady Kohyōe (see p. 95) was known as something of a wag; she is clearly the prime mover in the practical joke that has been played on Tōzammi with the knowledge of the Emperor and the Empress.

(659) See note 103.

(660) *Sugoroku* (backgammon): like *go*, this game was introduced from China. Each of two players had fifteen pieces (*uma*) which he moved across the board depending on throws of the dice; the first player to occupy his enemy's territory was the winner. *Sugoroku* was a quicker and less elegant game than *go* but far more widely played, especially for gambling. *Ōkagami* describes Michinaga and his nephew, Korechika, engaged in a keen contest of *sugoroku* that lasted all night. Though the game took place in the Palace, both men were naked except for their scanty loincloths (*Nisho nagara hadaka ni koshi karamasetamaite*).

(661) This particular misfortune is also listed under Depressing Things (section 24), where it is described in detail (pp. 22–23).

(662) Putting starch in laundered clothes was so plebeian an occupation that Shōnagon hesitates even to hint at its existence. She points out, however, that her notes were not intended for other people to see and that she would therefore be justified in including so inauspicious an item as parting-fire tongs (below), which were associated with death.

Atobi no hibashi (tongs used for the parting fires): the Festival of the Dead (Urabon), which corresponded in some ways to All Souls' Day in the West, was celebrated from the 13th to the 16th of the 7th Month (App. 1). Sticks of peeled hemp (known as *mukaebi* or *sakihi*) were lit on the first day of the festival so that the souls of the dead might find their way to earth; on the last day, fires (*okuribi* or *atobi*, which I translate as 'parting fires') were again lit, this time to speed the ghostly visitors on their way back. On the 15th a special Buddhist service (Urabone) was held in intercession for the dead who were suffering in hell, especially for those who were undergoing the ordeal of Headlong Falling (*Tōken no Ku*).

The wooden tongs (*hibashi*) used for the parting fires clearly deserved to be included among Things Without Merit. The tongs used for the welcoming fires (*mukaebi*) could be used again at the end of the festival, but afterwards they had to be thrown away because of their inauspicious connotations. Kaneko believes that parting-fire tongs (*atobi no hibashi*) may have been a set expression to describe something useless (*Hyōshaku*, p. 684).

Yo ni naki koto naraneba minahito shiritaramu: lit. 'because they are (663) not things that are not in the world, all people must know [them]'.

Shōnagon is clearly defending herself from some criticism that she (664) has received or expects to receive (e.g. 'Why do you write about such vulgar subjects as starching laundered clothes?'). Her answer is that she originally had no intention of letting anyone read her notes. See also p. 112 for a suggestion made in 995 or 996 by someone who had either read or heard her notes, and p. 267 for the possible way in which part of the notes came into circulation between 995 and 996. It is probable, though by no means certain, that the present passage was written in 996 after Shōnagon knew that parts of her notes were being read or, at least, discussed.

Kamorizukasa (or *Kamonzukasa*) (Housekeeping Office): Govern- (665) ment office under the Ministry of the Treasury (Ōkura Shō, App. 7a) in charge of furnishings used in the Palace buildings and gardens.

Indeed it is. Since the present festival takes place in the spring, and (666) since there was no Sacred Dance of the Return (note 672), it must be the one held at Iwashimizu (not Kamo) Shrine. At the Iwashimizu festival the Imperial envoys faced south towards Iwashimizu; at the Kamo festival (in the 11th Month) they faced north towards Kamo. For the importance of directions see note 38; for the Special Festivals, note 66; for the rehearsal, note 315.

It was usual after large Court banquets to let commoners come and
help themselves to the left-overs. The custom (known as *toribami*) is
typical of the many informal aspects of Palace life. The *tori* in *toribami*
may mean 'bird', suggesting the image of hungry sparrows picking
crumbs off the ground; this would accord with the contemporary
aristocratic picture of *hoi polloi*.

(668) *Hitakiya* (fire-huts): small, roofless huts built in the Palace gardens
to house the bonfires that provided illumination, especially during
nocturnal festivals and ceremonies.

(669) *Beijū mo* (even the musicians): the *beijū* (Index-Glossary) ranked so
low in the social hierarchy that they were not normally allowed to
move about in the Emperor's presence. I have moved this passage
forward several sentences to what appears to be its logical place.

(670) *Udo Hama* (Udo Beach): folk-song from the eastern provinces. Its
racy character is typical of popular songs of the time (cf. p. 82):

Udo Hama ni	At Udo Beach
Suruga naru	In Suruga,
Udo Hama ni	Ay, at Udo Beach!
Uchiyosuru nami wa	The wave that beats against the shore
Nanakusa no imo	Is mistress of the seven herbs.
Koto koso yoshi	Oh, how good!
Koto koso yoshi	Oh, how good!
Nanakusa no imo	The mistress of the seven herbs—
Koto koso yoshi	Oh, how good!
Aeru toki isa	But what does she do when she meets her
Sa wa nenan ya	herbs?
Nanakusa no imo	Sleep with them? Oh does she now!
Koto koso yoshi	The mistress of the seven herbs—
	Oh, how good!

For 'seven herbs' see note 5; here they may well have a phallic connotation.

(671) Another folk-song from the east:

Chidori yue ni	Be mindful of the plovers
Hama ni ideasobu	That come to play upon the beach!
Chidori yue ni	Ay, be mindful of the plovers,
Aya mo naki	Do not cast your net
Komatsu ga ure ni	Over the branches of the little pines,
Ami na hari so	For that would be a foolish act.

The basic text has Koma Yama (Mount Koma) instead of Komatsu
(Little Pines); but this must be a mistake (*Hyōshaku*, p. 688) since the
Mount Koma song belonged to the category of *saibara* (Index-
Glossary), which were never sung at the Kamo festival.

Kaeridachi no Mi-Kagura (Sacred Dance of the Return): a *kagura* (672)
performed by the dancers after their return to the Palace. This encore
took place when the festival was held at the Kamo shrines, but not
when the dancers came from the more distant shrine in Iwashimizu.

The director (*ninjō*) of the dancers and musicians was usually a (673)
Guards officer of the 6th Rank. The singers and dancers included
noblemen of the 4th, 5th, and 6th Ranks; in a very rank-conscious
society it was of course a particular satisfaction to be obeyed by people
who were usually giving the orders.

Shōnagon is probably referring to a poem by Fujiwara no Tadafusa (674)
(Index-Glossary) contained in the *Shūi Shū*:

Mezurashiki	Ah, upon this festive day
Kyō no Kasuga no	When the eight young maidens dance at Kasuga
Ya otome wo	Even the Gods must be overwhelmed with joy.
Kami mo ureshi to	
Shinobazarame ya	

This became a precedent and Sacred Dances of the Return were held (675)
after the Iwashimizu Festival until the end of the Kamakura period.
The reason the ladies did not expect the Emperor to keep to his decision (*sa shi mo ya arazaramu*) was that the extra performance involved
a break with traditional usage and such breaks were not lightly made
in the Heian period.

Mo wo kashira ni uchikazukite ('they lifted their skirts over their (676)
heads'): in order to avoid being recognized. The ladies had several
under-skirts, petticoats, etc., beneath their *mo* and were in no danger
of revealing their bodies.

For the political background and for Shōnagon's reputation of being (677)
partial to the 'enemy' faction see note 606. 'Stir and movement'
refers specifically to the Korechika-Takaie disgrace and to Sadako's
becoming a nun (all in 996).

Owing to Bedchamber intrigues that Michinaga fostered after his (678)
brother's death, Sadako was obliged to leave the Imperial Palace. In

996 (4th Month) she moved into the Smaller Palace of the 2nd Ward (Ko Nijō In), which had been built as her private residence in 992.

(679) *Sachūjō* (Captain of the Left Guards Division): either Fujiwara no Tadanobu or Fujiwara no Masamitsu. The visit takes place about the 7th Month of 996, some sixteen months after Michitaka's death (App. 4). The *Sangenbon* texts, however, have *Uchūjo* (Captain of the Right Guards Division); in this case the gentleman in question is Minamoto no Tsunefusa, who became Captain in this Division in the 7th Month of 996.

(680) *Shion hagi* (purple and dark red): see note 19 for these colour combinations.

(681) *Oboshimesaretaru kai mo naku*: lit. '[Her Majesty's] thinking [thus] has no result. . . .'

(682) I.e. to Michinaga, the leader of the 'Opposition'.

(683) *Koko nite sae hikishinobu mo amari nari. Hitozute no ōsegoto nite aranumeri* . . .: lit. 'It was excessive to conceal [a letter] even here. It did not seem to be the letter of an intermediary. . . .'

(684) From the *Rokujō* poem quoted in note 312. The mountain rose (*yamabuki = kerria japonica*) points to the same poem, because its yellow colour is designated by a word (*kuchinashi-iro*) that is homonymous with 'does not speak'.

(685) I.e. with tears. The conceit is based on the following *Kokin Shū* poem:

Yo no naka no	Before we even learn
Uki mo tsuraki mo	How sad, how fleeting is this world of ours,
Tsugenaku ni	We know already of the world of tears.
Mazu shiru mono wa	(*More lit.*, 'The thing that one knows first
Namida narikeri	of all is tears.')

(686) For the significance of this lapse see *W.S.P.*, pp. 182–3. The line quoted by the Empress is *iwade omou zo* (note 312); it is the earlier part of the poem (*uta no moto*) that Shōnagon cannot remember.

(687) *Nikuki uta naredo*: lit. 'though it was a hateful (unpleasant) poem'.

(688) *Nazonazo* (riddles): the game was played by two teams, left and right, who tried to solve each other's riddles and conundrums. Preparations

for matches (*awase*) of this kind usually continued for several weeks (*W.S.P.*, pp. 151–2). During the competition two participants, one from each team, would exchange riddles; then another pair would make an exchange, and so forth. Victory went to the team whose members had solved more riddles and received the greater number of winning tokens (note 691) from the judge.

The answer to the present very simple riddle is 'crescent moon', because *hari* means 'drawing', 'stretching', *yumi* 'bow', and *yumi-harizuki* 'crescent moon' (lit. 'bow-draw-moon'). No self-respecting courtier could fail to know the answer, since the same riddle had been asked by Emperor Daigo (reg. 897–930) and recorded in *Utsubo Monogatari*. It is precisely because the answer is so obvious that the player fails to answer and loses the first point for his team.

Isa shirazu. Saraba na tanomare so: 'Well, I do not know. If it is thus, (689) pray do not depend on me.'

Kuchi hikitarete: lit. 'his mouth drooping'; but 'pout' better conveys (690) the player's annoyance at being given such an easy riddle.

Kazu sase: lit. 'put out a token (counter)'. Tokens (*kazusashi*) were (691) given to each team as it scored a point in a competition. Sometimes valuable gold and silver ornaments were used instead of simple counters.

Oboenu koto wa sa koso are: lit. 'as for not knowing it is indeed thus'; (692) the Ikeda-Kishigami text has *oboenu toki wa shika koso wa are* ('when one does not know, it is indeed thus') His team-mates assume that he did in fact know the answer but refused to give it because it was too obvious.

Kore wa wasuretaru koto ka wa. Minahito shiritaru koto ni ya: lit. 'Can (693) this be a thing one forgets? It must be a thing that everyone knows.' Ikeda-Kishigami (p. 203) give the following gloss. Shōnagon realizes that the failure of the man in the Empress's story is different from hers: he failed to answer the riddle because it was too familiar, whereas she actually forgot the poem. Kaneko (*Hyōshaku*, p. 710) comments on the modesty of the conclusion: Shōnagon forgot the missing line because it was too easy, and the man failed to answer the riddle for the same reason; but, whereas she actually forgot the answer, he merely pretended to have done so (*izure mo furugoto wo anadotta shippai de wa aru ga, nazo no hanashi wa shitte ite anadotta no, jibun no wa anadotte wasureta . . .*). Shōnagon's lapse is obviously the more serious of the two.

Because he is bending over the board, the upper part of his costume reaches up and covers his face (*kubi no kao ni kakareba*).

(695) *Tsurubami* (bark of an oak): used to produce a dark dye and therefore associated with mourning.

(696) Presumably it is the unfamiliarity of the sight that makes it frightening for a woman.

(697) I.e. before they are properly fledged.

(698) The present Japanese custom of a daily bath did not become current, even in aristocratic circles, until a much later period. Thus in his advice to his descendants Fujiwara no Morosuke writes: 'Next choose a[n auspicious] day for your bath; bathe once every five days' (*Hyō-shaku*, p. 718).

(699) The following four sections (142–5) correspond to Ippon 1–3, 5 in the *Sangenbon* version (Ikeda–Kishigami ed.); they are not included in the *Shunchobon* text.

(700) *Darani* (incantations): see note 596 and 'Depressing Things', p. 22.

(701) *Hichiriki* (flageolet): a shrill pipe used in Shintō services. See p. 190 for details.

(702) *Kōshiri*: the word is totally unknown. According to some commentaries, it is a contraction of *kawa-shiri* ('river-bottom') and refers to boating excursions at the mouth of a river (probably the Kamo); but, if so, it is not clear why it belongs in this section.

(703) A Senior Secretary in the Ministry of Ceremonial belonged to the 6th Rank (note 123). When a new Secretary was appointed to the Ministry, a former incumbent might be retired; in this case he would normally be promoted in rank. No prestige attached to such a promotion, however, and the retired official would not be allowed access to the Senior Courtiers' Chamber, a privilege usually enjoyed by members of the 5th Rank. Hence he is listed among 'vulgar-seeming things' (*iyashige naru mono*).

(704) *Mushirobari no kuruma* (straw-mat carriage): a lowly member of the ox-carriage hierarchy; it was covered with straw or rush matting (cf. palm-leaf carriage).

Shōnagon has already expressed her doubts about these garments and their wearers in section 47 (Unsuitable Things). (705)

It appears that straw mats manufactured in other provinces were (706) sometimes known as Izumo mats and that these were in fact superior to the genuine Izumo product, which tended to be roughly plaited and coarse.

Kurabeuma (horse-races) were included in the Court calendar. They (707) took place annually in the 5th Month and also during the Kamo Festival. As in all Heian competitions, the participants were divided into left and right teams. The races were held individually between two riders, one from each team, the aim being not only to outride one's opponent but to unhorse him.

Because it can break so easily. In Heian times women manufactured (708) their own cords (*motoyui*). Sometimes they were made of silk or hemp, but here Shōnagon clearly refers to the fragile paper variety.

I.e. without knowing that he (or she) is there. But the passage is (709) obscure.

For the unhappy implications of this delay see note 185. (710)

Furi (or, according to *Sangenbon*, *uri*): probably a type of small musk- (711) melon (*cucumis melo*) known as *himeuri*. Drawing faces on melons was a common pastime, especially for women and children.

Women and children of the leisured class often kept baby sparrows (712) and other little birds as pets. The squeak of a mouse was a *chū-chū* sound used to attract pet birds.

Ito chiisaki chiri nado: lit. 'such a thing as a very small piece of dirt (713) (dust)'.

I.e. cut at shoulder length. So great was the aesthetic value attached (714) to a woman's hair that nuns were not expected to take the tonsure, but simply cut their hair at about the level of their shoulders.

Also listed among 'Things That Arouse a Fond Memory of the Past'. (715) See note 141.

Hiyohiyo (cheeping): this is the form given in the texts that I have
consulted; the modern onomatopoeia is *piyopiyo*.

(717) Also listed among 'Elegant Things'. See note 236.

(718) *Hitobae suru mono* ('presumptuous things'): commentators disagree
about this heading. The main theories are: (i) the syllable *so* has been
dropped, and the first words should be *hitosobae suru* = presume on
another's kindness, take advantage of another's affection; (ii) *bae*
(*hae*) is the *renyōkei* of *hayu* ('to shine', 'be brilliant', 'jovial', etc.) and
hitobae means 'to be(come) jovial (elated, triumphant, etc.) in the
presence of other people'; (iii) *hae* = *hiku* ('to pull', etc.).

The first interpretation does not seem to cover the second and third
paragraphs in this section, but it does apply to the main contents, i.e.
to those about spoilt children.

In contrast to the previous section, the present one is focused on the
less endearing aspects of little children.

(719) *Aofuchi* (pool of green water): frightening because it seems so
deep.

Kurogane (iron): because the word means 'dark metal'.

Ikazuchi (thunder): the probable etymology is 'solemn (or majestic)
hammer'.

Fusūgumo (cloud of ill omen): any peculiarly shaped cloud was
regarded as a portent (see *W.S.P.*, p. 128).

Hokoboshi (halberd star): the 7th star of Ursa Major. It appears to
be shaped like a sword, and the direction in which the sword pointed
was believed to be highly inauspicious.

Ōkami (wolf): homonymous with the word meaning 'Great
Divinity', which often referred to the Sun Goddess; here 'frightening'
has the sense of 'awe-inspiring'.

Ushi (cow): the basic text (*ushi wa same*) is obscure. *Same* refers to
horses or cows with white, fish-like eyes. Kaneko prefers the *Bōhon*
text, which has *ushi kasame* ('The cow. The *kasame* crab'); according
to this theory, 'cow' (*ushi*) is included because it is homonymous
with 'sad'.

Ikari (anchor): another obscure entry. Some texts have *inizushi*,
which may be a corruption of *izushi* (rice cakes with mussels). Kaneko
and Ikeda-Kishigami follow the *Beppon* text and give *ikari*, which
has the double meaning of 'anchor' and 'anger'. But what is so
frightening about an anchor? Beaujard (*Notes de chevet*, p. 185)
believes that *inizushi* is a corruption of *inoshishi* (boar), but here again
there seems nothing frightening about the actual word.

Hijikasaame ('elbow shower'): a sudden, unexpected shower; since one is not prepared for the rain, one has to protect oneself with an 'elbow hat' (*hijikasa*) (i.e. by covering one's head with the sleeves of one's robe) instead of with the usual headgear (*kasa*). By Shōnagon's time the word had become established in poetic usage.

Kuchinawa-ichigo (snake strawberries): i.e. Indian strawberries (*duchesnea indica*); so called because they seemed to crawl along the ground and were popularly believed to be poisonous.

Ikisudama (*ikiryō*) (living ghost): according to current superstition, a person's spirit could torment his enemies and cause their death even while the tormentor was still alive and consciously unaware of what his spirit was perpetrating. The most famous 'living ghost' in literature is Lady Rokujō in *The Tale of Genji*: consumed with jealous hatred, her unappeased spirit attacks one after another of Genji's wives and mistresses.

Bōtan (peony): perhaps included in this list because the Japanese word is hard and rather unattractive.

Ushioni (cow-headed devil): one of the two devils who guard the entrance to the Buddhist hell; the other one (*mezu*) has a horse-head.

The words in this list that are not mentioned above have been included for their associations or their sounds or both. The order and selection of 'things with frightening names' is different in the *Sangenbon* texts. Some of those given in the *Shunchohon* version are omitted; the following are added:

Aranora: a rough field.

Ransō: a rough voice (*or* a green robe as worn by men of the 6th Rank).

Kanamochi: unknown, but possibly a corruption of *kanemochi* (Chinese hawthorn).

Ichigo (strawberries): written with three Chinese characters (mean- (720) ing 'cover', 'dish', 'child') that have a total of thirty strokes, an absurdly large number (Shōnagon implies) for such a small, simple thing as a strawberry. Even in modern Japanese many common words (e.g. those for 'rose', 'velvet', 'fan', 'mackerel', 'gargle') are written with bizarre combinations of unusual Chinese characters, which convey neither the sound nor the meaning. These so-called *ateji* ('false substitute characters') represent a gratuitous, though at times rather fascinating, complication in an already tortuous system of writing.

Tsuyugusa (dew-plant): a kind of hare's ear, a common wild plant, written with the characters for 'wild duck', 'sole of the feet', and 'plant' (total strokes: 37); it was used to produce a common dye.

127

Mizubuki (prickly water-lily): written with a single Chinese character which, though simple (seven strokes), is most unusual and therefore seems inappropriate for such a humble plant.

Kurumi (walnut): written then as now with the characters for
'barbarian' (*go, ko, u*) and 'peach tree' (*tō; momo*), which have
no connexion, in either sound or meaning, with the word they
represent.

Monjō Hakase (Doctor of Literature): academic people were generally held in low regard by the people of Shōnagon's world (see
note 398 and *W.S.P.*, p. 172).

Kōgōgū no Gon no Taifu (Provisional Senior Steward in the Office
of the Empress's Household): an impressive collection of Chinese
characters (six characters with a total of fifty-four strokes) for a not
very lofty post.

Yamamomo (red myrtle): this is the *myrica rubrica* (red myrica),
a Linnaean genus of shrubs including the bog myrtle. It is written
with characters meaning 'purple willow' (*kawayanagi*) and 'plum
tree' (*ume*), but the word itself evidently means 'mountain peach
tree'. So here we have a case in which neither the word's apparent
etymology nor the characters used to write it give any clue about its
meaning.

Itadori (knotweed): this is the *polygonum cuspidatum* (pointed
polygonum). It is written with the characters for 'tiger' (*tora*) and
'stick' (*tsue*).

Sangenbon also has the following:

Kumo (spider): written with two rare characters having a total of
twenty-six strokes.

Tokugō no Shō: Master of Literature; this was a scholar (ranking
below Doctor of Literature) who had passed his examinations in
Chinese composition. Once again the title is more impressive than
the status.

(721) This is Ippon 4 in the *Sangenbon* version (Ikeda–Kishigami ed.); it
does not appear in *Shunchobon*. The list consists of words written
with unfamiliar characters or combinations of characters; they are:
itameshio, akome, katabira, keishi, yusuru, okefune. The last word has
not been identified.

(722) Here *mono* obviously means both 'thing' and 'person' (see note 102).

(723) *Ōne*: radishes were one of the dishes presented to the Emperor during
the ceremony of Tooth Hardening (Hagatame) on the 3rd day of the
year (note 220).

Himemōchigimi (Ladies of the Escort): these were girls, belonging to the Palace Attendants' Office, who accompanied the Emperor on horseback during Imperial Processions. Normally they were of slight social importance, but they came into their own during the Processions.

The Great Purification (Ōharai), carried out on the last days of the (725) 6th and 12th Months, was one of the main Shintō observances of the year (App. 1). On the eve of the ceremony life-size figures (*miagamono*) of the Emperor, Empress, and Crown Prince were prepared and dressed by the Lady Chamberlains (note 348), who took measurements by breaking off suitable lengths of bamboo. This was known as *yoori* ('breaking the knots') and came to designate the entire preparation; it probably offered the only occasion on which such low-ranking women could approach the sacred person of the Emperor. On the day of the ceremony the substitute figures, to which all impurities had been magically transferred, were bathed in running water; thereby the ritual impurities that had accumulated during the previous six months were washed away. For the role of running water in Heian beliefs see also *W.S.P.*, p. 130.

Ki no Mi-Dokyō (seasonal Sacred Readings): so called because they (726) took place in two seasons, spring and autumn (notes 357, 360). The Master of Observances (Igōshi) was a priest who supervised the performance of the intricate Court ceremonies that accompanied the Readings.

Kasuga Matsuri (Kasuga Festival): this was held in the 2nd and 11th (727) Months at Kasuga Shrine in Nara (App. 1). On the day before the ceremony an officer of the Inner Palace Guards proceeded to the shrine as Imperial Messenger to make offerings to the Gods on behalf of the Emperor; here Shōnagon is referring to the Imperial Attendants (Toneri) who escorted him on his august mission.

This evidently refers to a solemn procession of students that took (728) place during a Ministers' Banquet (note 396). On these occasions the students recited congratulatory Chinese verses in honour of the new minister.

It is the people in the procession, not the procession itself, that is 'trivial'. In Shōnagon's time students and others connected with the academic world were generally regarded as 'trivial people' (see notes 398, 720, etc.); but on ceremonial occasions like this they came into their own.

On New Year's Day various types of spiced wine (*toso*) were prepared by the Palace Medicinal Office. After being tasted by specially appointed virgins known as *Kusuriko* (lit. 'medicine children'), they were offered to the Emperor as an elixir of long life. The purpose of this tasting was not (*pace* Beaujard, *S.S.S.T.*, p. 150) to avoid the danger of poisoning but to promote the Emperor's longevity by transferring the long life expectancy of the girls by means of the wine. *Toso* is still commonly drunk by Japanese families on New Year's Day, but there are no longer any virgin wine-tasters.

(730) The priests presented the wands from the exorcists (note 321) and had the privilege of pronouncing 'auspicious words' (i.e. wishes for a long and prosperous reign) to the Emperor (cf. p. 70).

(731) See note 431.

(732) The Palace Festivals (*Sechie*) included the Accession Ceremony, the festival of the blue horses (note 8), the Iris Festival, etc. On these occasions some of the Palace Girls (note 202) were privileged to serve at the Emperor's table, an office normally performed only by Assistant Attendants.

(733) Because they received special awards (note 396).

(734) See note 592.

(735) Shōnagon refers to the *ichimegasa* ('market woman's hat'); this was the least elegant form of headgear, yet became important when it rained.

(736) *Inari*: a group of three Shintō shrines built in 711 on the slopes of a hill a couple of miles south of the capital (App. 9c); they were dedicated to the gods of the five grains. Pilgrims used to pick branches of cryptomeria (*shirushi no sugi*), which grew near the shrines, and wear them on their head-dress to show that they had made the auspicious visit. The Middle Shrine (Naka no Mi-yashiro) was the most important but for a proper visit one had to go all the way up to the top shrine. The Shrine Festival was celebrated on the 1st day of the Horse in the 2nd Month (see App. 3).

(737) I.e. about 10 a.m. (App. 3).

(738) I.e. about 2 p.m. (App. 3).

Naniwazu watari no tōkaranu: lit. 'not far from the ferry of Naniwa' NOTES (739)
(see note 80).

Artificial light in a Heian house was usually too poor for accurate work (740) like sewing. See *W.S.P.*, p. 34.

Kesōbito nado wa sa shi mo isogumajikeredo onozukara mata sarubeki (741) *ori mo ari*: lit. 'in the case of a lover, although one need not hurry so very much, there are, as a matter of course, occasions when again it must be there'.
    The rules for replying to love-poems were less rigorous than those governing other types of correspondence (note 111).

Michitaka died in the 4th Month of 995 (App. 4); the present events (742) occur about two months later. Empress Sadako and her ladies moved from the Imperial Palace to the Empress's Office on the 28th of the 6th Month, just before the ceremony of the Great Purification (note 725). The move was made for reasons of ritual purity. The Empress returned to the Palace on the 8th of the following month.

Aitandokoro (Dining Hall of the High Court Nobles): this was part (743) of the Government Offices of the Great Council of State (Dajōkan Chō or Kan no Tsukasa, App. 9e). It included kitchens and a dining hall used by the High Court Nobles.

Ubeubeshiki tokoro no senzai ni wa yoshi: lit. 'they were good in the (744) garden of [this] right (appropriate) place'.
    The flowers are *kanzō* (*hemerocallis fulva*).

One of the functions of the Bureau of Divination (Onyō Ryō) in the (745) Ministry of Central Affairs was to keep time by means of clepsydrae. This important duty was entrusted to the Time Office (Tokizukasa), which was staffed by two Doctors of the Clepsydra (Rokoku Hakushi) assisted by twenty Time Watchers (Tokimori). At the last quarter of each watch (i.e. every two hours, App. 3) the Time Watchers would go to the courtyard outside Seiryō Palace and inscribe the time on a board, which an officer of the Guards then attached to a post (*toki no kui*) (see *W.S.P.*, p. 132); at each new watch a fixed number of strokes was sounded on a gong in the bell-tower of the Bureau of Divination, which was directly to the north of the Government Offices of the Great Council of State; this could be heard throughout the Palace enclosure, but obviously it was louder in a place like the Aitandokoro, where Shōnagon was now staying (App. 9e). During the course of

131

each of the night watches an officer would strum his bowstring to keep away the evil spirits; then, after naming himself, he would announce the time in a stentorian voice (p. 236).

(746) 'Recited' (*zu shi*) suggests that this is a quotation from a poem, but the passage is obscure. I have followed *Hyōshaku*, p. 752.

(747) Shōnagon is thinking of the following *Kokin Shū* poem:

Natsu to aki to	There in the sky,
Yukikau sora no	Where the paths of summer and autumn cross,
Kayoiji wa	A cooling wind will blow from many sides.
Katae suzushiki	
Kaze ya fukuramu	

We are still at the beginning of the 7th Month, which corresponds to early autumn in the Western calendar (note 3). *Katae* ('from the side') suggests that the autumn winds are only just beginning.

(748) I.e. the Weaver and the Herdsman (note 55). The Tanabata Festival was celebrated on the 7th of the 7th Month.

(749) The visit takes place in 996, on the last day of the 3rd Month (App. 4). Tadanobu did not become Imperial Adviser until about one month later (24th of the 4th Month). Shōnagon frequently anticipates promotions in this way (cf. note 597). In the following section (161) she gives Tadanobu his correct (lower) title, which suggests that the two sections (160-1) were written at different times.

(750) *Ningen no shigatsu*: lit. 'the Fourth Month of men'. From Po Chü-i's poem:

Jen chien szu yüeh fang fei chin	The Fourth Month in this world of men
Shan szu t'ao hua shih sheng k'ai	Is when all flowers have lost their scent.
	But the peach trees by the mountain temple
	Have just put out their clouds of bloom.

In the traditional Far Eastern calendar the last day of the 3rd Month marked the end of spring (note 3). This of course called for special recitations of poetry. Tadanobu's quotation is especially appropriate because it also alludes to Michitaka's death ('when all the flowers have lost their scent'), which occurred in the 4th Month of the preceding year.

Nyōbō nado koso sayō no monowasure wa senu: lit. 'ladies certainly do not forget such things'. Yet, only four months later, Shōnagon her- self forgot a far more famous poem (section 136).

For the inconsistency in Tadanobu's title see note 749. (752)

For Heian bed-times see *W.S.P.*, pp. 149–50. (753)

Tsuyu no wakare no namida narubeshi: lit. 'they must be the tears of (754) parting of dew'. Tadanobu is quoting from a Chinese poem by Suga-wara no Michizane concerning the unhappy love of the Weaver and the Herdsman (note 55):

Lu ying pieh lei chu k'ung lo   The tears she sheds on parting will
turn to dew when morning comes...
Those tears, like pearls, that fall in
vain. . . .

Kono watari nite wa kakaru koto omoimawasazu iu wa kuchioshiki zo (755) *ka shi*: lit. 'when one says such a thing hereabouts without reflecting, it is certainly regrettable'. *Kakaru koto* ('such a thing') probably means 'a remark that reveals one's true feelings'. In other words, 'One always has to be on one's guard when you are about'.

See note 616. Because of his appalling ugliness the God of Mount (756) Kazuraki, to whom Tadanobu playfully compares himself, had to hide during the daytime. As Kaneko points out (*Hyōshaku*, p. 766), it is a rather trite joke and hardly worthy of a man of Tadanobu's parts. Possibly he has been thrown off balance by Shōnagon's recent comment and cannot find anything better to offer as a parting shot.

Waga kokoro nagara sukizukishi to oboeshi: lit. 'I knew despite my own (757) heart (i.e. I was forced to admit) that I was fanciful.' *Sukizukishi* meant 'fanciful, whimsical, curious, inquisitive', and referred to people who enjoyed novelties, mystifications, etc.

The secret language evolved by Shōnagon and Tadanobu varies with (758) the texts. I have used *Hyōshaku*, p. 760, which is the most com-prehensible version.

The terms are as follows (for the game of *go* see note 92).

te yurusu ('to yield one's hand'): to place one's pieces without pay-ing too much attention to one's opponent's strategy; a daring style of play in which one occasionally risks one's own position in the expecta-tion of later successes and in the hope that one's opponent will not be able to take advantage of one's temporary weakness. Thus a man and a woman who are on intimate terms may be prepared to risk 'showing their hands'.

kechi sasu ('to fill up the spaces'): to fill in the points that neither player can claim as his own territory. These spaces are known as *dame* ('false eyes'), and the process of filling them alternately with black and white stones is one of the last stages in a game of *go*. In the same way the physical intimacy of a couple ('tying the true lovers' knot') is the culminating stage in their relationship. '

te uku ('to keep one's hand'): the opposite of 'yielding one's hand'; a cautious style of play in which one is constantly on one's guard, closely observing one's opponent's moves. Here Shōnagon and Tadanobu refer to men and women who handle their partners with circumspection.

oshikobotsu ('to part the pieces'): the final stage in the game is to determine which of the players controls the larger territory, that is, has secured the greater number of viable 'eyes'. In order to facilitate the counting, the players 'break up' (*uchikobotsu*) the position, re-arranging the pieces in such a way that the territories controlled by the two sides are clearly visible. Just as in *go* 'parting the pieces' is the ultimate stage of the game (after 'filling up the spaces'), so in a love affair 'intolerable familiarity' (*aenaku chikō narinuru*) is the final stage (after physical intimacy).

(759) The exchange between Nobukata and Shōnagon is full of double meanings, based on the secret *go* language (note 758). When Nobukata asks whether she will yield her hand (*te wo yurushi*), he is in fact suggesting that their relations become more intimate. Next he tells her that he is as good a player (i.e. lover) as Tadanobu. Kaneko (*Hyōshaku*, p. 767) remarks on the unsubtle way in which Nobukata uses the secret language. Not surprisingly, Shōnagon rejects his overtures. 'If I played like that' means 'if I gave myself to every man who asked me'. Then comes an ingenious pun: *sadamenaki* means (i) not fixed, flighty, (ii) lacking a fixed 'eye' (i.e. a secure space as opposed to an insecure *dame*) in *go*. 'Roving eye' suggests some of the implications, but of course there is nothing in English corresponding to the use of 'eye' (*me*) in the game of *go*.

(760) *Hsiao K'uai-chi chih kuo ku miao . . .*: 'Hsiao of K'uai-chi, having visited the ancient tomb. . . .' As usual, Shōnagon gives the quotation in Japanese: *Shō Kaikei no kobyō wo sugishi*.

This is from a work by Ōe no Asatsuna (Index-Glossary) included in the preface to *Honchō Monzui* (Index-Glossary). Hsiao Yün was chief official of K'uai-chi in the sixth century A.D. The *Nan shih* ('History of the Southern Dynasties') records a visit that he made to the tomb of Chi Cha, a respected figure from the state of Wu in the sixth century B.C.

Misoji no ki ni oyobazu ('had not yet reached the term of thirty'): (761) i.e. he did not live to be thirty. This is a Chinese poem by Minamoto no Hideakira included in *Honchō Monzui*.

Yen Hui Chou hsien che	Yen Hui, the sage of Chou, had not yet
Wei chih san shih ch'i	reached the term of thirty;
P'an Yüeh Chin ming shih	And P'an Yüeh, great gentleman of Chin,
Tsao chu ch'iu hsing tz'u	Wrote his 'Song of Autumn Thoughts' at
Pi chieh shao yü wo	an early age
K'o hsi shih chien ch'ih	Both were some years younger than myself
	Who here observe my first grey hairs.
	So let me now rejoice
	That their sight has been delayed so long.

The poet, whose hair is turning white at the age of thirty-five, consoles himself by recalling two distinguished men of ancient times to whom this (or something worse) happened at even earlier ages. P'an Yüeh became white-haired at thirty-two; Yen Hui died in his twenties. In Japanese the quoted words are: *Imada misoji no go ni oyobazu*.

There is an interval of about one year from mid-996 (Tanabata (762) Festival) to mid-997 (Imperial Abstinence). The undatable events (like Nobukata's attempts to recite the 'term of thirty' poem) occurred at some time during this year. The unity of the section lies, of course, in the contrasting pictures of Tadanobu and Nobukata.

Sōkan (or Sakan) (Clerk) was the lowest of the four classes of officials (763) in a government department, the first three being Kami, Suke, and Jō (App. 7b). In the Inner Palace Guards (Konoe) he had the rank of Shōsō (Assistant Lieutenant). The official in question has been tentatively identified as a certain Ki no Mitsukata (Tanaka, op. cit., p. 279).

In his forties Chu Mai-ch'en (d. 116 B.C.) was still an impecunious (764) wood-cutter. When his wife threatened to leave him, Chu admonished her, saying, 'I am already forty, but I shall have riches and honours by the time I am fifty.' Despite these assurances his wife deserted him. Thanks to his tireless studies Chu achieved his ambition and became the governor of a province. His wife then returned to him but was so ashamed by the magnanimous way in which he received her that she hanged herself in remorse. The story appears in the *History of the Former Han Dynasty*.

135

Nobukata was in fact twenty-seven (or twenty-eight in the Japanese count). According to Kaneko (*Hyōshaku*, p. 768), Shōnagon is teasing him by pretending that he appears much older than he actually is.

(765) The original has 'forty-nine', but this is almost certainly a copyist's error for 'over forty'.

(766) Else he would hardly have told the Emperor something so unflattering about himself.

(767) I.e. Fujiwara no Yoshiko (Index-Glossary). Her father was Kinsue, the founder of the Kanin branch of the Fujiwara family. The *Shunchobon* text refers to him here as Kanin no Dajō Daijin (the Prime Minister of the Kanin Palace), but this must be a copyist's mistake since Kinsue did not become Prime Minister until 1021. This scene takes place in the 2nd Month of 998 (App. 4).

(768) *Ōkagami* (in its chapter about Fujiwara no Kaneie) refers to a young Shintō priestess (*miko*) at Kamo Shrine with the name of Uchifushi; this may well be the same person.

(769) A pun on the name of his mistress's mother (note 768) (*uchifusu* = 'to lie down'). The reason that Nobukata is ridiculed for his affair with Sakyō and finally breaks it off is probably connected with the humble birth of her mother; Uchifushi appears to have been a lower-class name.

(770) *Hito no iifurushitaru sama ni torinashitamau*: lit. 'You mistakenly treated [it] as a thing that people are accustomed to speaking about.' He is of course referring to his affair with Sakyō.

(771) Ideally a woman's hair reached the ground when she was standing (*W.S.P.*, p. 203). Artifice was frequently used when nature proved inadequate; *The Tale of Genji* refers to false hair that was nine feet long. The ideal colour for hair was a pure, glossy black; the false variety was apt to take on a reddish tint when it became old.

(772) Because he has little chance of making a successful career if he has only reached the post of Chamberlain of the 6th Rank (Rokui no Kurōdo) by the time his hair has turned white. On p. 90 (note 395) Shōnagon classes such Chamberlains among Splendid Things, but she is referring to younger men.

(773) *Soragoto suru hito*: lit. 'a man who tells lies'.

Musoji nanasoji yasoji naru hito: lit. 'a person who is sixty [or] seventy [or] eighty'. NOTES (774)

See note 371. The *Shunchobon* text includes this as the final item in the list of Unreliable Things; but it is obviously misplaced, and I have followed Kaneko and Ikeda-Kishigami in assigning it to a separate section. Perhaps we should understand some continuation like 'moves and delights me'. (775)

Shōnagon may be referring to private celebrations which were carried out near the Palace but which it was impossible, owing to protocol, for her and other members of the Court to attend. (776)

Because the temple (note 346) seems close but in fact takes a long time to reach because of the constant turns in the path. (777)

Gokuraku (Paradise) refers to the Pure Land (Jōdo) or Western Paradise, into which the believer who invokes the name of Amida Buddha will be reborn. The following statement is attributed to the great Amidist leader, Genshin (942–1017): 'Though [Paradise] be infinitely distant—separated by seas and mountains and thousands of millions of provinces—yet I tell thee: if only the path of thy spirit be smooth, thou canst reach it overnight.' (778)

When boats kept their course, they could cover a great distance in a surprisingly short time, whereas travel by land was slow and uncomfortable. (779)

(780)

	Section	Place	Province (District)	Literary association	Literal meaning
1.	168	Horikane	Musashi (Iruma)	*Tsurayuki Shū*	Hard to Dig
2.	„	Ōsaka	Yamashiro-Ōmi		Slope of Meetings
3.	„	Asuka	Yamato (Takechi)	*saibara*	
4.	„	Tama	Yamashiro (Tsuzuki)	*Kokin Shū*	Jewel
5.	„	Shōshō	Yamashiro (Heian Kyō)		Captain
6.	„	Sakura	Yamato (Takechi)	*saibara*	Cherry Blossom
7.	„	Kisakimachi	Yamashiro (Heian Kyō)		Empress's Quarters
8.	„	Chinuki	unidentified		Thousand Diggings

See p. 254 for a poem about this well. (781)

137

Reference to a *Manyō Shū* poem, recited by a Palace Girl to Prince Katsuragi (eighth century):

·Asaka Yama	The well of Mount Asaka,
Kage sae miyuru	Whose water mirrors the mountain's forms!
Yama no i no	How shallow is its heart,
Asaki kokoro wa	Unlike the one that beats beneath my breast!
Waga omowanaku ni	

The Nippon Gakujutsu Shinkōkai edition gives a more specific translation of the last part of the poem (*The Manyōshū*, p. 265):

> But no shallow heart
> Have I for you, O Prince!

The *asa* in *Asa*ka Yama ('Mountain of the Morning Perfumes') is homonymous with the word for 'shallow'.

(783) Shōnagon is thinking of the old *saibara*:

Asuka I ni	At the well of Asuka
Yadori wa subeshi	Let us stop and rest.
Kage mo yoshi	Its shade is pleasant,
Mimoi mo samushi	Its water fresh and cool,
Mimagusa mo yoshi	And excellent its forage for our horse.

The charm of the quotation lies mainly in the use of the archaic word, *mimoi*, for 'water'.

(784) *Kisakimachi* referred to the Empress's Residential Palace (Jōnei Den), and the well in question was situated to one side of the gallery that connected this building with Shōkyō Palace (App. 1f).

(785) Though these provinces were very uneven in size, the posts were both regarded as good ones; besides, the two provinces contained several places (such as Wakanoura in Kii) that were associated with poetry (App. 9a).

(786) These are all superior provinces (*jōkoku*). It is not clear why Shōnagon has listed these particular ones; possibly she was familiar with officials who had served in all these places. Concerning Shimotsuke see section 295 (App. 9a).

(787) The posts of Senior Secretary (Ministry of Ceremonial), Senior Lieutenant• (Outer Palace Guards), and Senior Scribe normally corresponded to the 6th Rank (App. 7b); for such an official to be appointed to the 5th Rank was an unusual honour.

When a Chamberlain of the 6th Rank was promoted, he auto- matically lost his right of attendance on the Emperor (note 395); hence their reluctance.

These are marks of ostentation, unwarranted for a man of this rank (788) and clearly condemned by Sei Shōnagon. Readers of *The Tale of Genji* will recall Murasaki's sarcastic descriptions of the efforts of parvenus like the Governor of Hitachi to decorate their houses in a style to which neither their rank nor their taste entitles them. Such uneducated efforts are bound to result in incongruities. The trees in the garden and the private carriages, for example, make an absurd contrast with the small, shingle-roofed house where the ambitious official lives. The effect is something like that of a Rolls Royce parked in front of a small, semi-detached villa in the suburbs. Shōnagon herself belonged to the provincial (5th Rank) class and was particularly sensitive to the pretensions of some of its members.

Sage-brush (*yomogi*) was the standard mark of the dilapidated Heian (789) dwelling. Book 15 of *The Tale of Genji*, which describes the red-nosed Suetsumuhana and her desolate household, is entitled *Yomogiu* (lit. 'land overgrown with sage-brush', i.e. waste land, or (Waley) 'The Palace in the Tangled Woods'). The forlorn dwelling of Lady Toshi-kage in *Utsubo Monogatari* is similarly surrounded by sage-brush (*natsu ni naru mama ni yomogi sae oihirogarite . . .*).
  It was customary to strew fine white sand on the gardens of Heian houses to protect people and carriages from mud, and also for aesthetic reasons (*W.S.P.*, p. 29).

Monokashikoge ni nadaraka ni suri shite: lit. 'repairing [things] (790) knowingly and smoothly'.

Because she is in her own home. The parents of Court ladies appear (791) to have been quite lax with their daughters.

Ii ni sashinozoku: lit. 'he peeps in [through the gate] in order to (792) say . . .'.

A rather obscure passage. *Ito iro ni idete iwanu mo omou kokoro naki* (793) *hito wa kanarazu ki nado ya suru*: lit. 'Even if nothing at all emerged in his appearance and he said nothing, would a man who did not love [one] do such a thing as invariably coming?'

Imijiki mi-kado wo koyoi raisō to akehirogete: lit. '[they] have tonight left the important gate wide open'. The meaning of *raisō to* is uncertain; Kaneko gives *karari to* ('completely', 'fully') and Ikeda-Kishigami *hirobiro to* ('widely'). Waley (*W.P.B.*, p. 75) takes it to be an emphatic slang expression.

(795) *Kayō naru ori* (such occasions): i.e. on beautiful, moving occasions when there is heavy snow, a splendid full moon, etc.

(796) From the *Shūi Shū* poem by Taira no Kanemori:

Yamazato wa	Here in my mountain home
Yuki furitsumite	The snow is deep
Michi mo nashi	And the paths are buried [in white].
Kyō komu hito wo	Truly would he move my heart—
Aware to wa mimu	The man who came today.

(797) On the arrival of male visitors ladies usually retired behind their curtains of state or blinds, from where they could see but not be seen.

Kaneko (*Hyōshaku*, pp. 796-7) refers admiringly to the endurance of the Heian gentlemen, who can spend an entire winter's night on an unheated veranda for the pleasure of viewing the snow while conversing with Court ladies.

(798) He refers to a Chinese poem in *Wakan Rōei Shū*:

Hsiao ju Liang Wang chih yüan	At dawn I walked into the garden of the King of Liang;
Hsüeh man ch'ün shan	
Yeh teng Yü kung chih lou	Snow lay upon the many hills.
Yüeh ming ch'ien li	At night I climbed the Tower of the Duke of Yü;
	The moon lit up the country for a thousand miles.

The hills in question had been artificially built in the king's garden. The correct quotation would be *yuki gunzan* ('cluster of hills') *ni miteri*; but the courtier (not having the benefit of modern commentaries) simply says *yuki nani no yama* ('such-and-such hills') *ni miteri*.

(799) *Setsugekka no toki*: lit. 'the time of snow, moon, flowers'. From a poem of Po Chü-i:

Ch'in shih chiu yu chieh p'ou wo	My friends—the zither, poetry and wine—
Yüeh hsüeh hua shih tsui i chün	Have all three left me;
	It's when I see the moon, the snow, the flowers,
	That I most recall my lord.

Watatsumi no
Oki ni kogaruru
Mono mireba
Ama no tsuri shite
Kaeru narikeri

A web of ingenious puns, whose general flavour I have tried to convey by a few simple word-plays in English. Lady Hyōe's composition is more like a conundrum than a proper poem.

Oki = (i) open sea, offing, (ii) embers, live coals, open fire;
Kogu = (i) to row, (ii) to burn, fry;
Kaeru = (i) to return, come home, (ii) frog.

Watatsumi is a pillow-word normally associated with *ama* (woman diver) (note 380).

According to *Kiyū Sōran* (an early commentary), someone had surreptitiously been cooking a frog to eat it; Kaneko (*Hyōshaku*, p. 799) dismisses the theory as 'preposterous' (*mukei*) and points out that a playful frog could very well have jumped into the fire by mistake.

Miare no Senji (High Priestess's Envoy) was the title given to the (801) attendants of the High Priestess of Kamo (note 382), Miare being the name of an important (Shintō) festival celebrated annually at the Shrine and Senji being a term applied to high-ranking female servants. This particular woman later became lady-in-waiting to Emperor Sanjō's principal consort.

For dolls see note 21. 'Girls should not play with dolls (*hiinaasobi*) after they are ten years old,' Shōnagon tells little Murasaki in *The Tale of Genji* (Ikeda, i. 376); but we know that grown-up Heian ladies enjoyed doing so.

Probably in the winter of 990, at about the time when Emperor Ichijō (802) celebrated his coming-of-age ceremony (see App. 4). This was the year in which Kaneie died and was succeeded by his son, Michitaka; Sadako, Michitaka's daughter, became an Imperial Lady (Nyōgo) of Emperor Ichijō's in the 5th Month and was promoted to the rank of Empress (Chūgū) after five months. Shōnagon's father also died in this year.

Several later dates have been suggested for Shōnagon's entry into Court service (Kaneko gives 991, Kishigami 993), but the description (on p. 92) of Sadako's installation as Chūgū suggests that Shōnagon was already at Court in 990, the year of the ceremony in question. There is the further evidence of section 43, in which Shōnagon writes that she has already been at Court for ten years (*totose bakari saburaite*, see note 231); this makes it probable that she entered Sadako's service in 990 or very shortly thereafter. At present, however, 993 is the most popular date among Japanese scholars for the beginning of Shōnagon's life at Court.

(803) Murasaki Shikibu was equally diffident: in her diary she writes that she hardly ever emerged from her room in the daytime (*hiru wa osaosa sashiidezu*).

(804) Because they were covered by her sleeves. In the winter the long sleeves of Heian robes served as a sort of muff.
  Usukōbai (light-pink hue): lit. 'light plum blossom'. Kaneko (*Hyōshaku*, p. 813) rather prosaically suggests that it was the cold which gave the Empress's hands their attractive colour.

(805) *Mishiranu satobigokochi ni wa*: lit. 'in my countrified (*or* unsophisticated) feelings which were not used to seeing [such things]'.

(806) *Tsubone-aruji* (lady in charge of my room): lady-in-waiting in charge of a number of younger maids-of-honour who lived in the same room or set of rooms.

(807) *Sore ni wa waza to hito mo izu*: lit. 'there was no one there on purpose'. Because the brazier was intended to throw out warmth for the entire room.

(808) *Shen* (Japanese: Jin): region in China that produced a type of aromatic wood imported into Japan and used for making braziers, etc.

(809) *On-fumi toritsugi tachii furumau sama nado tsutsumashige narazu mono ii ewarau. Itsu no yo ni ka sayō ni majirai naramu to omou sae zo tsutsumashiki*: lit. 'The manner in which they did such things as deliver letters and move about and deport themselves was not awkward-seeming, and they conversed and laughed. Even wondering when in the world I would mix (*or* join) thus was awkward.'

(810) The Empress and her brother are referring to the *Shūi Shū* poem quoted in note 796.

(811) *Soragoto nado notamaikakuru wo*: lit. '[When] he began to tell lies, etc.' See note 960.

Cf. note 127. Sneezing in Heian Japan had many of the same implications as in the West (see *W.S.P.*, p. 129), but in addition it suggested
that the last person who had spoken was not telling the truth.

> Ika ni shite
> Ika ni shiramashi
> Itsuwari wo
> Sora ni Tadasu no
> Kami nakariseba

> Usuki koso
> Sore ni mo yorame
> Hana yue ni
> Ukimi no hodo wo
> Shiru zo wabishiki

Sora = (i) heaven, sky, (ii) lie, falsehood.

Tadasu = (i) Shintō deity associated with Kamo and enshrined in
the nearby Tadasu Wood (Tadasu no Mori), (ii) to verify, inquire
into the truth of something.

The first poem is fairly clear. Shōnagon's reply, however, is most
obscure. Kaneko's interpretation is as follows (*Hyōshaku*, p. 811): If
I did not really love the Empress, the insincerity of my reply ('How
could I possibly not be fond of you?') might well be determined by
someone's sneezing in the next room; but, since in fact I do love her
deeply, it makes me wretched to think that something as trivial as a
sneeze should have made her judge me to be dishonest. Here is a more
literal translation:

> A shallow [feeling can] indeed
> Depend on that.
> [But] it is sad that I too should know
> Wretchedness
> Because of a sneeze (nose).

An earlier text gives *yorane* ('does not depend') instead of *yorame*
('does depend'); but this serves to remove all possible sense from
the poem.

Shiki was the name of a demon invoked by magicians and other
practitioners of the occult when they wished to put a curse on someone. Shōnagon implies that the ill-timed sneeze was due to a power
of this kind.

See note 812. He looks pleased with himself because everyone wishes
him good luck (cf. 'God bless you!' in the West). Kaneko (*Hyōshaku*,

p. 810) quotes the late Heian poet, Kenshō: 'Sneezing is altogether ominous. If someone sneezes at the New Year, everyone wishes him good luck.' It appears that in Shōnagon's day this custom was not restricted to any particular time of the year. Cf. p. 27 for Shōnagon's dislike of sneezers.

(816) *I(n)futagi* (hidden rhymes): popular game among the aristocracy; one of the players covered a character in some old Chinese poem, and the winner was the player who, from context, rhythm, etc., first guessed the hidden character.

(817) See notes 92, 758, 759. Because of the large size of the *go* board and because the stones cannot be moved to a new place once they have been played, the battle in its early stages can be carried out on several independent fronts. A player who decides that he is not making sufficient headway on one part of the board may switch his attention to another sector (*kakaguriariku*). In the present instance he is pleasantly surprised to find that his opponent's position in this new sector is weaker than it had appeared to be. The opponent is unable to keep the 'eyes' that determine the viability and value of any position and the greedy player succeeds in capturing a large number of stones. If he had played in a more conservative way and continued to concentrate on the original part of the board, he might have missed the opportunity.

In *go* as in chess a 'greedy' (*fukutsukeki*) player is one who is more interested in capturing his opponent's stones (pieces) than in slowly building up a strong position.

(818) *Miezarishi chōdo sōzoku no wakiizuru*: lit. 'utensils and clothes, which have not been seen, gush forth'. The parvenu governor with his absurd pretensions is a stock figure in Heian literature (cf. note 788).

(819) High ranks in the Imperial Guards were as a rule honorary positions reserved for members of the aristocracy. A provincial governor would naturally be more flattered to receive such an appointment than a young nobleman, who would take it for granted.

(820) Empresses (Kisaki) were usually chosen from the Imperial family itself or from among the daughters of the Chancellor, the Regent, or one of the Great Ministers. When Shōnagon writes about a High Court Noble's daughter who has been appointed to the rank of Empress, she may be thinking of Fujiwara no Takeko, the daughter of Naritoki (Index-Glossary and App. 6b), who was appointed First

144

Empress (Kōgō) to Emperor Sanjō though her father during his lifetime never advanced beyond the rank of Major Counsellor. This has
been used as evidence that *The Pillow Book* was not completed until at
least 1013, the date of the appointment in question; but the evidence
is inconclusive.

(*Nai*)*gubu* (Palace Chaplain): one of ten priests in charge of the Palace (821)
Oratory (Naidōjō), where they carried out readings of the scriptures,
made offerings to the Buddhist statues, etc. They were frequently on
night duty, and therefore tended to come into contact with the Court
ladies.

Kao ni shimitaru: lit. 'pierces one's face'. I have moved this sentence (822)
back a few lines to where it apparently belongs. In all the texts I have
consulted it comes after the passage about the rainy wind.

The padded garments (*wataginu*) were worn in the rainy season and (823)
then put aside during the hot summer months. As the summer
advanced, the weather became so stifling that even clothes of unlined
silk were uncomfortable. Then all of a sudden there was a cool, rainy
wind, and people had to throw their padded clothes over their silk
ones, making for the kind of incongruous combinations that frequently
struck Shōnagon's fancy.

Nyōbō to wa oboenu koe: lit. 'a voice that one does not think is a (824)
servant['s]'. It is probably the voice of a lady-in-waiting summoning
her young maid.

Samagashū wa arade kami no furiyararetaru: lit. 'the hair is scattered (825)
[down her shoulders] without being disordered'.

The stones that have been captured are put away in boxes. (826)

Section	Place	Province (District)	Literary association	Literal meaning	(827)
1.	182	Ukishima	Rikuzen (Miyagi)	*Rokujō*	Floating Isle	
2.	,,	Yasoshima	Ugo (Yuri)		Eight Thousand Isles	
3.	,,	Tawareshima	Higo (Uto)	*Ise Monogatari*	Joking Isle	
4.	,,	Mizushima	Bitchū (Oda) or Higo (Kikuchi)	*Manyō Shū*	Water Isle	

145

Section	Place	Province (District)	Literary association	Literal meaning
5. 182	Matsugaurashima	Rikuzen (Miyagi)	*Gosen Shū*	Pine Bay Islands
6. „	Magaki no Shima	Rikuzen (Miyagi)	*Kokin Shū*	Fence Island
7. „	Toyora no Shima	Nagato (Toyora)	*Rokujō*	Island of the Bay of Plenty
8. „	Tadoshima	Sanuki (Tado)		
9. 183	Soto no Hama	Mutsu (Tsugaru)	Surugamai	Outside Beach
10. „	Fukiage no Hama	Kii (Kaisō)	*Kokin Shū* and *Utsubo Monogatari*	Beach Exposed to the Sea Gales
11. „	Nagahama	Ise (Inae)	*Kokin Shū*	Long Beach
12. „	Uchide no Hama	Ōmi (Shiga)	*Manyō Shū* and *Shūi Shū*	Beach of Departure
13. „	Moroyose no Hama	Tajima (Mikata)	*Rokujō*	Beach of Meetings
14. „	Chisato no Hama	Kii (Hitaka)	*Ise Monogatari*	Beach of a Thousand Hamlets
15. 184	Ou no Ura	Shima	*Kokin Shū*	
16. „	Shiogama no Ura	Rikuzen (Miyagi)	*Ise Monogatari*	Salt Pan Bay
17. „	Shiga no Ura	Ōmi (Shiga)	*Manyō Shū*	
18. „	Nataka no Ura	Kii (Kaisō)	„ „	Bay of Renown
19. „	Korizuma no Ura	Settsu (Muko)	*Genji Monogatari*	The Bay Where There is No Learning from Experience
20. „	Waka no Ura	Kii (Kaisō)	*Manyō Shū*	The Bay of Poems
21. 185	Inabino	Harima (Kako)	„ „	
22. „	Katano	Kawachi (Kita Kawachi)	*Ise Monogatari*, etc.	
23. „	Komano	Yamashiro (Sōraku)		
24. „	Awazuno	Ōmi (Shiga)	*saibara*	Millet Ferry Plain
25. „	Tobuhino	Yamato (Sō no Kami)	*Kokin Shū*	The Plain of the Flying Flame
26. „	Shimejino	Yamashiro		Plain of Mushrooms (?)
27. „	Sagano	Yamashiro (Kadono)		Thanks-to-the-Emperor Plain (?)
28. „	Sōkeino	unidentified		
29. „	Abeno	Settsu (Higashi Nara)		
30. „	Miyagino	Rikuzen (Miyagi)	„ „	
31. „	Kasugano	Yamato (Sō no Kami)	„ „	

146

Section		Place	Province (District)	Literary association	Literal meaning
32.	185	Murasakino	Yamashiro (Otagi)		Plain of Violets
33.	186	Tsubosaka	Yamato (Takaichi)		Bowl Slope
34	,,	Kasagi	Yamashiro (Sōraku)		Hat-Placing [Temple]
35.	,,	Hōri	Yamashiro (Kadono)		Wheel of the Law
36.	,,	Kōya	Kii (Ito)		High Plain
37.	,,	Ishiyama	Ōmi (Shiga)		Stone Mountain
38.	,,	Kokawa	Kii (Naka)		Powder River
39.	,,	Shiga	Ōmi (Shiga)		

Chisato: note 827 (no. 14): Literal meaning.   (828)

The section on plains seems to be incorrectly placed in the texts I (829) have consulted, where it comes in the middle of the sections on Buddhist and other writings or (in the *Sangenbon* version) after the section on wells a great deal earlier; I have put it at the end of the sections on geographical places, where it more logically belongs.

Saga Plain (note 827, no. 27), a few miles north of the capital, was a popular place for courtly excursions. *Sōkei* (note 827, no. 28) probably means 'expressing thanks to the Emperor (upon receiving an official appointment)'; the place itself is unknown.

Mount Kōya (note 827, no. 36) was and remains the site of the complex (830) of temples first established in 816 by Kōbō Daishi (Index-Glossary), one of the greatest figures in the history of Japanese Buddhism, who was responsible, among his multifarious accomplishments, for the introduction of Shingon to Japan in 806. It was popularly believed that Kōbō Daishi had supernaturally survived his death and continued to live in the temple he had founded on the top of Mount Kōya.

Over half of the seven temples listed by Shōnagon (nos. 33, 37-39) were dedicated to Kannon. The others were dedicated to Miroku Bosatsu (no. 34), Kokuzō Bosatsu (no. 35), and Dainichi (no. 36).

Because the *Lotus Sutra* (*Saddharma Puṇḍarīka Sūtra*), the principal (831) sutra of the Tendai Sect, was the most popular and influential of all the scriptures in Heian Japan. The Japanese (and Sanskrit) names of the titles mentioned in this section are:

(1) *Senju Kyō* (*Nīlakaṇṭha Dhāraṇī*),
(2) *Fugen Jūgan*, the Ten Great Vows set forth by the Bodhisattva Samantabhadra; refers to the section of the *Fugen Gyōgan Bon*

147

(*Samantabhadra-caryā-praṇidhāna*) in the *Kegon Kyō* (*Avatam-saka Sūtra*),

(3) *Zuigu Kyō* (*Mahāpratisara Dhāraṇi*),

(4) *Sonshō Darani* or *Butchō Sonshō Darani Kyō* (*Uṣṇiṣavijaya Dhāraṇi*),

(5) *Amida no Taiju* or *Amida Nyorai Kompon Darani* (*Daśāmrita Dhāraṇi*),

(6) *Senju Darani*, being one section of the *Senju Kyō*.

(832) *Wen hsüan* (*Monzen*): the first and foremost literary anthology in China, compiled *c.* 530 by Hsiao T'ung, the Prince of Liang (501–31). It originally consisted of thirty chapters and included poems, essays, and stories written during the 750-odd years since the end of Chou.

(833) The Bodhisattva Kannon (who changed sex while moving from China to Japan) was regarded as being polymorphic. Among her six main representations (Roku Kannon) were those of Nyoiri(n) Kannon, in which the goddess holds a jewelled wheel that can grant the wishes of her petitioners, and Senju Kannon, in which she is represented as having 1,000 hands (though in actual sculpture the number is usually reduced to forty).

(834) *Fudōson* (the Great Immovable One): a terrifying deity, mainly associated with Shingon. His frightening appearance was intended to protect believers by scaring away evil spirits. Fudō, who belongs to a group of deities derived from Tantric Buddhism, is frequently regarded as corresponding to the Indian deity, Acala.

The other Buddhas and Bodhisattvas are:

(1) Yakushi Butsu (Bhaiṣajya Guru), the healing Buddha,

(2) Shaka (Gautama Buddha), the historical Buddha,

(3) Miroku (Bodhisattva Maitreya), the Bodhisattva of the Future Coming,

(4) Fugen (Bodhisattva Samantabhadra), guardian deity of wisdom and contemplation,

(5) Jizō (Bodhisattva Kṣitigarbha), guardian deity of children,

(6) Monju (Bodhisattva Mañjuśrī), guardian deity of wisdom and intellect.

Some of the texts omit Monju from the list. Amida (Amitabha), the great Buddha of the Western Paradise, is conspicuously absent from *The Pillow Book*, though frequently mentioned by Murasaki Shikibu and other contemporaries.

The titles are as follows: *Sumiyoshi, Utsubo, Tono Utsuri, Tsuki*
Matsu Omina, Katano no Shōshō, Umetsubo no Shōshō, Hitome,
Kuniyuzuri, Umoregi, Dōshin Susumuru Matsu ga E, Komano no
Monogatari. Other texts of *The Pillow Book* list the following addi-
tional *monogatari: Monourayami no Chūjō, Otokiki, Kawahori no*
Miya, Tōgimi.

This is an intriguing section for the literary historian, since among
the works listed by Shōnagon only *Utsubo* is extant in its Heian
version. *Kuniyuzuri* is the title of one long section of *Utsubo Monogatari,* but it may also have been a separate work. *Tono Utsuri* may
possibly have been the title of the section of *Utsubo* now called *Kura-
biraki. Sumiyoshi, Katano no Shōshō,* and *Komano no Monogatari* are
all mentioned in *The Tale of Genji.*

It is clear that a large number of *monogatari* were circulating in
Shōnagon's time. We know the titles of about forty works of vernacular
prose fiction that were being read in the late tenth century. Of these
only four survive; it is fortunate that one of them should be *The Tale
of Genji.*

Darani: see note 700.

Kemari (kick-ball): an elegant game, popular among Heian courtiers.
The aim was to prevent a leather ball from touching the ground (see
W.S.P., pp. 152-3). I have avoided the translation 'foot-ball' because
of its hearty, muscular connotations.

The following are the names and provenances of these dances (see
W.S.P., p. 196):

(1) Suruga Mai (eastern provinces of Japan),
(2) Motomego (eastern provinces of Japan),
(3) Taiheiraku (T'ang China),
(4) Tori no Mai (India),
(5) Batō (Annam),
(6) Rakuson (Korea),
(7) Komahoko (Korea).

Despite its name Taiheiraku (Dance of Peace) was a sword dance
performed by four dancers in armour. Its origin is an episode that
occurred in the second century B.C., and it is to this episode (described
in the *Shih chi*) that Shōnagon refers. During an encounter between
the governor of P'ei (the future founder of the Han dynasty) and
Hsiang Yi, one of the latter's adherents (Hsiang Chuang) attempted
to assassinate the governor in the course of a sword dance. 'But

Hsiang Po rose and danced, constantly shielding and protecting the governor of P'ei with his own body so that Hsiang Chuang could not attack him.' (Watson, i. 52.) The murder plot was abortive.

(840) The following are the names of the tunes and their provenances or the instruments on which they were usually played:

    (1) Fukō Jō (*biwa*),
    (2) Ōshiki Jō (*biwa* or flute),
    (3) Sogō(kō) (India),
    (4) Uguisu no Saezuri (China),
    (5) Sōfuren (China).

(841) The *sō no fue* was a rather formidable instrument (*S.S.T.B.*, p. 130, gives 'orgue à bouche'), and the player had to puff out his cheeks in order to fill the air chamber.

(842) *Sore wa yokobue mo fukinashi ari ka shi*: lit. 'as for that there really are [ugly *or* ungraceful] ways of blowing (cross-) flutes also'.

(843) *Hichikiri* (flageolet): see note 701. The long cricket (*kutsuwamushi*) (Index-Glossary) makes a particularly shrill chirp.

(844) *Tada imijū uruwashiki kami motaramu hito mo*: lit. 'it was really terrible, and even people who (probably) have beautiful hair . . .'. In Heian times people's hair stood on end (*kami tachiagaru*) when they were deeply impressed by something, rather than when they were frightened (cf. p. 228).

(845) The Special Festival at Kamo (note 66) took place during the height of winter in the 11th Month.

    Kazashi no hana: artificial flowers that the participants in the Special Festivals wore in their head-dress—wistaria for the Imperial envoys, cherry blossom or yellow rose for the dancers and musicians.

    Aozuri: white robes decorated (like modern *yukata*) with blue patterns.

(846) As a rule the envoys (*tsukai*), who followed the dancers in the Kamo procession, were chosen from among the Imperial Guards (note 66), but on this occasion high provincial officials (*zuryō*) had been selected for the honour. Shōnagon's scorn for the *zuryō* (*me tomarazu nikuge naru*) is typical of contemporary attitudes (*W.S.P.*, pp. 79-83) and was not mitigated by the fact that her own father belonged to this class.

The basic texts give 'the mulberry sashes of Kamo Shrine' (*Kamo no* NOTES
Yashiro no yūdasuki); but almost certainly 'mulberry sash' is a (847)
copyist's error for 'princess pine' (*himekomatsu*), and Shōnagon is
referring·to the well-known *Kokin Shū* poem by Fujiwara no
Toshiyuki:

Chihayaburu	The princess pines that grow outside
Kamo no Yashiro no	All-powerful Kamo Shrine—
Himekomatsu	Ten thousand years may pass away
Yorozuyo fu tomo	And yet their colour will not fade.
Iro wa kawaraji	

Himekomatsu is the short pine or *pinus parriflora*. *Chihayaburu* ('swift
and mighty', 'all-powerful') is a stock epithet (*makura kotoba*) used
in poetry before the names of gods and shrines.

An introductory note in *Kokin Shū* explains that Toshiyuki's poem
was associated with the winter festival at Kamo, and *Ōkagami* con-
firms Toshiyuki's authorship of the poem which was recited during
the festival. The copyist's error undoubtedly results from the fact
that there is a love poem in *Kokin Shū* starting with the same two lines
as Toshiyuki's and containing the word *yūdasuki*, which we find in
early texts of *The Pillow Book*. This poem was not, however, associated
with the Special Festival at Kamo, and it seems unlikely that Shōnagon, who had frequently attended the ceremony, could have made
such an elementary error.

Section 199 begins with the characters for *mi-yuki* (Imperial Pro- (848)
gress); they seem to belong in the present paragraph, and I have
omitted them from the beginning.

Ōtoneri Ryō (Bureau of Imperial Attendants): Bureau under the (849)
Ministry of Central Affairs (App. 7a). It was in charge of the Imperial
Attendants (*Ōtoneri*), who served the Emperor in the Palace and
during Imperial Processions. The Assistant Directors (*Suke*) belonged
to the Senior 6th Rank, Lower Grade. Those holding the cords of the
Imperial palanquin were known as Mitsuna no Suke.

Kinō wa yorozu no koto uruwashūte: lit. 'Yesterday everything was (850)
beautiful.' The Return Procession was on the 2nd Day of the Dog in
the 4th Month. 'Yesterday' refers to the 2nd Day of the Bird, when
the actual festival took place.

The 4th Month was the beginning of summer and usually quite hot.

Cf. p. 49. (851)

151

Mi-koshi tagoshi nado: lit. 'shoulder palanquin, hand palanquin, etc.'.
(852) These were the conveyances used by the High Priestess within the precincts of the Shrine. When she left the Shrine, she travelled by ox-carriage. The porters (in red clothes) are now carrying back the empty palanquins.

(853) For the traditional association between *hototogisu* and *u no hana* see note 194. See also p. 42.

(854) *Monoguruhoshi made mieshi*: lit. 'they went to the extent of looking crazy'.

(855) After the Kamo Festival a special banquet was held in the palace of the High Priestess. The guests of honour were princes of the blood and top-ranking officials like the Chancellor; in addition a number of gentlemen were invited as 'extra guests' (*enga*).

(856) The gentleman refers to a love poem by Mibu no Tadamine (Index-Glossary) in the *Kokin Shū*:

> Kaze fukeba   The fleecy clouds that scatter on the peak,
> Mine ni wakaruru   Blown asunder by the mountain winds—
> Shiragumo no   Surely your heart is not all cold like them.
> Taete tsurenaki
> Kimi ga kokoro ka

Taete = (i) breaking, coming asunder, (ii) intently, wholly, all.

(857) *Ue wa tsurenaku kusa oishigeritaru*: lit. '[places] where the surface is casual (i.e. does not reveal what is below) and where the grass grows in profusion'.
    This appears to be an allusion to a *Shūi Shū* love poem in which the marsh-image is used to contrast the lover's casual exterior (*ue koso tsurenakere*) with the strong emotions (*shita wa e-narazu omou kokoro*) that it conceals.
    Shūi Shū: . . . *ue koso tsurenakere shita wa e-narazu*; *Makura no Sōshi*: . . . *ue wa tsurenaku . . . shita wa e-narazarikeru*.

(858) In the Palace buildings the irises were usually left hanging until the 9th Month (note 113), but in some houses they were kept all winter.

(859) The original has 'yesterday, the day before yesterday, today'. This type of departure from the normal chronological or numerical order is an idiosyncrasy of Shōnagon's. Cf. p. 1, where she speaks of the crows flying 'in threes and fours and twos'.

Shōnagon deviates from conventional standards of male beauty, NOTES
which prescribed narrow eyes (*hikime*) for men as well as for women (860)
(*W.S.P.*, p. 144).

Large winter cherries (*hōzuki*) were used as toys or dolls. (861)

Like Mme de Sévigné, Shōnagon believed that one could always (862)
judge the master by his servants' behaviour.

Mashite ika bakari naru kokochi nite sate miruramu: lit. 'all the more, (863)
with what feelings must he being thus (i.e. he who is in a shabby
carriage) see [the very elegant carriage]?'

I.e. the First Avenue (note 72). (864)

Traffic congestions and altercations of this kind were a normal occur- (865)
rence at Heian processions and ceremonies. Known as *kuruma-arasoi*,
they figure frequently in contemporary literature (see *W.S.P.*, p. 36).
The present encounter was a very mild one and Shōnagon obviously
enjoyed it (. . . *koso okashikere*).

Shōnagon's visitor was a *jige* (note 35). (866)

The Empress's message contains the first three lines (seventeen (867)
syllables) of a poem:

> Mikasa Yama
> Yama no ha akeshi
> Ashita yori.

Shōnagon's reply caps it, in linked verse style, by providing two final
lines (fourteen syllables):

> Ame naranu na no
> Furinikeru ka na.

The exchange is more ingenious than poetic. *Mikasa* can be taken to
mean 'three umbrellas' and clearly refers to Shōnagon's visitor. The
word was also used to designate the Inner Palace Guards, to which the
gentleman in question evidently belonged. 'Dawn first shed its light'
means that rumours have been circulating since the morning. Shōnagon's reply is an attempt to convince the Empress that the rumours
are false. It contains a play of words on *furu* = (i) to rain, (ii) to
spread rumours. 'Though innocent of rain' refers to a woman's virtue;
but in view of her many love affairs Shōnagon can hardly have
expected the Empress to take this protestation too seriously. *Nureginu*

has the double meaning of (i) wet clothes (connected here with the umbrella-rain imagery), (ii) false accusation, unfounded rumour.

(868) I.e. in the former residence of Taira no Narimasa (note 33). This scene takes place in the 5th Month of 1000 (App. 4). The Iris Festival was on the 5th day.

(869) I.e. Prince Atsuyasu, who was six months old.

(870) The flour used for *aozashi* cakes was made from unripe ('green') wheat.

(871) The phrase 'from across the fence' (*masegoshi ni*) means 'from outside'; it comes from a *Rokujō* poem:

> Masegoshi ni   Stretching his neck across the fence,
> Mugi hamu koma no   The little colt can scarcely reach the wheat.
> Hatsuhatsu ni   So I myself cannot attain
> Oyobanu koi mo   The object of my love.
> Ware wa suru ka na

The link between the poem and the *aozashi* cake (note 870) is the word 'wheat' (*mugi*).

The Empress's poem

> Minahito no
> Hana ya chō ya to
> Isogu hi mo
> Waga kokoro woba
> Kimi zo shirikeru

is rather cryptic. 'To hurry about searching for flowers and butterflies' (*hana ya chō ya to isogu*) means 'to be busy with festive activities'. Possibly Sadako implies that on this day of the Iris Festival, when all the other ladies are busy with elaborate preparations for the joyful occasion, only Shōnagon, by presenting her with a simple green wheat cake 'from across the fence', shows that she has understood her mistress's somewhat melancholy mood. As Kaneko points out (*Hyōshaku*, pp. 890-1), this was a time when things were not going too well for Empress Sadako, owing to the elevation of Akiko to the rank of Chūgū and to the growing hostility of the Michinaga faction (note 606).

(872) Lady Chūnagon had arranged her hair in such a way that instead of hanging down over her shoulders it fell forward, partly covering her face. Her companions regret that she has adopted such a messy and

unfeminine style. The lady's resemblance to the Quiver-Bearers, however, has nothing to do with her hair, but derives from her red dress (note 248).

Minamoto no Narinobu was appointed Uchūjō (Middle Captain of (873) the Inner Palace Guards, Right Division) in the 10th Month of 998; this section and the following one probably belong to the end of that year (App. 4).

The *Shunchobon* text gives 'handwriting' (*te*) instead of 'looks' (874) (*omote*); the latter is from the *Shōhon* text.

The Minister (*Kyō*) was the top official in each of the eight Ministries (875) (App. 7b). The incumbent in question was Fujiwara no Masamitsu, who received the appointment in the 10th Month of 998 (App. 4).

I.e. with Minamoto no Narinobu, Michinaga's adopted son (note 873). (876) Narinobu's great acoustic talent (section 214) was to tell *who* was speaking; Masamitsu's lay in distinguishing *what* they said.

Black-lacquered (*kuronuri*) boxes and tiled inkstones (*kawara-suzuri*) (877) were inelegant types of writing equipment.

Inochi wo nobubekameru. Ge ni kotowari ni ya: lit. 'it seems as if it is (878) going to prolong one's life; can that really be reasonable?'

	Section	Place	Province (District)	Literary association	Literal meaning	(879)
1.	218	Nashiwara no Eki	Ōmi (Kurimoto)	*Rokujō*	Pear-Tree Plain	
2.	,,	Higure no Eki	unidentified		Sunset Relay	
3.	,,	Mochizuki no Eki	Shinano (Saku)		Full-Moon Relay	
4.	,,	Noguchi no Eki	Tamba (Funai), etc.		Entrance-to-the-Plain Relay	
5.	,,	Yama no Eki	Yamato, Echigo, etc.		Mountain Relay	
6.	219	Funaoka	Yamashiro (Ōtagi)	*Rokujō*	Boat Hill	
7.	,,	Kataoka	Yamato (Kita Katsuragi)	*Manyō Shu,* *Rokujō*	Side Hill	
8.	,,	Tomooka	Yamashiro (Otokuni)	*kagura*	Strap Hill	
9.	,,	Katarai no Oka	Mutsu (?)		Conversation Hill	
10.	,,	Hitomi no Oka	Yamashiro (Kadono)		See-People Hill	

155

	Section	Place	Province (District)	Literary association	Literal meaning
11.	220	Furu	Yamato (Yamabe)	*Manyō Shū*	
12.	„	Ikuta	Settsu (Muko)	„ „	
13.	„	Tatsuta	Yamato (Ikoma)	„ „	
14.	„	Hanafuchi	Rikuzen (Miyagi)		Flower Pool
15.	„	Mikuri	Echigo (Nutari)		Water-Bur
16.	„	Miwa	Yamato (Shiki)	*Kokin Shū, Tsurayuki Shū*	
17.	„	Koto no Mama	Tōtōmi (Ogasa)	*Kokin Shū*	Answered Prayers
18.	„	Aridōshi	Izumi (Sennan)		Ants' Passage

(880) The commentators have not yet identified this reference. There were several posting-houses with the name of Yama.

(881) Shōnagon is probably thinking of the following lines of a *kagura*:

Kono sasa wa	This bamboo grass—
Izuko no sasa zo	From what place does it come?
Tonerira ga	From Tomo Hill, from Tomo Hill—
Koshi ni sagareru	Where the drover goes,
Tomo Oka no sasa	A strap suspended from his waist.

(882) This is probably an error for Katakoi no Oka (Hill of Unrequited Love) in Mutsu, which is the subject of a poem in the *Rokujō* anthology.

(883) Miwa Shrine at the foot of Mount Miwa in Yamato (Shiki) was famous for the cryptomeria (*sugi*) that grew at its entrance. There is a play on the word *shirushi* = (i) sign, mark (the tree marks the site of the shrine), (ii) virtue, efficacy (prayers to the god of Miwa Shrine are efficacious). A poem of Ki no Tsurayuki has the words,

It is the *sugi* tree	Miwa no yama
That marks Mount Miwa's heights.	Miyuru shirushi wa
	Sugi ni zo arikeru;

a *Kokin Shū* poem about Miwa also refers to the famous cryptomeria (see note 1008).

(884) *Koto no mama* can be taken to mean literally 'prayers that are fully answered'. This is the basis of a punning *Kokin Shū* poem that starts,

Negigoto wo	This is indeed a shrine
Sanomi kikikemu	Where every prayer's been glibly answered [by
Yashiro koso	the God].

Sa nomi ('in such an indiscriminate / glib way') has a decidedly disrespectful tone.

156

In the collected works of Ki no Tsurayuki we read that one day, when NOTES (885) he was riding back to the capital, his horse suddenly became ill. The local inhabitants informed him, 'This is the doing of the God who dwells in these parts. For all these many years he has had no shrine, and there is nothing to mark his presence here. Yet he is a fearful God, and this is how he always lets people know of his existence.' Since Tsurayuki had no suitable offering to present to the irate deity, he simply washed his hands (to acquire ritual purity) and, 'facing the hill, where no sign of the God existed', dedicated the following poem to him:

Kakikumori	How could I have known
Ayame mo shiranu	That in this cloudy, unfamiliar sky
Ōzora ni	There dwelt the Passage of the Ants?
Aridōshi woba	
Omoubeshi ya wa	

Thereupon the God, appeased by this belated recognition of his existence, promptly restored the poet's horse to health.

In *Aridōshi*, a Nō play by Zeami, the God (who first appears as a shrine attendant) is angered when Tsurayuki rides his horse within the sacred precincts; he is appeased by a poem and ends the play by performing some auspicious Shintō dances at Tsurayuki's request.

Aridōshi Shrine had obviously disappeared in Tsurayuki's time; it was subsequently rebuilt near present-day Ōsaka.

The legend of Aridōshi probably dates in its present form from the (886) eighth century (*Hyōshaku*, pp. 907–8), but it is an amalgam of various ancient traditions. Part I of *Zappōzō Kyō* (*Samyukta-Ratna-Pitaka Sūtra*, 'The Sutra of the Collection of Varied Jewels') refers to the exile of old people and also describes the puzzles of the piece of wood and of the two snakes. The story of the jewel and the cats occurs in a Chinese Buddhist work, *Sotei Jien* (*Tsu tʻing shih yüan*), which was compiled during the Sung period; in this version, however, the jewel has nine, instead of seven, curves. The story in which a king tests the level of intelligence in a foreign state by posing various problems (usually three) is an old one, being told *inter alia* in the thirty-three-chapter Han compilation, *Sengoku Saku* (*Chan kuo tsʻe*, 'Schemes of the Warring States'), and in the Japanese chronicle, *Bidatsu Tennō Ki*.

The entire legend is brought up to date and Japanized by the hero's rank of Chūjō (Middle Captain of the Inner Palace Guards). The Captain's filial piety makes him a standard Confucian-type hero and a striking contrast to the officer described in section 286.

I.e. which end of the log grew nearer the trunk of the tree from which (887) it was cut?

Yamato in the *Shunchobon* text, *Hi no Moto no Kuni* in *Sangenbon*.
(888) *Morokoshi* ('the land of T'ang') is invariably used for China.

(889)   Nanawata ni
                         Magareru tama no
                         O wo nukite
                         Aridōshi tomo
                         Shirazu ya aramu

The god's poem (whose source is unknown) is a typical example
of early pseudo-etymology: almost certainly Aridōshi Shrine in
Izumi became associated with the legend because of its name, not
vice versa.

(890) Compare Shōnagon's description of the corresponding scene at dawn
(p. 1) when the clouds are purplish.

(891) According to a current superstition (of Chinese origin), it was
dangerous for women to see shooting stars. Also there is a pun on
yobai = (i) shooting star (in *yobaiboshi*), (ii) clandestine visit by a man
to a woman's room at night.

(892) *Asa ni saru iro* ('the tints that leave at dawn'): this is traditionally
believed to have come from a poem by Sung Yü (fl. 290–223 B.C.),
included in the *Wen hsüan* anthology:

Tan wei ch'ao yün   At dawn [they] make the morning clouds.
Mu wei hsing yü   At night [they] make the driving rain.

But there may be some other source, since this does not seem very
close to the words quoted by Shōnagon.

(893) Shōnagon is presumably thinking not so much of the sparks themselves as of the tumult (uproar, chaos) they produce since they may
result in a fire.

(894) After the fire has really got under way, it leaves the category of
'tumultuous things' (*sawagashiki mono*) and is classed as 'extremely
frightening' (*semete osoroshiki mono*, p. 212).

(895) See p. 193 for a description of such a scene.

(896) *Nyōkan*: see Index-Glossary. Being of low rank, they can never look
really elegant.

Since the front of the leather sash (*kawa no obi*) is very elegant, the plain back looks shabby by contrast.

Because he does not care about the people and things of this (898) world.

Probably refers to Ōmiya no Me, a Shintō deity and one of the pro- (899) tectors of the Imperial House. In private households prayers were addressed to this goddess in order to secure her protection at the time of the Seasonal Changes, etc.; but evidently they were not taken very seriously and were often recited in a disrespectful, half-joking way by one of the family officials (*Hyōshaku*, p. 915).

Kannari no Jin (Thunder Guard): another name for the Inner Palace (900) Guards, derived from the fact that, when there were violent thunder-storms, members of the Inner Palace Guards Headquarters would arm themselves with bows and arrows and post themselves in Seiryō and Shishin Palaces to protect the distinguished inhabitants from harm.

The wrestling of their attendants is not the formal type of ceremony mentioned in note 592, but a rough, impromptu affair.

The implication is that children have become more precocious than (901) in the past.

Shōnagon refers to *gohei*, sacred strips of pendant paper which are cut (902) in a special way and either hung at a Shintō shrine or outside a house, or attached to a wand (*nusa*). They belong to the ancient indigenous cult of Japan and are supposed to confer special sanctity on the place where they are suspended. These pieces of paper originally repre-sented strips of cloth that were among the offerings made to the Shintō deities; later they came to represent the deities themselves (Sansom, *Short Cultural History*, pp. 58–59).

The women described in this section are sorceresses (*miko*) who were consulted in case of illness and whose methods of cure included the use of Shintō incantations and paraphernalia.

Oshie nado subeshi: lit. 'they may do such a thing as teaching'. Kaneko (903) (*Hyōshaku*, p. 918) points out that such behaviour is typical of lower-class families in all periods, since the wives work and therefore tend to acquire opinions of their own.

These were all particularly respected posts, usually occupied by the
(904) most successful members of the Fujiwara clan during their progress
up the administrative ladder.

(905) Here *kindachi* refers, not simply to the sons of top members of the
nobility, but to all senior courtiers (*denjōbito*) who ranked below the
High Court Nobles (*Kandachime*).

(906) But note how disrespectfully Shōnagon refers to Palace Chaplains
towards the end of section 178.

(907) Above the ranks (*i*) there were four orders (*hon*), which were assigned
to Imperial Princes and Princesses.

(908) Because her high Shintō office precluded participation in Buddhist
services. Waley (*The Tale of Genji*, p. 299) refers to the numerous
speech-taboos imposed on the High Priestess: all words pertaining to
Buddhism were forbidden, bonzes for example being ironically
referred to as *kaminaga* ('long hair') and the sutras as *somegami*
('stained paper'). This type of exclusivism was becoming more and
more unusual in Shōnagon's day, when the tendency was to syncretize
the two religions (*W.S.P.*, pp. 92-93).
   The High Priestess in question is Princess Senshi (Index-
Glossary).

(909) I.e. Fujiwara no Kaneie's daughter, Yukiko (Index-Glossary).

(910) *Mi wo kaetaramu hito nado wa kaku ya aramu to miyuru mono*: lit.
'people who seem [to be such that one wonders:] would someone who
has been reborn (reincarnated, lit. changed body) have [changed]
thus?'

(911) Cf. p. 90. The name *zōshiki* (Subordinate Official) means 'various
colours' and derived from the fact that, whereas the colours worn
by gentlemen of higher rank were stipulated in the legal codes, these
lowly officials were free to wear any colour that was not specifically
prohibited.

(912) These belts (*kawa no obi, sekitai*) were part of the Court uniform, but
were not usually worn by gentlemen on night watch.

(913) The Imperial Bathing Room (Mi-Yudono) was in the north-west
corner of Seiryō Palace (App. 9g), directly north of the Imperial

Washing Room (note 536). Outside (to the north) was the east-west NOTES
gallery and beyond this the bridle-path (*medō*), a narrow pathway for
the use of riders.

Tada sugi ni suguru mono: lit. 'things that do nothing but pass and (914)
pass'. For the *sugi ni suguru* construction see NI 6 in my *Dictionary of
Selected Forms in Classical Japanese Literature*.

In each month a certain number of days, varying from three to four- (915)
teen, were fixed as inauspicious (*kuenichi*). There was a total of eighty
in the course of the year, and it was impossible (*Hyōshaku*, p. 929)
to remember all of them.

The women were planting rice—hardly an exotic occupation in Japan, (916)
but one that no elegant Court lady would admit to recognizing.

> Hototogisu yo (917)
> Ore yo ka yatsu yo
> Ore nakite zo
> Ware wa ta ni tatsu

A folk-song. The season of the *hototogisu*'s song corresponded with
one of the busiest times in the farmer's year, the planting of the seed-
lings in the paddy-fields.

The woman is quoting from a seventh-century *Rokujō* poem by a wife (918)
of Emperor Temmu:

Hototogisu	Sing not too loudly,
Itaku na naki so	*Hototogisu.*
Nagakoe wo	Leave those long songs of yours
Satsuki no tama ni	Until they're threaded with the Fifth-Month
Aenuku made ni	jewels.

'Fifth-Month jewels' (*Satsuki no tama*) refers to the herbal balls prepared for the Iris Festival. The poet wishes to preserve the *hototogisu*'s precious songs throughout the year. In the Fourth Month the
hototogisu was reputed to sing softly in the shade of the trees; from the
Fifth Month he sang loudly and clearly from the tree-tops.

For Nakatada's humble childhood and Shōnagon's attitude to him (919)
see p. 77. When writing this passage, she probably forgot that it was
Empress Sadako who stressed Nakatada's mean upbringing.

A village about one mile west of the capital; it was the site of Kōryū (920)
Ji, a Shingon temple built in 603 on the orders of Shōtoku Taishi.

Shōnagon is thinking of a *Kokin Shū* autumn poem, which contains
a typical lament about the rapid passage of time:

Kinō koso	Only yesterday, it seems,
Sanae torishi ka	They were pulling out the sprouts.
Itsu no ma ni	And now already autumn's stolen up,
Inaba soyogite	And rice leaves rustle in the wind.
Akikaze zo fuku	

In Shōnagon's time, as today, the light-green rice sprouts were pulled
from the seed-bed in the spring (at about the time of the Kamo
Festival) and planted in the paddy-fields by hand (note 916); in the
autumn, when the ears were formed, the field was drained and harvest-
ing began.

(922) *Katana ka nani ni ka* (a knife or something of the sort): Shōnagon
again shows her unfamiliarity with agricultural matters. She is
obviously referring to a scythe.

(923) Sections 243-4, which correspond to sections 228-9 in Ikeda-
Kishigami, occur only in the *Sangenbon* texts.

(924) *Gōshi* (lacquered bowls): red-lacquered bowls with lids, used com-
munally by courtiers who took their meals in the Imperial Palace.
Since they were not changed for many years, they tended to lose some
of their pristine cleanliness, and this, according to Kaneko (*Hyōshaku*,
p. 934), was the reason that gentlemen came to avoid eating in the
Palace.

(925) This is almost identical with the last paragraph of section 92; but
here Shōnagon is interested not so much in the awkwardness of the
situation as in whether or not an unfaithful son-in-law feels sorry for
the wife he has deserted.

(926) *Tomi no o* (kite's tail): refers to the end of each of the shafts of an ox-
carriage. For the cord of the young man's short-sleeved jacket see
note 530.

(927) Beaujard (*Notes de chevet*, p. 250) quotes Bossuet's 'Il n'y a rien de plus
triste à la nature que d'être haï'.

(928) ... *Oya nareba zo ka shi to aware nari*: lit. '[one thinks,] "It is certainly
because they are parents ..." and this is sad.'

(929) *Onna no me ni mo* (even other women): the implication (a rather
dubious one) is that women are less critical than men when it comes to
judging a girl's appearance.

Kanarazu omoubeki hito toubeki hito: lit. 'people whom one must necessarily love, people whom one must visit'. (930)

Saredo keshikaranu yō ni mo ari. Mata onozukara kikitsukete urami mo (931) *zo suru. Ai nashi*: lit. 'nevertheless it seems outrageous; moreover [if the victim] hears of it, he automatically feels resentment; this is charmless'.

This passage is very obscure. Both texts and commentaries differ (932) widely; I have followed *Hyōshaku*, p. 944. The *Sakai* and *Maeda* texts give *Yoki wa sa shi mo kotowari nikuge naru mo tsune ni medachite mamoraruru yo* (which has only *mamoraruru* in common with the *Shunchobon* and *Sangenbon* versions):
'It is only natural that one should be so attracted by a face with good features; but ugly faces also draw one's attention (and are gazed upon).'

See note 835 about *monogatari*; also *W.S.P.*, pp. 262-3, which sug- (933) gests how hard it could be to obtain copies.

For the absence of privacy regarding letters see *W.S.P.*, p. 188. (934)

For the interpretation of dreams (*yumeawase, yumetoki*) see *W.S.P.*, (935) p. 129.
A famous example of dream interpretation concerns Fujiwara no Kaneie, who dreamt that he saw Ōsaka Barrier covered with snow. This was interpreted (correctly, as it turned out) to mean that he would attain the post of Chancellor, because *Kampaku* (Chancellor) is written with characters signifying 'barrier' and 'white' (*Hyōshaku*, p. 948).

Monoawase (object match): lit. 'comparison of objects'. See note 688 (936) for *awase*. Among the 'objects' used in these games were flowers, roots, seashells, birds, insects, fans, and paintings.

Ito tsurenaku nan tomo omoitaranu sama nite, tayumesugusu mo okashi: (937) lit. 'it is also interesting when he passes the time in putting me off my guard with a very casual manner as if he were thinking of nothing'. Shōnagon enjoyed both the eager and the casual approaches in her male victims.

Probably in the 4th or 5th Month of 996, at the height of the Kore- (938) chika crisis (App. 4).

163

The Empress refers to the *Kokin Shū* poem,

Waga kokoro	Inconsolable my heart
Nagusame kanetsu	As I gaze upon the moon that shines
Sarashina ya	On Sarashina's Mount Obasute.
Obasute Yama ni	
Teru tsuki wo mite	

For Mount Obasute see note 62 (no. 32).

The Empress implies that Shōnagon manages to comfort herself too easily, and contrasts her with the inconsolable poet who gazed at the moon in Sarashina. The other ladies express the idea that Shōnagon's method of curing her world-weariness is far too cheap; prayers for warding off evil (*sokusai no inori*) normally involved making expensive gifts to Buddhist priests.

(940) *Jumyō Kyō* (Sutra of Longevity): a short sutra frequently recited or copied in order to ward off personal dangers and to secure a long life. The Empress refers to this particular sutra because of (*a*) Shōnagon's feeling that she cannot go on living for another moment (p. 217), (*b*) the ladies' comment about a prayer for warding off evil (p. 218). The statement that the paper is of poor quality belongs, of course, to the 'Please step into my filthy hovel' class of modesty.

(941)

Kakemaku mo
Kashikoki kami no
Shirushi ni wa
Tsuru no yowai ni
Narinubeki ka na

There is a play of words on *kami* = (i) deity (in this case referring to the Empress), (ii) paper (i.e. the paper that the Empress sent to Shōnagon). Shōnagon refers to her earlier remark that the sight of some good paper makes her feel she can stay a little longer on earth. The crane is a standard symbol of longevity in the Far East, and numerous Japanese poems refer to his thousand-year (*chiyo*, *chitose*) life expectancy.

(942) *Sōshi* (collection of notes): collection of miscellaneous notes, impressions, anecdotes, etc., of which Shōnagon's *Pillow Book* (*Makura no Sōshi*) is the only extant example from the Heian period. Shōnagon must have received this paper from the Empress well after the notebooks mentioned in section 326 (note 1155), and it seems likely that she had already started writing her *Pillow Book* by this time. According to some authorities, *sōshi* was a general term referring to bound books as opposed to rolled scrolls.

If the messenger in red had been found, Shōnagon would have NOTES
asked him whether he came from the Empress; since he has dis- (943)
appeared, she prefers not to let the people in her house know what she
is thinking.

The action described in this section takes place in 994, the year before (944)
Michitaka's death, when he and his immediate family were at the very
height of their power and glory (App. 4). Michitaka's dedication ceremony is reminiscent of the one arranged by Michinaga at Hōjō
Temple in 1022 (*W.S.P.*, pp. 61-62). For Dedication of the Sutras
see note 159. The Full Canon (*Issaikyō*) was a compilation of all the
sutras containing the statements of Gautama Buddha with commentaries. Originally it consisted of 5,084 volumes, but later it reached
the grand total of 8,534. The copying and recitation of this vast collection was, of course, a major event in the capital. Shakuzen Temple
had been founded by Michitaka himself in his father's Hōkō Palace
four years earlier (see note 494). Only a very small proportion of this
section (the longest single section in *The Pillow Book*) deals with the
religious ceremony itself; Shōnagon's real interest lay elsewhere.

Nijō no Miya (Palace of the Second Ward): This was the building in (945)
which Empress Sadako frequently resided when she left the Imperial
Palace enclosure; it was situated quite near Shakuzen Temple (App.
9d) and was therefore convenient for attending the present services.

The cherry trees usually came into bloom in the 2nd Month of the (946)
lunar calendar; the plum blossoms appeared about one month earlier.
The vile custom of decorating trees with artificial paper blossoms was
already well established in Shōnagon's time; despite her usual fastidiousness, she does not object to it in the slightest.

For colour combinations see note 23. (947)

Here *satobito* refers to anyone who lived outside the Palace. (948)

Nani ka shiryūgoto ni wa kikoemu: lit. 'why should I say this behind (949)
your back?' For similar examples of Michitaka's mock humility see
pp. 117 and 134.

Oko nari tote, kaku waraimasu ga hazukashi: lit. 'it is shameful that (950)
you laugh thus, thinking it is foolish'.

This is presumably a letter from the Emperor to Empress Sadako. (951)

165

An example, according to Kaneko (*Hyōshaku*, p. 988), of Shōnagon's conceit about her powers of aesthetic observation. But perhaps he is simply expressing a regret that other people are not present to enjoy the beauty of the scene (cf. p. 220).

(953) This was a standard gift presented to distinguished messengers; the long robe (*hosonaga*), also a woman's garment, was a mark of particular favours.

(954) Cf. note 348. It appears that Michitaka's third daughter occupied the post of Mistress of the Robes before his fourth daughter. The second daughter was Fujiwara no Genshi (note 415).

(955) From an anonymous *Shūi Shū* separation poem:

Sakurabana	Sadly I behold them,
Tsuyu ni nuretaru	The cherry blossoms moistened by the dew,
Kao mireba	Like tearful lovers
Nakite wakareshi	Forced to say farewell.
Hito zo koishiki	

Shōnagon changes the perfective tense of the original (*wakareshi*) to the future (*wakaremu*) and adds the word 'faces'.

(956) Minamoto no Kanezumi (Index-Glossary) was a poet and provincial governor. The present line does not appear among his extant works. There is, however, a *Gosen Shū* poem by the priest, Sosei, that does contain the words in question:

Yamamori wa	Let him tell me what he will,
Iwaba iwanamu	The mountain warden of these parts!
Takasago no	I'll pick a spray of cherry blooms
Onoe no sakura	On Takasago's Mount Onoe,
Orite kazasamu	And wear them as a chaplet on my head.

Either Shōnagon has confused the authors, or there is a non-extant poem by Kanezumi that may be similar to Sosei's.

(957) I.e. his idea that the ruined paper blossoms should be removed while it was still dark.

(958) Possibly an allusion to the *Shūi Shū* poem by Hitomaro which contains the syllepsis, 'both the rain and my tears come pouring down' (Ame mo namida mo / Furi ni koso fure). But the Empress's phrase

(*furi ni koso furu naritsure*) is a fairly standard one, and she may
not be referring to any particular poem. Whether or not this is a
quotation, the Empress is subtly indicating that she understands
her father's motive in ordering the rain-drenched blossoms to be
removed.

This is a pun on *asagao* = (i) morning face, i.e. one's dishevelled (959)
appearance on getting up in the morning, (ii) 'morning face', i.e. the
althea flower (notes 297, 299). Now that the sun has risen it is 'unseasonal' for Shōnagon to look as if she has just woken up; the 2nd
Month is unseasonal for the althea.

In the tenth century the suggestion that someone was telling a false- (960)
hood (*soragoto*) had far less damaging implications in Japan than in
the West and was usually more in the nature of a joke than of an
accusation.

The Empress alludes to Tsurayuki's poem, (961)

Yamada sae	The time has come
Ima wa tsukuru wo	To till the rice fields in the hills,
Chiru hana no	Oh, do not blame the wind
Kagoto wa kaze ni	For scattering the blossoms [far and wide below]!
Ōsezaranamu	

Quoting, with a few changes, from the first two lines of the poem,
Empress Sadako suggests that Shōnagon should not blame the wind
for removing the blossoms when she knows perfectly well who the
real culprit is.

'Simple remark' (*tadakoto*) normally referred to a conversational (962)
statement that did not include any quotation from Chinese or
Japanese.

The speaker (*kowakagimi*) is generally taken to be Korechika's son, (963)
Fujiwara no Matsugimi, but, since he was only two years old at
the time of this scene, he must have been an unusually precocious
child; some commentators accordingly believe that this is in fact
the name of one of Empress Sadako's ladies-in-waiting. For a discussion of this and other ambiguities in the present passage see
Ōhashi Kiyohide, 'Tōjō Jimbutsu', in *Kokubungaku* (November
1964), pp. 53-57.

Hana no kokoro hiraketari ya ('Have the flowers laid bare their hearts?'): the Empress is quoting from Po Chü-i:

Chiu yüeh hsi feng hsing	In the Ninth Month the west wind
Yüeh leng shuang hua ning	quickens;
Szu chün chʻiu yeh chʻang	[Under] the cold moon, flowers of frost
I yeh hun chiu sheng	have formed.
Erh yüeh tung feng lai	When I think upon my lord, the spring
Tsʻao chʻe hua hsin kʻai	day seems long.
Szu chün chʻun jih chʻih	My soul, nine times, rises towards him in
I jih chʻang chiu hui	one night.

In the Second Month the east wind comes,
Tearing at the plants till the flowers lay bare their hearts.
When I think upon my lord, the spring day passes slowly.
My heart, nine times, leaps up to him in one night.

Sadako is asking Shōnagon whether she misses her lord (i.e. herself); Shōnagon replies that she does miss her (*yoru ni kokonotabi noboru kokochi shihaberu*, 'I feel my heart rising nine times towards you in the night') and implies that she will soon return. The phrase *chʻang . . . hui* ('my heart . . . leaps up') refers to the painful uncertainties of love.

(965) The following scene is a 'flashback' describing what happened during and immediately after the move mentioned on p. 219; if the narrative were in normal time sequence, this scene would of course come *before* the story of the cherry blossoms.

(966) Cf. p. 193.

(967) 'Ill-natured' (*haragitanashi*) might seem a strong word to describe Shōnagon's suggestion that the serving-women (*tokusen*) should be seated before herself and her companions; but, in view of Heian class attitudes, the idea that the normal order of procedure might be reversed was nothing short of indecent.

(968) *Waraite* (we laughed): but some texts (including Kaneko, p. 965) give *wabite* (we were sorry). Normally carriages were lit at night by pine-torches; but this one was intended for servants and therefore left suitably murky.

Four passengers were the normal complement of a carriage (*W.S.P.*, pp. 36–37). (969)

Uemo was one of the three ladies-in-waiting who travelled with Sei (970) Shōnagon in the last carriage.

Sama ashūte, kaku noritaramu mo kashikokarubeki koto ka wa: lit. 'can (971) it really have been a clever thing to have (probably) got into [the carriages] in such an unseemly way?'

This scene takes place on about the 19th. Shōnagon had left the Palace (972) in the 2nd Ward on the 8th or 9th of the month.

About 4 a.m. See App. 3. (973)

Karabisashi: elaborate *hisashi* in the Chinese style (see Index- (974) Glossary and note 38).

Fujiwara no Korechika and his younger brother, Takaie. (975)

The original is obscure and elliptical. *Kushikoki kao mo naki ka to* (976) *oboyuredo* means literally 'although I think I cannot have had an impressive face'. But there is no contradiction between this and the clause that follows (viz. 'when we had all got into our carriages'); in order to justify the use of the concessive *oboyuredo* it seems necessary to interpolate something like 'it was the best I could do'.

Kusushi: doctor attached to the Bureau of Medicine (Tenyaku Ryō); (977) this Bureau, which was under the Ministry of the Imperial Household (App. 7a), was in charge of curing people of the 5th Rank and above (see *W.S.P.*, p. 133). The *Sangenbon* texts refer to Shigemasa (whose full style was Tamba Sukune no Sukemasa) as Director of the Bureau of Medicine (Tenyaku no Kami).

'Forbidden colours' (*kinjiki*) were those, like dark purple, that could (978) be worn only by members of the Imperial family or High Court Nobles. *Ebizome* (light purple, grape colour) was not included among the forbidden colours. Yamanoi's remark, in which he refers to a Palace Girl by a man's name, is entirely facetious.

Nagi no hana (onion-flower decoration): onion-shaped metal finial on (979) the roof of an Imperial palanquin. The onion was regarded as an auspicious decoration because of its long-lived flowers.

The *Shunchobon* text gives *kami ashikaramu hito mo* ('even those with ugly hair'). Kaneko (*Hyōshaku*, p. 971) bases his text on a later gloss, which has *kami ashikaranu hito mo* ('even those with attractive hair'), Ik'eda-Kishigami (p. 295) have *kami ashikaran* (= *ashikaramu*) *hito mo*, and their note suggests, rather unconvincingly, that Shōnagon may be referring to herself. I have followed Kaneko, whose text makes somewhat better sense and fits in with the similar passage on p. 190 (note 844), where even the ladies whose hair is most beautifully groomed feel it standing on end when they hear the flageolets.

(981) This refers to ceremonial Court music of the *gagaku* type, which had been imported from the Continent and which was preserved in Japan long after it disappeared in its country of origin.

(982) In order to keep their long hair in place, ladies often tucked it under their jackets, especially when travelling; but the shaking of the carriage was apt to disarrange it. For reddish (i.e. false) hair see note 771.

(983) There appears to have been a young Fujiwara gentleman of this name. Possibly he was reputed to have an eye for women; this would explain the need to get Shōnagon and her companions out of their carriages secretly. Some commentators suggest this may refer to Kiyowara no Munetaka, a brother of Shōnagon's, but the context makes it unlikely.

(984) *Izura tote*: lit. 'saying, "Where?"'

(985) *Zōgan* (elephant-eye silk): Chinese silk decorated with delicate gold and silver designs.

(986) *Miya no Daibu* (Master of the Household): i.e. Master of the Office of the Empress's Household (App. 7b); refers here to Fujiwara no Michinaga, who later became Empress Sadako's greatest political enemy. See *W.S.P.*, p. 62.

(987) *Tomi no Kōji no Udaijin*: the Minister of the Right of Tomi Street, i.e. Fujiwara no Akitada. According to Fujiwara no Yukinari, who was Akitada's fourth cousin, Sei Shōnagon's father was actually Fujiwara no Akitada and not, as is more generally believed, Kiyowara no Motosuke. In that case Lady Saishō would be Shōnagon's niece. But there is little evidence to support the theory. Akitada died in 965 at the age of sixty-seven, and 965 is the probable date of Shōnagon's birth.

This passage provides a good illustration of the type of jealousy that NOTES (988) prevailed among the ladies at Court. All of them vied for the favours of the Empress and therefore tended to resent her particular affection for Shōnagon. (Murasaki Shikibu's diary suggests that she suffered from similar jealousy at Empress Akiko's Court.) When the Empress tells Saishō to go and see what is happening in the gentlemen's hall, the lady realizes that her mistress intends to put Shōnagon in her place on the straw mat. She replies rather bluntly that there is room for three people on the mat (i.e. herself, Lady Chūnagon, and Shōnagon). Sadako's 'Very well then' is a shorthand way of saying, 'Well, if you feel so strongly about it, you may as well stay where you are.' She then invites Shōnagon to sit near her on the mat. This irks some of the other ladies-in-waiting who are seated on a lower level, where they cannot observe the ceremony so well, and they vent their annoyance by denigrating Shōnagon, whose social position is of course inferior to that of Ladies Saishō and Chūnagon. First, one of them compares her to a page-boy (*kodoneri*), who is not normally allowed into the Imperial presence even though he may be favoured on special occasions. Another jealous lady compares her to a mounted escort (*umasae*), implying that, despite the Empress's partiality, Shōnagon's social relationship to Lady Saishō is like that of an inferior attendant to his master. There is a reference here to the fact tha Saishō's father, Atsusuke, was Director of the Bureau of Horses, Right Division (Uma Ryō no Kami). Shōnagon wisely refuses to allow this backbiting to spoil her pleasure.

... *nado iedo, soko ni iriite miru wa, ito omotadashi. Kakaru koto nado* (989) *wo mizukara iu wa, fukigatari ni mo ari, mata, Kimi no on-tame ni mo karogaroshū, ka bakari no hito wo sae oboshikemu nado, onozukara mono shiri, yo no naka modoki nado suru hito wa, ainaku kashikoki on-koto ni kakarite, katajikena-keredo, aru koto nado wa, mata ikage wa. Makoto ni mi no hodo ni sugitaru koto mo arinubeshi*: lit. 'though they said such things, it was very glorious / honourable to see [the ceremony] having entered there. To say such a thing oneself is boasting; moreover, for Her Majesty also, people who naturally know things and who criticize everything [no doubt] maliciously [express their criticism] concerning [Her] August [Majesty] for lightly doing such a thing as favouring/ loving even such a person [as myself]; and, though she was [too] good to me, how can I (moreover) [be silent about] a (sort of) thing that happened? Truly there must have been things that were excessive for someone of [my] status.'

Viz. Michitaka's three sons, Michiyori, Korechika, and Takaie (the (990) Middle Captain).

171

Military paraphernalia might seem inappropriate for a Buddhist ceremony; but the function of the Guards was almost entirely ceremonial
and it was the elegance of the uniform that counted.

(992) This is one of the great days in Michitaka's life and he does not want
its memory to be spoiled by subsequent complaints that the women
were uncomfortable in their formal costumes.

    I have followed the *Shunchobon* commentary (*Ima yori irai, kyō wa
kaku kyūkutsu naru me mitsu to mōshitamau na to nari. Onoono mo
karaginu nite gyōgi tadashiki yue nari*), but there are numerous variants
and interpretations of this passage. They are discussed in Ikeda-
Kishigami, p. 359.

(993) *Oboroge no koto ka(wa)*: lit. 'is [that] an ordinary thing?'

(994) They wept for joy. For a discussion of male weeping see *W.S.P.*,
pp. 145-6.

(995) Michitaka refers facetiously to the fact that Buddhist priests wear
robes of the same red colour as Shōnagon's jacket.

(996) *Sei Sōzu* (Bishop Sei): see note 60 for Sōzu.

    The names of Buddhist priests were read in the Sino-Japanese (*on*)
pronunciation; *Sei*, which is the Sino-Japanese reading of the first
element of what is generally believed to be the author's family name
(*Kiyowara*), lends itself to Korechika's witticism in a way that would
be impossible with Japanese (*kun*) names like Ono, Izumi, and
Murasaki.

(997) *Jizō Bosatsu*: see note 834. The numerous stone images of Jizō in
Japan represent him as a Buddhist priest with shaven head, clad in
bonze's vestments and carrying a rosary. Ryūen was the Empress's
brother (note 436); hence his presence among the ladies-in-waiting.
Despite his high ecclesiastical rank, he was only fifteen years old.

(998) The flowers were artificial (cf. note 946).

(999) *Ekō* (Prayer for Salvation): comprises sixteen characters from the
Kammuryōju Kyō (Skr. *Amitāyur Buddha Dhyāna Sūtra*). Anesaki
gives the following translation:

> His light pervades the world in all the ten directions,
> His grace never forsakes anyone who invokes his name.

Masaharu Anesaki, *History of Japanese Religion*, p. 178.

Minamoto no Norimasa: see Index-Glossary. He was appointed Secretary of Ceremonial (*Shikibu no Zō*) in 993, at which time he held the post of Chamberlain of the 6th Rank. Later he became Governor of Owari and Tajima Provinces. Norimasa's younger sister was Korechika's wife.

Kurōdɔ no Ben (Chamberlain-Controller): see Index-Glossary. The gentleman in question is Takashina no Sanenobu, the Minor Controller of the Right, who had become Chamberlain of the 5th Rank three months before the present ceremony. He was the Empress's maternal uncle (see App. 6d).

Reference to an old love poem (included in the *Zoku Gosen Shū* anthology):

Michinoku no	Though close at hand
Chika no shiogama	The Chika kilns
Chikanagara	In Michinoku's land,
Karaki wa hito ni	People can still not meet their salty taste.
Awanu narikeri	

Lit 'the saltiness does not meet people', i.e. even though the salt-kilns are close, their salty flavour does not reach people in the vicinity. There is a play of words on Chika = (i) place name, (ii) close. The poem applies to a situation in which, although two people happen to be near each other (like Empress Sadako and the Empress Dowager during the present ceremony), they are still unable to meet.

Such a reduction in retinue was normal on the return from cere- monies, festivals, etc.

Sukuse (karma): if it had rained on the previous day, much of the ceremony would have been ruined. Michitaka attributes his good luck with the weather to an accumulation of merit in previous incarnations (cf. note 506).

Kujō Shakujō (Nine Articles of the Pilgrim's Staff): sacred Buddhist text in nine articles; it was recited by pilgrims, who rattled their staffs (*shakujō*) at the end of each article.

Ekō: see note 999. 'Invoking the Sacred Name' (*Nembutsu*) refers to the increasingly popular practice in Heian Buddhism of meditating on the name of Amida (Amītabha) Buddha and intoning the Namu Amida Butsu ('I call on Thee, Amida Buddha') formula. This was to become the basis of the popular Amidist sects that developed in the thirteenth century. See *W.S.P.*, pp. 101-2.

Uta: the differentiation between 'song' and 'poem' was tenuous. An important part of Japanese poetry was associated with music and dance.

(1008) From the *Kokin Shū* poem:

> Waga iori wa
> Miwa no yamamoto
> Koishiku wa
> Toburaikimase
> Sugi tateru kado

> My hut is at Mount Miwa's base.
> Come, if you wish to see me,
> To the gate where grows the *sugi* tree.

For Mount Miwa, its shrine, and the *sugi* see note 883.

(1009) For an example of *kagura-uta* see note 544.

(1010) *Imayō-uta* (songs in the modern style): a type of poetry that became popular from the middle of the Heian period; originally the form was fairly fluid, but by Shōnagon's time it had been fixed at four (sometimes eight) lines in the seven-and-five-syllable metre. 'Modern style' songs were often chanted at Court banquets.

(1011) *Fūzoku (-uta)* (popular songs): refers to ancient songs of the *saibara* type that were enjoyed in Court circles; many were of provincial origin. For an example see note 316.

(1012) *Sashinuki* (trousers): see note 623.

(1013) *Kariginu* (hunting costume): see note 122.

(1014) *Shitagasane* (under-robe): see note 623.

(1015)

Name of Shrine	Province (District)	Shintō Deities enshrined
1. Matsunoo	Yamashiro (Kadono)	Ōyamakui, Wakeikazuchi
2. Yawata (Hachiman)	Yamashiro (Tsutsuki)	Yawata (Hachiman)
3. Ōharano	Yamashiro (Otokuni)	Takemikazuchi, Futsunushi, Ame no Koyane, etc.
4. Kamo	Yamashiro (Otagi)	Wakeikazuchi, Tamayori, Hime, etc.
5. Inari	Yamashiro (Kii)	Uga no Mitama, Saruda hiko, etc.
6. Kasuga	Yamato (Sōnokami)	Takemikazuchi, Futsunushi, Ame no Koyane, etc.
7. Sahodono	Yamato (Sōnokami)	
8. Hirano	Yamashiro (Kadono)	Kudo, Imaki, Aidono Hime, etc.
9. Mikomori	Yamato (Yoshino)	

Hachiman, the God of War, enshrined at Yawata, was identified with
Ōjin, the fifteenth Emperor of Japan, whose traditional dates are 201– (1016)
310, but who actually lived and reigned towards the end of the fourth
century. Concerning an Imperial visit to the shrine see note 597.

Nagi no hana: see note 979. (1017)

Sahodono, lit. 'Hall of Help and Protection', appears to have been an (1018)
ancillary building to the great Kasuga Shrine, and was apparently
used by Fujiwara retainers when attending celebrations in the shrine
and at Kōfuku Temple.

Mi-koshi (sacred palanquin): portable shrine in which the God is (1019)
carried during certain festivals and other important occasions.

Poem by Ki no Tsurayuki in the *Kokin Shū*: (1020)

Chihayaburu	Even the arrowroot that trails the sacred hedge
Kami no igaki ni	At the shrine of the all-powerful Gods
Hau kuzu mo	Cannot withstand the autumn's strength
Aki ni wa aezu	And turns its colours [to the season's hues].
Utsuroinikeri	

According to Kaneko (*Hyōshaku*, p. 1006), this is because the name (1021)
Mi-ko-mori could be taken to mean 'honourable protector of children'.
The correct etymology, however, is probably *Mi-kumari* ('sharing
the waters').

Place	Province (District)	Literary association	Literal meaning	(1022)
1. Karasaki	Ōmi (Shiga)	*Manyō Shū*	China Cape	
2. Ika ga Saki	,, ,,	*Kagerō Nikki* (?)		
3. Miho ga Saki	Suruga or Izumo		Cape of Three Protections	

Azumaya (Azuma cottage): cottage of the type found in the eastern (1023)
provinces (Azuma). It was square and thatched with strips of cypress.

In the *Shunchobon* texts this section is incongruously placed between (1024)
those about unlined clothes and under-robes (261 and 262) (App. 5).

Cf. p. 28, in which Shōnagon discusses honorific usage. (1025)

Saredo hito woba shiraji. Tada sa uchioboyuru nari: lit. 'Nevertheless I (1026)
(probably) do not care about other people. It is only that I think thus.'

175

The 'to' in my translation corresponds fortuitously to the particle *to*
(1027) in the original. Even in Heian Japanese, however, the abbreviated
form never came close to being such a solecism as 'intend . . . -ing' is
in English. The *-muzu* contraction of *-mu to su* was well established
by Shōnagon's time, at least in conversation. For example, in *Taketori
Monogatari* ('the ancestor of the *monogatari*') we find *inamuzu* for
inamu to su. In *Tosa Nikki* (935) the process of abbreviation has gone
still further and we find *makarazu* for *makaramu to su*. The *Pillow
Book* itself contains several of the forms that Shōnagon so roundly
condemns (e.g. *kaeramuzuramu* for *kaeramu to suramu*, *komozuru* for
komu to suru), but this may be due to the carelessness of copyists.

(1028) These were standard marginal comments made by copyists, the
second one (*jōhon no mama*) corresponding to our *sic*. Such notes are
bound to be distracting when placed in the body of the text and
Shōnagon prefers that they be omitted, at least from works of fiction.

(1029) The vowel-changes that Shōnagon condemns are hitotsu → hitetsu
and motomu → mitomu. Cf. her amusement at Narimasa's use of
chūsei for *chiisai* (note 42).

(1030) It is all right for a gentleman to use an occasional slang or provincial
expression as long as he does so with tongue in cheek; but, if it has
become a natural part of his vocabulary, he is bound to be despised.

(1031) Cf. note 745.

(1032) The times announced correspond to 3 a.m. and 1.30 a.m. (App. 3).

(1033) The *Engi Shiki* (supplementary civil code) specified the number of
strokes to be sounded on the gong at each new watch: nine for the
Rat and the Horse, eight for the Ox and the Sheep, etc. (App. 3).
These inexperienced officers, instead of announcing the exact quarter
of the watch (as in note 1032), simply state the number of gong-
strokes that accompany it. I have tried to make the distinction clearer
by adding the words 'quarter' and 'strokes' in my translation.

(1034) About midnight.

(1035) Emperor Ichijō was a keen flautist (*W.S.P.*, p. 45). For music at
night see *W.S.P.*, pp. 150, 189.

(1036) I.e. of Prince Munehira, Emperor Murakami's son, who served as
Minister of Military Affairs (App. 7a) and became a lay priest.

Minamoto no Kanesuke, the Governor of Iyo, descended from a brother of Emperor Seiwa (reg. 858-76), the main ancestor of the Minamoto clan. His daughter was originally one of Fujiwara no Takaie's wives and she had at least two children by him; after her husband's disgrace she transferred her affections to the handsome young Narinobu, only to be abandoned by him a few years later. Kaneko suggests (*Hyōshaku*, p. 1017) that the reason for Narinobu's leaving her was not fickleness but his increasing determination to enter a monastic life, a step that he took in 1001 at the age of twenty-two.

Hyōbu = Military Affairs. No doubt she had a father, brother, or (1038) other close relative in the Ministry of Military Affairs. The lady's full last name was therefore something like Taira no Hyōbu, but the other ladies teased her by using her original family name, which was presumably a rather humble one. (The Tairas, like the Minamotos, had Imperial antecedents; see Index-Glossary.)

This was unusual. The names of most of the Court ladies consisted (1039) of the offices, ranks, provinces, etc. with which their close relations were associated (e.g. Shikibu, Uma, Sammi, Naishi, Izumi, Sagami, Ise), or pseudonyms like Murasaki and Sei, or personal names like Yoshiko and Akiko. One of the few well-known ladies to use her family name (*sō*) was Akazome Emon.

This section belongs to the year 1000 (App. 4); the month is un- (1040) certain, but it must be the 2nd, 3rd, or 8th.

Shōnagon is offended by the idea that Narinobu, who had come to (1041) visit her, should so easily have been put off by her pretence at being asleep and that he should have been satisfied to spend the night with such an inferior creature as Hyōbu. Her reaction, in other words, is what men often describe as 'feminine'.

Shōnagon is coyly referring to herself. (1042)

Moto yori no yosuga: lit. 'an affinity from the beginning', i.e. his (1043) principal consort.

Cf. note 145. (1044)

For *Komano no Monogatari* see p. 188. The episode of the old bat- (1045) fan (about which we know nothing since the work is not extant) seems to have made a particular impression on Shōnagon.

177

From the *Gosen Shū* poem:

(1046)   Yūyami wa   The evening now is dark,
           Michi mo mienedo   The path has disappeared from sight,
           Furusato wa   As I go towards my native town.
           Moto koshi koma ni   Yet I ride without a care—
           Makasete zo kuru   My horse has come this way before.

(1047) Shōnagon refers to *Ochikubo Monogatari*, 'The Tale of Room Below',
a romance in four scrolls written towards the end of the tenth century
(authorship unknown) and telling the story of an unfortunate young
lady who is mistreated by her stepmother but eventually rescued by
the hero, Ukon no Shōshō. Captain Katano (Katano no Shōshō)
figures as an unsuccessful rival for the heroine's hand, but the extant
version of *Ochikubo Monogatari* contains no reference to his being
criticized by the hero. 'Captain Ochikubo' is clearly Ukon no Shōshō,
and the extant version does in fact contain a scene in which he pays
the heroine a 'third-night visit' (*W.S.P.*, p. 216) in the rain and has to
wash the muck off his feet (*mazu mizu mote on-ashi sumasu*).

(1048) Possibly an allusion to the *Manyō Shū* poem:

           Waga inochi   Until my life becomes extinct,
           Mata kemu kagiri   How can she vanish from my thoughts—
           Wasureme ya   She whom I cherish more each day?
           Iya hi ni ke ni wa
           Omoimasu tomo

Wasureme ya, the quoted line, means 'Can I (*or* he) forget?'

(1049) *Rōsō* (short green robe): worn by men of the 6th Rank. For its derogatory connotations see *W.S.P.*, p. 66. As a rule Shōnagon would not
have welcomed a gentleman visitor below the 5th Rank.

(1050) Even by Heian standards (*W.S.P.*, p. 182) this is a rather laconic com-
munication. Its implication, however, would instantly be grasped by
any perceptive member of Court society: 'There is nothing special for
me to say, except to ask how you are enjoying this moonlight.'

(1051)   Reference to the opening lines of a *Kokin Shū* poem:

           Aketáteba   When dawn appears,
           Semi no orihae   The ceaseless cry of the cicadas
                                    [Greets my ears] . . .

(1052) This is obviously a quotation, but the source is unknown. According
to some of the early commentaries, the gentleman is referring to a

Kokin Shū poem in which the writer compares his growing love (*masaru waga koi*) to Yodo River, whose waters swell in the rain. But the wording is totally different.

Because the tip of the writing-brush was frozen; but, as Kaneko (1053) remarks (*Hyōshaku*, p. 1022), this is surely an exaggeration. It is also hard to understand how Shōnagon could have observed the delicate indentations and other details of the letter from where she was standing (note 1054).

Yoso nite miyaritaru mo: lit. 'though I was looking [from] outside'. (1054)

The *Hyōshaku* text puts sections 274–6 together under 'Resplendent (1055) Things' (*kirakirashiki mono*). I follow Ikeda-Kishigami and the other texts that give them as three separate sections. See App. 5.

Kujaku Kyō: abbreviation of *Butsumo Daikuzaku Myōō-gyō* (Sanskrit: (1056) *Mahāmayūrīvidyārājñi Sūtra*) (Sutra of the Great Peacock Queen, the Holy Mother of Buddha).

Rite of incantation (note 586) devoted to a group of fierce Shingon (1057) gods known as the Five Great Venerables (Godaison).

Go Saie (Assembly of Purification). annual Buddhist services held at (1058) Court from the 8th to the 14th of the 1st Month. Readings of the Sutra of the Victorious King (*Saishōō Kyō*) (Sanskrit: *Suvarṇa Prabhāsa Sūtra*) were performed in order to assure the safety of the country during the coming year.

Sonshōō no Mi-zuhō (rite of the Holy and Victorious King): based on (1059) the *Sonshō Darani* (note 831) and addressed to the Holy and Victorious Buddha-Head (Sunshō Butchō, Uṣṇiṣavijaya Rāja).

Shijōkō no Mi-zuhō (rite of the Flourishing and Shining Spirit) (N.B. (1060) the Sanskrit text has been lost and cannot be identified): rite of incantation aimed at averting natural calamities and military insurrections; the prayers were usually addressed to Konrin Butchō (the Golden-Wheeled Buddha-Head, Suvarṇoṣṇiṣacakravartin).
　Shingon services had a particular aesthetic appeal for Shōnagon and the people of her circle (see *W.S.P.*, p. 100).

Kannari no Jin: see note 900. (1061)

I.e. 'Proceed to the Imperial Palace' or 'Return to barracks'. (1062)

This section lists three famous painted scenes that were kept in the Palace: (i) *Kongen Roku* ('Original Records of the Earth'), a ten-chapter Chinese topography (*K'un yüan lu*), which, though no longer extant, is identified in an entry of *Nihon Kiryaku* dated 949, (ii) *Kansho* (*Han shu*) ('History of the Han') (*N.B.* scenes illustrating Chinese works were very popular in Shōnagon's time), (iii) *Tsukinami* ('The Months'), the yearly round of Court observances.

(1064) *Rei narazu mi-kōshi mairasete*: lit. 'it was not customary [but] they had caused [the maids] to close the (honourable) lattices'.

(1065) *Kōrōhō no yuki wa ika naramu* ('How is the snow on Hsiang-lu peak?'): the Empress refers to some famous lines of Po Chü-i:

Jih kao shui tsu yu jung ch'i	The sun has risen in the sky,
Hsiao ko ch'ung ch'in pu p'a han	but still I idly lie in bed;
I-ai szu chung i chen t'ing	In my small tower-room the
Hsiang-lu feng hsüeh po lien k'an . . .	layers of quilts protect me
	from the cold;
	Leaning on my pillow, I wait
	to hear I-ai's temple bell;
	Pushing aside the blind, I
	gaze upon the snow of
	Hsiang-lu peak . . .

The poem was well known in Heian Kyō. It had been imitated by Sugawara no Michizane; and, as Shōnagon points out, it was often rendered in Japanese form, i.e. as an *uta*. Once again, it is not Shōnagon's erudition that distinguishes her from the other ladies but her ability to rise instantly to the occasion.

(1066) *Nao kono miya no hito ni wa, sarubeki nameri*: lit. 'after all she seems to be appropriate as the person (i.e. servant) of the Empress'.

(1067) This section probably belongs to 992, but some authorities prefer 994 (App. 4). Cf. section 132, in which 'leaving home because of an abstinence' is listed among 'Boring Things'.

(1068) *Kakaru mo ari*: lit. 'there are also such'.

(1069)   Sakashira ni
            Yanagi no mayu no
            Hirogorite
            Haru no omote wo
            Fusuru yado ka na

Shōnagon compares the leaves of the unsightly willow tree to human eyebrows (*mayu*); the eyebrow image leads directly to the word 'face' in 'lose face' (*omote wo fusuru*). *Mayu* also has the sense of cocoon, and there is a further implicit comparison between cocoons and the downy buds of the willow. Like so many of Shōnagon's verses, the present *uta* is more ingenious than poetic.

> Ika ni shite （1070)
> Suginishi kata wo
> Sugushikemu
> Kurashiwazurau
> Kinō kyō ka na

It has been hard enough for the Empress to get through the past two days (lit. 'yesterday and today'). How, she wonders, can she have managed to exist during the long period before Shōnagon came into service? The exchange of this type of romantic poetry between ladies at Court was entirely conventional and should not be taken as evidence of Lesbian attachments (see *W S P*, p. 220 n.).

An allusion to the *Goshūi Shū* poem, （1071)

Kururu ma wa	Evening comes
Chitose wo sugusu	And still I pine away;
Kokochi shite	Truly the time seems long,
Matsu wa makoto ni	Long as the pine tree's life:
Hioaohikarikeri	I feel as though I'd waited for a thousand years.

There is the usual pun on *matsu* = (i) to wait (pine), (ii) pine tree.

Mashite ōsegoto no sama ni wa, oroka naranu kokochi suredo: lit. （1072) 'though still less did I feel indifferent about the form of the Empress's message'.

> Kumo no ue ni （1073)
> Kurashikanekeru
> Haru no hi wo
> Tokorogara tomo
> Nagametsuru ka na

'One who lives above the clouds' refers, of course, to the Empress. High members of Court society were commonly known as 'people above the clouds' (*kumo no uebito*).

This is probably a reference to Fukakusa no Shōshō. He fell in love （1074) with the famous ninth-century poetess and beauty, Ono no Komachi, but she said that she would trust and accept him only after he had spent every night outside her house for one hundred nights. Captain Fukakusa almost managed to pass the test; but he succumbed on the

ninety-ninth night and accordingly failed to win Komachi. His unappeased spirit returns to torment her in *Kayoi Komachi*, a famous
Nō play.

In a type of insincere hyperbole that was common in Court circles
Shōnagon suggests that she too may be unable to survive her last
night away from the object of her devotion (i.e. the Empress).

(1075) Because, says Kaneko (*Hyōshaku*, p. 1031), Shōnagon's reply poem
was more concerned with her own unhappy feelings than with those
of the Empress.

(1076)
> Yama chikaki
> Iriai no kane no
> Koegoto ni
> Kouru kokochi no
> Kazu wa shiruramu

The 'mountain' (which is really more of a hill) is Otowa Yama;
Kiyomizu Temple is situated about half-way up the slope.

(1077) *Toriwasuretaru tabi nite*: lit. 'being a time / journey when I had for-
gotten to take [paper]'. There is a pun on *tabi* = (i) time, (ii) journey.
Kiyomizu was only a few miles from the Imperial Palace, but such
was the slowness of transport in Shōnagon's day (*W.S.P.*, pp. 37–38)
that the word 'journey' was quite appropriate for describing a visit to
this temple.

The lotus petal is artificial, like those on page 232. Possibly Shōnagon selected it from among the petals that had been used in the
Buddhist rite of scattering flowers (*sange*). Both red and purple were
associated with sunset and therefore appropriate for evening poems
(note the Empress's reference to vespers). The fact that Shōnagon
does not quote her reply suggests she was not particularly proud of it.

(1078) *On-Butsumyō* (Naming of the Buddhas): see note 325. The present
section cannot be dated.

(1079) *Rinrin to shite kōri shikeri* ('piercing cold, it spreads like ice'). This is
from a ninth-century Chinese poem by Kung Ch'eng-i, included in
Wakan Rōei Shū:

Ch'in tien chih i ch'ien yü li	[The moon,] piercing cold,
Lin lin ping p'u	Spreads like ice over the thousand
Han chia chih san shih liu kung	leagues of the realm of Ch'in,
Ch'eng ch'eng fen shih	And lucently adorns the thirty-six
	palaces of Han with silver grains.

Presumably during the friend's absence at Court; but the passage is somewhat obscure.

Keshikaranu kokoro ni ya aramu: lit. 'I wonder whether this is [not] (1081) a strange feeling.' Although this immediately follows the statement about liking people of good birth (*yoki hito*), Heian ideas about society (*W.S.P.*, p. 68) were such that it cannot possibly refer to it. Rather it refers to the entire section, in particular to Shōnagon's fancies about the type of home life she would enjoy after retiring from Court service.

The original has *omotage ni nado mo araneba* ('because it does not look (1082) heavy'); but this seems illogical, and in my translation I have assumed that *araneba* is a copyist's error for *aranedo*. Kaneko (*Hyōshaku*, p. 1041) solves the difficulty by the following rather elaborate inter-pretation: 'Because it did not look heavy, one would have expected to feel uneasy; but in fact I did not feel uneasy, for the boat looked just [as safe as] a little house.'

The image is not as original as it might seem: Japanese children make (1083) toy boats (*sasabune*) out of bamboo leaves.

Reference to a *Shūi Shū* poem by the early eighth-century priest, (1084) Mansei:

Yo no naka wo	This world of ours—
Nani ni tatoemu	To what shall I compare it?
Asaborake	To the white waves behind a boat
Kogiyuku fune no	That disappear without a trace
Ato no shiranami	As it rows away at dawn.

Yoroshiki hito wa, norite arikumajiki koto koso, nao oboyure: lit. 'after (1085) all, I certainly think that people of fair/average standing should not travel on [boats]'.

Umi wa nao yuyushi to omou ni, maite ama no kazuki shi ni iru wa uki (1086) *waza nari*: lit. 'whereas I think that the sea is after all fearful, all the more wretched an action is that of women divers who enter [the sea] (in order to do) diving'. Since ancient times the Japanese have used women divers (*ama*), partly because they can hold their breath longer than men, partly because they are more resistant to the cold.

Me mo aya ni asamashi: lit. 'it is amazing to the extent of making one (1087) doubt one's eyes'. I have moved this passage (*otoshiirete . . . asamashi*) back a few sentences in order to improve the sequence of ideas and to avoid repetition.

NOTES (1088) *Shiotaru* has the double sense of (i) dripping with salt water (like the diving women), (ii) being sorrowful, weeping (like the outsider).

(1089) For being old and ugly, according to Kaneko (*Hyōshaku*, p. 1045); but perhaps the real reason was that they were embarrassingly provincial (*W.S.P.*, pp. 81-82).

(1090) Dōmei (Azari) (Index-Glossary), the eldest son of Fujiwara no Michitsuna, was noted for the beauty of his sutra-chanting and for his skill at poetry. In the present poem

> Watatsumi ni
> Oya wo oshiirete
> Kono nushi no
> Bon suru miru zo
> Aware narikeru

there may be a play on the word *bon* = (i) the Festival of the Dead, (ii) the splash that the old couple made on hitting the water. The poem may also suggest the irony of the fact that, after pushing his parents into the sea, the lieutenant attended a service that was particularly concerned with interceding with those who were undergoing the Ordeal of Headlong Falling (*Tōken no Ku*) in Hell (note 662).

For the Confucian significance of this anecdote see *W.S.P.*, pp. 96-97.

(1091) The lady in question was the grandmother of Dōmei, the poet-priest mentioned in section 286. She is best known as the author of *Kagerō Nikki*, one of the most famous of the Heian diaries; her real name, however, is not given and she is usually called Michitsuna no Haha (Michitsuna's mother). She was the daughter of Fujiwara no Tomoyasu, the Governor of Mutsu, and became one of the many mistresses of Fujiwara no Kaneie. Her diary describes her unhappy relations with Kaneie during the years 954-74.

Fujiwara no Tomoyasu
|
Michitsuna no Haha ⊤ Fujiwara no Kaneie
|
Michitsuna
|
Dōmei

Michitsuna was frequently known as the Lord of Ono (Ono-dono), Ono being a village in the district of Kadono, north of the capital, where he had a residence.

Fumon Temple (Fumon Ji) is unidentified; from Shōnagon's wording it does not appear to have been well known even in her own day.

Takigi koru   (1092)
Koto wa kinō ni
Tsukinishi wo
Kyō wa Ono no e
Koko ni kutasamu

The poem is an ingenious web of puns and allusions. 'Cutting firewood' (*takigi koru*) alludes to a passage in the *Lotus Sutra* in which
the Buddha is described as having gained wisdom by serving the old
hermit, Asita ('picking fruits for him and drawing water, cutting
firewood and preparing food'); in the present context it refers to the
previous day's recitation of the Eight Lessons (which were devoted
to the *Lotus Sutra*). During the service of the Eight Lessons there was
a procession of priests carrying firewood and buckets of water.

'The axe's handle rots away' alludes to the story of Wang Chih
(note 309) and implies that, since the axe is no longer needed today,
they will let it rot away (i.e. they will devote themselves to mundane
pleasures). There is a pun on Ono – (i) the name of Michitsuna's
villa, (ii) axe.

The present poem appears in *Kagerō Nikki*. The following translation is by Edward Seidensticker (*The Kagerō Nikki: Journal of a 10th
Century Noblewoman*, p. 225): 'Yesterday ended our services; and
now let us stay at Ono till the wood of our axe-handle rots.'

Kokomoto wa: lit. '[the poems] hereabouts', i.e. the poems described (1093)
in section 286 ff. In fact Shōnagon was not present when any of these
poems were written or recited.

The unhappy lady is Princess Izu, a daughter of Emperor Kammu. (1094)
Her son by Prince Aho was the famous poet and courtier, Ariwara no
Narihira. The following episode occurs in *Kokin Shū*: 'When the
Princess, Lord Narihira's mother, was residing in Nagaoka, His
Lordship was serving at Court and could not go to see her. One day in
the 12th Month a letter suddenly arrived from the Princess. When
Narihira opened it, he found that there was no message but simply the
following poem:

Oinureba   Now I am old,
Saranu wakare mo   And fear we'll never meet again.
Ari to ieba   Oh, how my wish to see you grows and grows!
Iyoiyo mimaku
Hoshiki kimi ka na

185

Mata homuru mama ni iisokonaitsuru mono woba: lit. 'moreover, how they speak wrongly when praising!'

(1096) From the rank (*Dainagon*) by which Korechika is designated it would appear that the events in this section occurred at some time between 992 (8th Month) and 994 (8th Month), when the Emperor was about thirteen years old (App. 4).

The Emperor's official tutor in literature was Ōe no Masahira, but prior to his exile in 996 Korechika occasionally gave him instruction.

(1097) See note 1032 and App. 3. The fourth quarter of the Hour of the Ox began at 3.30 a.m.

(1098) *Koe meiō no neburi wo odorokasu* ('the prudent monarch rises from his sleep'): from a poem by Miyako no Yoshika (d. 879), included in both *Honchō Monzui* and *Wakan Rōei Shū*:

Chi jen hsiao ch'ang	When the cock-man cries the
Sheng ching ming wang chih mien	advent of the day,
Fu chung yeh ming	The prudent monarch rises from
Hsiang ch'e an t'ien chih t'ing	his sleep.
	When in the night the bell of Fu
	rings out,
	Its sound pervades the darkness
	of the sky.

The 'cock-man' (*chi jen*) was an official in charge of delivering fowls for sacrifice; his head-dress was decorated with a cock's comb. For all official ceremonies he announced the daybreak and the hour when the ceremony was to start. The bell of Fu (*Fu chung*) was named after a family that in the ancient times of Chou had been responsible for casting bells.

The top lines refer to the conscientious Emperor who, as soon as dawn had been announced, would get up and busy himself with affairs of state instead of idling away his time in bed.

(1099) *Yūshi nao nokori no tsuki ni yukeba* ('as the traveller journeys by the dying moon's faint light'): from a poem by Chia Tao (fl. 793–865), included in *Wakan Rōei Shū*:

Chia jen chin shih yü ch'en chuang	At dawn when bells of Wei begin
Wei kung chung tung	to ring,
Yu tzu yu hsing yü ts'an yüeh	The lovely girl adorns herself
Han-ku chi ming	with care.
	When cocks crow at the barrier
	of Han Ku,
	The traveller journeys by the
	dying moon's faint light.

Wei was the name of a palace (Wei Kung); for the barrier of Han Ku
see note 637.

For Mistress of the Robes see notes 348 and 954. The bishop is (1100)
Empress Sadako's brother, Ryūen. Mama was a name commonly
given to nurses in the Heian period; a woman with this mammalian
name also appears in *The Tale of Genji*.

Hito no ie ni shiri wo sashiirete: lit. 'thrusting my buttocks into other (1101)
people's houses', i.e. imposing myself on people's hospitality. The
phrase has a crude ring and emphasizes the low social status of the
speaker.

> Mimagusa wo   (1102)
> Moyasu bakari no
> Haru no hi ni
> Yodono sac nado
> Nokorazaruramu

Shōnagon's poem is riddled with puns and would be quite incomprehensible to anyone unaware of the double meanings involved. The
unfortunate recipient of the poem would have had little chance of
understanding it even if he had been able to read the words.

Moyasu = (i) to make (something) sprout, (ii) to burn.
Hi = (i) sun, (ii) fire.
Yodono = (i) the Plain of Yodo (south of the capital), (ii) bedroom.

If we interpret the poem according to the first set of meanings
(sprout . . . sun . . . Yodo Plain), *mimagusa* (fodder) is likely to evoke
the word *nukusa* (new grass).

Using the second set of meanings (burn . . . fire . . . bedroom), we
get the following translation, which is of course immediately relevant
to the situation:

> If the spring-time fire is strong enough
> To make the fodder burn,
> Even the bedroom of a house like yours
> Could ill survive its heat.

Tanjaku (record-slip): narrow strip of paper or tag used among other (1103)
things for noting the amount of rice or other alms to be given to people.
By Shōnagon's time decorated *tanjaku* were also being used in Court
circles for writing poems. The poor man in the present section
obviously believes that Shōnagon has written down the amount of
rice he will receive as charity; instead all he gets is a callous, mocking

poem, which he cannot even understand. For 'good' people's attitude to the lower orders, of which this is a peculiarly unattractive example, see *W.S.P.*, p. 85.

(1104) *Katame mo akitsukōmatsurade wa*: lit. 'neither of my eyes is open', i.e. I am totally illiterate. As Kaneko remarks (*Hyōshaku*, p. 1056), the poem was almost certainly written in phonetic *kana* (i.e. without any Chinese characters), which makes the man's inability to read it even more striking.

(1105) Like many sections in *The Pillow Book* this reads like a character sketch for a possible story or novel. On the other hand, Shōnagon may be describing some real person.

The wicked stepmother theme was common in Heian fiction, but the unfortunate stepchild was usually a girl (e.g. note 1047).

(1106) Jōchō was famous for his great height (note 60); Lord Suisei (Suisei-kimi) has not been identified, but he was presumably known for his small stature. When Jōchō wore a long robe (*uchigi*), it looked like a jacket; conversely, when the diminutive Suisei wore a short jacket (*akome*); it covered him like a robe.

(1107)   Omoi dani
         Kakaranu yama no
         Sase-mogusa
         Tare ka Ibuki no
         Sato wa tsugeshi zo

This is a play on words and has very little poetic value. The central pun depends on the double use of *sato* = (i) village, (ii) (telling you) that (it was) thus (*sa to*). If we take the second sense, the last line of the translation becomes 'Who can have told you that I had such plans?' and the poem means, 'I have never even dreamt of going to Shimotsuke. Who can have told you such a thing?'

Ibuki is a mountain in the eastern province of Shimotsuke (App. 9a). Its environs were known for a particular type of sage-brush (*sase-mogusa*) that was used for moxabustion. The syllable *hi* in *omo(h)i* evokes the idea of burning (as in moxabustion) and is represented by the word 'fiery' in my translation.

It seems strange that anyone should have supposed that Shōnagon would leave the capital for such a wild and distant place as Shimotsuke; but at least it gave her the opportunity to compose a rather ingenious *uta*.

188

In the *Sangenbon* edition of *Makura no Sōshi* this section comes at
the end of the entire book and reads, 'Is it true that you are going to the
provinces?' Clearly the editors believed that this passage referred to
Shōnagon's final departure from the capital after the termination of
her service at Court; but such an interpretation seems rather dubious
(see Ikeda-Kishigami, p. 12).

Chikae kimi   (1108)
Tōtōmi no
Kami katete
Muge ni Hamana i.
Hashi mizariki ya

Here the central pun is on *hashi* = (i) bridge, (ii) scrap, fragment. If
hashi is taken in the second sense, the poem implies, 'Do you really
suppose that I have not had the slightest idea (scrap of an idea) about
your affair with the other woman?' and the last line of the translation
would then be 'For do you think I've never had an inkling [of your
faithless deeds]?'

Rather than ask the question bluntly, which would be a heinous
solecism, Shōnagon introduces the poetic conceit of Hamana
Bridge. This was a famous bridge in Tōtōmi Province, where the
man's father served as governor; it figures frequently in classical
poetry. *Kami* has the double sense of (i) gods, (ii) (provincial)
governor.

'I feel rather nervous [lit. 'my breast is rushing']. Why do you suppose (1109)
that is?' says the man.

'Because you are afraid that someone will find us here,' would be
the crude, prosaic reply. Instead Shōnagon produces an elegant poem,
in which she once more uses the image of Ōsaka (*Au-Saka*, Lovers'
Slope, notes 540, 640).

Ōsaka wa
Mune nomi tsune ni
Hashirii no
Mitsukuru hito ya
Aramu to omoeba

There are puns on *hashiri* = (i) gushing forth (see p. 173 for a
reference to water gushing out of Ōsaka Well), (ii) rushing (in the
phrase, *mune hashiru* = 'my heart is fluttering', i.e. 'I feel uneasy'),
and on *mi* = (i) seeing (in *mitsukuru*), (ii) water.

Shōnagon refers to *mo* (Index-Glossary) that are made of material (1110)
decorated with waves, shells, coral, etc.

189

This curious fashion (*katakkata no yudake*) was probably related to the custom of *idashiginu* (note 147). When travelling by carriage, people would frequently wear asymmetrical robes, which had very wide, low-hanging sleeves on one side and sleeves of ordinary width on the other; they would then let the wide sleeves trail conspicuously outside the carriage.

The reader should remember that even ordinary Court robes had very wide, heavy sleeves; the extra-wide sleeves known as *yudake* to which Shōnagon refers in this section must have been exceedingly cumbersome.

(1112) The Board of Censors (Danjō Dai) was entrusted with the investigation of offences committed in the capital and with numerous other police duties. By Shōnagon's time its functions had almost entirely been taken over by the Imperial Police; yet the office retained certain uncomfortable associations, and it seemed an inappropriate place of employment for a good-looking young aristocrat.

The Middle Captain in question is Minamoto no Yorisada (Index-Glossary), the son of Prince Tamehira; he was appointed Senior Assistant President (Daihitsu) in the Board of Censors in 992; he became a Captain in the Middle Palace Guards in 998, and the present section was presumably written after that date.

(1113) These were all the standard attributes of feminine beauty in the Heian period (*W.S.P.*, p. 203).

(1114) But according to Kaneko (*Hyōshaku*, p. 1067), the unfortunate lady was suffering from gastric convulsions.

Mune yamu refers to illness of the stomach as well as of the chest.

(1115) As a rule the voluminous hair of Heian women hung loosely over their shoulders (*W.S.P.*, loc. cit.), but this was inconvenient for someone who was ill in bed.

(1116) Cf. p. 5.

(1117) *Hito yori nao sukoshi nikushi to omou hito*: lit. 'a person whom I regard as still a little more unpleasant than others'.

(1118) Shōnagon seems to be suggesting that the reason one dislikes the child is that one imagines what a bad effect the ill-natured nurse must have had on his character, but the passage is obscure.

(1119) That is, she places her bedding closer to Shōnagon's than usual.

See p. 156. The river is the Hasegawa, which flows near the foot of the
hill on which Hase Temple was built.

Hito no shōsoko, ōsegoto nado: lit. 'such things as the message of an (1121)
[ordinary] person or the message of a superior'.

Some offence of a sexual nature, explains one of the commentaries (1122)
(*Hyōshaku*, p. 1073). It may have been an injudicious liaison.

The over-robes of the Court costumes worn by gentlemen of the 4th (1123)
and 5th Ranks were black and light vermilion respectively; the 6th
Rank over-robes were dark green. The same over-robes were used
during the night watch, but *sashinuki* were substituted for *ue no
hakama* (Index-Glossary).

Neko no tsuchi ni oritaru yō nite: lit. 'being like a cat that has descended (1124)
to earth (i.e. gone out of doors)'. The expression is obscure, but
evidently implies that elegant cats remain indoors. If a cat leaves the
house and goes outside (*tsuchi ni oritaru*), it loses its dignity; this is
the sort of thing that women should avoid.

Normally the soup and vegetables were eaten together with the rice; (1125)
to finish each of the dishes separately and with such speed was unspeakably ill-mannered (*W.S.P.*, p. 86).

Nani no kimi (a certain lady): the *Shunchobon* texts give *Naka no Kimi* (1126)
(a woman's name); I have followed *Sangenbon* (Ikeda-Kishigami,
p. 226).

Cf. p. 30. (1127)

From the *Shūi Shū* poem by Hitomaro: (1128)

Nagatsuki no	If you but came and lingered by my side,
Ariake no tsuki no	Like the moon that lingers in the dawning sky
Aritsutsu mo	During the Long-Night Month,
Kimi shi kimasaba	What need for me to languish as I do?
Ware koime ya mo	

The Long-Night Month (Nagatsuki) is the 9th. Hitomaro's poem ends
with a combination of particles that gives it the form of a rhetorical
question expecting a negative reply.

Rei no ushi yori mo shimozama ni uchiiite: lit. 'speaking coarsely even (1129)
more than [to] the usual oxen'.

Takashina no Naritō (Index-Glossary) served as Governor of Mino and Tamba, and later became the Assistant Director of the Crown Prince's Household (4th Rank). Shōnagon refers to him by the distinguished title of Ason.

(1131) See *W.S.P.*, pp. 233-4. This is one of the many passages in *The Pillow Book* where Shōnagon gives her idea of the perfect lover (cf. pp. 29-30).

(1132) *Tsumi uramu to okashikere*: lit. 'it is certainly amusing [to wonder] whether he will acquire a load of sin'.

(1133) Sections 318-20 correspond to sections 292-4 in the Ikeda-Kishigami (*Sangenbon*) text; they do not occur in the texts belonging to the *Shunchobon* tradition (App. 5).

(1134) *Kaku tsukaitsuru dani akazu oboyuru ōgi*: lit. 'the fan which, even when one was using it thus, seemed insufficient'.

(1135) *Minami narazu wa hingashi no hisashi*: lit. 'the eastern ante-room if it is not the southern one'. (See note 38.)
    This section describes a summer evening in the women's quarters of an elegant mansion. The woman behind the curtain of state is the mistress of the house, the visitor is presumably her lover.

(1136) For the nuances of olfactory impressions see *W.S.P.*, pp. 191-3.

(1137) *Oto mo tatezu*: lit. 'it does not even make any noise'.

(1138) See note 1099.

(1139) *Ōri* (mud-shield): long leather flaps hanging down on both sides of the horse.

(1140) *Senju Darani* (Magic Incantation of the Thousand Hands): one section of the *Senju Kyō* (Thousand Hand Sutra) (note 831), which was especially associated with Shingon. It was recited to ward off illnesses, discord, slander, and other evils.

(1141) *Mono no ke ni itō nayamu hito*: lit. 'a person suffering painfully from an evil spirit'. For a discussion of Heian beliefs about evil spirits (*mono no ke*) as a cause of illness, and about the method of curing such illness by exorcism, see *W.S.P.*, pp. 135-9. Heian exorcist practices were closely associated with Shingon and were frequently of Indian origin.

Tok(k)o (wand): a type of mace, particularly connected with Shingon NOTES
and used by priests, exorcists, etc., who brandished it in all directions (1142)
while reciting their prayers and magic formulae.

The groans and wails come from the evil spirit, which has temporarily (1143)
been transferred to the medium and is now being painfully subdued
by the priest's incantations.

4 p.m. (App. 3). (1144)

Kaneko (*Hyōshaku*, p. 1089) remarks on the similarity between the (1145)
priest's well-chosen, rather pompous words and those of many
fashionable doctors in modern times.

Cf. p. 184. (1146)

Boys normally celebrated their coming of age between the ages of ten (1147)
and fifteen; during this ceremony (*gembuku*) their hair, which until
then they had worn loose, was trimmed and tied into a knot, and the
boys received an adult head-dress (*kan*). The older pages mentioned
by Shōnagon have evidently not yet been through the *gembuku* even
though they have started growing beards; hence the phrase *omowazu
ni* (unexpectedly, to one's surprise).

High clogs (*ashida*) were a rough, rustic form of footwear and looked (1148)
incongruous with a *hakama*. The same type of incongruity can be
found in modern Japan, where students sometimes wear *geta* (clogs)
at the same time as a *hakama*.

Even if they were in a hurry, well-bred people walked in a slow, (1149)
dignified manner.

Many *yin-yang* beliefs and practices became associated in Japan with (1150)
Shintō (*W.S.P.*, pp. 124 ff.), and conversely many Shintō services,
such as *harae* (purification), were performed by the *yin-yang*
practitioners known as Onyōji (Masters of Divination). Such was the
complexity of Heian eclecticism, however, that Buddhist priests also
performed services like *harae* which had no connexion whatsoever
with their own religion.

The paper head-dress (*kami-kōburi*) to which Shōnagon refers was
a triangular hat fixed to the front of the head and tied in the back. It
was worn by Shintō priests, exorcists, and others, but not normally
by Buddhist priests, whose heads were completely shaven. When

performing an essentially non-Buddhist service like *harae*, however, Buddhist priests frequently did wear these triangular hats. This produced an ugly, incongruous effect, much as if a Roman Catholic priest were to don a magician's cap in order to perform a primitive type of service.

(1151) Cf. note 115 for the prejudice against daytime naps.

(1152) Shōnagon obviously found it more unpleasant to see ugly people when they were lying down than when they were up and about. I have omitted one redundant section in this passage: *ware nikuge nari tote, okiirubeki ni mo arazu ka shi* ('ugly people really need not stay up all night for fear that people will see them lying down and find them unattractive').

(1153) Because the scarlet colour hides their dark skin. For the importance of white skin see *W.S.P.*, p. 203.

(1154) This section occurs only in the *Bōhon* text and is of dubious authenticity; it is included by both Kaneko and Ikeda-Kishigami as their final sections.

Minamoto no Tsunefusa served as Governor of Ise from 995 (12th Month) to 996 (12th Month), and he can certainly not have seen the entire manuscript on this occasion (see App. 4 and note 1155). He was not appointed Middle Captain of the Left Guards Division (Sachūjō) until the end of 998, which is therefore the earliest possible date for the writing of this section; Tsunefusa remained Middle Captain until 1015, when he became Provisional Middle Counsellor.

If the incident is to be included, it should in any case come before section 326, which is clearly intended as a conclusion to the entire book.

(1155) It appears that Korechika also presented Emperor Ichijō with a quantity of paper (good paper being in short supply even at Court) and that the Emperor had decided to use his allotment for making a copy of the huge Chinese historical work, *Shih chi* (Index-Glossary).

Korechika became Minister of the Centre in the 8th Month of 994; he was forced out of the capital about a year and a half later. It seems improbable that Shōnagon started writing her *Pillow Book* before the winter of 994. (See App. 4 and note 942.)

(1156) *Makura ni koso wa shihaberame* ('make them into a pillow'): i.e. a pillow book. Here we have one likely explanation of the title of

Shōnagon's book (for a detailed discussion of the title and its possible origins see Ikeda-Kishigami, pp. 6–7, where about a dozen distinct theories are suggested). *Makura no sōshi* ('pillow book') referred to a notebook or collection of notebooks kept in some accessible but relatively private place, and in which the author would from time to time record impressions, daily events, poems, letters, stories, ideas, descriptions of people, etc. (For *sōshi* see note 942.) The phrase *makura no sōshi* does not appear to have been original with Sei Shōnagon; but her work is the only extant one of its type with that title as well as being by far the oldest surviving book of the typically Japanese genre known as *zuihitsu*.

Beaujard suggests (*S.S.S.T.*, p. 314) that the title *Makura no Sōshi* may have been given to the book because *makura* ('pillow') is close to *makkura* ('complete darkness'); in this case the word would refer to the extreme obscurity of Shōnagon's work and also perhaps to the opening words of section 326. Apart from being far-fetched, this theory takes it for granted that Shōnagon's early readers found her book peculiarly hard to understand—an entirely unwarranted assumption. It also ignores the probability that the phrase *makura no sōshi* was frequently used in Shōnagon's time to describe books like hers.

In later times the name *makura no sōshi* came to designate books of erotic illustrations depicting the standard forms of sexual intercourse; such books were frequently included in a bride's trousseau as a remedy for her supposed innocence in these matters.

Okashi . . . medetashi ('charming . . . splendid'): *okashi* (Index- (1157) Glossary) is the most common of all Shōnagon's adjectives, occurring 439 times in *The Pillow Book*, in which adjectives appear altogether 3,660 times; *medetashi* is the fourth most frequent adjective, occurring 129 times. Tanaka Shigetarō has calculated in *Kokubungaku* (November 1964, p. 141) that proportionately *okashi* is used five times as often in *The Pillow Book* as in *The Tale of Genji*.

See App. 10. (1158)
The clause ending with *iidashitaraba koso* ('if I had indeed spoken about poems . . .'), though grammatically appearing to express a contrary-to-fact condition, must surely be understood to have a weak causal sense; possibly *-taraba* is a copyist's error for *-tareba*. Yamanaka (op. cit., p. 114) and other scholars question the authenticity of this passage.

Ayashū ('strangely') (*Sangenbon* texts) seems to make better sense (1159) than *meyasuku* ('pleasantly') (*Shunchobon* texts).

Since Shōnagon's judgement tended to be the exact opposite of other
(1160) people's, it was only natural that they should praise a book (her own)
which she considered to be deficient in so many respects.

(1161) *Hito ni miekemu*: lit. 'that it should have been seen by people'.

APPENDIX 1

ANNUAL OBSERVANCES AND OTHER CEREMONIES
MENTIONED IN *THE PILLOW BOOK*

Day	First Month
1st	New Year's Day (Chōga) (note 4)
2nd	Tooth-Hardening (Hagatame) (note 220)
1st day of the Hare	Presentation of Hare-Wands (Uzue) (note 321)
7th	Festival of Young Herbs (Wakana no Sekku) (note 5)
7th	Festival of the Blue Horses (Aouma no Sechie) (note 8)
8th–14th	Assembly of Purification (Go-Saie) (note 1058)
9th–11th	Period of (provincial) appointments (Jimoku) (note 19)
15th	Full-Moon Gruel (Mochigayu) (note 16)
18th	Archery contests (Noriyumi) (note 451)
	Second Month
11th	The Examination (Reken) (note 611)
1st day of the Fire	Worship of Confucius (Shakuten) (note 612)
1st day of the Monkey	Kasuga Festival (Kasuga Matsuri) (note 727)
(During four consecutive days)	Seasonal Sacred Readings (Ki no Mi-Dokyō) (note 360)
	Third Month
3rd	Peach Festival (Momo no Sekku) or Jōmi (including Winding Water banquets, displays of dolls, etc.) (note 21)
13th	The Chancellor's pilgrimage to Kasuga Shrine (note 402)
2nd day of the Horse	Special Festival at Iwashimizu Shrine (Rinji no Matsuri) (note 66)
	Fourth Month
2nd day of the Bird	Kamo Festival (Kamo Matsuri) (note 24)

197

Day	
5th	*Fifth Month* Iris Festival (Ayame no Sekku) (note 206)
14th	*Sixth Month* Feast of the Sacred Spirit (Goryō E) (note 323)
Last day	Great Purification (Ōharai) (note 725)
7th	*Seventh Month* Weaver Festival (Tanabata Matsuri) (note 55)
13th–16th	Festival of the Dead (Urabon) (note 662)
28th–29th	Wrestling tournament (Sumai) (note 592)
11th	*Eighth Month* The Inspection (Kōjō) (note 611)
1st day of the Fire	Worship of Confucius (Shakuten) (note 612)
(During four consecutive days)	Seasonal Sacred Readings (Ki no Mi-Dokyō) (note 360)
9th	*Ninth Month* Chrysanthemum Festival (Kiku no Sekku) (note 56)
1st day of the Monkey	*Eleventh Month* Kasuga Festival (Kasuga Matsuri) (note 727)
2nd day of the Ox	Dais Rehearsal (Chōdai no Kokoromi) (note 430)
2nd day of the Tiger	Banquet with songs and dances (note 432)
2nd day of the Hare	Attendants' Dance (Warawamai) (note 432)
2nd day of the Hare	Festival of the First Fruits (Niinami no Matsuri) (note 419)
2nd day of the Hare	Lesser Abstinence (Omi) (note 411)
2nd day of the Dragon	Gosechi Dances (Gosechi no Mai) (note 432)
Last day of the Bird	Special Festival at Kamo Shrine (Rinji no Matsuri) (note 66)
19th–22nd	*Twelfth Month* Naming of the Buddhas (Butsumyō) (note 325)
Last day	Festival of the Spirits (Tama Matsuri) (note 220)
Last day	Great Purification (Ōharai) (note 725)

198

APPENDIX 2

CHARACTERS IN *THE PILLOW BOOK*

The following are the principal characters mentioned by Sei Shōnagon; for identifications see Index-Glossary.

1. FUJIWARA NO KORECHIKA

Section 22: visits Seiryō Palace and recites the Mount Mimoro poem (p. 16).

Section 77: recites a poem by Po Chü-i (p. 70).

Section 95: orders Shōnagon to write a poem for the Night of the Monkey (p. 110).

Section 122: picks up his father's shoes (p. 134).

Section 177: visits Empress Sadako, his sister, on a snowy day and embarrasses Shōnagon, who has just come into waiting (p. 181).

Section 256: attends the Dedication Service at Shakuzen Temple and helps Shōnagon and her companions out of their carriage; teases Shōnagon about her robe (p. 232).

Section 291: recites a Chinese poem about an emperor rising from his sleep; impresses Shōnagon with another Chinese quotation (p. 251).

Section 326: gives the Empress some notebooks, which Shōnagon later receives and uses to write her *Pillow Book* (p. 267).

2. FUJIWARA NO MICHINAGA

Section 122: makes obeisance to Michitaka, his brother (pp. 134–5).

Section 256: refuses to be seen twice in the same under-robe (p. 230).

3. FUJIWARA NO MICHITAKA (the Chancellor)

Section 22: adapts a poem for Emperor Enyū (p. 17).

Section 37: attends the Eight Lessons for Confirmation (p. 37).

Section 100: is delighted by his daughters' beauty; teases Shōnagon; encourages everyone to get drunk; insists that his daughter must go to the Emperor (p. 116).

Section 122: jokes with the ladies-in-waiting; Michinaga, his brother, makes obeisance to him (p. 134).

Section 256: orders that a Dedication of the Full Canon be held at Shakuzen Temple; teases the Empress; orders his men to remove cherry blossoms

199

secretly from the Empress's garden; praises the Empress's ladies-in-waiting; declares that he must have a good karma (p. 219).

4. FUJIWARA NO MICHIYORI

Section 100: escorts the Emperor to the Palace (p. 119).
Section 256: jokes about Shigemasa (p. 228).

FUJIWARA NO SADAKO: see Sadako.

5. FUJIWARA NO SAISHŌ

Section 22: has difficulty in remembering Kokin Shū poems (p. 17).
Section 79: exchanges Chinese quotations with Tadanobu (p. 78).
Section 136: explains why the grass has been allowed to grow in the Empress's garden (p. 149).
Section 256: Michitaka compares her to Shōnagon; she resents the Empress's partiality for Shōnagon (p. 230).
Section 280: copies a poem for the Empress (p. 244).

6. FUJIWARA NO TADANOBU

Section 78: maligns Shōnagon and puts her to the test (p. 71).
Section 79: pays her an abortive visit; exchanges Chinese quotations with Lady Saishō (p. 76).
Section 80: attempts to discover Shōnagon's whereabouts (p. 79).
Section 87: comments on the Imperial instruments (p. 99).
Section 89: impresses the younger ladies-in-waiting by his scent (p. 99).
Section 121: serves as Imperial messenger after the Imperial visit to Yawata (p. 133).
Section 128: quotes a very appropriate poem after the memorial service for Michitaka; urges Shōnagon to have a closer relationship with him (p. 139).
Section 160: tells Shōnagon he intends to recite a poem by Po Chü-i (p. 166).
Section 161: recites a Chinese poem by Sugawara no Michizane; resents being teased by Shōnagon; recalls their conversation several months later; uses a secret go language with Shōnagon; Shōnagon admires his recitation of a Chinese poem (p. 167).

7. FUJIWARA NO TAKAIE

Section 98: gives the Empress a fan (p. 112).
Section 256: helps the ladies in and out of their carriages during the service of Dedication (p. 226).

8. FUJIWARA NO YUKINARI

Section 51: converses with Ben no Naishi; is disliked by Court ladies; avoids looking at Shōnagon; secretly watches Shōnagon and Lady Shikibu in their room (p. 52).

Section 77: plays the flute (p. 70).

Section 126: sends Shōnagon some square cakes and a Submission (p. 136).

Section 129: he and Shōnagon exchange notes that lead to their famous poems about Ōsaka Barrier; he praises Shōnagon for her talents (p. 140).

Section 130: accompanies the group of men who bring a branch of bamboo to the Empress's Office, and praises Shōnagon for her skill in recognizing the allusion (p. 142).

9. ICHIJŌ (the Emperor) (selected entries)

Section 22: orders Shōnagon and the other ladies to write down some old poems; tells a story about Emperor Enyū, his father (p. 16).

Section 28: plays the flute with Takatō, and makes sure that Suketada will not hear a song that makes fun of him (p. 30).

Section 51: surprises Shōnagon and Lady Shikibu in their bedroom (p. 54).

Section 83: praises Shōnagon at the end of the snow-mountain episode (p. 90).

Section 87: takes the Mumyō flute to the Empress's rooms (p. 98).

Section 100: dazzles Shōnagon as he leaves the Palace in his Court robes (p. 119).

Section 101: praises Shōnagon for her quotation of a Chinese poem (p. 120).

Section 121: returns from the shrine at Yawata and halts his palanquin before the gallery of the Empress Dowager, his mother (p. 133).

Section 131: teases Tōzammi about the mysterious letter she has received (p. 144).

Section 161: is impressed by Shōnagon's knowledge of a Chinese story (p. 170).

10. MINAMOTO NO MASAHIRO

Section 52: behaves in a peculiar way during the roll-call; leaves his shoes on the serving-board (p. 56).

Section 104: speaks and behaves in other strange ways (p. 121).

11. MINAMOTO NO NARINOBU

Section 12: jokes about Bishop Jōchō (p. 13).

Section 214: has an amazing memory for voices (p. 200).

Section 271: visits Shōnagon on a rainy night, but she refuses to see him (p. 237).

12. MINAMOTO NO NOBUKATA

Section 160: fails to recognize Tadanobu's Chinese quotation (p. 167).

Section 161: fails to remember Tadanobu's conversation with Shōnagon; tries to use Tadanobu's secret *go* language when speaking to Shōnagon; endears himself to Shōnagon by reciting a Chinese poem in Tadanobu's style, but later she makes fun of him for continually referring to the poem (p. 168).

Section 162: Shōnagon teases him about his liaison with Lady Sakyō; he resents Shōnagon's attitude, yet eventually breaks with Sakyō (p. 170).

13. MINAMOTO NO TSUNEFUSA

Section 78: tells Shōnagon about Tadanobu's test (p. 73).

Section 80: Shōnagon confides to him where she is staying (p. 78).

Section 325: removes Shōnagon's notes, which are then circulated at Court (p. 267).

14. RYŪEN

Section 87: asks the Empress, his sister, for her flute (p. 98).

Section 129: is impressed with the Yukinari-Shōnagon exchange of poems and shows them to the Empress (p. 141).

Section 256: stays with the women during the service of Dedication (p. 232).

15. SADAKO (the Empress) (selected entries)

Section 8: moves to Narimasa's house; reprimands her ladies about their appearance; tells Shōnagon not to tease Narimasa (p. 6).

Section 51: surprises Shōnagon and Lady Shikibu in their bedroom (p. 54).

Section 82: sends a message to Shōnagon asking her to return into service (p. 81).

Section 83: scolds her ladies for making fun of the beggar-nun and tells them to give the woman a new robe; plays a trick on Shōnagon by ordering that the snow mountain be removed secretly (p. 82).

Section 86: makes elaborate arrangements for the Gosechi dances (p. 94).

Section 88: holds her black lute lengthwise and impresses Shōnagon with her beauty (p. 99).

Section 95: reprimands her ladies for not producing any poems about their *hototogisu* expedition; agrees not to oblige Shōnagon to write any more poems (p. 108).

Section 97: tells Shōnagon that she should try to come first in everyone's affections (p. 112).

Section 98: receives a fan from Takaie, her brother (p. 112).

Section 99: puts Nobutsune to the test in poetry (p. 113).

Section 100: impresses Shōnagon as being even more beautiful than the Shigei Sha (p. 116).

Section 122: declares that it is better to become a Buddha than to be a Chancellor (p. 135).

Section 128: holds a memorial service for Michitaka, her father, and is impressed by Tadanobu's quotation (p. 139).

Section 130: congratulates Shōnagon on recognizing a Chinese quotation (p. 143).

Section 131: teases Tōzammi about the mysterious letter she has received (p. 144).

Section 136: despite her ladies' suspicions about Shōnagon, begs her to return to Court; tells a story that illustrates how easily one can forget familiar things (p. 149).

Section 177: treats Shōnagon, who has newly come into her service, with great consideration; Shōnagon wonders how such beauty can exist in this world; tries to prevent Korechika, her brother, from embarrassing Shōnagon (p. 178).

Section 211: teases Shōnagon about the gentleman with an umbrella (p. 198).

Section 212: sends a poem to Shōnagon during the Iris Festival (p. 199).

Section 255: sends Shōnagon twenty rolls of paper; later she sends her a straw mat as a joke (p. 218).

Section 256: attends the Dedication Service at Shakuzen Temple and invites Shōnagon to sit close to her (p. 219).

Sections 280-1: sends Shōnagon poems urging her to return to the Palace (pp. 244-5).

Section 292: laughingly asks her ladies how they could be so mad as to tease the poor man who has lost his house in a fire (p. 253).

Section 306: sends a priest to perform Sacred Readings for a girl who is ill (p. 256).

Section 326: gives some notebooks to Shōnagon 'to make into a pillow' (p. 267).

16. TACHIBANA NO NORIMITSU

Section 78: is proud about the success of Shōnagon, his 'younger sister', in passing Tadanobu's test (p. 74).

Section 80: tries to hide Shōnagon's whereabouts from Tadanobu; receives a piece of seaweed from her, but cannot understand its significance; expresses his dislike of poetry; parts from Shōnagon on bad terms (p. 79).

17. TAIRA NO NARIMASA

Section 8: the Empress and her ladies move into his house; Shōnagon makes fun of his gate; he pays her an abortive visit at night; Shōnagon makes fun of his way of speaking; he tells Shōnagon that his brother would like to meet her (p. 6).

APPENDIX 3

CHINESE ZODIAC

The twelve signs or 'branches' (*jūni shi*) were as follows:

(i) Rat (Ne), (ii) Ox (Ushi), (iii) Tiger (Tora), (iv) Hare (U), (v) Dragon (Tatsu), (vi) Snake (Mi), (vii) Horse (Uma), (viii) Sheep (Hitsuji), (ix) Monkey (Saru), (x) Bird (Tori), (xi) Dog (Inu), (xii) Boar (I).

They referred to: (*a*) time (e.g. Hour of the Snake = 10 a.m. to midnight), (*b*) direction (e.g. Dragon-Snake = south-east), (*c*) day of the month (e.g. 1st Day of the Snake), (*d*) year (e.g. Year of the Snake = 6th year of any sexagenary cycle).

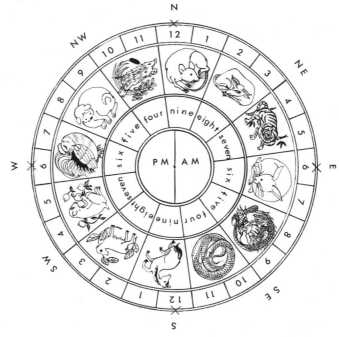

Information given on the diagram,[1] from the outside to the inside, is as follows: (1) the compass directions, (2) the hours of the day and night (mid-

---

[1] This diagram and the illustrations and maps in Appendixes 8 and 9 were drawn by Mrs. Nanae Momiyana.

204

night at the top, noon at the bottom), (3) drawings of the twelve 'branches', each corresponding to one watch (*toki*) or two Western hours, (4) the number of strokes of the gong sounded at each new watch (see notes 745, 1033).

Months (see note 3) were either twenty-nine or thirty days long, with an intercalary month added about once every three years. Days were designated either by their order in the month (e.g. 3rd day of the 5th Month) or in terms of the twelve branches of the Chinese Zodiac and the ten calendar signs (*jikkan*) as follows:

THE SEXAGENARY CYCLE

	Rat	Ox	Tiger	Hare	Dragon	Snake	Horse	Sheep	Monkey	Bird	Dog	Boar
1. Elder brother of wood (*kinoe*)	1	..	51	..	41	..	31	..	21	..	11	..
2. Younger brother of wood (*kinoto*)	..	2	..	52	..	42	..	32	..	22	..	12
3. Elder brother of fire (*hinoe*)	13	..	3	..	53	..	43	..	33	..	23	..
4. Younger brother of fire (*hinoto*)	..	14	..	4	..	54	..	44	..	34	..	24
5. Elder brother of earth (*tsuchinoe*)	25	..	15	..	5	..	55	..	45	..	35	..
6. Younger brother of earth (*tsuchi no to*)	..	26	..	16	..	6	..	56	..	46	..	36
7. Elder brother of metal (*kanoe*)	37	..	27	..	17	..	7	..	57	..	47	..
8. Younger brother of metal (*kanoto*)	..	38	..	28	..	18	..	8	..	58	..	48
9. Elder brother of water (*mizunoe*)	49	..	39	..	29	..	19	..	9	..	59	..
10. Younger brother of water (*mizunoto*)	..	50	..	40	..	30	..	20	..	10	..	60

If, for example, a month started on the 15th day of the sexagenary cycle (as shown above), the 3rd day of that month would be designated as: (1) the (1st) Day of the Dragon, (2) the (1st) Day of the Elder Brother of Metal, (3) a combination of (1) and (2). In any given month there was a maximum of three days named after each of the twelve 'branches' and three days named after each of the ten calendar signs. These days could be identified by the prefixes *jō*, *chū*, and *ge* for the 1st, 2nd, and 3rd respectively. Thus the Jōmi Festival (see Index-Glossary) was so named because originally it fell on the 1st Day of the Snake (Mi).

APPENDIX 4

CHRONOLOGY

Dates are given according to the lunar calendar; '23.6', for example, means the 23rd day of the 6th lunar month. (For the discrepancy between the lunar and Julian calendars see note 3.) Era names (*nengō*) are given in brackets after the Western years; thus 'Kanna 2' means the 2nd year of the *nengō* that started in A.D. 985. Italicized entries are from *The Pillow Book*; datable sections are ' listed at the end of the Chronology.

986 (*Kanna 2*)

23.6   Emperor Kazan secretly visited Kazan Temple and took holy orders.
Emperor Ichijō acceded to the Throne (aged six).

24.6   Fujiwara no Kaneie, the father of Michitaka, was appointed Regent and became Head of the (Fujiwara) Clan.

6th Month   *Shōnagon heard the Eight Lessons at Ko Shirakawa* (section 37; note 167).

5.7   Emperor Ichijō's mother, Fujiwara no Senshi, became Empress Dowager.

22.7   The enthronement ceremony of Emperor Ichijō took place.

987 (*Eien 1*)

7.1 (?)   *Shōnagon visited the Imperial Palace to view the Ceremony of the Blue Horses* (section 3; note 10).

14.10   Emperor Ichijō visited the residence of the Regent, Fujiwara no Kaneie.

15.12   Emperor Ichijō made a pilgrimage to Kamo Shrine.

988 (*Eien 2*)

25.3   Emperor Ichijō celebrated the sixtieth birthday of the Regent, Fujiwara no Kaneie.

16.9   Fujiwara no Kaneie held a banquet at his new residence in Nijō.

27.10   The Priestly Retired Emperor, Enyū, visited Fujiwara no Kaneie in Nijō.

989 (*Eiso 1*)

16.2   Emperor Ichijō made a pilgrimage to Enyū Temple.

22.3   Emperor Ichijō made his first pilgrimage to Kasuga Shrine.

20.12   Fujiwara no Kaneie was appointed Prime Minister.

990 (*Shōryaku 1*)

5.1   Emperor Ichijō, aged ten, celebrated his coming-of-age ceremony.

25.1   Fujiwara no Sadako, Michitaka's daughter, became an Imperial consort at the age of fourteen.

11.2   Fujiwara no Sadako was appointed Imperial Lady (Nyōgo).

?   *Shōnagon probably entered Court service during this year as Empress Sadako's lady-in-waiting* (section 177; note 802).

5.5   Fujiwara no Kaneie was appointed Chancellor.

8.5   Fujiwara no Kaneie took holy orders, and Fujiwara no Michitaka succeeded him as Chancellor.

13.5   Fujiwara no Michitaka became Head of the (Fujiwara) Clan.

26.5   Fujiwara no Michitaka was appointed Regent.

6th Month   Kiyowara no Motosuke, Shōnagon's father, died in Higo at the age of eighty-two.

2.7   Fujiwara no Kaneie died at the age of sixty-one.

Between 3rd and 8th Months (?)   *Fujiwara no Nobutaka and Fujiwara no Takamitsu made a pilgrimage to Mitake* (section 112; note 553).

5.10   Fujiwara no Sadako was appointed Second Empress; Fujiwara no Nobuko became First Empress.

991 (*Shōryaku 2*)

1st Month   Emperor Ichijō visited his father, the Priestly Retired Emperor, Enyū, in Enyū Temple where he lay ill.

3.2   The Priestly Retired Emperor, Enyū, died at the age of thirty-two.

7.9   Fujiwara no Tamemitsu was appointed Prime Minister.

16.9   Fujiwara no Senshi, the widow of Emperor Enyū, being in ill health, took holy orders and received the name Higashi Sanjō no In.

3.11   Higashi Sanjō no In moved into the residence of her brother, Fujiwara no Michinaga.

(12th Month   Shōnagon entered Court service, according to Kaneko Motoomi.)

992 (*Shōryaku 3*)

6.2   The one-year period of mourning for Emperor Enyū came to an end; *Shōnagon described this as 'a most moving time'; a practical joke was played on Tōzammi* (section 131; note 649).

3rd Month (?)   *Shōnagon visited a friend's house to perform abstinence* (section 280; note 1067).

6th Month   Fujiwara no Tamemitsu, the Prime Minister, died at the age of fifty.

8th Month (?)   *At some time between 992 (8th Month) and 994 (8th Month) Fujiwara no Korechika visited the Palace and Emperor Ichijō was awakened by a rooster* (section 291; note 1096).

12th Month   *Empress Sadako, residing at the Southern Palace, ordered a dress to be sewn in a hurry* (section 91; note 445).

7.12   Empress Sadako returned to the Imperial Palace from the Southern Palace.

993 (*Shōryaku 4*)

3.1   Emperor Ichijō made his annual New Year visit to his mother, Higashi Sanjō no In.

22.1   There was an Imperial banquet attended by Higashi Sanjō no In and Empress Sadako.

22.4   Fujiwara no Michitaka was appointed Chancellor and resigned as Regent.

Summer   There was an epidemic of smallpox and an amnesty was proclaimed.

Intercalary 20.10   Sugawara no Michizane was posthumously appointed Prime Minister.

(Early spring or early winter   Shōnagon entered Court service, according to Ikeda Kikan, Kishigami Shinji, etc.)

Between 993 (4th Month) and 994 (8th Month)   *Fujiwara no Michitaka came out through the black door and his brother, Michinaga, did obeisance to him* (section 122; note 599).

15.11 (?)   *Empress Sadako sent Gosechi dancers to the Palace* (section 86; note 414).

27.11   Emperor Ichijō made his first pilgrimage to Ōhara No.

22.12   *A screen depicting the horrors of hell was taken to Empress Sadako's Palace; Korechika recited a Chinese poem* (section 77; note 325).

994 (*Shōryaku 5*)

23.1   Fujiwara no Michitaka held a great banquet.

17.2   Fires broke out in Koki Palace and other palaces.

2nd Month   *Shōnagon attended services at Shakuzen Temple* (section 256; note 944).

3rd Month   *Emperor Ichijō ordered Empress Sadako's ladies to write poems* (section 22; note 74).

3rd Month (?)   *Empress Sadako played the lute* (section 88; note 440).

9.5   Lady Senyōden, the Crown Prince's consort, gave birth to a son, the future Emperor Goichijō.

5th Month   *Fujiwara no Tadanobu visited the Empress's apartments in Seiryō Palace and impressed her ladies with his scent* (section 89; note 441).

7.8   Fujiwara no Michitaka organized a wrestling tournament.

28.8   Fujiwara no Korechika was appointed Minister of the Centre.

After 8th Month   *Fujiwara no Korechika presented some notebooks to Empress Sadako, who gave them to Shōnagon 'to make into a pillow'* (section 326; note 1155).

Autumn (?)   Shōnagon may have started writing *The Pillow Book* about this time.

13.11   Fujiwara no Michitaka fell ill.

12th Month   There was a solar eclipse, robberies occurred in the provinces, and a great epidemic broke out.

995 (*Chōtoku 1*)

2.1   Owing to illness, Fujiwara no Michitaka was unable to appear at Court.

9.1   Several residences on Nijō no Ōji were destroyed by fire, including those of Fujiwara no Michitaka and Fujiwara no Korechika.

19.1   Fujiwara no Michitaka's second daughter, the Shigei Sha, became a consort of the Crown Prince.

3.2   The palace attendants of Higashi Sanjō no In fought with those of Empress Sadako.

5.2   Fujiwara no Michitaka resigned as Chancellor.

12.2 (?)   *Fujiwara no Yukinari sent rice cakes to Shōnagon* (section 126; note 491).

18.2   *The Shigei Sha visited Empress Sadako, her sister* (section 100; note 613).

26.2   Fujiwara no Michitaka confirmed his resignation as Chancellor.

End of 2nd Month   *Fujiwara no Tadanobu and Shōnagon exchanged messages and he put her to the test* (section 78; note 333).

9.3   Owing to his father's illness, Fujiwara no Korechika assumed the duties of Imperial Examiner (Nairan).

6.4   Fujiwara no Michitaka took holy orders.

10.4   Fujiwara no Michitaka died at the age of forty-two.

27.4   Fujiwara no Michikane was appointed Chancellor.

28.4   Fujiwara no Michikane became Head of the (Fujiwara) Clan.

Between 995 (4th Month) and 996 (4th Month)   *Fujiwara no Takaie presented a fan to his sister, Empress Sadako* (section 98; note 479).

8.5   Fujiwara no Michikane died at the age of thirty-four.

4th and 5th Months   There was a great epidemic, in which many high officials died.

11.5   Fujiwara no Michinaga was appointed Imperial Examiner (Nairan).

5th Month (?)   *Shōnagon and her companions went to hear the* hototogisu *and failed to produce any poems* (section 95; note 454).

11.6   Fujiwara no Michiyori, Empress Sadako's brother, died at the age of twenty-five.

19.6   Fujiwara no Michinaga was appointed Minister of the Right and became Head of the (Fujiwara) Clan.

28.6   Empress Sadako moved into the Empress's Office.

6th Month   *Shōnagon and the other ladies-in-waiting moved with the Empress into the Dining Hall of the High Court Nobles and visited the Time Office* (section 159; note 742).

8.7   Empress Sadako returned to the Palace.

24.7   There was a dispute between Fujiwara no Michinaga and his nephew, Fujiwara no Korechika.

27.7   There was a fight between the attendants of Fujiwara no Michinaga and those of Fujiwara no Korechika's brother, Takaie.

10.9   *Empress Sadako held a memorial service for her father, Fujiwara no Michitaka, in the Empress's Office; after the service Fujiwara no Tadanobu quoted a Chinese poem, deeply impressing the Empress and Shōnagon* (section 128; note 626).

21.10   Emperor Ichijō made a pilgrimage to Iwashimizu Hachiman Shrine at Yawata.

22.10   *Emperor Ichijō visited his mother, Higashi Sanjō no In, on his return from Yawata* (section 121; note 597).

995–6   *Shōnagon observed examples of Masahiro's strange behaviour* (section 104; note 532).

996 (*Chōtoku 2*)

16.1   The attendants of Fujiwara no Korechika and Fujiwara no Takaie shot at the Priestly Retired Emperor, Kazan.

11.2   The Doctors of Law (Myōbō Hakase) determined the guilt of Fujiwara no Korechika and Fujiwara no Takaie.

End of 2nd Month   *Fujiwara no Tadanobu visited Shōnagon in Umetsubo Palace and was disappointed not to find her* (section 79; note 344).

3rd Month   *Emperor Ichijō took the Mumyō flute to Empress Sadako's rooms* (section 87; note 433).

30.3   *Fujiwara no Tadanobu and Minamoto no Nobukata visited Shōnagon in the Palace* (section 160; note 749).

Between 995 (12th Month) and 996 (12th Month)   *Minamoto no Tsunefusa discovered Shōnagon's notes and they came into circulation* (section 325, note 1154).

24.4   Empress Sadako, being pregnant, moved to the Palace of the Second Ward; Fujiwara no Korechika was appointed Provisional Governor-General of the Government Headquarters in Kyūshū, and Fujiwara no Takaie was appointed Provisional Governor of Izumo Province.

1.5   Empress Sadako took holy orders.

1.5   Fujiwara no Takaie left the capital.

4.5   Fujiwara no Korechika left the capital.

15.5   Fujiwara no Korechika and Fujiwara no Takaie were detained in Harima and Tajima Provinces respectively.

4th or 5th Month   *Shōnagon told the Empress that beautiful paper or straw mats consoled her when she felt depressed; later she received twenty rolls of paper from the Empress and used it to write her notes* (section 255; note 938).

About 7th Month   *Shōnagon was visited at home by a gentleman who advised her to return to the Empress* (section 136; note 679).

9.8   Fujiwara no Yoshiko became an Imperial Concubine.

7.10   Fujiwara no Takaie requested permission to return to the capital.

10.10   Fujiwara no Korechika, who had secretly returned to the capital, was ordered to be expelled from the city and sent to his post.

10th Month   Empress Sadako's mother, the widow of Fujiwara no Michitaka, died.

1.11   Fujiwara no Michinaga made a pilgrimage to Kasuga Shrine.

2.12   Fujiwara no Motoko became an Imperial Concubine.

16.12   Empress Sadako gave birth to her first child, Princess Osako.

All year   There were rice shortages and famines.

During the year (?)   *Minamoto no Masahiro behaved strangely when serving as Chamberlain on duty during the roll-call* (section 52; note 270).

997 (*Chōtoku 3*)

25.3   Owing to the illness of Higashi Sanjō no In, a general amnesty was proclaimed.

5.4   Thanks to the amnesty, Fujiwara no Korechika and Fujiwara no Takaie were recalled to the capital.

21.4   Fujiwara no Takaie returned to the capital.

22.6   Emperor Ichijō visited Higashi Sanjō no In because of her illness.

22.6   Empress Sadako moved to the Empress's Office with Princess Osako.

6th or 7th Month   *Shōnagon and her companions amused themselves in the garden of the Empress's Office and visited the guard-house of the Left Guards* (section 72; note 317).

8th Month (?)   *Lady Ukon played the lute in the Empress's Office* (section 96; note 475).

Autumn   *Shōnagon received a message from Empress Sakado recalling the visit to the guard-house and asking her to return to the Palace* (section 82; note 368).

Between 997 (1st Month) and 998 (1st Month)   *Fujiwara no Nobutsune came to the Empress's Palace and was ridiculed by Shōnagon* (section 99; note 483).

2.11   The Government Headquarters in Kyūshū reported the repulsion of the southern barbarians.

12th Month   Fujiwara no Korechika returned to the capital.

998 (*Chōtoku 4*)

2nd Month   *Empress Sadako moved to the Empress's Office. Minamoto no Nobukata had a liaison with Lady Sakyō, but broke with her after being teased by Shōnagon* (section 162; note 767).

2nd or 3rd Month   *Fujiwara no Yukinari and Shōnagon exchanged poems about Ōsaka Barrier* (section 129; note 633).

3rd Month   *Fujiwara no Yukinari saw Shōnagon in her bedroom* (section 51; note 264).

5.7   Empress Sadako was ill.

18.7   Emperor Ichijō was ill.

20.7   Owing to Emperor Ichijō's illness, a general amnesty was proclaimed.

After 10th Month   *Fujiwara no Masamitsu overheard Shōnagon making an objectionable remark* (section 215; note 875).

10.12   *There was a heavy fall of snow; snow mountains were built outside the Palace, and Shōnagon predicted that the one outside the Empress's Office would last until the 15th day of the New Year* (section 83; note 371).

After 10th Month   *Shōnagon was impressed by Minamoto no Narinobu's ability to recognize people's voices* (section 214; note 873).

3.1 Empress Sadako returned to the Palace, but without the usual ceremonial.

9.2 Fujiwara no Akiko, Michinaga's daughter, celebrated her coming-of-age ceremony at the age of eleven and was appointed to the 3rd Rank.

Last day of 2nd Month *Shōnagon was challenged by a poem from Fujiwara no Kintō and other gentlemen* (section 102; note 520).

End of 2nd Month (?) *Shōnagon stayed at home secretly and Fujiwara no Tadanobu tried to discover where she was* (section 80; note 357).

5th Month *Shōnagon astonished some courtiers by recognizing a Chinese reference* (section 130; note 642).

14.6 The Imperial Palace burnt down.

16.6 Emperor Ichijō moved to the Smaller Palace of the First Ward.

6th Month (?) *Shōnagon wrote that she had been serving for ten years in the Palace* (section 43; note 231).

9.8 Owing to her pregnancy, Empress Sadako moved from the Empress's Office to the house of Taira no Narimasa.

9.8 *Shōnagon accompanied Empress Sadako to the house of Taira no Narimasa and found many occasions to tease their host* (section 8; note 33).

1.11 Fujiwara no Akiko entered the Palace.

7.11 Empress Sadako gave birth to Prince Atsuyasu at the house of Taira no Narimasa.

7.11 Fujiwara no Akiko was appointed Imperial Concubine.

1.12 The Great Empress Dowager died at the age of fifty-five.

1000 (*Chōhō 2*)

12.2 Empress Sadako moved to the Smaller Palace of the First Ward.

20.2 *Emperor Ichijō was given a music lesson by Fujiwara no Takatō* (section 28; note 133).

25.2 Empress Sadako was appointed First Empress, Fujiwara no Akiko became Second Empress, and Fujiwara no Nobuko became Great Empress Dowager.

3rd Month *The dog, Okinamaro, was punished for attacking the Emperor's cat* (section 9; note 45).

27.3 Empress Sadako returned to Taira no Narimasa's house.

5.5 *Herbal balls were presented to Empress Sadako and Empress Akiko; Shōnagon exchanged poems with Empress Sadako* (section 212; note 868).

8.8 Empress Sadako returned to the Imperial Palace.

8th Month (?)   *Minamoto no Narinobu visited Shōnagon on a rainy night, but she pretended to be asleep* (section 271; note 1040).

27.8   Empress Sadako returned to the house of Taira no Narimasa.

29.8   *Jōchō visited the Palace on his appointment as Intendant of Yamashina Temple, and Shōnagon joked about him with Minamoto no Narinobu* (section 12; note 59).

11.10   Emperor Ichijō moved into the rebuilt Palace.

15.12   Empress Sadako gave birth to a second princess.

16.12   Empress Sadako died from childbirth at the age of twenty-four.

27.12   Empress Sadako was buried in Rokuhara.

Date	Section
986 (6th Month)	37
987 (1st Month) (?)	3
990 (?)	177
990 (between 3rd and 8th Months) (?)	112
992 (2nd Month)	131
992 (3rd Month) (?)	280
992 (8th Month) (?)	291
992 (12th Month)	91
Between 993 (4th Month) and 994 (4th Month)	122
993 (11th Month) (?)	86
993 (12th Month)	77
994 (2nd Month)	256
994 (3rd Month)	22
994 (3rd Month) (?)	88
994 (5th Month)	89
994 (after 8th Month)	326
995 (2nd Month) (?)	126
995 (2nd Month)	100
995 (end of 2nd Month)	78
Between 995 (4th Month) and 996 (4th Month)	98
995 (5th Month) (?)	95
995 (6th Month)	159
995 (9th Month)	128
995 (10th Month)	121
995-6	104
996 (end of 2nd Month)	79
996 (3rd Month)	87
996 (3rd Month)	160
Between 995 (12th Month) and 996 (12th Month)	325
996 (4th or 5th Month)	255
996 (about 7th Month)	136
996 (?)	52

Date	Section
997 (6th or 7th Month)	72
997 (8th Month) (?)	96
997 (autumn)	82
Between 997 (1st Month) and 998 (1st Month)	99
998 (2nd Month)	162
998 (2nd or 3rd Month)	129
998 (3rd Month)	51
998 (after 10th Month)	215
998 (12th Month)	83
998 (after 10th Month)	214
999 (2nd Month)	102
999 (2nd Month)	80
999 (5th Month)	130
999 (6th Month) (?)	43
999 (8th Month)	8
1000 (2nd Month)	28
1000 (3rd Month)	9
1000 (5th Month)	212
1000 (8th Month) (?)	271
1000 (8th Month)	12

Section	Date
3	987 (1st Month)
8	999 (8th Month)
9	1000 (3rd Month)
12	1000 (8th Month)
22	994 (3rd Month)
28	1000 (2nd Month)
37	986 (6th Month)
43	999 (6th Month) (?)
51	998 (3rd Month)
52	996 (?)
72	997 (6th or 7th Month)
77	993 (12th Month)
78	995 (end of 2nd Month)
79	996 (end of 2nd Month)
80	999 (2nd Month)
82	997 (autumn)
83	998 (12th Month)
86	993 (11th Month) (?)
87	996 (3rd Month)
88	994 (3rd Month) (?)
89	994 (5th Month)
91	992 (12th Month)
95	995 (5th Month) (?)

215

Section	*Date*
96	997 (8th Month) (?)
98	Between 995 (4th Month) and 996 (4th Month)
99	Between 997 (1st Month) and 998 (1st Month)
100	995 (2nd Month)
102	999 (2nd Month)
104	995–6
112	990 (between 3rd and 8th Months) (?)
121	995 (10th Month)
122	Between 993 (4th Month) and 994 (4th Month)
126	995 (2nd Month) (?)
128	995 (9th Month)
129	998 (2nd or 3rd Month)
130	999 (5th Month)
131	992 (2nd Month)
136	996 (about 7th Month)
159	995 (6th Month)
160	996 (3rd Month)
162	998 (2nd Month)
177	990 (?)
212	1000 (5th Month)
214	998 (after 10th Month)
215	998 (after 10th Month)
255	996 (4th or 5th Month)
256	994 (2nd Month)
271	1000 (8th Month) (?)
280	992 (3rd Month) (?)
291	992 (8th Month) (?)
325	Between 995 (12th Month) and 996 (12th Month)
326	994 (after 8th Month)

APPENDIX 5

FINDING LIST

This list, in addition to giving page numbers and titles, shows the correspondences between the 326 sections of my translation and the sections of the principal texts that I have used, viz. (i) the 301 sections of Kaneko Motoomi's *Makura no Sōshi Hyōshaku*, (ii) the 348 sections of Ikeda-Kishigami's *Makura no Sōshi* (Nihon Koten Bungaku Taikei ed.), (iii) the 329 sections of Tanaka Shigetarō's *Makura no Sōshi* (Nihon Koten Zensho ed.). It also indicates, in the last column, the 52 datable sections (D) and the 164 sections that consist of lists (L).

	TRANSLATION		ORIGINAL			
Section	Page	Title	Kaneko	Ikeda–Kishigami	Tanaka	
1	1	In Spring It Is the Dawn	1	1	1	
2	1	These Are the Months	2	2	2	L
3	1	Especially Delightful Is the First Day	3	3	3	D
4	4	On the Third Day of the Third Month	3	4	3	
5	4	How Delightful Everything Is	3	5	3	
6	5	Different Ways of Speaking	4	6	4	L
7	5	That Parents Should Bring up Some Beloved Son	5	7	5	
8	6	When the Empress Moved	6	8	6	D
9	9	The Cat Who Lived in the Palace	7	9	7	D
10	12	On the First Day of the First Month	8	10	8	
11	13	I Enjoy Watching the Officials	9	11	9	
12	13	The Eastern Wing of the Palace of Today	10	12	10	D
13	13	Mountains	11	13	11	L
14	14	Peaks	12	15	13	L
15	14	Plains	13	16, 113	14, 109	L
16	14	Markets	14	14	12	L
17	14	Pools	15	17	15	L
18	14	Seas	16	18	16	L
19	15	Ferries	17	20	18	L
20	15	Imperial Tombs	18	19	17	L
21	15	Buildings	19	22	20	L

217

TRANSLATION			ORIGINAL			
				Ikeda–		
Section	Page	Title	Kaneko	Kishigami	Tanaka	
22	15	The Sliding Screen in the Back of the Hall	20	23	21	D
23	20	When I make Myself Imagine	20	24	22	
24	21	Depressing Things	21	25	23	L
25	24	Things about Which One Is Liable to Be Negligent	22	26	24 .	L
26	25	Things That People Despise	23	27	25	L
27	25	Hateful Things	24	28, 63, 121, 187, 262	26, 60, 117, 182, 246	L
28	30	The Smaller Palace of the First Ward	25	245	230	D
29	31	Things That Make One's Heart Beat Faster	26	29	27	L
30	31	Things That Arouse a Fond Memory of the Past	27	30	28	L
31	32	Things That Give a Pleasant Feeling	28	31	29	L
32	32	A Palm-Leaf Carriage Should Move Slowly	29	32	30	
33	33	Oxen Should Have Very Small Foreheads	29	50–52	48–50	
34	33	The Driver of an Ox-Carriage	29	53–55	51–53	
35	33	A Preacher Ought to Be Good-Looking	30	33	31	
36	36	When I Visited Bodai Temple	31	34	32	
37	36	Smaller Shirakawa	32	35	33	D
38	40	It Is So Stiflingly Hot	33	36	34	
39	42	Flowering Trees	34	37	35	L
40	43	Ponds	35	38	36	L
41	44	Festivals	36	39	37	L
42	45	Trees	37	40	38	L
43	47	Birds	38	41	39	L, D
44	49	Elegant Things	39	42	40	L
45	49	Insects	40	43	41	L
46	50	In the Seventh Month	41	44	42	
47	50	Unsuitable Things	42	45, 312	43, 294	L
48	51	I Was Standing in a Corridor	43	46	44	
49	52	The Women Who Work in the Office of Grounds	44	47	45	
50	52	Gentlemen Should Always Have Escorts	44	48	46	
51	52	Once I Saw Yukinari	45	49	47	D
52	55	The Roll-Call of the Senior Courtiers	46	56	54	D
53	56	It Is Hateful When a Well-Bred Young Man	47	57	55	
54	57	Small Children and Babies	48	58	56	
55	57	Nothing Can Be Worse	48	59	56	

218

| | TRANSLATION | | | ORIGINAL | |
Section	Page	Title	Kaneko	Ikeda–Kishigami	Tanaka	
56	58	Travelling in My Carriage One Day	49	60	57	
57	58	Once When I Was Passing	49	60	57	
58	58	Waterfalls	50	61	58	L
59	59	Rivers	51	62	59	L
60	59	Bridges	52	64	61	L
61	59	Villages	53	65	62	L
62	60	Herbs and Shrubs	54	66	63	L
63	61	Anthologies	55	68	65	L
64	61	Poetic Subjects	56	69	66	L
65	61	Flowering Shrubs	57	67	64	L
66	63	Unsettling Things	58	70	67	L
67	63	Things That Cannot Be Compared	59	71–72	68	L
68	63	To Meet One's Lover	60	73	69	
69	64	A Lover's Visit	61	74	70	
70	65	Rare Things	62	75	71	L
71	65	The Women's Apartments along the Gallery	63	76–77	72–73	
72	68	It Was during One of Her Majesty's Periods of Residence	64	78	74	D
73	69	Things Not Worth Doing	65	79	75	L
74	69	Things That Make One Sorry	66	..	..	L
75	70	Pleasant-Seeming Things	67	80	76	L
76	70	People Who Are Treated Well	68	..	..	L
77	70	On the Day after the Naming of the Buddhas	69	81	77	D
78	71	The Captain First Secretary, Tadanobu	70	82	78	D
79	75	On the Twenty-Fifth of the Second Month	71	83	79	D
80	78	When I Stayed away from the Palace	72	84	80	D
81	80	Things That Give a Pathetic Impression	73	85	81	L
82	81	Then a Few Months after Our Visit	74	86	82	D
83	81	Once When Her Majesty Was Residing	75	87	83	D
84	90	Splendid Things	76	88	84	L
85	93	Graceful Things	77	89	85	L
86	94	For the Gosechi Celebrations	78	90–92	86–88	D
87	98	One Day When the Emperor Visited Her Majesty's Rooms	79	93	89	D
88	99	A Group of Senior Courtiers	80	94	90	D
89	99	Once in the Fifth Month	..	202	192	D
90	100	One of Her Majesty's Wet-Nurses	81	240	226	

TRANSLATION			ORIGINAL			
Section	Page	Title	Kaneko	Ikeda–Kishigami	Tanaka	
91	100	Annoying Things	82	95	91	L, D
92	102	Embarrassing Things	83	96	92	L
93	103	Surprising and Distressing Things	84	97	93	L
94	104	Regrettable Things	85	98	94	L
95	104	It Was during the Abstinence of the Fifth Month	86	99	95	D
96	111	It Was a Clear, Moonlit Night	..	100	96	D
97	111	One Day When There Were Several People in the Empress's Presence	87	101	·97	
98	112	His Excellency the Middle Counsellor, Takaie	88	102	98	D
99	112	Once during a Long Spell of Rainy Weather	89	103	99	D
100	114	When the Lady of the Shigei Sha Entered the Crown Prince's Palace	90	104	100	D
101	120	One Day a Messenger from the Imperial Palace	91	105	101	
102	120	On the Last Day of the Second Month	92	106	102	D
103	121	Things That Have a Long Way to Go	93	107	103	L
104	121	Masahiro Really Is a Laughing-Stock	94	108	104	D
105	123	Barriers	95	111	107	L
106	123	Forests	96	112, 207	108, 196	L
107	123	On the Last Day of the Fourth Month	97	114	110	
108	124	Hot Springs	98	..	..	L
109	124	Things That Especially Attract One's Attention on Some Occasions	99	115	111	L
110	124	Things That Lose by Being Painted	100	116	112	L
111	124	Things That Gain by Being Painted	101	117–18	113–14	L
112	124	Moving Things	102	119, Ippon 26	115, Ippon 26	L, D
113	126	During the Long Rains in the Fifth Month	..	Ippon 27	Ippon 26	
114	126	In the First Month When I Go to a Temple	103	120	116	
115	130	Gloomy-Looking Things	104	122	118	L
116	131	Things That Give a Hot Feeling	105	123	119	L
117	131	Shameful Things	106	124	120	L
118	132	Things That Have Lost Their Power	107	125	121	L
119	133	Among the Ceremonies of Incantation	108	126	122	

TRANSLATION			ORIGINAL			
				Ikeda–		
Section	Page	Title	Kaneko	Kishigami	Tanaka	
120	133	Awkward Things	109	127	123	L
121	133	When the Emperor Returned from His Visit to Yawata	109	128	123	D
122	134	One Day We Heard That His Excellency	110	129	124	D
123	135	I Remember a Clear Morning	111	130	125	
124	135	On the Sixth of the Month	112	131	126	
125	136	In the Second Month Something Takes Place	113	132	127	
126	136	One Day a Man from the Office of Grounds	114	133	128	D
127	138	One Night the Empress's Ladies-in-Waiting	114	134	129	
128	139	On the Tenth Day of Each Month	116	135	130	D
129	140	One Evening Yukinari, the Controller First Secretary	117	136	131	D
130	142	On a Dark, Moonless Night in the Fifth Month	118	137	132	D
131	143	A Year after Emperor Enyū's Death	119	138	133	D
132	145	Boring Things	120	139	134	L
133	145	Distractions at Boring Times	121	140	135	L
134	145	Things without Merit	122	141	136	L
135	146	Outstandingly Splendid Things	123	142	137	L
136	149	When His Excellency, the Chancellor, Had Departed	124	143	138	D
137	152	On the Tenth Day of the First Month	125	144	139	
138	153	Two Handsome Men	126	145–6	140–1	
139	154	Frightening Things	127	147	142	L
140	154	Things That Give a Clean Feeling	128	148	143	L
141	154	Things That Give an Unclean Feeling	129	..	..	L
142	154	Things That Seem Better at Night Than in the Daytime	..	Ippon 1	Ippon 1	L
143	155	Things That Should Not Be Seen by Firelight	..	Ippon 2	Ippon 2	L
144	155	Things That Are Unpleasant to Hear	..	Ippon 3	Ippon 3	L
145	155	Things That Look Pretty but That Are Bad Inside	..	Ippon 5	Ippon 5	L
146	155	Things That Give a Vulgar Impression	130	149	144	L
147	156	Things That Make One Nervous	131	150	145	L

TRANSLATION   ORIGINAL

Section	Page	Title	Kaneko	Ikeda–Kishigami	Tanaka	
148	156	Adorable Things	132	151	146	L
149	157	Presumptuous Things	133	152	147	L
150	158	Things with Frightening Names	134	153	148	L
151	159	Words That Look Commonplace but That Become Impressive When Written in Chinese Characters	135	154	149	L
152	159	Words Written in Chinese Characters for Which There Must Be a Reason Though One Cannot Really Understand It	..	Ippon 4	Ippon 4	L
153	159	Squalid Things	136	155	150	L
154	160	Trivial Things That Become Important on Special Occasions	137	156	151	L
155	160	People Who Seem to Suffer	138	157	152	L
156	161	Enviable People	139	158	153	L
157	163	Things That One Is in a Hurry to See or to Hear	140	159	154	L
158	163	Things That Make One Impatient	141	160	155	L
159	165	While We Were in Mourning for the Chancellor	142	161	156	D
160	166	One Day Captain Tadanobu, the Imperial Adviser, Came to Call	143	161	157	D
161	167	It Was Late at Night	144	161	157	
162	170	The Name 'Kokiden'	145	162	157	D
163	171	Things That Recall the Past but Serve No Useful Function	146	163	158	L
164	172	Unreliable Things	147	164	159	L
165	172	The Lotus Sutra	148	165	160	
166	172	Things That Are Distant Though Near	149	166	161	L
167	173	Things That Are Near Though Distant	150	167	162	L
168	173	Wells	151	168	163	L
169	173	Provincial Governors	152	172	167	L
170	173	Provincial Governors Awaiting Permanent Appointments	153	173	168	L
171	173	Gentlemen of the Fifth Rank	154	174, 177	169, 172	L
172	174	When a Woman Lives Alone	155	178	173	
173	174	When a Court Lady Is on Leave	156	179	174	

TRANSLATION   ORIGINAL

Section	Page	Title	Kaneko	Ikeda–Kishigami	Tanaka	
174	176	It Is Delightful When There Has Been a Thin Fall of Snow	157	181	176	
175	177	One Evening during the Reign of Emperor Murakami	158	182	177	
176	178	One Day Lady Miare no Senji	159	183	178	
177	178	When I First Went into Waiting	160	184	179	D
178	183	People Who Look Pleased with Themselves	161	185–6	180–1	L
179	184	Winds	162	197–9	190	L
180	185	On the Day after a Fierce Autumn Wind	163	200	191	
181	186	Charming Things	164	201	192	L
182	187	Islands	165	204	193	L
183	187	Beaches	166	205	194	L
184	187	Bays	167	206	195	L
185	187	Plains	173	169	164	L
186	187	Temples	168	208	197	L
187	188	Scriptures	169	209	198	L
188	188	Writings in Chinese	170	211	200	L
189	188	Buddhas	171	210	199	L
190	188	Tales	172	212	201	L
191	188	Mystic Incantations	174	213	202	L
192	189	Recitations of the Scriptures	175		..	L
193	189	Concerts	176	214	203	L
194	189	Games	177	215	204	L
195	189	Dances	178	216	205	L
196	189	String Instruments	179	217	206	L
197	189	Tunes	180	..	..	L
198	190	Wind Instruments	181	218	207	L
199	190	Things Worth Seeing	182	219–22	208	L
200	193	In the Fifth Month	183	223	209	
201	194	During the Hot Months	184	224	210	
202	194	The Irises That Were Used on the Fifth Day	185	230	216	
203	194	One Has Carefully Scented a Robe	186	231	217	
204	195	When Crossing a River	187	232	218	
205	195	Things That Should Be Large	188	233	219	L
206	195	Things That Should Be Short	189	234	220	L
207	195	Things That Belong in a House	190	235	221	L
208	196	One Day I Passed a Handsome Man	191	236	222	
209	196	Though an Imperial Progress Is a Splendid Sight	192	..	..	
210	196	Nothing Annoys Me So Much	193	237	223	

223

TRANSLATION			ORIGINAL			
				Ikeda–		
Section	Page	Title	Kaneko	Kishigami	Tanaka	
211	198	There Was a Man in the Corridor	194	238	224	
212	199	When the Empress Was Staying in the Third Ward	195	239	225	D
213	199	One Bright, Moonlit Evening	196	273	257	
214	200	Captain Narinobu Has an Amazing Memory	197	274	258	D
215	200	I Have Never Come across Anyone with Such Keen Ears	198	275	259	D
216	200	I Hate Seeing a Dusty, Dirty-Looking Inkstone	199	..	..	
217	202	Letters Are Commonplace	200	..	..	
218	202	Posting Stations	201	242	228	L
219	202	Hills	202	249	234	L
220	202	Shrines	203	243–4	229	L
221	205	Things That Fall from the Sky	204	250–1	235	L
222	205	The Sun	205	252	236	
223	205	The Moon	206	253	237	
224	205	Stars	207	254	238	L
225	206	Clouds	208	255	239	L
226	206	Tumultuous Things	209	256	240	L
227	206	Slovenly Things	210	257	241	L
228	206	People Who Express Themselves Inelegantly	211	258	242	L
229	207	People with a Knowing Look	212	259	243	L
230	207	High Court Nobles	213	170	165	L
231	208	Other Senior Courtiers	214	171	166	L
232	208	Priests	215	175	170	L
233	208	Women	216	176	171	L
234	208	Palaces Where One Can Serve As a Lady-in-Waiting	217	Ippon 25	Ippon 24	L
235	209	People Who Have Changed As Much As If They Had Been Reborn	218	246	232	L
236	209	One Day, When the Snow Lay Thick on the Ground	219	247	233	
237	210	One Morning, When the Door Leading to the Long Corridor Had Been Opened	220	248	234	
238	210	Things That Do Not Linger for a Moment	221	260	244	L
239	210	Things of Which People Are Rarely Aware	222	261	245	L
240	210	On Some Evenings in the Fifth or Sixth Month	223	..	..	
241	210	When I Was Going to the Kamo Shrines	224	226	212	

| TRANSLATION | | | ORIGINAL | | | |
Section	Page	Title	Kaneko	Ikeda–Kishigami	Tanaka	
242	211	Towards the End of the Eighth Month	225	227	213	
243	212	Shortly after the Twentieth of the Ninth Month	..	228	214	
244	212	Once When I Went to Kiyomizu	..	229	215	
245	212	Very Dirty Things	226	263	247	L
246	212	Extremely Frightening Things	227	264	248	L
247	212	Things That Give One Confidence	228	265	249	L
248	213	After Lengthy Arrangements	229	266	250	
249	213	To Feel That One Is Disliked by Others	230	267	251	
250	214	Men Really Have Strange Emotions	231	268	252	
251	214	Sympathy Is the Most Splendid of All Qualities	232	269	253	
252	215	It Is Absurd of People to Get Angry	233	270	254	
253	215	Features That I Particularly Like	234	271	255	
254	216	Pleasing Things	235	276	260	L
255	217	One Day, When Her Majesty Was Surrounded by Several Ladies	236	277	261	D
256	219	On about the Twentieth of the Second Month	237	278	262	D
257	233	Holy Things	238	279	263	L
258	234	Songs	239	280	264	L
259	234	Trousers	240	281	265	L
260	234	Hunting Costumes	241	282	266	L
261	234	Unlined Clothes	242	283	267	L
262	234	Under-Robes	244	284	268	L
263	235	Fan Frames	245	285	269	L
264	235	Cypress Fans	246	286	270	L
265	235	Deities	247	287	271	L
266	235	Capes	248	288	272	L.
267	235	Houses	249	289	273	L
268	236	Bad Things	243	195	188	L
269	236	I Enjoy Hearing the Officers Call out the Time	250	290	274	
270	237	At Noon When the Sun Is Shining Brightly	251	291	275	
271	237	Captain Narinobu Is a Son of His Reverend Highness	252	292	276	D
272	240	On One Occasion a Man	253	293	277	
273	241	One Day the Sky, Which until Then Had Been Quite Clear	253	294	277	

	TRANSLATION		ORIGINAL			
				Ikeda–		
Section	Page	Title	Kaneko	Kishigami	Tanaka	
274	242	Resplendent Things	254	295	278	L
275	242	The Thunder Guards Are Awe-Inspiring	254	296	279	
276	242	Screens	254	297	280	L
277	243	One Has Taken a Round-about Way	255	298	281	
278	243	One Day, When the Snow Lay Thick on the Ground	256	299	282	
279	243	The Boys Employed by Masters of Divination	257	300	283	
280	244	Once in the Third Month	258	301	284	D
281	245	Once When I Had Gone to Kiyomizu Temple	259	241	227	
282	245	On the Twenty-Fourth of the Twelfth Month	260	302	285	
283	246	It Is Delightful for the Master of a Household	261	303	286	
284	247	People Who Irritate Others	262	304	287	L
285	247	Times When One Should Be on One's Guard	263	305–6	288	L
286	249	A Certain Lieutenant	264	307	289	
287	249	The Lord of Ono's Mother	265	308	290	
288	250	I Am Greatly Moved and Delighted	266	309	291	
289	250	Once I Wrote down a Poem	267	310	292	
290	250	If a Servant Girl	268	311	293	
291	250	One Evening Korechika	269	313	295	D
292	252	One Day I Was in the Apartment	270	314	296	
293	253	A Young Man Has Lost His Mother	271	315	297	
294	253	I Enjoy the Remark	272	..	..	
295	253	'Is It True That You Are Going to Shimo-tsuke?'	273	318	300	
296	254	One of the Ladies-in-Waiting	274	316	298	
297	254	One Day I Was with a Man	275	317	299	
298	254	Women's Coats	276	Ippon 6	Ippon 6	L
299	254	Chinese Jackets	277	,, 7	,, 7	L
300	254	Ceremonial Skirts	278	,, 8	,, 8	L
301	255	Loose Coats	279	,, 9	,, 9	L
302	255	Materials	280	,, 10	,, 10	L
303	255	Patterns	281	,, 11	,, 11	L
304	255	I Cannot Stand a Woman Who Wears Sleeves of Unequal Width	282	..	..	
305	256	It Is Very Unpleasant to See	283	45	43	
306	256	Illnesses	284	188–90	183	L
307	257	Disagreeable Things	285	121	117	L

TRANSLATION   ORIGINAL

Section	Page	Title	Kaneko	Ikeda– Kishigami	Tanaka	
308	257	I Cannot Bear Men to Eat	286	196	199	
309	258	It Is Very Annoying	287	Ippon 28	Ippon 26	L
310	259	Things That Are Hard to Say	288	110	106	L
311	259	Ceremonial Court Dress	289	. .	. .	
312	259	Everyone Should Behave As Elegantly As Possible	290	. .	. .	
313	259	The Way in Which Carpenters Eat	291	. .	. .	
314	260	I Cannot Bear People	292	. .	. .	
315	260	One Night in the Ninth Month	293	180	175	
316	260	It Often Happens That a Court Lady	294	Ippon 29	Ippon 27	
317	261	A Young Bachelor	295	191	184	
318	262	It Is Noon on a Summer Day	. .	192	185	
319	262	The Floor-Boards in the Ante-Room	. .	193	186	
320	263	At First Dawn a Carriage Passes	. .	194	187	
321	263	A Handsome Young Gentleman	296	. .	. .	
322	264	The House Had a Spacious Courtyard	297	Ippon 23	Ippon 24	
323	266	It Is Pleasant When One Can Employ	298	„ 24	. .	
324	266	Things That Are Unpleasant to See	299	109	105	L
325	267	When the Middle Captain	301	319	301	D
326	267	It Is Getting So Dark	300	319	301	D

APPENDIX 6

GENEALOGIES

In the following six genealogical tables the people whose names appear in capital letters are Emperors. Numbers are for identifying names in the Index-Glossary and in the following charts.

(a) EMPERORS AND MINAMOTOS

1st generation: NIMMYŌ
2nd generation: MONTOKU, KŌKŌ
3rd generation: 1. UDA
4th generation: Prince Sadazumi, Prince Atsumi, DAIGO
5th generation: 2. Kanchō
3. Shigenobu
4. Masanobu
5. MURAKAMI
6. Tadaakira
6th generation: 7. Nobukata
8. Michikata
9. Senshi (Saiin)
10. ENYŪ
11. Prince Tamehira
12. Prince Munehira
13. Toshikata
14. Tsunefusa
7th generation: 15. Tadataka
16. Narimasa
17. Norimasa
18. ICHIJŌ
19. Yorisada
20. Narinobu
21. SANJŌ
22. KAZAN
8th generation: 23. Prince Atsuyasu
24. Princess Osako

(b) FUJIWARAS (1)

1st generation: Fuyutsugu
2nd generation: 25. Yoshifusa
3rd generation: 26. Akiko
27. MONTOKU

228

```
4th generation:  28. Tadahira
5th generation:  29. Akitada
                 30. Tadagimi
                 31. Morotada
                 32. Morosuke
                 33. Saneyori
6th generation:  34. Atsusuke
                 35. Chūnagon no Kimi
                 36. Naritoki
                 37. Yoshiko (Senyōden no Nyōgo)
                 38. MURAKAMI
7th generation:  39. Murasaki Shikibu
                 40. Nobutsune
                 41. Nobutaka
                 42. Noritaka
                 43. Saishō no Kimi
                 44. SANJŌ
                 45. Nagaakira
                 46. Sanekata
                 47. Sukemasa
                 48. Takatō
                 49. Kintō
8th generation:  50. Takamitsu
```

FUJIWARAS (2)

```
1st generation:  Morosuke
2nd generation:  51. Yasuko
                 52. MURAKAMI
                 53. Kinsue
                 54. Koretada
                 55. Tadagimi
                 56. Kaneie
                 57. Tamemitsu
                 58. Shigeko (Tōzammi)
3rd generation:  59. Asamitsu
                 60. Masamitsu
                 61. ENYŪ
                 62. Senshi (Saiin)
                 63. Sanenari
                 64. Yoshiko (Kokiden no Nyōgo)
                 65. ICHIJŌ
                 66. Yoshichika
                 67. Tadanobu
                 68. Kiminobu
4th generation:  69. KAZAN
                 70. Yukinari
```

) FUJIWARAS (3)

1st generation: Kaneie
2nd generation: 71. Michitsuna
           72. Michitaka
           73. Michikane
           74. Yukiko
           75. SANJŌ
           76. Akiko (Higashi Sanjō no In)
           77. ENYŪ
           78. Michinaga
3rd generation: 79. Dōmei
           80. Michiyori
           81. Korechika
           82. Takaie
           83. Ryūen
           84. Yorichika
           85. Chikayori
           86. Genshi (Shigei Sha)
           87. Sadako
           88. ICHIJŌ
           89. Akiko (Jōtōmon In)
4th generation: 90. Matsugimi

(c) KIYOWARAS

1st generation: TEMMU
12th generation: 91. Motosuke
13th generation: 92. Shōnagon

(d) TAKASHINAS

1st generation: Takashina no Moronao
4th generation: 93. Naritō
           94. Sanenobu
           95. Akinobu
           96. Takako
           97. Michitaka
           98. Sadako

ALPHABETICAL LISTING

Given name	Family chart	Generation on chart	Number on chart
Akiko (daughter of Yoshifusa)	Fujiwara (1)	3rd	26
Akiko (Higashi Sanjō no In)	Fujiwara (3)	2nd	76
Akiko (Jōtōmon In)	Fujiwara (3)	3rd	89
Akinobu	Takashina	4th	95
Akitada	Fujiwara (1)	5th	29
Asamitsu	Fujiwara (2)	3rd	59

Given name	Family chart	Generation on chart	Number on chart
Atsusuke	Fujiwara (1)	6th	34
Atsuyasu	son of Emperor	8th	23
Chikayori	Fujiwara (3)	3rd	85
Chūnagon no Kimi	Fujiwara (1)	6th	35
Dōmei	Fujiwara (3)	3rd	79
Enyū	Emperor	6th	10 (see also 61 and 77)
Genshi (Shigei Sha)	Fujiwara (3)	3rd	86
Higashi Sanjō no In	see Akiko		
Ichijō	Emperor	7th	18 (see also 65 and 88)
Jōtōmon In	see Akiko		
Kanchō	grandson of Emperor	5th	2
Kaneie	Fujiwara (2)	2nd	56
Kazan	Emperor	7th	22 (see also 69)
Kiminobu	Fujiwara (2)	3rd	68
Kinsue	Fujiwara (2)	2nd	53
Kintō	Fujiwara (1)	7th	49
Kokiden no Nyōgo	see Yoshiko		
Korechika	Fujiwara (3)	3rd	81
Koretada	Fujiwara (2)	2nd	54
Masamitsu	Fujiwara (2)	3rd	60
Masanobu	Minamoto	5th	4
Matsugimi (Michimasa)	Fujiwara (3)	4th	90
Michikane	Fujiwara (3)	2nd	73
Michikata	Minamoto	6th	8
Michimasa	see Matsugimi		
Michinaga	Fujiwara (3)	2nd	78
Michitaka	Fujiwara (3)	2nd	72 (see also 97)
Michitsuna	Fujiwara (3)	2nd	71
Michiyori	Fujiwara (3)	3rd	80
Montoku	Emperor	3rd	27
Morosuke	Fujiwara (1)	5th	32
Morotada	Fujiwara (1)	5th	31
Motosuke	Kiyowara	12th	91
Munehira	son of Emperor	6th	12
Murakami	Emperor	5th	5 (see also 38 and 52)
Murasaki Shikibu	Fujiwara (1)	7th	39
Nagaakira	Fujiwara (1)	7th	45
Narimasa	Minamoto	7th	16
Narinobu	Minamoto	7th	20
Naritō	Takashina	4th	93
Naritoki	Fujiwara (1)	6th	36
Nobukata	Minamoto	6th	7
Nobutaka	Fujiwara (1)	7th	41
Nobutsune	Fujiwara (1)	7th	40
Norimasa	Minamoto	7th	17
Noritaka	Fujiwara (1)	7th	42
Osako	daughter of Emperor	8th	24
Ryūen	Fujiwara (3)	3rd	83

Given name	Family chart	Generation on chart	Number on chart
Sadako	Fujiwara (3)	3rd	87 (see also 98)
Saiin	see Senshi		
Saishō no Kimi	Fujiwara (1)	7th	43
Sanekata	Fujiwara (1)	7th	46
Sanenari	Fujiwara (2)	3rd	63
Sanenobu	Takashina	4th	94
Saneyori	Fujiwara (1)	5th	33
Sanjō	Emperor	7th	21 (see also 44 and 75)
Sei Shōnagon	see Shōnagon		
Senshi (Saiin)	daughter of Emperor	6th	9 (see also 62)
Senyōden no Nyōgo	see Yoshiko		
Shigei Sha	see Genshi		
Shigeko (Tōzammi)	Fujiwara (2)	2nd	58
Shigenobu	Minamoto	5th	3
Shōnagon	Kiyowara	13th	92
Sukemasa	Fujiwara (1)	7th	47
Tadagimi	Fujiwara (1)	5th	30 (see also 55)
Tadahira	Fujiwara (1)	4th	28
Tadanobu	Fujiwara (2)	3rd	67
Tadataka	Minamoto	7th	15
Takaakira	Minamoto	5th	6
Takaie	Fujiwara (3)	3rd	82
Takako	Takashina	4th	96
Takamitsu	Fujiwara (1)	8th	50
Takatō	Fujiwara (1)	7th	48
Tamehira	son of Emperor	6th	11
Tamemitsu	Fujiwara (2)	2nd	57
Toshikata	Minamoto	6th	13
Tōzammi	see Shigeko		
Tsunefusa	Minamoto	6th	14
Uda	Emperor	3rd	1
Yasuko	Fujiwara (2)	2nd	51
Yorichika	Fujiwara (3)	3rd	84
Yorisada	Minamoto	7th	19
Yoshichika	Fujiwara (2)	3rd	66
Yoshifusa	Fujiwara (1)	2nd	25
Yoshiko (Senyōden no Nyōgo)	Fujiwara (1)	6th	37
Yoshiko (Kokiden no Nyōgo)	Fujiwara (2)	3rd	64
Yukiko	Fujiwara (3)	2nd	74
Yukinari	Fujiwara (2)	4th	70

APPENDIX 5a

EMPERORS AND MINAMOTOS

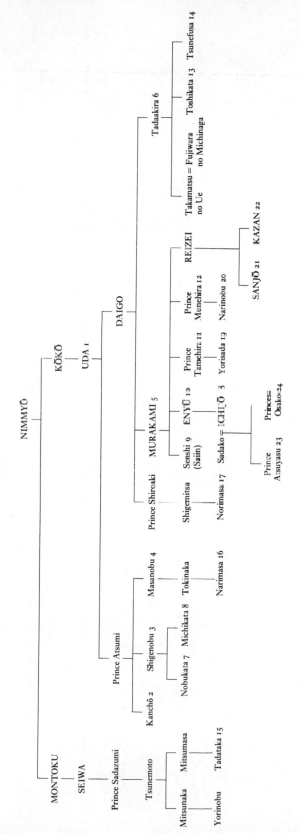

APPENDIX 6b

FUJIWARAS (1)

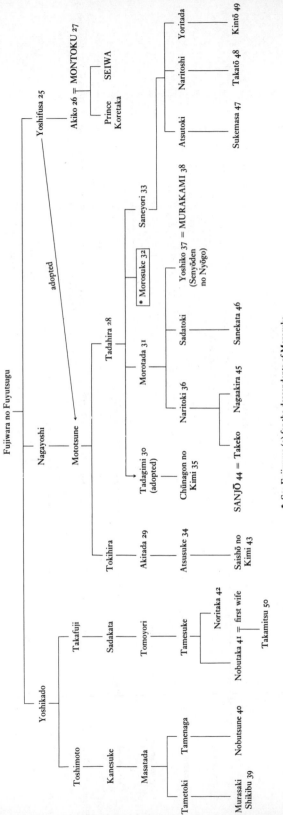

* See Fujiwaras (2) for the descendants of Morosuke.

APPENDIX 6b

FUJIWARAS (2)

Fujiwara no Morosuke

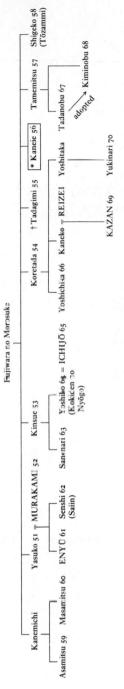

* See Fujiwara (3) for the descendants of Kaneie.
† Adopted by his grandfather. Tadahira (no. 28).

FUJIWARAS (3)

Fujiwara no Kaneie

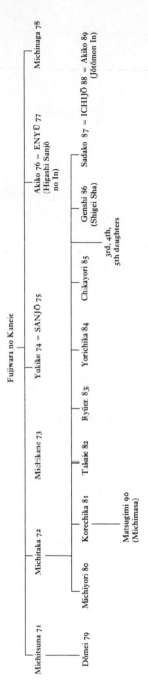

233

APPENDIX 6c

KIYOWARAS

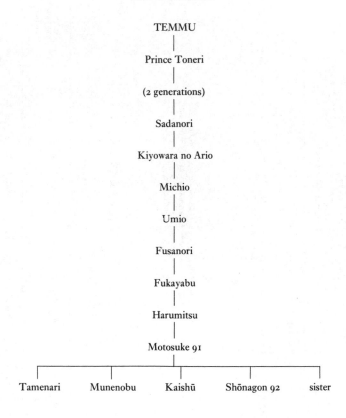

TEMMU
|
Prince Toneri
|
(2 generations)
|
Sadanori
|
Kiyowara no Ario
|
Michio
|
Umio
|
Fusanori
|
Fukayabu
|
Harumitsu
|
Motosuke 91
|
Tamenari — Munenobu — Kaishū — Shōnagon 92 — sister

APPENDIX 6d

TAKASHINAS

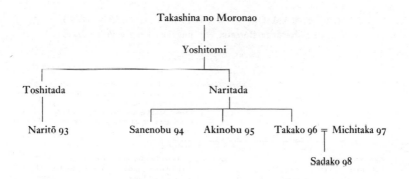

APPENDIX 7

GOVERNMENT

(a) DIAGRAM OF THE CENTRAL GOVERNMENT
(showing Ministries, Bureaux, etc., mentioned in *The Pillow Book*)

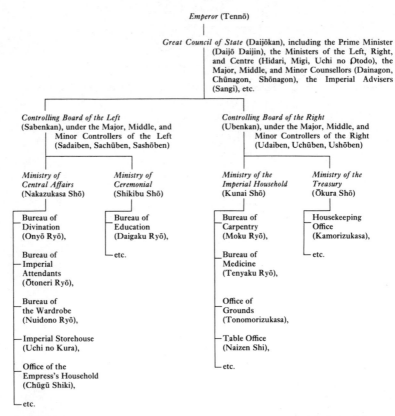

Emperor (Tennō)

Great Council of State (Daijōkan), including the Prime Minister (Daijō Daijin), the Ministers of the Left, Right, and Centre (Hidari, Migi, Uchi no Ōtodo), the Major, Middle, and Minor Counsellors (Dainagon, Chūnagon, Shōnagon), the Imperial Advisers (Sangi), etc.

Controlling Board of the Left (Sabenkan), under the Major, Middle, and Minor Controllers of the Left (Sadaiben, Sachūben, Sashōben)

Controlling Board of the Right (Ubenkan), under the Major, Middle, and Minor Controllers of the Right (Udaiben, Uchūben, Ushōben)

Ministry of Central Affairs (Nakazukasa Shō)

Bureau of Divination (Onyō Ryō),

Bureau of Imperial Attendants (Ōtoneri Ryō),

Bureau of the Wardrobe (Nuidono Ryō),

Imperial Storehouse (Uchi no Kura),

Office of the Empress's Household (Chūgū Shiki),

etc.

Ministry of Ceremonial (Shikibu Shō)

Bureau of Education (Daigaku Ryō),

etc.

Ministry of the Imperial Household (Kunai Shō)

Bureau of Carpentry (Moku Ryō),

Bureau of Medicine (Tenyaku Ryō),

Office of Grounds (Tonomorizukasa),

Table Office (Naizen Shi),

etc.

Ministry of the Treasury (Ōkura Shō)

Housekeeping Office (Kamorizukasa),

etc.

N.B. The other four Ministries were as follows: under the Controlling Board of the Left: Ministry of Civil Administration (Jibu Shō) and Ministry of Popular Affairs (Mimbu Shō); under the Controlling Board of the Right: Ministry of Justice (Kyōbu Shō) and Ministry of War (Hyōbu Shō).

APPENDIX 7 (cont.)

(b) OFFICES AND RANKS

Ranks	Great Council of State (Dajōkan)	The Eight Ministries (Shō)	Government Bureaux (Ryō)	Office of the Empress's Household (Chūgū Shiki)	Palace Attendants' Office (Naishi no Tsukasa)	Inner Palace Guards (Konoe)	Middle and Outer Palace Guards (Hyōe, Emon)	Imperial Police (Kebiishi)	Great and Superior Provinces (Taikoku, Jōkoku)	Medium and Inferior Provinces (Chūkoku, Gekoku)	Government Headquarters in Kyūshū (Dazai Fu)	Ezo (Eastern) Headquarters
1st (Ichii)	Prime Minister (Daijō Daijin)											
2nd (Nii)	Ministers of the Left, Right, and Centre											
3rd (Sammi)	Major and Middle Counsellors				Chief Attendant (Naishi no Kami)	Major Captains (Taishō)		Chief (Bettō)			Governor-General (Sotsu)	
4th (Shii)	Imperial Advisers, Major Controllers	Minister (Kyō)		Master (Daibu)	Assistant Attendants (Naishi no Suke)	Middle Captains (Chūjō)	Captains (Kami)				Senior Assistant Governor-General (Daini)	
5th (Goi)	Middle and Minor Controllers, Minor Counsellors	Senior and Junior Assistant Ministers (Tayū, Shō)	Director (Kami)	Assistant Master (Suke)	Junior Assistants (Shōji)	Minor Captains (Shōshō)	Assistant Captains (Suke)	Assistant Director (Suke)	Governor (Kami)		Junior Assistant Governor-General (Shōni)	General (Shōgun)
6th (Rokui)	Senior Scribes (Taishi)	Senior and Junior Secretaries (Daijō, Shōjō)	Assistant Director (Suke)	Senior Stewards (Daijin)		Lieutenants (Shōgen)	Senior Lieutenants (Daijō)	Lieutenants (Hōgan)	Assistant Governor (Suke)	Governor (Kami)	Senior and Junior Secretaries (Taigen, Shōgen)	
7th (Shichii)	Junior Scribes (Shōshi)	Senior Recorders (Dairoku)	Doctors (Hakase), Senior and Junior Secretaries (Daijō, Shōjō)	Junior Stewards (Shōjin)		Assistant Lieutenants (Shōsō)	Junior Lieutenants (Shōjō)	Junior Lieutenants (Shōjō)	Senior and Junior Secretaries (Daijō, Shōjō)		Senior Clerks (Daisakan)	Divisional Commanders (Gungen)
8th (Hachii)		Junior Recorders (Shōroku)	Senior and Junior Clerks (Daisakan, Shōsakan)	Senior and Junior Clerks (Daisakan, Shōsakan)			Senior and Junior Assistant Lieutenants (Daisakan, Shōsakan)	Senior and Junior Assistant Lieutenants (Daisakan, Shōsakan)	Senior and Junior Clerks (Daisakan, Shōsakan)	Secretaries (Jō)	Junior Clerks (Shōsakan)	Regimental Commanders (Gunsō)

APPENDIX 8

ILLUSTRATIONS

(a) CLOTHES

Men's Clothes: 1-6 *sokutai* (full Court costume)
1. *ue no kinu* (over-robe)
2. *hirao* (ribbon attached to sword-belt)
3. *hakama* (trouser-skirt)
4. *kutsu* (shoes)
5. *shaku* (baton)
6. *kōburi* (head-dress)

7-10 *naoshi* (ordinary Court costume)
7. *naoshi* (Court cloak)
8. *sashinuki* (loose laced trousers)
9. *kawahori* (fan)
10. *eboshi* (head-dress)

11-13 *kariginu* (hunting costume)
11. *kariginu* (hunting cloak)
12. *ōgi* (fan)
13. *eboshi* (head-dress)

Women's Clothes: 14-21 *full Court costume* (front view)
14. *karaginu* (Chinese jacket)
15. *uchigi* (robe)
16. *hitoeginu* (unlined dress)
17. *hakama* (trouser-skirt)
18. *mo* (skirt with long train)
19. *hitoegasane* (matched set of unlined dresses)
20. *ōgi* (fan)
21. *saishi* (hair ornament)

22-24 *full Court costume* (back view)
22. *hitoeginu* (unlined dress)
23. *karaginu* (Chinese jacket)
24. *mo* (skirt with long train)

237

(b) HOUSES, FURNISHINGS, ETC.

Outside: 1-4 reconstruction of a *shinden* mansion and its garden by Mr. Mori Osamu (N.B. this reconstruction of Higashi Sanjō Dono is taken from *Nihon Emakimono Zenshū*, vol. xii).
   1. *shinden* (main building)
   2. *tai no ya* (wing)
   3. *watadono* (corridor)
   4. *kado* (gate)

Inside: 5-18 schematic redrawing of the section from *Makura no Sōshi Emaki* that illustrates the Shigei Sha's visit to her sister (see Plate 4, Vol. I)
   5. *shitone* (cushion)
   6. *ugemberi no tatami* (straw mat with floral design)
   7. *chōdai* (curtain-dais)
   8. *kichō* (curtain of state)
   9. *shishi* (lion)
   10. *nageshi* (beam)
   11. *byōbu* (screen)
   12. *hioke* (brazier)
   13. *kōraiberi no tatami* (straw mat with white and black design)
   14. *sōji* (sliding-door)
   15. *sudare* (blinds)
   16. *sunoko* (open veranda)
   17. *takatsuki* (tray)
   18. *tatejitomi* (garden fence)

19-27 schematic redrawing of the section from *Makura no Sōshi Emaki* illustrating the scene in which Shōnagon makes an allusion to a passage from Chinese literature about bamboo (see Plate 7, Vol. I)
   19. *sunoko* (open veranda)
   20. *kōran* (balustrade)
   21. *tsumado* (side door)
   22. *shitomi* (latticed shutters)
   23. *yarido* (sliding-door)
   24. *sudare* (blinds)
   25. *kichō* (curtain of state)
   26. *sōji* (sliding-door)
   27. *nageshi* (beam)

(c) VEHICLES

1. *nagi no hana no mi-koshi* (Imperial palanquin with onion-flower decoration)
2. *birōge no kuruma* (palm-leaf carriage).
3. *ajiro no kuruma* (wickerwork carriage).
4. *idashiginu* (see Index-Glossary).

238

(d) MISCELLANEOUS

1. *musubibumi* (knotted letter)
2. *tatebumi* (twisted letter)
3. *kusudama* (herbal ball)
4. *uzuchi* (hare-stick)
5. *go* (see Index-Glossary)
6. *sugoroku* (backgammon)
7. *biwa* (Japanese lute)
8. *kin* (7-string zither)
9. *wagon* (6-string zither)
10. *sō no koto* (13-string zither)
11. *sō no fue* (13-pipe flute)

ALPHABETICAL LISTING

Word	Chart	Number
ajiro no kuruma	c	3
birōge no kuruma	c	2
biwa	d	7
byōbu	b	11
chōdai	b	7
oboshi	a	10, 13
go	d	5
hakama	a	3, 17
hioke	b	12
hirao	a	2
hitoegasane	a	19
hitoeginu	a	16, 22
idashiginu	c	4
kado	b	4
karaginu	a	11, 14, 23
kawahori	a	9
kichō	b	8, 25
kin	d	8
kōburi	a	6
kōraiberi no tatami	b	13
kōran	b	20
koto	d	8, 9, 10
kusudama	d	3
kutsu	a	4
mi-koshi	c	1
mo	a	18, 24
musubibumi	d	1
nageshi	b	10, 27

Word	Chart	Number
nagi no hana no mi-koshi	c	1
naoshi	a	7
ōgi	a	12, 20
saishi	a	21
sashinuki	a	8
shaku	a	5
shinden	b	1
shishi	b	9
shitomi	b	22
shitone	b	5
sōji	b	14, 26
sō no fue	d	11
sō no koto	d	10
sudare	b	15, 24
sugoroku	d	6
sunoko	b	16, 19
tai no ya	b	2
takatsuki	b	17
tatami	b	6, 13
tatebumi	d	2
tatejitomi	b	18
tsumado	b	21
uchigi	a	15
ue no kinu	a	1
ugemberi no tatami	b	6
uzuchi	d	4
wagon	d	9
watadono	b	3
yarido	b	23

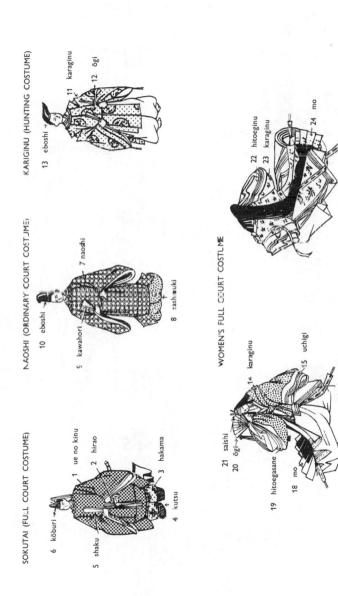

SOKUTAI (FULL COURT COSTUME)

1 ue no kinu
2 hirao
3 hakama
4 kutsu
5 shaku
6 kōburi

NAOSHI (ORDINARY COURT COSTUME)

7 naoshi
8 sashinuki
9 kawahori
10 eboshi

KARIGINU (HUNTING COSTUME)

11 karaginu
12 ōgi
13 eboshi

WOMEN'S FULL COURT COSTUME

14 karaginu
15 uchigi
16 hitoeginu
17 hakama
18 mo
19 hitoegasane
20 ōgi
21 saishi
22 hitoeginu
23 karaginu
24 mo

84. CLOTHES

241

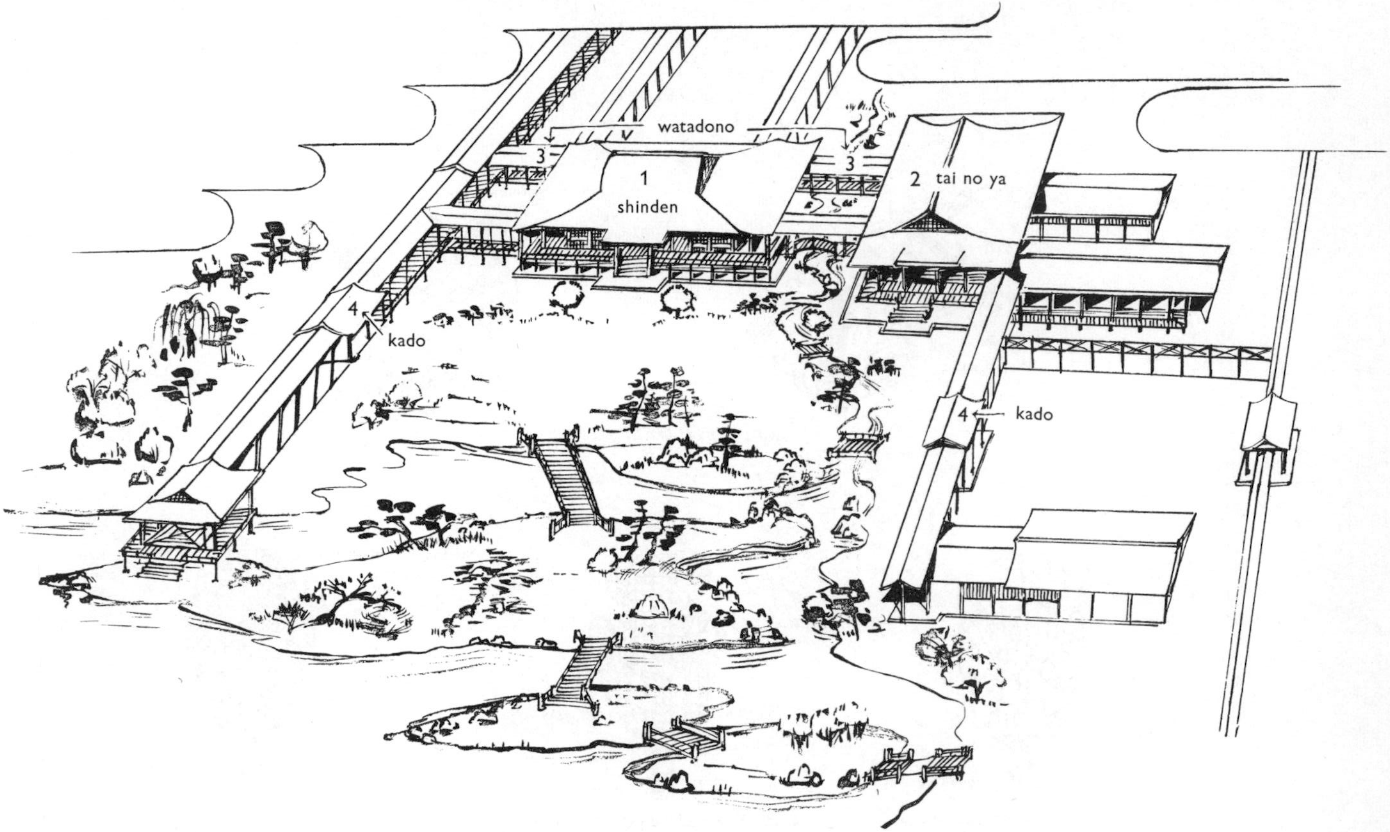

2 tai no ya

3

watadono

1 shinden

3

kado

4

4 kado

4

8b. (NOS. 1-4). SHINDEN MANSION AND GARDEN

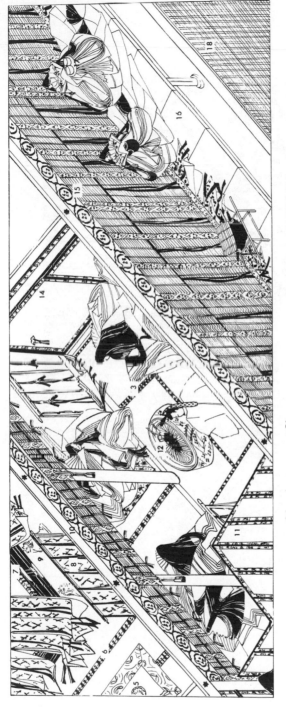

8*b*. (NOS. 5–18). INTERIOR OF A SHINDEN MANSION

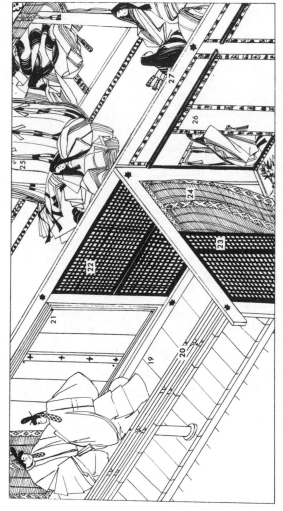

8b. (NOS. 19-27). INTERIOR OF A SHINDEN MANSION

244

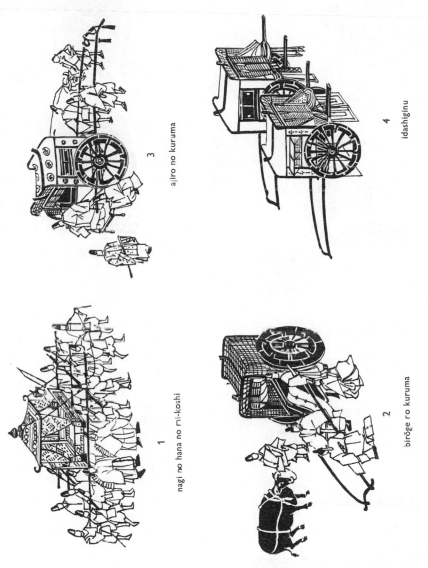

ajiro no kuruma

3

idashiginu

4

nagi no hana no ni-koshi

1

birōge ro kuruma

2

8c. VEHICLES

245

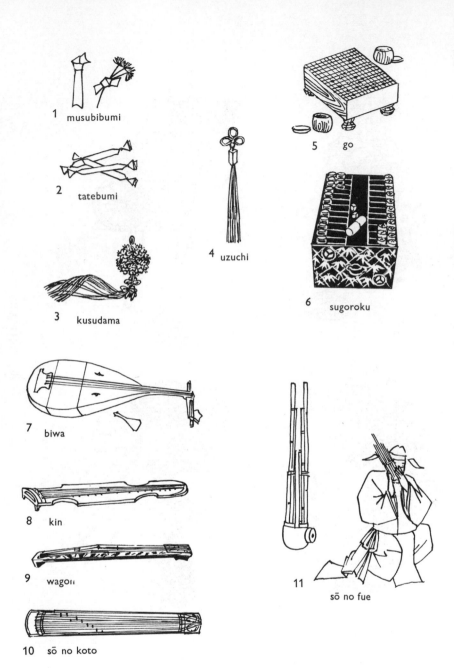

1 musubibumi

2 tatebumi

3 kusudama

4 uzuchi

5 go

6 sugoroku

7 biwa

8 kin

9 wagon

10 sō no koto

11 sō no fue

8*d*. MISCELLANEOUS

246

APPENDIX 9

MAPS

(a) PROVINCES OF JAPAN

Alphabetical Listing				Geographical Listing			
Aki	58	Kii	43	1. Rikoku		36. Tajima	
Awa	23, 51	Kōzuke	11	2. Rikuchū		37. Tamba	
Awaji	49	Mikawa	28	3. Rikuzen		38. Yamashiro	
Bingo	55	Mimasaka	47	4. Ugo		39. Settsu	
Bitchū	54	Mino	18	5. Uzen		40. Kawachi	
Bizen	48	Musashi	20	6. Echigo		41. Izumi	
Bungo	65	Nagato	60	7. Iwashiro		42. Yamato	
Buzen	64	Noto	14	8. Iwaki		43. Kii	
Chikugo	63	Ōmi	33	9. Hitachi		44. Harima	
Chikuzen	61	Ōsumi	69	10. Shimotsuke		45. Inaba	
Echigo	6	Owari	29	11. Kōzuke		46. Hōki	
Echizen	16	Rikuchū	2	12. Shinano		47. Mimasaka	
Etchū	13	Rikoku	1	13. Etchū		48. Bizen	
Harima	44	Rikuzen	3	14. Noto		49. Awaji	
Hida	17	Sagami	24	15. Kaga		50. Sanuki	
Higo	66	Sanuki	50	16. Echizen		51. Awa	
Hitachi	9	Satsuma	68	17. Hida		52. Tosa	
Hizen	62	Settsu	39	18. Mino		53. Iyo	
Hōki	46	Shima	31	19. Kai		54. Bitchū	
Hyūga	67	Shimōsa	21	20. Musashi		55. Bingo	
Iga	32	Shimotsuke	10	21. Shimōsa		56. Izumo	
Inaba	45	Shinano	12	22. Kazusa		57. Iwami	
Ise	30	Suō	59	23. Awa		58. Aki	
Iwaki	8	Suruga	26	24. Sagami		59. Suō	
Iwami	57	Tajima	36	25. Izu		60. Nagato	
Iwashiro	7	Tamba	37	26. Suruga		61. Chikuzen	
Iyo	53	Tango	35	27. Tōtōmi		62. Hizen	
Izu	25	Tosa	52	28. Mikawa		63. Chikugo	
Izumi	41	Tōtōmi	27	29. Owari		64. Buzen	
Izumo	56	Ugo	4	30. Ise		65. Bungo	
Kaga	15	Uzen	5	31. Shima		66. Higo	
Kai	19	Wakasa	34	32. Iga		67. Hyūga	
Kawachi	40	Yamashiro	38	33. Ōmi		68. Satsuma	
Kazusa	22	Yamato	42	34. Wakasa		69. Ōsumi	
				35. Tango			

(b) HOME PROVINCES (KINAI = YAMASHIRO, YAMATO, IZUMI, KAWACHI, SETTSU) AND NEIGHBOURING PROVINCES

Alphabetical Listing		Geographical Listing
Biwa Ko	2	1. Hieizan
Hasedera	6	2. Biwa Ko
Heian Kyō	3	3. Heian Kyō
Hieizan	1	4. Yodogawa
Kōya San	9	5. Nara
Kumano	10	6. Hasedera
Mitake	8	7. Yoshino
Nara	5	8. Mitake
Yodogawa	4	9. Kōya San
Yoshino	7	10. Kumano

(c) HEIAN KYŌ AND ITS SURROUNDINGS[1]

Alphabetical Listing		Geographical Listing
Chisoku In	4	1. Kuramadera
Inari no Jinja	8	2. Kamo no Jinja
Iwashimizu no Hachiman Gū	10	3. Murasaki No
Kamo no Jinja	2	4. Chisoku In
Kuramadera	1	5. Ninna Ji
Murasaki No	3	6. Uzumasa
Ninna Ji	5	7. Ōsaka no Seki
Ōsaka no Seki	7	8. Inari no Jinja
Otoko Yama	9	9. Otoko Yama
Uzumasa	6	10. Iwashimizu no Hachiman Gū

(d) HEIAN KYŌ

Alphabetical Listing		Geographical Listing
Agata no Ido	3	1. Daidairi
Daidairi	1	2. Ichijō no Miya
Hōkō In	14	3. Agata no Ido
Ichijō ni Miya	2	4. Somedono no Miya
Ichijō no Ōji	6	5. Sekai
Ima Dairi, see Ko Ichijō In		6. Ichijō no Ōji
Kanin	18	7. Kyōgoku Dono
Kiyomizudera	24	8. Ko Ichijō In
Kōbai	22	9. Sugawara no In
Ko Ichijō In	8	10. Ono no Miya
Ko Nijō In	13	11. Reizei no In

[1] The maps in Appendixes 9c–f are adapted from R. K. Reischauer's *Early Japanese History*, Volume B, published in 1937 by Princeton University Press, with whose permission they are reproduced.

Alphabetical Listing		Geographical Listing
Ko Rokujō In	23	12. Nijō no Miya
Kyōgoku Dono	7	13. Ko Nijō In
Nijō no Miya	12	14. Hōkō In
Nijō no Ōji	16	15. Shakuzen Ji
Ono no Miya	10	16. Nijō no Ōji
Reizei no In	11	17. Suzaku Ōji
Sekai	5	18. Kanin
Shakuzen Ji	15	19. Tō Sanjō In
Somedono no Miya	4	20. Yamanoi
Sugawara no In	9	21. Suzaku In
Suzaku In	21	22. Kōbai
Suzaku Ōji	17	23. Ko Rokujō In
Tō In	25	24. Kiyomizudera
Tomi no Kōji	26	25. Tō In
Tō Sanjō In	19	26. Tomi no Kōji
Yamanoi	20	

(e) DAIDAIRI (GREATER IMPERIAL PALACE)

Alphabetical Listing		Geographical Listing
Dairi	8	1. Kita no Jin
Daijōkan Chō	17	2. Ōkura Shō
Hyōbu Shō	18	3. Nuidono Ryō
Jōtō Mon	5	4. Sakon Efu
Kita no Jin	1	5. Jōtō Mon
Naizen Shi	7	6. Ukon Efu
Naka no Mikado, see Taiken Mon		7. Naizen Shi
Nakazukasa Shō	14	8. Dairi
Nuidono Ryō	3	9. Shiki no Mi-zōshi
Ōkura Shō	2	10. Saemon Fu
Onyō Ryō	15	11. Sahyō Efu
Ōtoneri Ryō	20	12. Yōmei Mon
Saemon Fu	10	13. Tenyaku Ryō
Sahyō Efu	11	14. Nakazukasa Shō
Sakon Efu	4	15. Onyō Ryō
Shikibu Shō	19	16. Taiken Mon
Shiki no Mi-zōshi	9	17. Daijōkan Chō
Taiken Mon	16	18. Hyōbu Shō
Tenyaku Ryō	13	19. Shikibu Shō
Tsuchi Mikado, see Jōtō Mon		20. Ōtoneri Ryō
Ukon Efu	6	
Yōmei Mon	12	

(f) DAIRI (IMPERIAL PALACE)

Alphabetical Listing		Geographical Listing
Fujitsubo	6	1. Umetsubo
Giyō Den	14	2. Tōka Den
Gyōke Sha, *see* Umetsubo		3. Jōgan Den
Higyō Sha, *see* Fujitsubo		4. Senyō Den
Jijū Den	11	5. Shigei Sha
Jōgan Den	3	6. Fujitsubo
Jōkyo Den, *see* Shōkyō Den		7. Koki Den
Jōnei Den	8	8. Jōnei Den
Koki Den	7	9. Seiryō Den
Seiryō Den	9	10. Shōkyō Den
Senyō Den	4	11. Jijū Den
Shigei Sha	5	12. Ummei Den
Shishin Den	13	13. Shishin Den
Shōkyō Den	10	14. Giyō Den
Tōka Den	2	15. Tsukumodokoro
Tsukumodokoro	15	
Umetsubo	1	
Ummei Den	12	

(g) SEIRYŌ DEN (EMPEROR'S RESIDENTIAL PALACE)

Alphabetical Listing		Geographical Listing
Araumi no Sōji	3	1. medō (bridle path)
Asagarei no Ma	8	2. Kurodo
Daihandokoro	9	3. Araumi no Sōji
Go-Chōzu no Ma	5	4. Mi-Yudono
Hi no Omashi	10	5. Go-Chōzu no Ma
Kokiden no Ue no Mi-Tsubone	6	6. Kokiden no Ue no Mi-Tsubone
Kosōji	7	7. Kosōji
Kurodo	2	8. Asagarei no Ma
medō (bridle path)	1	9. Daihandokoro
Mi-Yudono	4	10. Hi no Omashi
Tenjō no Ma	11	11. Tenjō no Ma

9a. PROVINCES OF JAPAN

251

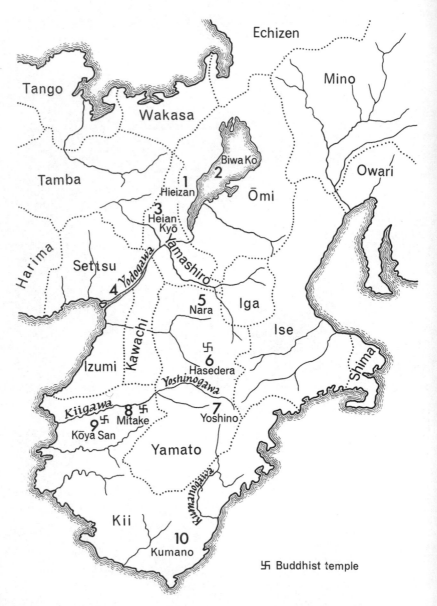

9*b*. HOME PROVINCES (KINAI) AND NEIGHBOURING PROVINCES

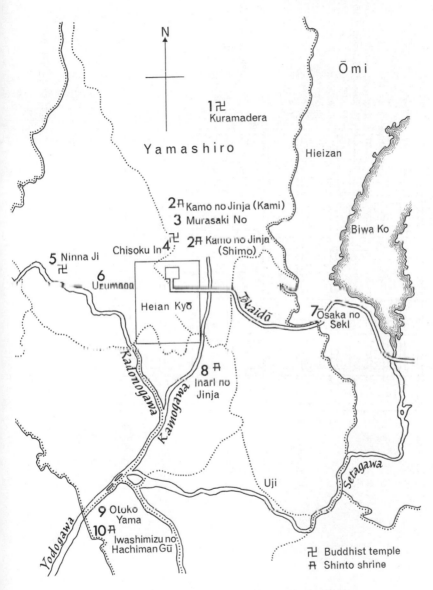

9c. HEIAN KYŌ AND ITS SURROUNDINGS

Ōmi

Kuramadera

Yamashiro

Hieizan

卍 1 Kuramadera

开 2 Kamo no Jinja (Kami)
3 Murasaki No

Biwa Ko

Chisoku In 卍 4   开 2 Kamo no Jinja (Shimo)

5 Ninna Ji 卍
6 Uzumasa

Heian Kyō

Byōdō

7 Osaka no Seki

开 8 Inari no Jinja

Uji

Kamogawa

Katsuragawa

Setagawa

9 Otoko Yama
开 10 Iwashimizu no Hachiman Gū

Yodogawa

卍 Buddhist temple
开 Shinto shrine

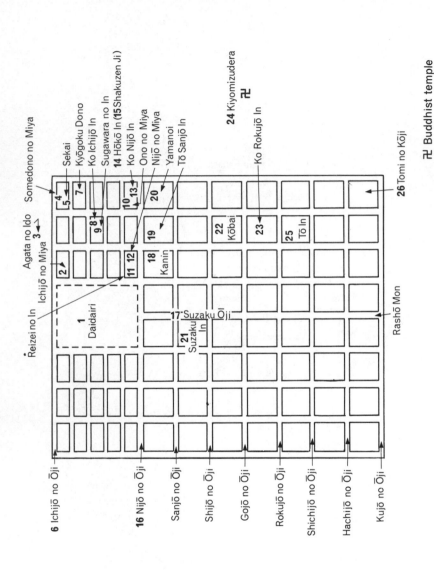

Reizei no In

Agata no Ido
3↘

Ichijō no Miya

Somedono no Miya

Sekai
Kyōgoku Dono
Ko Ichijō In
Sugawara no In
14 Hōkō In (**15** Shakuzen Ji)
Ko Nijō In
Ono no Miya
Nijō no Miya
Yamanoi
Tō Sanjō In

24 Kiyomizudera
卍

26 Tomi no Kōji

1 Daidairi

4
5
7
8
9
10 **13**
20
2
11 12
18 Kanin
19
22 Kōbai
23
25 Tō In

Ko Rokujō In

17 Suzaku Ōji

21 Suzaku In

Rashō Mon

6 Ichijō no Ōji
16 Nijō no Ōji
Sanjō no Ōji
Shijō no Ōji
Gojō no Ōji
Rokujō no Ōji
Shichijō no Ōji
Hachijō no Ōji
Kujō no Ōji

9d. HEIAN KYŌ

卍 Buddhist temple

254

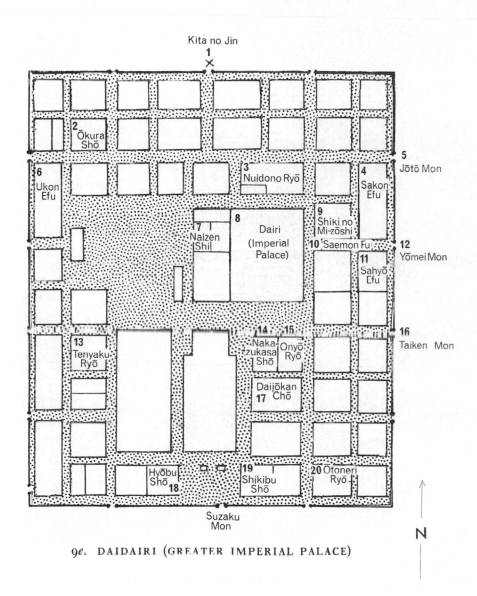

Kita no Jin
1
×

2 Ōkura Shō

5 Jōtō Mon

6 Ukon Efu

3 Nuidono Ryō

4 Sakon Efu

9 Shiki no Mi-zōshi

7 Naizen Shi

8 Dairi (Imperial Palace)

10 Saemon Fu 12 Yōmei Mon

11 Sahyō Efu

16 Taiken Mon

13 Tenyaku Ryō

14 15 Naka-zukasa Shō Onyō Ryō

17 Daijōkan Chō

Hyōbu Shō 18

19 Shikibu Shō

20 Otoneri Ryō

Suzaku Mon

N

9e. DAIDAIRI (GREATER IMPERIAL PALACE)

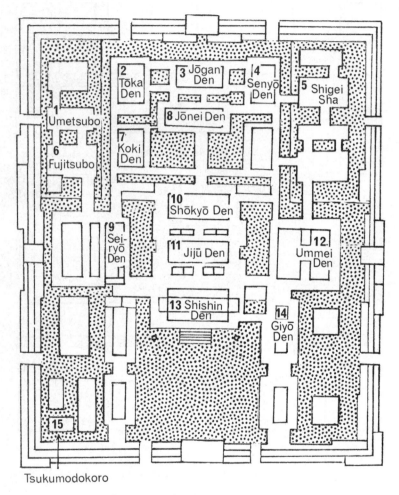

Tsukumodokoro

9f. DAIRI (IMPERIAL PALACE)

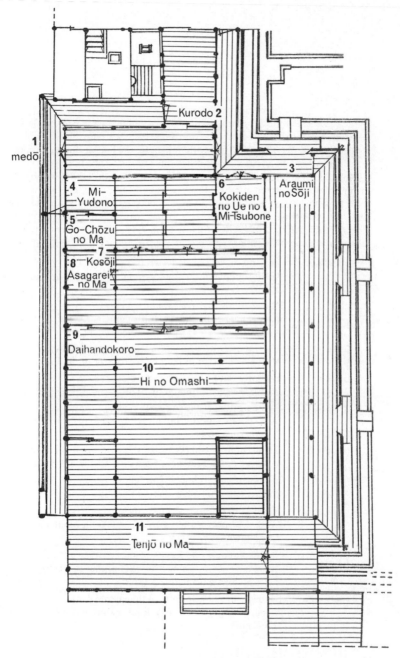

1
medō

Kurodo **2**

3
Araumi
no Sōji

4
Mi-
Yudono

6
Kokiden
no Ue no
Mi-Tsubone

5
Go-Chōzu
no Ma

7
8 Kosōji
Asagarei
no Ma

9
Daihandokoro

10
Hi no Omashi

11
Tenjō no Ma

9*g*. SEIRYŌ DEN (EMPEROR'S RESIDENTIAL PALACE)

257

APPENDIX 10

POEMS

Of the 132 poems whose first lines in the original and in the English translation are given below, 91 are quoted (69 from Japanese, 22 from Chinese) and 41 are original. Of the 69 quoted from the Japanese, the largest number appear in the *Kokin Shū* and *Kokin Rokujō* anthologies (19 and 13 poems respectively). Of the 22 Chinese poems, exactly one half are by Po Chü-i, who was by far the most popular foreign poet in Heian Japan. Of the 41 original poems, the largest numbers were written by Shōnagon herself (17 poems) and by the Empress (7 poems). It should be noted that many of the quoted poems were not included in anthologies until after *The Pillow Book* was written. The following is a complete list of the *Pillow Book* poems.

1 (note 64). Inugami no (By Isaya River)
Kokin Shū poem quoted by Shōnagon in reference to Mt. Toko.

2 (note 65). Mukashi mishi (Like Mount Asakura)
Rokujō poem quoted by Shōnagon in reference to Mt. Asakura.

3 (note 79). Tsuki mo hi mo (The days and months flow by)
Manyō Shū poem quoted by Korechika to the Empress.

4 (note 81). Toshi fureba (The years have passed)
Kokin Shū poem quoted by Shōnagon to the Emperor.

5 (note 84). Shio no mitsu (Like the sea)
Love poem (source unknown) quoted by Michitaka to Emperor Enyū.

6 (note 138). Sau nashi no nushi (Who can stand next to this fine fellow)
Mocking poem recited at Court to ridicule Suketada.

7 (note 163). Motomete mo (Though you bid me come)
Poem written by Shōnagon to a friend.

8 (note 175). Naoki ki ni (The straightest tree)
Gosen Shū poem quoted by Michitaka in reference to an unknown lady.

9 (note 179). Shiratsuyu no (The *asagao* bloom)
Muneyuki poem quoted by Shōnagon in reference to Yoshichika's becoming a priest.

10 (note 186). Sakurao no (The sprouts of the cherry-flax)
Rokujō poem quoted by a lover on his way home in the morning.

258

11 (note 196).   Yü jung chi mo lei lan kan (Her face, delicate as jade, is
                  desolate beneath the heavy tears)
                  Chinese poem (Po Chü-i) quoted by Shōnagon in reference
                  to the pear blossom.

12 (note 202).   Wagimoko ga (Grievous indeed to see)
                  Gosen Shū poem to which Shōnagon alludes in reference
                  to Sayama Pond.

13 (note 204).   Musashi naru (Pull out the water-bur)
                  Rokujō poem to which Shōnagon alludes in reference to
                  Hara Pond.

14 (note 205).   Oshi takabe (The mandarin duck)
                  Popular song quoted by Shōnagon in reference to Hara
                  Pond.

15 (note 216).   Izumi naru (One thousand branches grow)
                  Rokujō poem to which Shōnagon alludes in reference to
                  the camphor tree.

16 (note 217).   Kono dono wa (Rich indeed has this palace grown)
                  Saibara quoted by Shōnagon in reference to the *hinoki*
                  cypress.

17 (note 219).   Ashibiki no (Climbing the arduous mountain path)
                  Manyō Shū poem to which Shōnagon alludes in reference
                  to the white oak.

18 (note 220).   Tabibito ni (When the leaves of the *yuzuriha*)
                  Rokujō poem quoted by Shōnagon in reference to the
                  yuzuriha leaves.

19 (note 221).   Kashiwagi ni (Not knowing what I did)
                  Yamato Monogatari poem to which Shōnagon alludes in
                  reference to the oak.

20 (note 225).   Takashima ya (In Takashima even the herons of Yurugi
                  Wood)
                  Rokujō poem to which Shōnagon alludes in reference to
                  the heron.

21 (note 227).   Ha no ue no (The mandarin ducks, the husband and his
                  mate)
                  Rokujō poem quoted by Shōnagon in reference to the
                  mandarin duck.

22 (note 228).   Aki kureba (Autumn is here)
                  Rokujō poem quoted by Shōnagon in reference to the
                  plover.

23 (note 229).   Saitama no (In Saitama)
                  Manyō Shū poem quoted by Shōnagon in reference to the
                  wild duck.

259

24 (note 259).	Arare furi (Oh, the willow tree)
	Manyō Shū poem to which Yukinari alludes in reference to his relations with Shōnagon.
25 (note 278).	Yo no naka wa (What in this world of ours can last)
	Kokin Shū poem to which Shōnagon alludes in reference to Asuka River.
26 (note 279).	Momoshiki no (Ah, the keen-eared stream of Mimito)
	Rokujō poem to which Shōnagon alludes in reference to Mimito River.
27 (note 281).	Nukigawa no sese no (As Nuki River gently flows along)
	Saibara to which Shōnagon alludes in reference to Nuki River.
28 (note 281).	Sawadagawa (If you cross the stream of Sawada)
	Saibara to which Shōnagon alludes in reference to Sawada River.
29 (note 283).	Michinoku ni (Alas, how sad)
	Kokin Shū poem to which Shōnagon alludes in reference to Natori River.
30 (note 284).	Karikurashi (After the long day's hunt)
	Kokin Shū poem quoted by Shōnagon in reference to the River of Heaven.
31 (note 291).	Kuan shen an o li ken ts'ao (I see that this, my life)
	Chinese poem (*Wakan Rōei Shū*) to which Shōnagon probably alludes in reference to shrubs that grow in precarious places.
32 (note 303).	Iwa-tsutsuji (I plucked a rhododendron)
	Goshūi Shū poem quoted by Shōnagon in reference to the rhododendron.
33 (note 304).	Chieh ti ch'iang wei ju hsia k'ai (Under the steps)
	Chinese poem (Po Chü-i) to which Shōnagon probably alludes in reference to roses.
34 (note 307).	Omowanu to (He whom I loved)
	Rokujō poem to which Shōnagon alludes in reference to a person whom one no longer loves.
35 (note 312).	Kokoro ni wa (He who does not speak his love)
	Rokujō poem quoted by Shōnagon in reference to people who do not put their feelings into words.
36 (note 316).	Arata ni ouru (Come, lads, let's pluck the rice-flowers from the freshly-planted fields)
	Folk-song quoted by Shōnagon in describing the Special Festival.
37 (note 319).	Ch'ih leng shui wu sañ fu hsia (Fresh is the pond)
	Chinese poem (by Minamoto no Hideakira) quoted by a group of courtiers on their way to the Empress's palace.

38 (note 329). Hu wen shui shang p'i p'a sheng (Suddenly we hear the lute's voice on the water)
Chinese poem (Po Chü-i) quoted by Korechika after a concert in the Palace.

39 (note 337). Lan sheng hua shih chin chang hsia (With you it is flower time)
Chinese poem (Po Chü-i) quoted by Tadanobu in a letter to Shōnagon.

40 (note 337). Kusa no iori wo (Who would come to visit)
Last two lines of a Japanese poem written by Shōnagon to Tadanobu in reply to his Chinese quotation (no. 39).

41 (note 355). Ts'ui hua pu lai hsi sui yüeh chiu (How many months, how many years, have passed)
Chinese poem (Po Chü-i) quoted by Lady Saishō in reference to the desolation of the West City.

42 (note 363). Kazuki suru (Tell no man where she lives)
Poem written by Shōnagon to Norimitsu.

43 (note 363). Shiranami no (How should I have a fixed abode)
Wakan Rōei Shū poem to which Shōnagon probably alludes in her poem to Norimitsu (no. 42).

44 (note 365). Kuzureyoru (Smoothly runs the river of Yoshino)
Poem written by Shōnagon to Norimitsu.

45 (note 365). Nagaruru wa (Between Mount Imo and Mount Se)
Kokin Shū poem to which Shōnagon probably alludes in her poem to Norimitsu (no. 44).

46 (note 369). Asaborake (Faintly I saw her by the dawn's pale light)
Utsubo Monogatari poem quoted by the Empress in reference to her ladies-in-waiting.

47 (note 373). Yoru wa tare to ka nemu (Who shall share my bed to-night)
Popular song sung by the old beggar-nun.

48 (note 373). Otoko Yama no (The maple leaves of scarlet)
Popular song sung by the old beggar-nun.

49 (note 379). Koko ni nomi (That mountain in our garden)
Poem recited by Shōnagon to Tadataka.

50 (note 380). Urayamashi (Lucky indeed is she)
Poem recited by the old beggar-nun to the ladies-in-waiting.

51 (note 385). Yama toyomu (I thought I heard the woodman's axe)
Poem written by the High-Priestess of Kamo to the Empress.

52 (note 420). Ashihiki no (The mountain well is frozen hard)
Poem recited by Captain Sanekata to Lady Kohyōe.

53 (note 422).	Usu-kōri (Frail as a string of bubbles is that ice) Reply poem recited by Shōnagon for Lady Kohyōe.
54 (note 429).	Tsukasa masare to (The envoys billow forth like waves) Song sung by the courtiers at the time of the Gosechi dances.
55 (note 440).	Yu pao pʻi pʻa pan che mien (She lifts her lute, and I can see but half her face) Chinese poem (by Po Chü-i) quoted by Shōnagon in reference to the Empress's beauty.
56 (note 444).	Akane sasu (When you have gone away) Poem written by the Empress to one of her nurses.
57 (note 467).	Hototogisu (If only I had known) Poem written by Kiminobu to Shōnagon.
58 (note 470).	Hototogisu (More than the cuckoo's song she went to hear) Poem composed jointly by the Empress (last two lines) and Shōnagon (first three lines).
59 (note 473).	Motosuke ga (Surely it is not you) Poem written by the Empress to Shōnagon.
60 (note 473).	Sono hito no (Were I not known to be the daughter of that man) Poem written by Shōnagon in reply to the Empress.
61 (note 476).	Wei chien chiang hsin chʻiu yüeh pai (Wordless we gaze into the river and the moon's white light) Chinese poem (by Po Chü-i) to which Shōnagon probably alludes in reference to the autumn moon.
62 (note 503).	Yamazakura (Ah, what fond memories she summons forth) *Kokin Shū* poem quoted by Michitaka in reference to Shōnagon's robe, which is protruding under a blind.
63 (note 519).	Ta-yü ling chih mei tsao lao (Early have they scattered—the blossoms on the plum trees of Ta-yü peak) Chinese poem (by Ki no Haseo) quoted by Shōnagon in reference to a plum-branch that has lost its blossoms.
64 (notes 523 and 526).	Sora samumi (As though pretending to be blooms) Poems composed jointly by Kintō and other gentlemen (last two lines) and Shōnagon (first three lines).
65 (note 544).	Komomakura (Ah, what sweet repose) The Song of Takase Pool, which Shōnagon recalls while crossing Yodo Ferry.
66 (note 610).	Tsumedo nao (Pluck them or pinch them as you may) Poem recited by Shōnagon to some children who are arranging flowers.

67 (note 628).	Pi chin ku tsui hua chih ti (This golden valley, this earth) Chinese poem (by Sugawara no Fumitoki) quoted by Tadanobu in reference to Michitaka's death.
68 (note 640).	Yo wo komete (There may be some who are deceived) Poem written by Shōnagon to Yukinari.
69 (note 640).	Au saka wa (I have heard it said) Poem written by Yukinari in reply to Shōnagon (no. 68).
70 (note 650).	Mina hito wa (All, once more, in flowery clothes are decked) Kokin Shū poem quoted by Shōnagon in reference to Emperor Enyū's death.
71 (note 653).	Kore wo dani (Here we keep our sombre, oak-dyed clothes) Poem sent to Tōzammi from the Palace.
72 (note 670).	Udo Hama ni (At Udo Beach) The Song of Udo Beach sung by the musicians on the day of the rehearsal for the Special Festival.
73 (note 671).	Chidori yue ni (Be mindful of the plovers) The Song of the Little Pines sung as an accompaniment to the dancing during the rehearsal for the Special Festival.
74 (note 674).	Mezurashiki (Ah, upon this festive day) Shūi Shū poem to which Shōnagon probably alludes in reference to the dances at the Special Festival.
75 (note 685).	Yo no naka no (Before we even learn) Kokin Shū poem quoted by Shōnagon in reference to weeping.
76 (note 747).	Natsu to aki to (There in the sky) Kokin Shū poem quoted by Shōnagon in reference to the absence of an autumn breeze.
77 (note 750).	Jen chien szu yüeh fang fei chin (The Fourth Month in this world of men) Chinese poem (by Po Chü-i) quoted by Tadanobu, who intends to recite it on the following day.
78 (note 754).	Lu ying pieh lei chu k'ung lo (The tears she sheds on parting will turn to dew when morning comes) Chinese poem (by Sugawara no Michizane) quoted by Tadanobu in reference to leaving Shōnagon and other ladies-in-waiting at dawn.
79 (note 761).	Yen Hui Chou hsien che (Yen Hui, the sage of Chou, had not yet reached the term of thirty) Chinese poem (by Minamoto no Hideakira) recited by Tadanobu in a manner that greatly impresses Shōnagon.

80 (note 782).   Asaka Yama (The well of Mount Asaka)
                 Manyō Shū poem to which Shōnagon alludes in reference
                 to the mountain well.

81 (note 783).   Asuka I ni (At the well of Asuka)
                 Saibara quoted by Shōnagon in reference to the well of
                 Asuka.

82 (note 796).   Yamazato wa (Here in my mountain home)
                 Shūi Shū poem quoted by a lady-in-waiting in reference
                 to a gentleman visitor.

83 (note 798).   Hsiao ju Liang Wang chih yüan (At dawn I walked into the
                 garden of the King of Liang)
                 Chinese poem (in *Wakan Rōei Shū*) quoted by a gentleman
                 who has visited some ladies-in-waiting on a snowy
                 night.

84 (note 799).   Ch'in shih chiu yu chieh p'ou wo (My friends—the zither,
                 poetry, and wine—have all three left me)
                 Chinese poem (by Po Chü-i) quoted by Lady Hyōe to
                 Emperor Murakami.

85 (note 800).   Watatsumi no (What do I see in the open sea)
                 Poem recited by Lady Hyōe to Emperor Murakami.

86 (note 813).   Ika ni shite (How, if there were no God Tadasu in
                 the sky)
                 Poem written by the Empress to Shōnagon.

87 (note 813).   Usuki koso (A simple sneeze might give the lie)
                 Poem written by Shōnagon in reply to the Empress.

88 (note 847).   Chihayaburu (The princess pines that grow outside)
                 Kokin Shū poem chanted by the musicians during the
                 Special Festival.

89 (note 856).   Kaze fukeba (The fleecy clouds that scatter on the
                 peak)
                 Kokin Shū poem quoted by a gentleman who passes
                 Shōnagon in a carriage.

90 (note 867).   Mikasa Yama (Since dawn first shed its light over Mount
                 Mikasa's peak)
                 Poem composed jointly by the Empress (first three lines)
                 and Shōnagon (last two lines).

91 (note 871).   Masegoshi ni (Stretching his neck across the fence)
                 Rokujō poem quoted by Shōnagon in reference to her love
                 for the Empress.

92 (note 871).   Minahito no (Even on this festive day)
                 Reply poem written by the Empress to Shōnagon.

93 (note 881).   Kono sasa wa (This bamboo grass)
                 Kagura to which Shōnagon probably alludes in reference
                 to Tomo Hill.

94 (note 883). Miwa no yama (It is the *sugi* tree)
Poem by Ki no Tsurayuki to which Shōnagon alludes in reference to the sacred shrine of the cryptomeria.

95 (note 884). Negigoto wo (This is indeed a shrine)
Kokin Shū poem quoted by Shōnagon in reference to the shrine of Koto no Mama.

96 (note 885). Kakikumori (How could I have known)
Poem by Ki no Tsurayuki to which Shōnagon alludes in reference to the God of Aridōshi.

97 (note 889). Nanawata ni (Who is there who does not know)
Poem (source unknown) quoted by Shōnagon in reference to the God of Aridōshi.

98 (note 892). Tan wei chʿao yün (At dawn they make the morning clouds)
Chinese poem (by Sung Yü) to which Shōnagon may be alluding in reference to the clouds that turn white at dawn.

99 (note 917). Hototogisu yo (Ah, *hototogisu*)
Folk-song sung by some peasant women whom Shōnagon sees in a field.

100 (note 918). Hototogisu (Sing not too loudly)
Rokujō poem quoted by one of Shōnagon's companions in reference to the *hototogisu*'s song.

101 (note 921). Kino koso (Only yesterday, it seems)
Kokin Shū poem quoted by Shōnagon in reference to the rice harvest.

102 (note 939). Waga kokoro (Inconsolable my heart)
Kokin Shū poem quoted by the Empress in reference to Shōnagon's ability to console herself.

103 (note 941). Kakemaku mo (Thanks to the paper that the Goddess gave)
Poem written by Shōnagon to the Empress.

104 (note 955). Sakurabana (Sadly I behold them)
Shūi Shū poem quoted by Shōnagon in reference to some faded cherry blossoms.

105 (note 956). Yamamori wa (Let him tell me what he will)
Gosen Shū poem that Shōnagon would have liked to quote to some workmen who are removing cherry blossoms from a tree.

106 (note 958). Ame mo namida mo (Both the rain and my tears come pouring down)
Shūi Shū poem to which the Empress may be alluding in reference to the disappearance of the cherry blossoms.

265

107 (note 961).   Yamada sae (The time has come)
Poem by Ki no Tsurayuki quoted by the Empress to
Michitaka in reference to the disappearance of the
cherry blossoms.

108 (note 964).   Chiu yüeh hsi feng hsing (In the Ninth Month the west
wind quickens)
Chinese poem (by Po Chü-i) quoted by the Empress to
Shōnagon in reference to their relationship.

109 (note 1002).   Michinoku no (Though close at hand)
Zoku Gosen Shū poem quoted by the Empress Dowager to
the Empress in reference to their failure to meet.

110 (note 1008).   Waga iroi wa (My hut is at Mount Miwa's base)
Kokin Shū poem quoted by Shōnagon in her list of
songs.

111 (note 1020).   Chihayaburu (Even the arrowroot that trails the sacred
hedge)
Kokin Shū poem quoted by Shōnagon in reference to
moonlight.

112 (note 1046).   Yūyami wa (The evening now is dark)
Gosen Shū poem quoted by Shōnagon in reference to
moonlight.

113 (note 1048).   Waga inochi (Until my life becomes extinct)
Manyō Shū poem to which Shōnagon may be alluding in
reference to a secret visit by a man.

114 (note 1051).   Aketateba (When dawn appears)
Kokin Shū poem quoted by Shōnagon in reference to the
non-arrival of a next-morning letter.

115 (note 1065).   Jih kao shui tsu yu jung ch'i (The sun has risen in the sky,
but still I idly lie in bed)
Chinese poem (by Po Chü-i) quoted by the Empress in
reference to the thick snow.

116 (note 1069).   Sakashira ni (Ah, what a house this is)
Poem written by Shōnagon about an ugly willow tree.

117 (note 1070).   Ika ni shite (So hard to bear)
Poem written by the Empress to Shōnagon.

118 (note 1071).   Kururu ma wa (Evening comes)
Goshūi Shū poem quoted by Lady Saishō in reference to
the Empress's poem to Shōnagon (no. 117).

119 (note 1073).   Kumo no ue ni (How sadly have I viewed these long spring
days)
Poem written by Shōnagon to the Empress.

120 (note 1076).   Yama chikaki (Count each echo of the temple bell)
Poem written by the Empress to Shōnagon.

121 (note 1079). Ch'in tien chih i ch'ien yü li ([The moon,] piercing cold)
Chinese poem (by Kung Ch'eng-i) quoted by a gentleman
who is travelling in a carriage with a lady.

122 (note 1084). Yo no naka wo (This world of ours)
Shūi Shū poem quoted by Shōnagon in reference to the
waves that disappear behind a boat.

123 (note 1090). Watatsumi ni (A man who drowned his parents in the
ocean's depths)
Poem written by Dōmei about a lieutenant who drowned
his parents.

124 (note 1092). Takigi koru (Yesterday we finished cutting firewood)
Poem written by the Lord of Ono's mother about a
Buddhist service at Ono Villa.

125 (note 1094). Oinureba (Now I am old)
Kokin Shū poem quoted by Shōnagon, who has been
moved by its sentiments

126 (note 1098). Chi jen hsiao ch'ang (When the cock-man cries the advent
of the day)
Chinese poem (by Miyako no Yoshika) quoted by Korechika in reference to the Emperor's being awakened by
a rooster.

127 (note 1099). Chia jen chin shih yu ch'en chuang (At dawn when bells
of Wei begin to ring)
Chinese poem (by Chia Tao) quoted by Korechika to
Shōnagon in reference to the moonlight.

128 (note 1102). Mimagusa wo (If the vernal sun burns strong enough)
Poem written by Shōnagon to a man who has lost his
house in a fire.

129 (note 1107). Omoi dani (The fiery sage-brush near the mountain's foot)
Poem written by Shōnagon in reply to someone who asked
whether she was leaving for the provinces.

130 (note 1108). Chikae kimi (Swear it, my lord, upon the Gods)
Poem written by Shōnagon for a lady who is being deceived
by her lover.

131 (note 1109). Ōsaka wa (Never is the mind at ease)
Poem written by Shōnagon in reply to a nervous lover.

132 (note 1128). Nagatsuki no (If you but came and lingered by my side)
Shūi Shū poem quoted by a lady while she watches her
departing lover.

BIBLIOGRAPHY

WORKS IN JAPANESE

Texts of *The Pillow Book*

Ikeda Kikan and Kishigami Shinji, *Makura no Sōshi*, Nihon Koten Bungaku Taikei ed., Tokyo, 1958.
Ikutoku Zaidan, ed., *Maedabon Makura no Sōshi*, Tokyo, 1927.
Kaneko Motoomi, *Makura no Sōshi Hyōshaku*, Tokyo, 1927.
Kaneko Takeo, *Makura no Sōshi*, Koten Hyōshaku ed., Tokyo, 1958.
Kurihara Takeichirō, *Makura no Sōshi*, Yōchū Kokubun Teihon Sōshū ed., Tokyo, 1928.
Mutō Motonobu (Genshin), *Makura no Sōshi Tsūshaku*, Tokyo, 1911.
Onoe Hachirō, ed., *Emaki Makura no Sōshi*, Tokyo, 1929.
Tanaka Shigetarō, *Makura no Sōshi*, Nihon Koten Zensho ed., Tokyo, 1954.

Other Works

Fujiki Kunihiko, *Heian Jidai no Kizoku no Seikatsu*, Tokyo, 1960.
Hisamatsu Senichi, *Nihon Bungaku Shi*, Tokyo, 1956.
Ikeda Kikan, *Heianchō no Seikatsu to Bungaku*, Tokyo, 1953.
—— *Kenkyū Makura no Sōshi*, Tokyo, 1963.
—— *Makura no Sōshi ni· Kansuru Ronkō*, Tokyo, 1946.
—— *Makura no Sōshi no Keitai ni Kansuru Ichikōsatsu*, Tokyo, 1932.
Kishigami Shinji, *Sei Shōnagon*, Tokyo, 1962.
Kitayama Keita, *Genji Monogatari Jiten*, Tokyo, 1957.
Kokubungaku, no. 182, *Sei Shōnagon no Bungaku to Kankyō*, Tokyo, 1964.
Kuroita Katsumi, *Kokushi no Kenkyū*, Tokyo, 1939.
Murai Jun, *Makura no Sōshi no Bumpō to Kaishaku*, Tokyo, 1956.
Nihon Emakimono Zenshū ed., Vol. XII (*Murasaki Shikibu Nikki Emaki, Makura no Sōshi Emaki*), Tokyo, 1961.
Shimada Taizō, *Makura no Sōshi Senshaku*, Tokyo, 1930.

WORKS IN WESTERN LANGUAGES

Aston, William, *Shinto: The Way of the Gods*, London, 1905.
—— *Japanese Literature*, London, 1899.
Beaujard, André, *Les Notes de chevet de Séi Shōnagon'*, Paris, 1934.
—— *Séi Shōnagon': son temps et son œuvre*, Paris, 1934.
Brower, Robert, and Miner, Earl, *Japanese Court Poetry*, Stanford, 1961.

de Bary, William Theodore, *et al.*, ed., *Sources of the Japanese Tradition*, New York, 1958.
Eliot, Sir Charles, *Japanese Buddhism*, London, 1959.
Frank, Bernard, *Kata-imi et kata-tagae: étude sur les interdits de direction à l'époque Heian*, Tokyo, 1958.
Keene, Donald, *Anthology of Japanese Literature*, New York, 1955.
Kobayashi Nobuko, *The Sketch Book of the Lady Sei Shōnagon*, London, 1930.
Kuni Matsuo and Steinilber-Oberlin, *Les Notes de l'oreiller*, Paris, 1928.
Morris, Ivan, *The World of the Shining Prince: Court Life in Ancient Japan*, London, 1964.
—— *Dictionary of Selected Forms in Classical Japanese Literature*, New York and London, 1966.
Nippon Gakujutsu Shinkōkai, *The Manyōshū*, Tokyo, 1940.
Omori, Annie, and Kochi Doi, *Diaries of Court Ladies of Old Japan*, Boston, 1935.
Purcell, Dr. T. A., and Aston, William, *A Literary Lady of Old Japan*, Transactions of the Asiatic Society of Japan, XVI. 3, Tokyo, 1888.
Reischauer, Edwin, and Fairbank, John, *East Asia: The Great Tradition*, Boston, 1958.
Reischauer, R. K., *Early Japanese History*, Princeton, 1937.
Revon, Michel, *Anthologie de la littérature japonaise, des origines au xxᵉ siècle*, Paris, 1928.
Sansom, G. B., *A History of Japan* (Vol. I: to 1334), London, 1958.
—— *A Short Cultural History of Japan*, London, 1931.
—— *An Historical Grammar of Japanese*, London, 1928
Seidensticker, Edward, *The Kagerō Nikki: Journal of a 10th Century Noblewoman*, Tokyo, 1955
Waley, Arthur, *The Pillow-Book of Sei Shōnagon*, London, 1928.

INDEX-GLOSSARY

This glossary of words, phrases, and proper names in *The Pillow Book of Sei Shōnagon* serves as an index to the notes accompanying my translation. To save space I have omitted most of the words that appear in:

(i) Kenkyusha's *New Japanese-English Dictionary* (1954 ed.),
(ii) my *Dictionary of Selected Forms in Classical Japanese Literature* (Columbia University Press, 1966).

I have, however, included Kenkyusha words if Sei Shōnagon used them, either occasionally or entirely, in a different sense from the modern ones. A major difficulty in reading Heian Japanese is the large number of 'false friends', common words like *sara, nao, tada, mazu, nakanaka, yagate, semete, kanashi*, and *kashikoshi* which, either by addition or by substitution, have now acquired meanings significantly different from those they had in Shōnagon's day. The reader should remember that, even though they had different meanings in the Heian period, this does not preclude the possibility that they may also have been used in the same way as today; *omou*, for example, was used in the senses of 'to love' and 'to worry', but it also meant 'to think'.

Homophones like *koto* ('particular', 'zither', 'word') always appear as separate entries. When a word (e.g. *kokorobae*) has a single origin but several different meanings, these meanings are all included in the same entry with numbers (1), (2), (3), etc. to distinguish them; there is no particular significance in their order but usually they appear in the order in which I found them in *The Pillow Book*, and the more important and common meanings may consequently come after rarer ones. Readers should also be warned that the meanings given for words and phrases in this glossary may not necessarily apply when these words and phrases occur in other classical texts; *kokoro koto nari*, for example, appears in *The Pillow Book* meaning 'to be alienated, estranged', but in *The Tale of Genji* it is used only in the sense of 'unusual, out of the ordinary'.

In my translations of proper names I have as a rule used those given in R. K. Reischauer's *Early Japanese History*. Occasionally, however, I have abbreviated his translations when they seem unduly cumbersome. For reasons explained in my notes I have not followed his translation of Kampaku ('Civil Dictator') and have translated this as 'Chancellor'; also I have preferred to write 'Emperor' rather than 'Sovereign'.

The nomenclature of flowering plants is based on *Index Kewensis*, Oxford, 1895, and *Supplements* I-XII, 1886-1955, to which the reader should refer for botanical details.

A number of English-Japanese entries have been included in the Index-Glossary. This is not intended as an aid to the intrepid student who wishes to compose Heian Japanese; the purpose is to help readers identify certain words like 'abstinence' and 'Chief Chamberlain' that occur frequently in my translation of *The Pillow Book*. Having found the Japanese equivalent in the Index-Glossary, they can then refer to the appropriate notes.

Owing to the plethora of unfamiliar words and proper names, classical Japanese literature is particularly difficult for the Western reader even after he has mastered the grammatical structure. Index-glossaries such as I have attempted here may help to make the riches of this literature more accessible. If numerous specialists engaged in the study of different works of classical literature were prepared to compile lists of this type for their own respective books, it is possible that they might eventually be combined into a fairly comprehensive dictionary of classical Japanese. This would be a boon for future students and would enormously facilitate the task of reading and translating pre-modern works.

abstinence—*monoimi, sōjin*
abura—light, taper
adopted son-in-law—*muko*
aenashi—unbearable
after-runner—*zuijin*
Agata no Ido—residence of the Tachibana family (App. 9d, no. 3)
ageburi—curtained pavilion
agura—stool
aigyō—charm, grace, amiability
aigyōzuku—to be charming, sweet, adorable
ai na—charmless, graceless (—*aigyo nashi*)
ai nashi—(1) strange, (2) untimely, out of place, (3) inexplicable, (4) unfortunate, (5) charmless, unamiable, malicious
Aitandokoro—Dining Hall of the High Court Nobles (note 743)
Ajari—*see* Azari
ajiki nashi—useless, uninteresting, time-wasting, not worth doing
ajiro—(1) wickerwork fish-net (note 100), (2) wickerwork ox-carriage (note 152) (App. 8c, no. 3)
akaginu—red costume worn by servants, messengers, etc.
akairo—purple-red (of woven materials)
akamu—to turn red, blush
akarasama ni—temporarily, for a short while
akaru—(1) to become clear, (2) to turn red
akashi—clear, light, bright
akashiraga—grey or white hair tinged with red; reddish grey
akegure—early dawn

akome—short under-jacket or waistcoat
aku—to dawn
akugaru—see *kokoro akugaru*
ama—woman diver (notes 363, 1086)
amabiko—(1) echo, (2) name of a bridge
amaguri—sweet chestnut (note 396)
amakaze—rainy (moist) wind
amazura—liana, liana syrup (note 237)
ameku—to shout, bawl
ame no ashi—rain-drop, rain
Amida—Amitabha, Buddha of the Western Paradise (note 834)
anagachi—reckless, immoderate
anakama—oh, how noisy [you are]! be quiet!
an(n)ai—(1) help, protection, guidance, (2) connexion, (3) inquiry, applying for information
anatagata—enemy party, rival faction
anatakonata ni—close by, in the neighbourhood
anazurawashi—(1) unimportant, insignificant, contemptible, held in scorn, (2) scornful, contemptuous
anazuru—(1) to scorn, despise, disdain, (2) to be negligent, off one's guard
ani hakariki ya—contrary to expectation, to one's surprise
ante-room—*hisashi*
ao—same as *ue no kinu*
aogu—see *uchiaogu*
Aoi Matsuri—Hollyhock (Kamo) Festival, *see* Kamo Matsuri
aoiro—yellowish green (notes 70, 395)
aokuchiba—(1) yellowish green (lit. green and withered leaf), (2) colour combination in which the outside of the

garment is yellowish green and the lining is green (or vice versa) (note 23)

aonibi—bluish grey

aouma—'blue' horses paraded before the Emperor at New Year (notes 8, 732) (App. 1)

aoyagi—willow-green (notes 23, 579)

aozashi—green-wheat cake (notes 870, 871)

aozuri—dark-blue pattern against a white background (note 845)

appointment—*jimoku*

arabatake—untilled field, uncultivated land

aragaigoto—dispute, controversy, question, quarrel

aragau—(1) to maintain, argue, (2) to be at variance, dispute

arakumashi—rude, wild, harsh

aramahoshi—(1) splendid, superb, (2) I wish that it were (*ara-mahoshi*)

arareji—material decorated with small, closely placed squares ('hail-stones')

Araumi no Sōji—'Rough Ocean' Screen in Seiryō Palace (note 73) (App. 9g, no. 3)

arawa—impertinent, impudent, forward

Archbishop—Sōjō

ariari(te)—at long last, after waiting for a long time

aridokoro—whereabouts

Aridōshi—shrine in Izumi Province (notes 879, 885, 886, 889)

arigatashi—strange, marvellous, rare

ariku—(1) to walk, stroll, go, visit, (2) to travel, sail

Ariwara no Narihira—(825-80) famous poet, known for his good looks and amorous exploits; classed as one of the Six Poetical Geniuses (notes 284, 1094)

aru kagiri—the best in the world, the best one can imagine

aruji—feast, entertainment

aruwa—or

asagao—(1) shrubby althea (notes 179, 297, 299), (2) campanula, (3) one's appearance in the morning (note 959)

Asagarei no Ma—Imperial Dining Room, room in Seiryō Palace where ceremonial meals were served (note 47) (App. 9g, no. 8)

asai—morning nap, staying late in bed

asaji—scattered reeds (of the *chigaya* variety)

asakaze—morning zephyr, breeze (notes 274, 287)

Asakura Yama—Mt. Asakura in Chikuzen Province (notes 62, 65)

asamashi—(1) amazing, astonishing, astounding, (2) stupid, silly, (3) wretched, lamentable, shameful

asamashigaru—(1) to be amazed, astounded, (2) to regard as wretched (shameful)

asaru—to be fashionable, smart

asaza—morning service (Buddhist)

ashi—ugly

ashida—high clogs (notes 561, 1148)

ashidaka—long-legged

ashige—dapple-grey

ashiki me miru—to have a bad experience

ashi no ke—beriberi

ashita—morning

asobi—music, concert

asobiwaza—game

asobu—(1) to play music, (2) to dance

Ason—hereditary title (His Lordship, Lord) (notes 460, 1130)

Assistant Attendant—Naishi no Suke, Tenji

Assistant Captain—Suke

Assistant Director—Suke

Assistant Governor—Suke

Assistant Master—Suke

Assistant Official (of the Emperor's Private Office)—Tokoro no Shū

aster—*shion*

Asukagawa—Asuka River in Yamato Province (notes 274, 278)

asuwa-hinoki—large-leaved cypress, *thuja dalobrata* (note 218)

atakataki—enemy

atarashi—(1) new, (2) regrettable, wasteful

ate(haka)—elegant, distinguished, noble

ateyaka—see *ate(haka)*

atobi—parting-fire, lit on the last day of the Urabon festival (note 662)

atsugoyu—to be very thick (heavy)

atsukawashi—sweltering, stifling, sultry

Atsuyasu, Prince—(999-1019) son of Emperor Ichijō and Sadako (notes 403, 509, 869) (App. 6a, no. 23)

Attendant—Shōji, Naishi

Attendants' Hall—Saburaidokoro

au—to bear, stand, endure, resist

avenue—*jō*

avoidance of unlucky direction—*katatagae*

Awa—superior province (*jōkoku*) in Shikoku (note 786) (App. 9b, no. 51)

awaawashi—light, frivolous, insincere

aware—(1) alas, (2) pitiful, moving, sad (notes 213, 549), (3) interesting, (4) splendid, fine, excellent (see also *Dictionary of Selected Forms in Classical Japanese Literature*)

awase—(1) match, competition (notes 688, 936), (2) see *yume-awase*, (3) vegetables

awasu—to match (exchange) entries in a competition (note 688)

Ayame no Sekku—Iris Festival (notes 54, 198, 206, 407, 410, 545, 732, 858, 868) (App. 1)

aya nashi—(1) incomprehensible, senseless, (2) unreasonable, foolish, useless

ayanikudatsu—to be mischievous, naughty

ayanikugaru—to loathe, hate, find detestable

ayaniku ni—in a cross (ill-tempered, malicious) way

ayanikushi—impudent, insolent

ayashi—(1) strange, suspicious, astonishing, grotesque, (2) plain, rough, (3) humble, common, vulgar, low-class, (4) unsightly, ugly, unbecoming, shameful, improper, scandalous, disgraceful, (5) absurd, preposterous, (6) see *kokoro ayashi*

ayashigaru—to regard (something) as strange

ayaugaru—to be frightened

ayu—to ooze out

ayumi—procession, progress (note 728)

Azari—Holy Teacher (note 586)

azumaya—Azuma-style cottage (note 1023)

backgammon—*sugoroku*

bakari—(1) period, (2) about, near

balustrade—*kōran*

bamboo blind—*mi-su*

ban—see *daihan* (1)

basket worm—*minomushi*

bat-fan—*kawahori* (2)

bathroom servant—*sumashi*

baton—*shaku*

bearded basket—*higeko*

bechi—separate, apart, different

beijū—low-ranking musician who accompanied dancers on the zither or flute (note 669)

Ben—Controller, official of the Controlling Boards in charge of work in the 8 Ministries (App. 7a)

Ben no Naishi—lady-in-waiting to Empress Sadako (notes 256, 257, 619)

Ben no Omoto—lady-in-waiting to Empress Sadako (note 619)

Bet(t)ō—(1) Intendant, priest in charge of certain important temples (note 61), (2) sexton, sacristan, (3) Director (of a government office) (note 490), (4) Chief of the Imperial Police

bin nashi—(1) awkward, inexpedient, inconvenient, troublesome, (2) improper irregular, outrageous

birōge no kuruma—palm-leaf carriage, large ox-carriage covered with palm leaf (note 34) (App. 8c, no. 2)

birth chamber—*ubuya*

Bishop—Sozu

hiwa—Japanese lute (App. 8d, no. 7)

Biwa Ko—large lake north-east of the capital (note 71) (App. 9b, no. 2)

Biwa Kō—see *I*ʳ*i I*ʰ*u Hsing*

Black Door—Kurodo

black lacquered head-dress—*eboshi*

blinds—*su(dare)*

'blue' horses—*aouma*

bō—visitors' lodgings in a temple, cell

bōbō to—see *hōhō to*

Bodai Ji—Temple of Bodhi (Supreme Enlightenment), east of the capital (note 162)

Bon—see Urabon

bonnō—bondage of the flesh, carnal passions (note 310)

Bosachi—Bodhisattva

bōtan—peony (note 719)

bō to—see *hō to* (3)

Bunjū—Collected Works of Po Chü-i (in 71 books)

Bureau of Carpentry—Moku Ryō

Bureau of the Wardrobe—Nui Dono

butō—ceremonial movement, dance (notes 58, 412)

Butsugen Shingon—'Secret Formula of the Sacred Eye' (note 596)

butsugu—offering (to Buddha)

273

Butsumyō—Naming of the Buddhas (notes 325, 1078) (App. 1)
byōbu—screen (App. 8b, no. 11)

calendars—notes 3, 4, 747, 750, App. 3
campanula—kichikō, asagao
Captain First Secretary—Tō no Chūjō
Captain of the Outer or Middle Palace Guard—Kami
cats (in the Palace)—note 44
central apartment—moya
ceremonial movement—butō
ceremony of incantation—zuhō
Chamberlain—Kurōdo
Chamberlain of the Fifth Rank—Goi no Kurōdo
Chamberlain of the Sixth Rank—Rokui no Kurōdo
chambermaid—shimoonna
Chancellor—Kampaku
Ch'ang Hên Ko—'The Song of Everlasting Regret', a poem by Po Chü-i, its Japanese name being Chōgonka (note 196)
chie—thousand branches
Chief Attendant—Naishi no Kami
Chief Chamberlain—Kurōdo no Tō
Chief of the Imperial Police—Bet(t)ō
chigaya—species of reed (similar to reed-mace)
chigo—baby, infant; child
chihiro—lacquered hearth with a stone base
Chikugo—superior province (jōkoku) in northern Kyūshū (note 786) (App. 9a, no. 63)
Chikuzen—superior province (jōkoku) in northern Kyūshū (notes 552, 554) (App. 9a, no. 61)
Chinese hisashi—karabisashi
Chinese jacket—karaginu
Chinese mirror—karakagami
chiribou—to be scattered, in disorder, dishevelled
Chisato no Hama—Chisato ('Thousand Villages') Beach in Kii Province (note 828)
Chisoku In—Chisoku Temple near the Kamo Shrines (note 235) (App. 9c, no. 4)
chōbami—game of dice (note 150)
chōdai—curtain-dais (note 208) (App. 8b, no. 7)

chōdai no kokoromi—dais rehearsal (note 430) (App. 1)
Chōga—New Year's Day (notes, 4, 54) (App. 1)
Chōgonka—see Ch'ang Hên Ko
chō zu—(1) to exorcize, (2) to punish, (3) to prepare, make ready
Chōyō—Chrysanthemum Festival (note 54)
Chrysanthemum Festival—Chōyō, Kiku no Sekku
Chūben—Middle Controller (note 256) (App. 7a)
chūgen—awkward, untimely
Chūgū—(Second) Empress (note 88)
Chūgū Shiki—Office of the Empress's Household (notes 33, 255, 720) (App. 7a)
Chūjō—Middle Captain of the Inner Palace Guards (notes 50, 60) (App. 7b)
chūkoku—medium province (note 324)
Chu Mai-ch'en—a poor Chinese scholar who achieved success at the age of 50 (note 764)
Chūnagon—Middle Counsellor (note 43) (App. 7a)
Chūnagon no Kimi—Lady Chūnagon, lady-in-waiting to Empress Sadako (note 603) (App. 6b, no. 35)
Circuit—Dō
Cloistered Emperor—Hōō
colour combinations—note 23
coming of age—gembuku
commoner—tadabito
Confucius (Analects)—note 262
Controller—Ben
Controller First Secretary—Tō no Ben
Court cloak—naoshi
Court lady—omoto
Court Noble—Kuge
Court ranks—notes 11, 907
Court robe—uchigi
covered rhymes—i(n)futagi
Crown Prince—Tōgū
'cuckoo'—hototogisu
curtain—katabira
curtain-dais—chōdai
curtain of state—kichō

daiban—see daihan
Daiben—Major Controller (note 256) (App. 7a)
Daibu—see Miya no Daibu

274

Daidairi—Greater Imperial Palace (App. 9d, no. 1)

Daigaku Ryō—Bureau of Education, a branch of the Ministry of Ceremonial (note 398) (App. 7a)

Daigyōdō—Great Procession round the image of Buddha (being one part of the Buddhist high mass)

daihan—(1) low rectangular table (usually about 8 feet long), (2) table in the Imperial Table Room

Daihandokoro—(1) Table Room, a room in Seiryō Palace, used by ladies-in-waiting (note 53) (App. 9g, no. 9), (2) kitchen

Dai Hannya Kyō—Sutra of Great Wisdom, Mahāprajñāpāramitā Sūtra

daiichi no kuni—first-class province (note 324)

Daijin—Minister (note 97)

Daijin—Senior Steward (note 33)

Daijō—Senior Secretary (in a Ministry) (note 123)

Daijō Daijin—Prime Minister (App. 7a)

Daijōkan—Great Council (of State) (note 396) (App. 7a)

Daijōkan Cho—Office of the Great Council of State (App. 9e, no. 17)

Daikan—the Great Cold, period beginning towards the end of the 1st Month (note 103)

daikyō—(1) banquet, (2) Ministers' Banquet (notes 396, 728, 733)

Dainagon—Major Counsellor (note 74) (App. 7a)

Daini—Senior Assistant Governor-General (note 134) (App. 7b)

Dainichi Nyorai—the Great Illuminator (note 596)

Dairi—Imperial Palace compound (App. 9e, no. 8)

daishōji—dining-table about 4 by 2 feet and about 1 foot high

Dajō Daijin—see Daijō Daijin

Dajōkan—see Daijōkan

Dajōkan Chō—see Daijōkan Chō

Danjō—Censor (note 1112)

darani—mystic Buddhist incantation (notes 700, 836)

dashiginu—see idashiginu

dates—App. 3

day of abstinence—(mono)imi no hi

days, names of—App. 3

Daytime Chamber—Hi no Omashi

Dazai Fu—Government Headquarters in Kyūshū (note 134) (App. 7b)

Dedication of (Buddhist) Images—Hotoke Kuyō

Dedication of Sutras—Kyō Kuyō

deep violet—futaai

dei no Shōshō—Minor Captain in attendance at the Imperial Games (note 583)

dice—chōbami

directions, names of—notes 38, 73, and App. 3

Director—Kami, Bet(t)ō

Display of Dolls—Hiina Asobi

Dō—Circuit, one of 7 administrative areas into which Japan was divided (App. 9a)

dō—dice-box

dochi—companion

Doctor (of Literature)—(Monjō) Hakase

dōdōji—young temple assistant

dog barrier—inufusegi

dogs—notes 46, 565

dokyō—(1) chanting the (Buddhist) scriptures, (2) see Mi-Dokyō

dokyō su—to chant (the Buddhist scriptures)

Doll (Festival)—Hiina Asobi (Display of Dolls)

Dōmei—(855-920) Buddhist priest and poet (notes 1090, 1091) (App. 6b, no. 79)

Dōshi—(Buddhist) Leader (note 325)

dyeing—note 27

eave-covered part of a room—hisashi

ebiiro—grape colour, light purple (note 978)

ebizome—see ebiiro

eboshi—man's lacquered head-dress or cap (note 125) (App. 8a, nos. 10, 13)

ebukuro—bag for provisions

Echigo—superior province (jōkoku) on the north-west coast (App. 9a, no. 6)

Efu—Imperial Guards

egachi ni—knowingly

Eight Lessons—Hakkō

Ekō—Prayer for Salvation (note 999)

emigoe—laughing (cheerful) voice

Emon—Outer Palace Guards (note 248) (App. 7b)

Emperor's Dining-Room—Mizushi-dokoro

275

Emperor's Private Office—Kurōdo-dokoro
Empress—Chūgū, Kōgō, Kisa(k)i
Empress Dowager—Nyōin, In
Empress's Office—Shiki (no Mizōshi *or* In)
emu—to smile, laugh
en—elegant, graceful, refined
enarazu—unspeakably, fantastically (note 857)
endatsu—to give an appearance of elegance; to pose as being elegant
endō—(1) spreading mats on the ground from the gate of a house to the main building, (2) path along which such mats have been spread
enga—extra guest (note 855)
Enutagi—serving-woman to Empress Yasuko (note 486)
envoy—*tsukai*
Enyū—(959-91) 64th Emperor, reg. 970-84 (notes 82, 649) (App. 6a, no. 10, and 6b, nos. 61 and 77)
en zu—to bear a grudge, feel resentment, be angry, jealous
esasu—to give (lit. to cause to obtain)
escort—*toneri*
ese—wretched, miserable, poor, worthless, trivial, displeasing
eseguruma—poor (humble) carriage
esemono—(1) person of mean (humble, low) station (note 93), (2) rude, impolite, wicked, inexcusable (person), (3) thing of no importance, trivial thing
esezaiwai—illusory happiness
eshi—painter
eu—to get drunk, become intoxicated
evil spirit—*mono no ke*
ewarau—to laugh, smile
exorcist—*genza*
extra guest—*enga*
eyō—plan, design
e zu—see *en zu*

Festival, the—Kamo Festival
Festival of the Dead—Urabon
Festival of the Spirits—Tama Matsuri
Festival of the Weaver Star—Tanabata Matsuri
Festival of Young Herbs—Wakana no Sekku
festivals—*see* Gosekku (the Five Festivals)
Fifth Rank Chamberlain—Kurōdo no Goi

fire-hut—*hitakiya*
First Avenue, the—Ichijō no Ōji
first-class province—*daiichi no kuni*
First Empress—Kōgō
First Man—Ichi no Hito
First Place—Ichi no Tokoro
First Secretary of the Emperor's Private Office—Tō
Five Festivals—Gosekku
formal skirt with train—*mo*
fubin—inconvenient, unpleasant
Fuboku Shū—abbreviation of *Fuboku Waka Shū*, an (unofficial) anthology of verse in 36 books, compiled by Fujiwara no Nagakiyo (notes 274, 537)
Fudan Kyō—*see* Fudan no Mi-Dokyō
Fudan no Mi-Dokyō—Perpetual Sacred Readings (note 371)
Fudō—the Immovable One (note 834)
Fugen—Bodhisattva Samantabhadra (notes 831, 834)
fuji—(1) wistaria, (2) colour combination in which the outside of the garment is violet or light blue and the lining is light green (note 23)
Fuji San—Mt. Fuji (note 62)
Fujitsubo—a building in the Imperial Palace compound (note 602) (App. 9f, no. 6)
Fujiwara—ruling family in Japan during most of the 10th and 11th centuries (note 83) (App. 6b)
Fujiwara no Akiko (1)—(961-1001) also known as Higashi Sanjō no In and Senshi, consort of Emperor Enyū and mother of Emperor Ichijō (notes 416, 597) (App. 6b, no. 76)
Fujiwara no Akiko (2)—(988-1074) also known as Jōtōmon In, consort of Emperor Ichijō (notes 72, 871) (App. 6b, no. 89)
Fujiwara no Akiko (3)—daughter of Fujiwara no Yoshifusa and consort of Emperor Montoku (notes 72, 81) (App. 6b, no. 26)
Fujiwara no Akitada—(898-965) Minister of the Right 960-5 (notes 87, 987) (App. 6b, no. 29)
Fujiwara no Asamitsu—(950-95) grandson of Morosuke; served as Major Counsellor (note 655) (App. 6b, no. 59)
Fujiwara no Atsushige—10th-century

276

poet who wrote mainly in Chinese (notes 643, 646)

Fujiwara no Atsusuke—son of Akitada; Director of the Bureau of Horses (note 988) (App. 6b, no. 34)

Fujiwara no Chikayori—6th son of Michitaka; Imperial Attendant and Guards Officer (notes 507, 508) (App. 6b, no. 85)

Fujiwara no Genshi—(981-1002) also known as the Shigei Sha, 2nd daughter of Michitaka; consort of the Crown Prince (notes 415, 416, 435, 954) (App. 6b, no. 86)

Fujiwara no Kaneie—(929-90) Minister of the Right 978-86, Regent 986-90, Chancellor 990 (notes 168, 494, 935, 1091) (App. 6b, no. 56)

Fujiwara no Kiminobu—(976-1026) fairly successful Court official (note 464) (App. 6b, no. 68)

Fujiwara no Kinsue—(956-1029) Minister of the Right and tutor to the Crown Prince 1017, Prime Minister 1021 9 (note 767) (App. 6b, no. 53)

Fujiwara no Kintō—(966-1041) high-ranking official, also known as a poet, musician, and compiler of anthologies (notes 62, 331, 522) (App. 6b, no. 49)

Fujiwara no Korechika—(973-1010) elder brother of Empress Sadako; rose to the rank of Minister of the Centre, but was exiled in 996 owing to the rivalry of Michinaga (notes 22, 74, 403, 505, 513, 602, 606, 660, 975, 990, 1096, 1155) (App. 2, no. 1, and App. 6b, no. 81)

Fujiwara no Koretada—(924-72) Regent 970-2 (notes 72, 628) (App. 6b, no. 54)

Fujiwara no Masamitsu—(957-1015) grandson of Morosuke; rose to be an Imperial Adviser (notes 50, 679, 875) (App. 6b, no. 60)

Fujiwara no Matsugimi—(992-1054) son of Korechika (notes 505, 963) (App. 6b, no. 90)

Fujiwara no Michikane—(961-95) brother of Michitaka, whom he succeeded as Chancellor for a short time in 995 (note 651) (App. 6b, no. 73)

Fujiwara no Michimasa—*see* Fujiwara no Matsugimi

Fujiwara no Michinaga—(966-1027) Minister of the Right 995-6, Minister of the Left 996-1017, Imperial Examiner 995-1016, Regent 1016-17; leader of the Fujiwara family and the most powerful political figure in Japan during the first decades of the 11th century (notes 74, 378, 510, 514, 528, 606, 655, 678, 682, 871, 876, 944, 986) (App. 2, no. 2, and App. 6b, no. 78)

Fujiwara no Michitaka—(953-95) Regent 990-3, Chancellor 993-5; elder brother of Michinaga, father of Empress Sadako and the leading political figure in Japan before Michinaga's rise to power (notes 83, 171, 445, 493, 494, 504, 506, 510, 514, 600, 604, 606, 626, 742, 750, 944, 949) (App. 2, no. 3, App. 6b, no. 72, and App. 6d, no. 97)

Fujiwara no Michitsuna—(955-1020) son of Kaneie, his mother being the author of *Kagerō Nikki* (note 1091) (App. 6b, no. 71)

Fujiwara no Michiyori—(970-95) eldest son of Michitaka (notes 22, 511, 513, 602, 978, 990) (App. 2, no. 4, and App. 6b, no. 80)

Fujiwara no Morosuke—(908-60) Minister of the Right 947-60 (notes 261, 698) (App. 6b, no. 32)

Fujiwara no Morotada—(918-69) Minister of the Left in 969 (notes 72, 88) (App. 6b, no. 31)

Fujiwara no Nagaakira—(b. 970) Gentleman-in-Waiting who became a priest at the age of 16 (note 170) (App. 6b, no. 45)

Fujiwara no Nakatada—hero of *Utsubo Monogatari* (notes 352, 369, 919)

Fujiwara no Naritoki—(941-95) Imperial Investigator in Mutsu and Dewa, who was posthumously appointed Prime Minister (notes 165, 655, 820) (App. 6b, no. 36)

Fujiwara no Nobuko—*see* Nobuko, Princess

Fujiwara no Nobutaka—(d. 1001) provincial governor, husband of Murasaki Shikibu (notes 552, 554) (App. 6b, no. 41)

Fujiwara no Nobutsune—government official who, despite his poor calligraphy, became Governor of Echigo

277

(notes 483, 484, 488, 489) (App. 6b, no. 40)

Fujiwara no Noritaka—(948-1014) Chamberlain and, later, Major Controller of the Left (note 266) (App. 6b, no. 42)

Fujiwara no Sadako—(976-1000) daughter of Michitaka and consort of Emperor Ichijō; 'the Empress' in *The Pillow Book* normally refers to Sadako, in whose Court Sei Shōnagon served for about 10 years (notes 22, 33, 83, 231, 460, 606, 678, 742, 871, 945, 964) (App. 2, no. 15, App. 6b, no. 87, and App. 6d, no. 98)

Fujiwara no Saishō—lady-in-waiting to Empress Sadako (notes 87, 987, 988) (App. 2, no. 5, and App. 6b, no. 43)

Fujiwara no Sanefusa—Chamberlain of the 6th Rank (note 51)

Fujiwara no Sanekata—(d. 998) Guards officer and poet (note 170) (App. 6b, no. 46)

Fujiwara no Sanenari—(975-1044) Guards officer and Imperial Adviser (notes 527, 644) (App. 6b, no. 63)

Fujiwara no Saneyori—(900-70) Minister of the Right 944-7, Minister of the Left 947-68, Chancellor 967-9, Regent 969-70 (note 72) (App. 6b, no. 33)

Fujiwara no Senshi—*see* Higashi Sanjō no In

Fujiwara no Shigeko—daughter of Morosuke, and Imperial Nurse to Emperor Ichijō (notes 651, 652, 653) (App. 6b, no. 58)

Fujiwara no Suetsuna—Minor Captain of the Inner Palace Guards (note 52)

Fujiwara no Sukemasa (1)—(944-98) Imperial Adviser and one of the Three Great Calligraphers; later, Minister of Military Affairs (note 169) (App. 6b, no. 47)

Fujiwara no Sukemasa (2)—Director of the Bureau of Imperial Stables and father of one of the Gosechi dancers (note 424)

Fujiwara no Suketada—government official who rose to be Governor of Yamato despite his mother's humble birth (note 137)

Fujiwara no Tadafusa—(d. 929) government official and poet (note 674)

Fujiwara no Tadagimi—adopted son of Tadahira, being in reality his grandson; served as Captain of the Middle Palace Guards, Right Division (note 603) (App. 6b, nos. 30 and 55)

Fujiwara no Tadahira—(880-949) Minister of the Right 914-24, Minister of the Left 924-36, Regent 930-41, Chancellor 941-9 (note 72) (App. 6b, no. 28)

Fujiwara no Tadanobu—(967-1035) successful official and poet, believed to have been Shōnagon's lover (notes 331, 441, 522, 628, 629, 632, 679, 749, 752, 756, 759, 762) (App. 2, no. 6, and App. 6b, no. 67)

Fujiwara no Tadasuke—(b. 944) Major Controller of the Right (note 256)

Fujiwara no Takaie—(979-1044) brother of Korechika; he was disgraced at the same time, but later returned to favour and rose to be Minister of the Treasury (notes 403, 479, 481, 505, 975, 990, 1037) (App. 2, no. 7, and App. 6b, no. 82)

Fujiwara no Takamitsu—(973-94) son of Nobutaka and stepson of Murasaki Shikibu; government official and provincial governor (note 552) (App. 6b, no. 50)

Fujiwara no Takatō—(949-1013) poet and musician (note 134) (App. 6b, no. 48)

Fujiwara no Tamemitsu—(942-92) Minister of the Right 986-91, Prime Minister 991-2 (notes 72, 174) (App. 6b, no. 57)

Fujiwara no Tokikara—Governor of Mino from 968 (note 486)

Fujiwara no Toshikata—high-ranking official and poet (notes 331, 528)

Fujiwara no Toshiyuki—(died *c.* 905) famous calligrapher and poet (note 847)

Fujiwara no Yasuchika—(b. 921) Imperial Adviser 987 (note 169)

Fujiwara no Yasuko—(926-64) principal consort of Emperor Murakami (note 486) (App. 6b, no. 51)

Fujiwara no Yorichika—5th son of Michitaka (notes 491, 514) (App. 6b, no. 84)

Fujiwara no Yoshichika—(957-1008) distinguished man of letters and official who retired to become a priest in 986 at the same time as his patron, Emperor Kazan (notes 172, 179) (App. 6b, no. 66)

Fujiwara no Yoshifusa—(804-72) Minister of the Right 848-57, Prime Minister 857-72, Regent 858-72 (notes 72, 81) (App. 6b, no. 25)

Fujiwara no Yoshiko (1)—(d. 967) a favourite of Emperor Murakami, also known as Senyōden no Nyōgo, noted for her beauty (note 88) (App. 6b, no. 37)

Fujiwara no Yoshiko (2)—(974-1053) consort of Emperor Ichijō, also known as Kokiden) (notes 378, 767) (App. 6b, no. 64)

Fujiwara no Yukiko—daughter of Kaneie, consort of Emperor Reizei, mother of Emperor Sanjō (note 909) (App. 6b, no. 74)

Fujiwara no Yukinari—(971-1027) successful official and noted calligrapher who appears frequently in *The Pillow Book* as a close friend of Shōnagon (notes 50, 256, 258, 327, 331, 615, 617, 638, 640, 987) (App. 2, no. 8, and App. 6b, no. 70)

fukagutsu—lacquered leather shoe (lit. deep shoe)

Fukakusa no Shōshō—unsuccessful suitor of the poetess Ono no Komachi (note 1074)

fukigatari—boasting, bragging

fukimono—wind instrument

fukisumasu—to be perfectly clear (serene)

fukiwataru—to blow from far away (over a great distance)

fukiwatasu—to cover (thatch) an entire surface

fukudamu—to be crumpled, baggy, bulging, disordered (of hair, clothes, etc.)

fukuraka—plump, full

fukusa—silk garment whose outside and lining are made of the same material and colour

fukutsukeshi—greedy, avaricious

Full Canon—Issaikyō

fumi—(1) book, (2) Chinese poem, (3) Chinese writings, (4) letter

fumikotoba—wording (words) of a letter

Fumizuki—Poem-Composing (Seventh) Month (notes 3, 55)

Fumon Ji—Fumon Temple (note 1091)

fumu—to thrust, strike

funabashi—boat bridge (note 285)

fun zu—to close, wrap, seal

furi—melon (note 711)

furihata—waving banner

furikaku—to be scattered, be in disorder

furiyaru—to shake away (off, over), scatter

furu—(1) to be old, (2) to be trite, commonplace, stale (note 379), (3) to spread rumours, reports, etc. (note 867)

furuburushi—old, elderly

furugoto—old poem

Furu no Taki—waterfall in Yamato (notes 274, 275)

furushi—(1) old, (2) expert, veteran

fusagaru—see *kokoro fusagaru*

fusayaka—profuse, abundant, hirsute

fushinamu—to fall down (and lie) in a row

fusōgumo—cloud of ill omen (note 719)

fusu—see *omote wo fusu*

fusubu—to smoulder (with jealousy), be jealous (envious)

futa—lid (notes 26, 376, 392)

futaai—violet colour made by mixing blue and scarlet (notes 26, 142)

futafuta to—flapping (sound)

futagu—to cover, stop up

futama a *ma* (see *ma*)

futatsu-kakego no suzuri—inkstones contained in two boxes that fit into each other

futo—(1) by chance, happens to, (2) slightly, just a moment, (3) at once, immediately, (4) suddenly, unexpectedly

futokorogami—pocket-paper (note 131)

fuyō—useless, in vain

fūzoku(uta)—popular song (notes 316, 1011)

gakumon—pursuit of literature, literary studies (pursuits)

gallery—*sajiki*

gammon—prayer, votive document (note 398)

gansan—first day of the year (note 547)

garden fence—*tatejitomi*

gari—place, house

-gata—about, in the (general) period of

Gebon—Lower Rank (in the Western Paradise) (note 478)

gekoku—inferior province (note 324)

279

gembuku—coming of age ceremony (note 1147)

Gen Chūjō—*see* Minamoto no Nobukata (1)

Gen Shōnagon—lady-in-waiting to Empress Sadako

Gen Shōshō—*see* Minamoto no Tsunefusa

gentleman—*tonobara*

Gentleman-in-Waiting—Jijū

gentleman of low rank—*jige*

gentleman of the 5th Rank—Taifu

genza—exorcist (note 32)

gerō—commoner (note 398)

gesu—(1) commoner, pauper, (2) servant

getai—negligence

Giyō Den—Giyō Palace, a building in the Imperial Palace compound, housing the Imperial treasures (note 439) (App. 9f, no. 14)

go—game introduced from China in the 8th century (notes 92, 660, 758, 759, 817, 826) (App. 8d, no. 5)

go-ban—tray (for the Emperor's meals)

go-bō—(Buddhist) priest

Go-Chōzu no Ma—Imperial Washing Room (note 536) (App. 9g, no. 5)

Godaison—the Five Great Venerables (note 1057)

gohei—sacred Shintō strips of paper (note 902)

gohō—power of exorcizing evil spirits by incantations, etc.

Gohō(-dōji)—Guardian Demon of Buddhism, in the form of a young boy (used by exorcists) (note 106)

Goi no Kurōdo—Chamberlain of the Fifth Rank (notes 156, 395)

Gokuraku—Paradise (note 778)

-gome—all of, inclusive

gon—temporary, provisional, or supernumerary appointment (note 60)

gōna—hermit crab

Gon Chūjō—Provisional Middle Captain (note 60)

Gon Chūnagon—Provisional Middle Counsellor

Gon Dainagon—Provisional Major Counsellor

Gon no Kami—Provisional Governor

Gon no Taifu—*see* Gon Tayū

Gon Tayū—Provisional Senior Steward (note 720)

goranjiwatasu—to read and pass on, circulate

Goryō E—Feast of the Sacred Spirit (note 323) (App. 1)

Go-Saie—Assembly of Purification (note 1058) (App. 1)

Gosechi dances—Gosechi no mai

Gosechi(e)—*see* Gosekku

Gosechi no mai—Gosechi dances, performed in the 11th Month (notes 99, 413, 414, 419, 423, 430, 432) (App. 1)

Gosekku—the Five (Palace) Festivals (note 54) (App. 1)

Gosen Shū—abbreviation of *Gosen Waka Shū*, 2nd official anthology of verse, in 20 books, compiled by Fujiwara no Koremasa and others, *c*. 950 (notes 62, 175, 199, 202, 274, 537, 827, 956, 1046)

gōshi—lacquered bowl with lid (note 924)

Goshūi Shū—abbreviation of *Goshūi Waka Shū*, 4th official anthology of verse, in 20 books, compiled by Fujiwara no Michitoshi, *c*. 1090 (notes 62, 303, 537, 1071)

gotachi—ladies, women

gotai—the five parts of the body, the whole body (note 535)

goya—matin, early morning (Buddhist) service (note 577)

goza—fine straw mat used by members of the nobility, etc.

gozen—outrider

grades (Court)—*see* ranks

Great Council of State—Daijōkan

Great Minister—Daijin

Great Purification—Ōharai

Gubu—Palace Chaplain (notes 821, 906)

gusoku su—to arrange, prepare, settle

gu su—(1) to consort, live as man and wife, (2) to accompany

gyōji—help, assistance, care, trouble, service

Gyōke Sha—*see* Umetsubo

haberu—(1) to serve, (2) to presume (note 129) (see also *Dictionary of Selected Forms in Classical Japanese Literature*)

Hachiman—God of War (notes 597, 1016)

hae—fly (note 242)

haebaeshi—glorious, grand, honourable; gay, attractive, gorgeous, brilliant, lively; cheerful, jovial, merry

280

hagae—changing (colour) of leaves (note 653)

hagatame—tooth-hardening (note 220) (App. 1)

hagi—(1) bush-clover, lespedeza, *lespedeza bicolor* (note 302), (2) green (colour), (3) colour combination in which the outside of the garment is dark red and the lining is green (notes 23, 680)

hagurome—tooth-blackening (note 149)

hahaki—broom

hahaso—notched oak, *quercus serrata*

hai—edge

haibushi—formal sitting posture

haifusu—to lie flat out (down)

haikaeru—to fade (of purple and other materials that have been dyed with camellia ashes)

hail-stone pattern—*arareji*

hair—notes 183, 349, 771, 844, 982, 1115

haizen—attendant who serves at the Emperor's table

haji—reserve

hajigamashi—shameful

hajikawasu—to treat each other with respect (reverence, reserve)

haji-suhō—orange (colour)

hajitomi—'half shutter', a hinged shutter (*shitomi*), the upper part of which can be raised to let in more light

hakabakashi—outstanding, remarkable

hakama—trouser-skirt, divided skirt (notes 623, 624) (App. 8a, nos. 3, 17)

hakanadatsu—to be simple, rough, poor, wretched

hakanashi—(1) transient, evanescent, ephemeral, (2) trivial, insignificant, (3) flimsy, frail

hakase—(1) professor, learned scholar, (2) *see* Monjō Hakase

hakashi—sword

Hakkō—Eight (Buddhist) Lessons (notes 159, 162)

hakodori—box-bird (note 226)

hakoyu—see *hikihakoyu*

hakuginu—white dress

Hakurakuten—Japanese name of the Chinese poet Po Chü-i (Po Lo-t'ien)

half shutter—*hajitomi*

hamaji—nut-grass, sedge, *cyperus rotundus*

Hamana no Hashi—Hamana Bridge in Tōtōmi Province (notes 274, 1108)

hamayū—crinum, *rhodea japonica*

Hamori no Kami—God of Leaves (note 221)

hampi—short-sleeved jacket (notes 530, 926)

hana—blue (= *hanada-iro*)

hanachitatsu—to exclude, ostracize, leave out

hana hiru—to sneeze (notes 127, 812, 815)

hanamuke—see *uma no hanamuke*

hanatsu—to open (a lattice, etc.)

hanau—see *hana hiru*

hanayagu—to be splendid (gorgeous, spectacular)

hanitsuchi—clay, mud

Han-ku—name of a barrier in China (notes 637, 1099)

Han shu—'History of the Han', by Pan Ku (A.D. 32–92) (notes 36, 1063)

hanzō—tub, bucket

hara—see *on-hara*

harae—(1) service of purification (notes 151, 1150), (2) purgation, indemnity, or penalty imposed on anyone who is held responsible for ritual uncleanness (note 270)

haragitanashi—ill-natured, malicious, cross-grained

Hara no Ike—pond in Kōzuke Province (note 205)

hara takashi—pregnant

hare-stick—*uzuchi*

hare-wand—*uzue*

harimushiro—straw mats used on carriages as a protection against rain

harp *koto*, *kin*, *wagon*

Hasedera Hase Temple, 8th-century Shingon temple south of Nara (notes 67, 200, 560, 577, 1120) (App. 9b, no. 6)

hashi—(1) area of veranda (*sunoko*), outer edge of a Heian building, (2) scrap, fragment

hashi—fire-irons

hashi—steps, stairs

hashibune—sampan, lighter

hashijikashi—paltry, mean, narrow

hashiribi spark (note 893)

hashirii—spouting well

hashirikau—to run helter-skelter (in all directions)

hashirikurabe—race, contest

hashiru—(1) to gush out (note 1109), (2) see *mune hashiru*

281

hashitamono—under-servant

hashita nashi—(1) unseemly, unbecoming, vulgar, (2) awkward, bungling, (3) severe, harsh, (4) heartless, indifferent

hata—again, also, moreover

hata—half, partly

hata—twenty

hatabaru—to be wide

hatagakuru—see *hatakakuru*

hataita—board fence, wooden wall

hatakakuru—to be partly hidden, half concealed

hatarakasu—to move

hate no toshi—anniversary of death

hatsu—to end

hatsuka ni—barely, slightly, faintly

Hatsuse—*see* Hasedera

hau—(1) to hang down, droop, (2) to draw out, stretch

hayachi—hurricane, high wind

haya(k)u—formerly, long since; at first, at the beginning

hayao—rope (used instead of a thole) to secure oars

hayariizu—to be carried away, go into an ecstasy

hayasu—see *uchihayasu*

hayō—see *haya(k)u*

hazame—crack, interstice

hazu—to be ashamed

hazukashi—(1) ashamed, shy (note 589), (2) remarkably (enviably) good, good enough to put others to shame

hazuru—to go beyond, exceed

hazusu—to release, fire

he—see *heo*

head-blind—*mokō (no su)*

head-dress of nobility—*kammuri*

hearth—*subitsu*

hedatsu—to intercept, hide

hei—wall

Heian Kyō—capital of Japan from 794 to 1869 (App. 9b, no. 3, App. 9d)

heidan—cold, square rice-cakes presented to dignitaries after the Examination and the Inspection (notes 613, 620)

heiman—curtain, hanging

Henjō—(816-90) poet-priest (notes 650, 654)

hen (wo tsugu)—(to play) a game of parts (note 334)

heo—thread used to attach a falcon or other bird

herbal ball—*kusudama*

hesu—to overwhelm, crush, outdo

hi—lamp

hichiriki—flageolet, pipe (notes 701, 843)

Hidan no Ōidono—*see* Hidari no Otodo

Hidari no Otodo—Minister of the Left (note 168) (App. 7a)

Hieizan—Mt. Hiei, mountain range northeast of the capital, headquarters of the Tendai sect of Buddhism (notes 72, 305) (App. 9b, no. 1)

hierarchy (Court)—notes 11, 907, App. 3

higaoboe—mistaken memory, memory playing one false, mistaken recollection, fault of memory

higagoto—mistake

Higashi Sanjō no In—*see* Fujiwara no Akiko (1)

higeko—bearded basket (note 405)

Higerō—low-ranking member of the Emperor's Private Office (notes 156, 395)

high clogs—*ashida*

High Court Noble—*kandachibe, kandachime, kugyō*

High Priestess of Kamo—Saiin

high-ranking ecclesiastic (priest)—*sōgō*

higoro ni nari—the days pass, time elapses

Higyō Sha—*see* Fujitsubo

hihitohi—all day long, the entire day

Hiina Asobi—Display of Dolls (lit. 'doll game') (notes 21, 141, 801) (App. 1)

hijikasaame—sudden shower (note 719)

hiji oru—to turn (be bent) at right angles

hikarimitsu—to shine (glitter) all over

hikau—to catch, seize, take hold of

hikiharu—to hold down, check, curb

hikiiregoe—affected (unnatural) voice

hikiiru—to retire, withdraw

hikikaesu—to turn inside out

hikikaku—see *kaku*

hikikazuku—see *kazuku*

hikikiru—to cover

hikikosu—to lift (something) up across (something else)

hikimono—stringed instrument (general term)

hikitatsu—(1) to close (a sliding door), (2) to withdraw, (3) to place, install

hikitoku—to unfasten, undo

hikitsukurou—see *tsukurou*

hikiyaru—(1) to push away (aside), (2) to tear off

282

hikiyurugasu—see yurugasu
hime—rice starch
Himemiya (no On-kata)—the Princess Imperial (note 40)
Himemōchigimi—Lady of the Escort (note 724)
himizu—iced water
himo sasu—to tie one's sash, cord, etc. in a special loose type of knot
himuro—ice chamber (note 237)
hinabu—to be countrified, provincial, rustic (note 462)
hinerimuku—to turn (twist) round
hingashi—east
hi no go-shōsoku—Court dress, formal attire
hinoki—cypress, chamaecyparis obtusa (note 217)
Hi no Omashi—Daytime Chamber, main room (moya) of Seiryō Palace (note 77) (App. 9g, no. 10)
hi no sōzoku—Court costume
hioke—round wooden brazier, covered with foil and decorated with paintings (note 2) (App. 8b, no. 12)
hiomushi—May-fly, ephemera
hira—flat (adj.)
hiraginu—plain (untwilled) silk (note 446)
hiramu—to flatten, make even (level)
hirao—wide, flat ribbon attached to the sword-belt on ceremonial occasions (App. 8a, no. 2)
hire—(1) fin, (2) shoulder sash worn by Court ladies (notes 66, 411, 569)
hirogoru—to be spread out (open)
hiroki mochii—flattened rice-cake
hiromeku—(1) to spread (stretch) out, sprawl, (2) to move here and there, scurry about
hiru—see hana hiru
hirumushiro—beach parsley, cnidium japonicum
hisage—wooden or metal vessel used for pouring liquids
hisagu—to close, shut
hisashi—(1) ante-room, portion of room or balcony covered by deep eaves and situated between the main part of the room (moya) and the open veranda (sunoko); it was usually divided into 4 sections (note 38), (2) hut, cabin, shed
His Excellency the Governor (of a province)—Kofudono

His Highness (Excellency)—Kindachi
His Lordship—Ason
His (Her) Majesty—(Ue no) On-mae
Hitachi—great province (taikoku) in the eastern part of the main island (note 373) (App. 9a, no. 9)
hitai—(1) forehead, (2) part that projects (juts) out of a cliff, etc.
hitaigami—forelock
hitaitsuki—face, expression, countenance
hitakiya—fire-hut (note 668)
hitaku—to rise, become high (of the sun)
hitamono—(1) earnest, intent, (2) worthy, talented, (3) proper, decent, respectable, suitable
hitobae su—(1) to make up to, presume upon, dally, flirt, coquet; (2) to take advantage of a situation in which others are present, let oneself go when others are present (note 718)
hitobitoshi—(1) pertaining to ordinary (other) people, (2) worthy, talented, (3) proper, decent, respectable, suitable
hitodamai—attendants' carriage (which followed the master's carriage in processions, etc.)
hitoegasane—matched set of unlined dresses (note 176) (App. 8a, no. 19)
hitoeginu—unlined dress (App. 8a, nos. 16, 22)
hitofushi—uncommon, worth noticing
hitoge nashi—(1) not human-seeming, (2) rough, coarse, common
hitogoto—malicious gossip, nasty remarks
hitohi—one day, the other day
hito mamoru—to escape notice, be inconspicuous
hitoma ni—when no one else is present, when one is alone
Hitomaro—see Kakinomoto no Hitomaro
hitomekasu—see hitonaminami
hitome omou—to avoid attracting attention
hitomori—one dish
hitonaminami—common, ordinary
hito no ko(domo)—child
hito no kotonashigao—officious air, the expression of someone who always wants to look after other people's affairs
hito no musume—young lady
hitori—incense-burner
hitorigotsu—to say to oneself, think aloud
hito su—to send a servant

283

hitowaroshi—unsightly, unbecoming, awkward

hitowatari—one tune (melody, piece)

hitoya—the other night, some nights ago

hitoyoroi—a pair

hitozuma—wife (notes 274, 287)

Hitsuji (no toki)—the Hour of the Sheep, about 2 p.m. (note 417) (App. 3)

hiwadaya—roof thatched with cypress bark

hiwarigo—partitioned (luncheon) box of cypress (note 406)

hiyohiyo to—peeping (cheeping) sound (of chicks, etc.) (note 716)

hizō—extreme, unusual, irregular

hōbuku—priestly robe (vestment)

hōchi-hōtō—thanksgiving offering

hodo—(1) vicinity, region, place, (2) time, period, (3) area, space

hodohodo ni tsukete—in accordance with rank

hodo sugu—to grow old

Hōgan—Lieutenant (of the Imperial Police) (note 249)

hōheishi—see *tsukai*

hōhō to—with a bang (booming sound)

hōka—short clog (lit. half-shoe)

hokahoka—distant, strange, unfamiliar

hokame su—to look away

Hoke Kyō—Lotus Sutra (notes 178, 399, 477, 831, 1092)

hokoboshi—the halberd star (note 719)

Hōkō In—Hōkō Palace, residence of Fujiwara no Kaneie, which in 990 was converted into a Buddhist temple (notes 494, 944) (App. 9d, no. 14)

hokorika—proud (self-satisfied, triumphant) look

hokorobi—loose bottom (of a curtain, etc.)

Hollyhock (Festival)—Aoi (Matsuri)

Holy Teacher—Azari

home—*sato*

Hon—Order (note 907)

Honchō Monzui—collection of Chinese poetry and documents in *kambun* (Sino-Japanese) compiled *c.* 1011 by Fujiwara no Akihira (notes 760, 761, 1098)

hone—frame, bone (note 480)

hō no kesa—patchwork surplice

honokiku—to overhear, hear by chance

Hōō—Cloistered Emperor (note 275)

hōō—phoenix (note 197)

Horse, Day of the—Uma no Hi

Hōshi—Master of the Buddhist Law

hōshigo—young (little) priest

hosobitsu—long, narrow chest (note 26)

hosodono—long, narrow corridor (note 250)

hosonaga—long robe (notes 623, 953)

hosoraka—slender, slim

hosotachi—narrow-bladed sword used for parades and other formal occasions

hosoyaka—see *hosoraka*

Hossō—Buddhist sect of the Nara period (note 61)

hō to—(1) abruptly, (2) altogether, completely, (3) noisily, with a clatter

hotohoto—almost, on the verge of

Hotoke Kuyō—Dedication of (Buddhist) Images

hotomeku—to tap, patter

hotōru—to be angry, heated

hototogisu—Japanese bird usually translated as 'cuckoo' (notes 25, 194, 467, 853, 917, 918)

hours, names of—notes 1032, 1033, App. 3

housekeeper—*osame*

Housekeeping Office—Kamorizukasa

hōzuki—see *nukazuki*

Hsiang Chung—name of an old man who figures in a well-known Taoist story and who is known in Japan as Sō Chū (note 164)

hunting costume—*kariginu, karisōzoku*

Hyōbu—lady-in-waiting to Empress Sadako (notes 1038, 1041)

Hyōbu Shō—Ministry of Military Affairs (App. 7a and 9e, no. 18)

Hyōe—(1) Middle Palace Guards (note 221) (App. 7b), (2) name of a talented Lady Chamberlain in the time of Emperor Murakami (note 800)

Hyūga—medium province (*chūkoku*) in eastern Kyūshū (note 444) (App. 9a, no. 67)

I—(Court) Rank (notes 11, 907) (App. 7b)

i—dam

iakasu—to spend the night without sleeping, to stay (up) all night

Ibuki—mountain in Shimotsuke Province (note 1107)

ibuseshi—(1) gloomy, sad, (2) uninteresting, (3) irksome

ichigo—strawberry (notes 306, 720)

Ichijō Dono—*see* Ichijō no Miya

284

Ichijō no Miya (Ichijō In)—Palace of the First Ward (note 72) (App. 9d, no. 2)

Ichijō (no) Ōji—the First Avenue, a wide street running from east to west across the capital, directly north of the Greater Imperial Palace (notes 72, 864) (App. 9d, no. 6)

Ichijō Tennō—(980-1011) 66th Emperor, reg. 986-1011; the Emperor to whom Sei Shōnagon usually refers in her book (notes 512, 597, 1035, 1096) (App. 2, no. 9, App. 6a, no. 18, and App. 6b, nos. 65 and 88)

ichimegasa—lacquered hat of medium height worn by women (note 735)

Ichi no Hito—the First Man, a designation of the Kampaku or Sesshō (notes 83, 402)

ichi no miya—eldest son of the Emperor

Ichi no Tokoro—the First Place, a designation of the Kampaku's or Sesshō's residence (note 83)

idashiginu—(1) style in which the bottom of the inner robe protrudes from below the opening of the outer robe or trouser-skirt (notes 23, 75), (2) style of letting one's sleeves hang outside the carriage in which one is travelling (notes 147, 176, 1111) (App. 8c, no. 4)

idashiguruma—see *idashiginu* (2)

idashiuchigi—see *idashiginu* (1)

Ide—village near the capital (note 443)

ideiru—to come and go

Ide no Chūjō—the Middle Captain of Ide (note 443)

idomikawasu—to exchange challenges

ie no ko—member of a household

ifutagi—see *infutagi*

igawarigawari—each in turn, one after another

Igishi—Master of Observances (note 726)

igitanashi—sleepy-head, lie-abed

iharu—to stretch oneself out, sprawl

iiakasu—to talk (with someone) until dawn

iiatsukau—to speak about, talk of, gossip

iiawasu—see *iikawasu*

iifuru—to request, apply

iifurusu—to be commonplace, trite

iigai nashi—(1) not worth saying, (2) unimportant, insignificant

iikaku—to speak, address oneself to

iikawasu—to converse, discuss

iiki su—to agree, plan, arrange

iikukumu—to tell, instruct

iikutasu—to deprecate, belittle

iinasu—(1) to affirm, assert, (2) to charge, accuse

iinonoshiru see *nonoshiru*

iiokosu—to send a message

iiotosu—to disparage, denounce, abuse

iiru—to enter, penetrate

iishirou—to quarrel, dispute

iitsuku—(1) to order, (2) to find fault with, give a bad name to

iiyaru—to speak, utter

ika de—(1) by all means, (2) (followed by negative) on no account

ikaga (wa) semu—what can one do about it? it cannot be helped

ikaku—to sprinkle

ikari—anchor (note 719)

ikari no o—anchor cord (note 409)

ikawaru—to take turns, alternate

ikazuchi—thunder (note 719)

ikisudama—living ghost (note 719)

ikiusu—to go and disappear, go and hide oneself

ikuka—how many days? how long?

Ima Dairi—Palace of Today (see Ko Ichijō In)

imamairi—newcomer

ima no koto—new thing, thing that has happened for the first time

imayō—modern style (fashion), present day

imayō-uta—modern song (poem) (note 1010)

imiji—(1) terrible, cruel, (2) striking, alarming, terrifying, (3) magnificent, splendid, impressive, superb, making a deep impression; skilful, excellent, (4) very, extreme, (5) important, precious, valuable, (6) self-important, pompous, (7) feeble, slender, dejected

imi no hi—see *monoimi no hi*

imo—(1) younger sister, (2) mistress (note 365)

i mo nezu—without sleeping, not getting a wink of sleep

Imose no Yama—Mt. Imose (in Yamato and Kii Provinces) (notes 62, 365)

Imperial Abstinence—On-Monoimi

Imperial Adviser—Saishō, Sangi

Imperial Attendant—Ōtoneri

Imperial Concubine—Kōi

285

Imperial Dining Room—Asagarei no Ma
Imperial Guards—Takiguchi
Imperial Lady—Nyōgo
Imperial Palace—Uchi, Ue, Dairi
Imperial Police—Kebiishi
Imperial Princess—Himemiya no On-kata
Imperial Stables (Office of)—Uma
Imperial Wardrobe (Office of the)—Mi-Kushige
In—(1) residence occupied by an abdicated emperor or empress, (2) Abdicated (Retired) Emperor or Empress, (3) *see* Nyōin
inakadatsu—to be rustic, countrified
Inakaeji—name of a famous flute (note 437)
inamu—to sit in a row
Inari no Jinja—Inari Shrine, south of the capital (notes 736, 1015) (App. 9c, no. 8)
incantation—*see* rite of incantation *and* mystic incantation
inesaga nashi—tossing (rolling about) in one's sleep, sleeping in an unsightly posture
infutagi—covered rhymes (note 816)
ingō—Palace name (note 72)
Inner Palace Guards—Konoe
Inner Palace Guards, Left Division—Sakon
Inner Palace Guards, Right Division—Ukon
inoshishi—boar (note 719)
Inshi—*see* Inzukasa
Intendant—Bettō
inu—to sleep
inufusegi—'dog barrier' (note 565)
inzukasa—official of the Empress Dowager's household
iori—dwelling, house
Ippon—First Order (note 907)
irau—to reply
iriiru—(1) to put in, install, (2) to live in retirement
Iris Festival—Ayame no Sekku, Tango
iritatsu—(1) to enter, penetrate, trespass, (2) to go in and out, be on close terms, be intimate
irizumi—dried charcoal
iro—(1) elegance, brilliance, (2) look, appearance, expression, (3) complexion, (4) 'forbidden colour' (note 978)

irofushi—formal, solemn, impressive
iro ni izu—to reveal by one's expression
iru—(1) to be, (2) to make obeisance
iru—to bring, lead, convey
isa—let me see! well now!
Ise—great province (*taikoku*) in central Honshū (note 1154) (App. 9a, no. 30)
Ise Monogatari—'The Tales of Ise', 9th-century collection of stories centred on Japanese poems, traditionally attributed to Ariwara no Narihira and largely concerned with his romantic exploits and his poetic reactions thereto (notes 62, 336, 827)
Ise no monogatari—tale from Ise (note 336)
Ise Shū—collected verse of the Court lady and poetess Ise no Go (d. 939) (note 62)
ishi—chair, seat
isogi—preparations, arrangements
Issai Butsugen . . .—the Eye of All the Buddhas . . . (note 596)
Issaikyō—the Full Canon (note 944)
itadori—giant knotweed, sorrel, *polygonum cuspidatum* (note 720)
itaku (*mo*)—in particular, especially
itarikashikoshi—thorough, efficient, effective
itawashū oboyu (*omou*)—to attach importance to, think highly of
itonamu—to prepare, plan
ito nashi—busy, occupied
itōshi—pathetic, pitiful
itōshigaru—to feel sorry for
ito tsukuru—to thread (a needle)
itsukushi—majestic, splendid, solemn, impressive
itsumadegusa—stone-crop, *sedum lineare* (note 292)
itsu to naku—always
iwai no tsue—see *uzue*
iwaku—to divide, separate
Iwashimizu no Hachiman Gū—the Iwashimizu Hachiman Shrine, a famous Shintō shrine south of the capital (notes 66, 315, 373, 597, 666, 672, 675, 1016) (App. 1 and App. 9c, no. 10)
iwatsutsuji—rhododendron, *rhododendron indicum*
Iyo—superior province (*jōkoku*) in Shikoku (notes 126, 1037) (App. 9a, no. 53)
iyosu—Iyo blind (note 126)

286

izariizu—to come out on one's knees, creep (crawl) out (note 496)

izarikaeru—see *izariizu*

izatoshi—easily.awakened. wakeful

Izumi—inferior province (*gekoku*) south of the capital (note 785) (App. 9a, no. 41)

Izumi Shikibu—(*c*. 970-*c*. 1030) Court lady and poetess who is generally believed to have written a famous diary describing her love affair with an Imperial Prince in 1003 (notes 303, 537)

Izumo—superior province (*jōkoku*) in the west of Japan which figures prominently in myth and legend (notes 84, 219, 706) (App. 9a, no. 56)

izushi—rice-cake with mussels (note 719)

jige—gentleman of low rank (notes 35, 866)

Jigoku-e—Hell painting (note 325)

Jijū—Gentleman-in-Waiting (note 170)

Jijū Den—Jijū Palace, a building in the Imperial Palace compound, formerly used as the Emperor's residence (App. 9f, no. 11)

Jikyōza—Lector (note 399)

jimoku—period of (official) appointments (notes 19, 661) (App. 1)

jin—(1) guard-house, barracks, (2) office, post

ji no hodo—time for vespers (evening prayers)

jinya—see *jin*

jisuri—printed in colour on plain white material

Jizō—Bodhisattva Kṣitigarbha (notes 834, 997)

Jō—Secretary in a Bureau (note 137)

Jō—Secretary in a Ministry

Jō—Lieutenant of the Guards or of the Imperial Police

jō—(1) avenue, (2) ward (note 72)

Jōchō—(934-1016) famous priest of the Hossō sect (notes 60, 1106)

jōgan member of the Great Council of State

Jōgan Den—Jōgan Palace, a building in the Imperial Palace compound (notes 348, 499, 500) (App. 9f, no. 3)

jōhon—original text (manuscript) (note 1028)

joju—woman serving in the Palace Attendants' Office (note 95)

jōkoku—superior province (note 324)

Jōkyō Den—*see* Shōkyō Den

Jōmi—festival celebrated on the 3rd day of the 3rd Month (notes 21, 50, 54, 141) (Apps. 1, 3)

Jōnci Den—Jōnei Palace, the Empress's Residential Palace (notes 425, 430, 784) (App. 9f, no. 8)

jōrō—noblewoman

Jōtō Mon—gate at the east of the Greater Imperial Palace (note 465) (App. 9e, no. 5)

Jōtōmon In—*see* Fujiwara no Akiko (2)

jōza—(1) priest who walks at the head of a religious procession, (2) superior of the Tōji (temple)

ju—Buddhist text in verse, *gâthâ* (note 562)

Jumyo Kyō—Sutra of Longevity (note 940)

kachiariki su—to go on foot

kachiji—travel by land (on foot)

kado—gate (App. 8b, no. 4)

kado ari—to be intelligent

kadokadoshi—intelligent

kae no ki—maple, *acer pictum*

Kaeridachi no Mi-Kagura—Sacred Dance of the Return (notes 672, 675)

kaeri(goto)—reply (letters, etc.)

kaeru—to fade

kaeru (toshi)—the following (year)

kaesa—return

kaesama ni—upside down, inside out, opposite, reverse

kaeshi(uta)—return poem (notes 111, 741)

kagayaku—to put out of countenance, shame

kagayou—(1) to shine, glisten, (2) to look proud, pretentious

Kagerō Nikki—'Gossamer Diary', diary by the mother of Fujiwara no Michitsuna, *c*. 974 (notes 200, 1022, 1091)

kagiri—(1) only, (2) see *aru kagiri*

kagishiru—to know by smell

kagura—sacred Shintō dance and music (notes 214, 544, 879, 881, 1009)

Kai—superior province (*jōkoku*) west of present-day Tokyo (note 786) (App. 9a, no. 19)

kai—conch-shell, conch (note 572)

287

kai—spoon

kaibami su—to peep in

kaiketsu—erased, eradicated, utterly vanished

kaikosu—to arrange the hair so that it hangs down in front (note 872)

kaikukumu—see *kukumu*

kaimasaguru—to fumble about with

kaineri—glossed (softened) silk

kaineri-gasane—under-robe of red glossed silk

kainogou—to wipe away, efface, eradicate

kairogu—to be graceful, elegant, fascinating, brilliant, flashing

kaitsuku—to cling, hold on

kaitsukuroi—assistant, attendant

kaja—young man who has recently celebrated his coming of age (i.e. *gembuku*, usually performed between the ages of 11 and 15)

kaji—type of Shingon prayer or incantation used by exorcists

kakagu—to turn up (a light), make bright

kakaguriariku—to become involved in (something) elsewhere (note 817)

kakaru—(1) to be connected with, (2) to go to, repair to

kaka to—cawing (sound of crows, etc.)

kakau—(1) to retain, preserve, (2) to be full of, redolent with

kakazuriariku—to walk about (to and fro)

kakeban—small table used to serve food, etc.

kakegane—latch, clasp

kakego—boxes made to fit into each other

kakewatasu—to hang in a row

kakeyari—tear, rent

kakiita—blackboard (used for writing memos, etc.)

kakikegasu—to make a slip of the pen (mistake in writing)

kakikurasu—to become dark (overcast)

Kakinomoto no Hitomaro—(died *c*. 710) famous poet (notes 202, 219, 958, 1128)

kakisusabu—to rake (scratch) idly (as a distraction)

kakisuu—to place, load, carry

kakitate—note, document, paper, list

kaku—(1) to lift up, raise, (2) to put (harness) on one's shoulders

kaku—(1) to mind, care, concern oneself, (2) to hang, suspend, dangle, sling

kaku—companion, follower

kakureusu—see *usekakuru*

kamatsuka—amaranth, Joseph's coat, Prince's feather, *amaranthus gangeticus* (note 298)

Kami—Captain of the Outer and Middle Palace Guards (App. 7b)

Kami—Governor of a province (note 1108) (App. 7b)

Kami—Director of a government bureau or office (App. 7b)

kami—paper (note 941)

kami—(1) hair, (2) mane

kami—deity (notes 941, 1015, 1108)

kami—thunder

kami-kōburi—triangular paper hat (note 1150)

Kaminazuki—Godless (Tenth) Month (note 3)

kamizama—(1) crown (of the head), (2) upwards

kammuri—another reading of *kōburi*

Kamo Matsuri—Kamo Festival (notes 24, 140, 289, 311, 459, 671, 707) (App. 1)

Kamo no Jinja—Kamo Shrines, Shintō shrines north of the capital at which an important festival ('the Festival') was held in the 4th Month (notes 24, 66, 140, 193, 235, 315, 382, 541, 666, 672, 847, 1015) (App. 9c, no. 2)

Kamonzukasa—*see* Kam(m)orizukasa

Kam(m)orizukasa—Housekeeping Office (note 665)

Kamo Shrines—Kamo no Jinja

Kampaku—Chancellor (notes 83, 171, 935)

kana—see *kan(n)a*

kanamari—metal bowl (jug, pitcher)

kanashi—(1) sweet, lovely, charming, (2) dear, precious, beloved

kanashiku su—to pet, love, make a fuss of

Kanchō—(916-98) important Buddhist dignitary (note 654) (App. 6a, no. 2)

Kandachibe—High Court Noble (note 96)

Kandachime—*see* Kandachibe

kandori—helmsman, steersman

kanegoto—prophecy, oracle, prediction

kangau—(1) to reconsider, reflect, correct, (2) to reprove, reprimand

kanii—campion, lychnic, *lychnis coronata*

Kanin—(1) Provisional Imperial Palace directly to the south-east of the Greater Imperial Palace (App. 9d, no. 18), (2) name given to Fujiwara no Kinsue, who resided there (note 767)

kanju—account of scrolls (note 652)

Kan Koku—Japanese name of Han-ku barrier

kan(n)a—Japanese phonetic script (note 337)

Kannari no Jin—Thunder Guard (notes 900, 1061)

kannin—official

Kannon—Bodhisattva Avalokiteśvara, Goddess of Mercy (notes 67, 377, 577, 830, 833)

Kannongyō—*Kannon Sutra* (note 577)

Kan no Tsukasa—Government Offices of the Great Council of State (note 743)

Kansho—Japanese reading of *Han shu* (q.v.)

kanzō—yellow day-lily, *hemerocallis fulva* (note 744)

kao no kinu—see *kinu* (2)

karaavi—sunflower, *helianthus annuus*

karauya—Chinese damask

karabisashi—*hisashi* (1) in the Chinese style, with the ends of the roof turned upwards (notes 500, 974)

karabitsu—T'ang-style chest on legs

karae—Chinese-style painting

karaginu—short, formal 'Chinese' jacket, worn over the *uchigi* (1) and having a contrasting colour (notes 76, 623) (App. 8a, nos. 11, 14, 23)

karakagami—elegant mirror imported from China or made in the Chinese style

karameku—to be in the Chinese style or taste, to look elegant (note 222)

karameku—to appear dried up (desiccated, emaciated)

kara no kagami—see *karakagami*

kara no mi-zo—see *karaginu*

karasu—crow (note 308)

karebamu—to seem (be) hoarse

kareno—lit. 'dried field', colour combination in which the outside of the garment is yellow and the lining is green (note 23)

kari—(1) wild goose, (2) duck

karibakama—cloth trouser-skirt worn as part of a hunting costume

kariginu—hunting costume, hunting cloak (notes 122, 1013) (App. 8a)

kari no ko—(1) duck egg, (2) duckling, (3) gosling (notes 236, 717)

karisome—decent, modest

karisōzoku—see *kariginu*

karma—*sukuse*

karobu—to be light

karogaroshi—undignified, indiscreet, rash

karoraka—light, nimble

karukaya—kind of pampas grass, *anthistiria arguens*

kasa—(1) large headgear of wickerwork or sedge used for walking or travelling, (2) top (cap) (of a writing-brush, etc.)

kasa—bark, shavings

kasame—type of crab (note 719)

kashigamashi—noisy, loud

Kashiko Fuchi—Pool of Kashiko (notes 62, 68)

kashikomari—disgrace, disfavour

kashikoshi—(1) illustrious, eminent, (2) important, significant, momentous, (3) splendid, impressive, awe-inspiring, (4) clever, wise; skilful (note 391)

kashira—(1) hair (of the head), (2) end (lit. 'head') (of a writing-brush, etc.)

kashiratsuki waroshi—to have one's hair in disorder

kashiwa(gi)—(Mongolian) oak, *quercus dentata* (note 221)

kashizuki—assistant, attendant

kashizuku—(1) to look after carefully, (2) to treat with respect, hold in awe, (3) to cherish, love dearly

Kasuga Jinja—Kasuga Shrine, clan shrine of the Fujiwara family in Nara (notes 61, 402, 674, 727, 1015, 1018) (App. 1)

Kasuga Matsuri—Kasuga Festival (note 727) (App. 1)

kasumikomu—to be shrouded in mist

kata—imperfection, abnormality, infirmity

kata—picture, painting

kata ashi—to be in an unlucky direction (cf. *katatagae*)

katabira—(1) curtains (note 39), (2) linen or hemp (summer) clothes

katachi—(1) appearance, (2) toilet, make-up

katae—(1) some, a certain amount, (2) half, (3) one side (note 747)

katafusagari—unlucky (forbidden, lit. blocked-up) direction (note 103)

289

katagi—engraving block used for printing designs on material

katahiku—to favour, be partial to

katai—beggar

kataki—(1) companion, (2) opponent

katakkata—one side

katakkata no yudake—see *yudake*

Katakoi no Oka—Katakoi Hill in Mutsu Province (note 882)

katakuna—unskilful, stupid

katame (mo) akazu—to be totally illiterate

katami ni—mutually, each other

katamoji—half (part) of a name (word)

katamon—material with a heavily figured design

katamu—see *tsukaikatamu*

Katano no Shōshō—(1) name of a tale (*monogatari*) that is no longer extant (note 835), (2) name of a character in *Ochikubo Monogatari* (note 1047)

kataoi—imperfect, incomplete

katarau—(1) to be intimate (friendly) with, court, woo, seduce, (2) to negotiate with, consult, confer, (3) to bring to one's side

kataritsugu—to make public, proclaim

Katasari Yama—Mt. Katasari (notes 62, 63)

katashi—see *arigatashi*

katashi—one side

katatagae—avoidance or conversion of unlucky directions by means of detours, etc. (notes 103, 347)

kata-tsu-kata—see *katakkata*

katatsuku—to leave (show) a mark

katawa—(1) wrong, improper, (2) deformed, maimed, (3) extraordinary, unusual

katawara itashi—(1) unpleasant, loathsome, unbearable, (2) pitiful, painful, awkward, embarrassing, ridiculous

katazama—direction

katōdo—supporter, ally, partisan, enthusiast

katori—stiff (raw) silk cloth

katsu—(1) the other side, on the other hand, rather, inclined to, (2) moreover

katsura—cinnamon, cassia, laurel

katsura—maple

Katsuragi—*see* Kazuraki

kau—see *kaku* (verbs)

kawaginu—fur robe

kawahori—(1) bat, (2) fan covered with paper on one side (note 144) (App. 8a, no. 9)

kawa no obi—black-lacquered leather belt (notes 897, 912)

kawarake—earthenware bowl for soup, etc.

kawara-suzuri—tiled inkstone (note 877)

kawatake—long-jointed (lit. river) bamboo, *phyllostachys bambusoides*

kawayabito—latrine cleaner

kawayōto—see *kawayabito*

kayatsu—that fellow

kayou—(1) to resemble, be similar, (2) to send

kayu no ki—elder-wood (used to stir the 7-herb gruel) (note 16)

kazami—loose coat worn by Palace Girls over their *akome* (notes 41, 623, 624)

Kazan In—ex-Emperor Kazan (968–1008), 65th Emperor, reg. 984-6 (notes 74, 172, 275, 276) (Apps. 6a, no. 22, and 6b, no. 69)

kazaridachi—long sword with decorated scabbard (worn by men of the 6th Rank and above)

kazashi—decoration of the hair or head-dress

kazashi no hana—artificial flower worn in the head-dress (note 845)

kazu—see *kazu(sashi)*

kazuke—reward given to a messenger (note 112)

kazuku—(1) to wear over another garment, (2) to put clothes on

kazura—crown, garland, chaplet

Kazuraki—mountain in Yoshino associated with a famous legend (notes 616, 756)

kazu(sashi)—counter, tally, token (note 691)

ke—wooden box

Kebiishi—Imperial Police (notes 249, 705, 1112) (App. 7b)

keburi—(1) smoke, (2) scent, aroma, fragrance

Kechien no Hakkō—Eight (Buddhist) Lessons for Confirmation (note 162)

Kechigan—Day of Conclusion, the last day of the Sacred Readings (note 360)

kechi sasu—to fill up the spaces in *go* (note 758)

kedakashi—proud, haughty

kedōshi—distant (from people)

kegiyoshi—clear, entire, complete

kehai—(1) manner, behaviour, (2) sign, indication

keishi—lacquered clogs

kei su—to report (say) to the Empress, Crown Prince, etc.

kejikashi—close, intimate

kemari—kick-ball (note 837)

Kemon—Submission, an official document submitted to a higher authority (notes 614, 615)

ke (ni)—more, superior

kenikushi—(1) curt, brusque, indifferent, with bad grace, (2) awkward, uncomfortable, hateful

kenja—see *genza*

keshiki—(1) circumstances, state of affairs, (2) appearance, looks, air, (3) thought, feeling, (4) see *keshiki yoshi*

keshikibamu—(1) to give oneself airs, (2) to get angry, excited, (3) to give a signal (hint, indication)

keshikidatsu—to become enlivened (active, excited)

keshiki yoshi—pleasing, charming, congenial

kesō—make up, toilet, dress, ornament

kesō—(1) plain, light, clear, outstanding, (2) public, open

kesōbito—lover

kesōbumi—love letter

kesō zu—to make one's toilet, paint one's face, adorn (embellish) oneself

kesumaji—extremely unpleasant (disagreeable, uninteresting)

keura—charming, pretty

kezayaka—vivid, bright, striking, clear; conspicuous, prominent

kezurigushi—combing (dressing) the hair

kezurihi—shaved ice (note 237)

kezuru—to comb

ki—(1) tree, (2) branch of a tree

ki—clothes

kichikō—campanula (modern *kikyō*), *platycodon grandiflorum* (note 297)

kichō—curtain of state, curtain-frame, wooden T-shaped frame with curtains (*katabira*) (notes 39, 181, 404, 797) (App. 8b, nos. 8, 25)

kieiru—(1) to swoon with grief, (2) to be embarrassed, put out, confused

Kii—superior province (*jōkoku*) south of the capital (note 785) (App. 9a, no. 43)

kikiatsumu—to catch (follow) (what a person is saying)

kikikaesu—to reply, return

kikinaosu—to reconsider, form a new opinion

kikinikushi—scandalous, outrageous

kikitodomu—(1) to listen attentively, (2) to object, find fault with (while listening)

kikiyoshi—easy to hear (understand)

kikobosu—to wear a garment in such a way that one part 'spills out' (i.e. protrudes from underneath a blind, etc.), thus helping to create a desired colour combination

kikoegotsu—to say (honorific) (see *Dictionary of Selected Forms in Classical Japanese Literature*)

kikoyu—(1) to speak, tell, (2) to write (send) a letter (honorific)

kiku—(1) to reply, (2) to hear (note 610)

kiku—chrysanthemum (note 610)

kikuchiba—tawny yellow

Kiku no Sekku—Chrysanthemum Festival (notes 54, 56) (App. 1)

Kimbu—highest peak in Yoshino, often visited by pilgrims (notes 32, 616)

kimemōsu—to discuss

Kimpu—see Kimbu

kin—type of zither (note 89) (App. 8d, no. 8)

Kinai—Home Provinces (note 62)

kinchō—brocade canopy or curtain

kindachi—(1) young nobleman or noblewoman, (2) title denoting the sons of certain top-ranking members of the nobility: His Highness, His Excellency, etc., (3) senior courtier who has not attained the rank of High Court Noble (note 905)

Ki no Haseo—(851-912) government official who wrote Chinese poetry (note 519)

Ki no Mi-Dokyō—seasonal Sacred Readings (see Mi-Dokyō)

Ki no Tomonori—(d. 905) poet, cousin of Tsurayuki (note 228)

Ki no Tsurayuki—(883-945) famous poet and critic (notes 279, 883, 885, 961, 1020)

kinu—(1) dress, clothing; bedclothes, (2) grain (of skin, etc.)

kinugachi—wearing many (layers of) clothes

kinuginu no fumi—next-morning letter (notes 185, 710)

kirakirashi—(1) resounding, ringing, sonorous, (2) glittering, resplendent, brilliant

kirimitsu—to be covered with mist

kiriwataru—see *kirimitsu*

Kisa(k)i—Empress (note 820)

Kisakimachi—Empress's Quarters (notes 780, 784)

Kisaragi—Clothes-Lining (Second) Month (note 3)

kishimeku—to squeak, grate

kishirou—to struggle, compete

kisugu—honest, sincere

kitanashi—(1) dirty, (2) ugly, unattractive, (3) wretched, miserable

Kita no Jin—guard-house next to one of the gates at the north of the Imperial Palace (note 59) (App. 9e, no. 1)

kita no kata—principal consort, official wife

kita-omote—back part of a house (note 121)

Kitano no Sammi—Gentleman of Kitano of the 3rd Rank, name given to Sugawara no Sukemasa (note 501)

kitaru—to wear (something) in such a way that it trails or hangs down low

kiwa—(1) social standing (level), (2) time, occasion

kiwagiwashi—(1) clear, conspicuous, prominent, (2) methodical, scrupulous, precise, exact

kiwayaka—(1) brisk, abrupt, (2) conspicuous, prominent

kiyare—tearing one's clothes

kiyasu—to melt

kiyoge—see *kiyoshi*

kiyoku (with neg.)—(not) in the least, (not) at all

Kiyomizudera — Kiyomizu Temple, famous temple in Kyōto, dedicated to Kannon, the Goddess of Mercy, in about A.D. 800 (notes 1076, 1077) (App. 9d, no. 24)

kiyora—see *kiyoshi*

kiyoshi—(1) neat, trim, dapper, elegant, handsome, attractive, pretty, beautiful, (2) clear, pure, limpid, clean

Kiyowara no Motosuke—(908-90) real or adoptive father of Sei Shōnagon; poet and provincial governor (notes 449, 471, 987) (App. 6c, no. 91)

knotted letter—*musubibumi*

ko—(1) former, (2) late

ko—hook

ko—(1) child, (2) egg

ko—term, period

kō—dark orange, tawny

kōbai—(1) red plum colour, (2) colour combination in which the outside of the garment is scarlet and the lining is violet (notes 23, 101)

Kōbai—Red Plum-Blossom (Palace) (note 72) (App. 9d, no. 22)

Kōbō Daishi—(774-835) great religious leader who introduced Shingon Buddhism to Japan (note 830)

kobokobo to—see *kōkō to*

koboru—to protrude in such a way as to be clearly visible

kobōshi—young priest

kōburi—(1) head-dress of nobility, ceremonial head-dress given to gentlemen of the 5th Rank and above (App. 8a, no. 6), (2) later, the rank itself (note 44)

kochitashi—(1) abundant, exaggerated, excessive, (2) too much to say, verbose

Kochōhai—see Chōga

kodani—bear ivy, *drymoglossum carnosum* (lit. tree-tick)

Kōdate no Mori—Kōdate Forest in Yamashiro Province (note 541)

kodoneri(-*wada* or -*warawa*) –messenger boy, page-boy (specifically one who served a Middle or a Minor Captain of the Inner Palace Guards) (note 988)

koe—(1) voice, (2) speech, language, way of speaking

koegoe shite—in a chorus, in unison

Kofudono—His Excellency the Governor (of a Province) (note 124)

Kōfuku Ji—Kōfuku Temple, clan temple of the Fujiwaras in Nara (note 61)

Kōgō—(First) Empress (note 820)

Kōgōgū—see Chūgū Shiki

kōgōshi—divine, heavenly, sacred

Kōgū—the Empress's Palace

kohaji—hook, fastener

kohajitomi—small half-shutter (*hajitomi*) (note 76)

kohigaki—fence made of strips of cypress (*hinoki*)

Kohyōe—lady-in-waiting to Empress Sadako (notes 420, 658)
Kōi—Imperial Concubine (note 88)
Ko Ichijō In—Smaller Palace of the First Ward (notes 45, 59, 72, 133, 165) (App. 9d, no. 8)
koisemu—to request importunately, insist on a request
kōji—preacher
Kojiki—'Record of Old Happenings', the first extant history of Japan, compiled c. 710 (notes 62, 79)
Kōjin—see Kōshin
kojitomi—small shutter (shitomi)
Kōjō—the Inspection (of low-ranking officials with a view to possible promotion) (notes 611, 612, 613) (App. 1)
Koki Den—(1) Koki Palace, the Empress's residence (notes 73, 378) (App. 9f, no. 7), (2) name given to Fujiwara no Yoshiko (2)
Koki Den no Ue no Mi-Tsubone—apartment in Seiryō Palace used by the Empress (notes 73, 269) (App. 9g, no. 6)
Kokin Rokujō—abbreviation of Kokin Waka Rokujō, (unofficial) anthology of Japanese verse in 6 books, compiled c. 950 (notes 62, 186, 199, 216, 220, 225, 227, 228, 274, 279, 296, 307, 312, 537, 684, 827, 871, 879, 882, 918)
Kokin Shū—abbreviation of Kokin Waka Shū, 'Collection of Old and New Japanese Poems', first official anthology of verse, in 20 books, compiled by Ki no Tsurayuki and others in 905; it contains 1,100 poems (notes 62, 64, 80, 81, 87, 94, 274, 278, 283, 284, 365, 503, 540, 650, 685, 747, 827, 847, 856, 883, 884, 921, 939, 1008, 1020, 1051, 1052, 1094)
Kōkō—(830-87) 58th Emperor, reg. 885-7 (note 275)
kokochi ashi—(1) in a bad mood, (2) ill, indisposed
kokochi ayashi—ill, out of sorts
kokochi wazurau—to feel unwell, be indisposed
kokomoto ni—actually, at present, now
Kokonoe—the Nine-Fold Enclosure, i.e. the Imperial Palace (note 14)
kokora—many, several
kokoro agaru—to have a swollen head, be proud (haughty), give oneself airs

kokoro akugaru—to be carried away (overwhelmed) with emotion
kokoro ari—to be kind-hearted
kokoro ayashi—ill-natured
kokorobae—(1) ready wit, (2) feeling, humour, mood, (3) meaning, significance, purport, (4) character, nature, disposition
kokorobase ari—to be alert, able
kokoro fusagaru—to be depressed, dejected
kokorogaku—to be in love (infatuated) with
kokorogurushi—pitiful, distressing, pathetic
kokoro hitotsu ni—entirely for one's own sake, exclusively for oneself
kokoro hitotsu yaru—to do (something) for one's own pleasure alone
kokoro iraru—to be cross, irritable, nervous
kokoro kashikoshi—(1) strong-minded, stout-hearted, (2) clever, (3) prudent, scrupulous
kokoro koto nari—(1) to be alienated, estranged, (2) to give a special (unusual) feeling
kokoro koto ni—(to pay) special attention, extra care
kokoro mijikashi—(1) quick-tempered, irritable, (2) quickly sated, quick to lose interest
kokoromōke—preparation, arrangement
kokoromoto nashi—(1) impatient, (2) slow-going, not quick enough, (3) precarious, questionable, (4) annoying, unpleasant, irritating, alarming
kokoro nashi—(1) dull-witted, dull, (2) heartless, inconsiderate
kokoro ni kakaru—to have (keep) in mind
kokoro nikushi—(1) important, consequential, (2) elegant, graceful, charming
kokoro no oni izu—to go against one's conscience, be pricked by one's conscience
kokoroochi—relief, security
kokoro okashi—good-natured, kind-hearted
kokoro omou—to be charmed, fascinated, moved
kokorootori su—to be disappointing, not to live up to expectations
kokoroshiri — knowledgeable, well-informed

kokoro shiru—to be familiar, know one's way about

kokoro su—to be careful

kokoro suku—see *suku*

kokoro to—of one's own accord

kokoro todomu—to be careful, attentive

kokoro tokimeki su—to have one's heart in one's mouth, feel one's heart beating quickly

kokorougaru—(1) to be sad (gloomy, sullen), (2) to regard as wretched (pitiable, miserable)

kokoroushi—sad

kokoro (wo) u—to understand, grasp

kokoro wo yaru—(to do something) to one's heart's content

kokoro yori hoka ni—unexpectedly

kokoro yuku—to satisfy, give a pleasant feeling

kokorozama—disposition, temperament

kokorozashi—(1) will, determination, (2) liking, fondness

kokorozukau—to be alert (anxious)

kokorozuki nashi—disagreeable, distasteful

kōkō to—loudly, with a clatter

komagoma to—one by one, piece by piece

komainu—'Korean dog' (notes 401, 595)

Komainu no Mai—Korean Dog Dance (note 595)

Komano no Monogatari—'The Tale of Komano', a non-extant work of prose fiction mentioned in both *The Tale of Genji* and *The Pillow Book* (notes 835, 1045)

Ko Manyō Shū—see *Manyō Shū* (note 295)

Komatsu—Little Pines, a folk-song (note 671)

komayaka—dark (colour)

Koma Yama—Mount Koma, an ancient song (note 671)

kōmeku—to make a reverberating (booming) sound

komo—water-oat, *zizania aquatica* (note 543)

komori—gardener

komu—to include

Kongen Roku—'Original Records of the Earth' (note 1063)

Kongōshu—Buddhist deity (note 32)

kongu—temple gong

Ko Nijō In—Smaller Palace of the 2nd Ward, private residence of Empress Sadako (note 678) (App. 9d, no. 13)

Ko Rokujō In—Smaller Palace of the 6th Ward (App. 9d, no. 24)

Konoe—Inner Palace Guards (notes 50, 72, 763) (App. 7b)

Konoe no mi-kado—gate of the Inner Palace Guards (note 318)

konomoshi—(1) pleasant, attractive, (2) loving, amorous

kōrai(beri)—lit. 'Korean edge', white material with black designs used as the border of *tatami* straw mats (App. 8b, no. 13)

kōran—balustrade (App. 8b, no. 20)

'Korean dog'—*komainu*

Korean Dog Dance—Komainu no Mai

Korechika—*see* Fujiwara no Korechika

Koretaka—(844–97) Prince Koretaka, son of Emperor Montoku (notes 72, 284)

korooi—about, approximately

kosaki—short cry of 'Make way!' (note 318)

Kosakon—lady-in-waiting to Empress Sadako

Koshi—old word for the remote northern area, comprising Echizen, Etchū, Echigo, Kaga, and Noto Provinces (notes 377, 387)

koshi—cords, strings (of *hakama*)

koshi—roof of a carriage

koshi—dark, deep (usually of violet or red colour)

Kōshin—Night of the Monkey (note 472)

Ko Shirakawa Dono—Smaller Shirakawa Palace, north-east of the capital (note 165)

Kosōji—the Little Screen, in Seiryō Palace (note 536) (App. 9g, no. 7)

koto—(1) the rest, (2) particular, different, outstanding, unusual

koto—(1) stringed instrument (generic term), (2) kind of zither (note 89) (App. 8d, nos. 8–10)

koto—word

kō to—see *kaka to*

kotobagaki—prose introduction to verse (note 91)

kotobazukuna ni—briefly, laconically

kotobito—other person, others

kotobuki—(1) auspicious words, magic formula, (2) congratulations, address of loyalty

kotodoki—another time, not now

kotodokoro—(1) elsewhere, outside, (2) abroad, foreign land

kotodomori—stammering, stuttering

kotogoto—other matter, other thing

kotogusa—habitual complaint, grumble; customary saying (as in 'he would often say . . .')

kotohito—see *kotobito*

kotonashibi ni—in a commonplace (banal) way, nonchalantly, carelessly

kotonashigao—see *hito no kotonashigao*

kotonashigusa—'nothing wrong' herb (note 293)

kotoneri—see *kodoneri*

Koto no Mama—shrine in Tōtōmi Province (notes 879, 884)

koto okonau—to direct, order, command

kotosogu—to simplify, make informal

kototakashi—positive, insistent

kototori—director

kotouruwashi—correctly (decorously) arranged

kotowari—natural, reasonable

kotowaru—to judge, estimate

kotoyō—(1) outlandish, unseemly, unbecoming, bad form, (2) rare, strange

kouchigi—wide-sleeved robe worn by women on formal occasions

kowagaru—to be obstinate, stiff, unyielding

kowagowashi—rigid, unbending, formal

kowakagimi—young lord (note 963)

kowashi—hard, solid, firm, rigid

kowazama—tone of voice, manner of speaking

kōyagami—heavy remade paper, manufactured in Kōyagawa (near the capital) and used in government offices for documents, etc.

Kōya paper—see *kōyagami*

Kōya (San)—Mt. Kōya in Kii Province, site of the headquarters of the Shingon sect of Buddhism (note 830) (App. 9b, no. 9)

koyona(shi)—unexcelled, extreme

koyumi—small bow (contest)

kōza—dais, platform

kozo—last year

kōzome—dyed dark orange

kōzome—reddish-yellow colour used for dyeing surplices, etc.

kō zu—(1) to become exhausted, tired, (2) to be perplexed

kozutau—to carry (transmit) from one tree to another

kubi(zuna)—collar

Kubon Rendai—Nine Ranks of Lotus Seats (note 478)

kuchiba—reddish-yellow

kuchigatashi—stubborn, firm

kuchi hikitaru—to pout (note 690)

kuchikigata—pattern of decaying wood (note 408)

kuchinawaichigo—Indian strawberry, *duchesnea (fragaria) indica* (note 719)

kuchioshi—(1) unsightly, unseemly, (2) bad, unpleasant, (3) regrettable, mortifying

kuchizusabu—to hum, murmur

kudamono—(1) fruit, (2) sweet, confectionery

kudari—auxiliary numeral for counting clothes

kudariseba—cramped, squeezed (of writing)

kudaru—to leave the capital (for the provinces)

kuenichi—inauspicious day (note 915)

Kuge—Court Noble, general term designating all officials of the Imperial Court

kugutsu—strolling player, minstrel

Kugyō—(1) see Kandachibe, (2) see Kuge, (3) see *tenjōbito*

Kujaku Kyō—'Peacock Sutra' (note 1056)

Kuji—Confucius (note 612)

Kujō Shakujō—Nine-Article Pilgrim's Staff (note 1005)

kukumu—to pile (fold) up, cover oneself with

kukuriagu—to raise (tuck) up and fasten

kukurimono—dappled material

Kumano—place south of Yoshino, site of 3 famous shrines (note 32) (App. 9b, no. 10)

kumo no uebito—high member of Court society (lit. 'person above the clouds') (note 1073)

Kunai Shō—Ministry of the Imperial Household (App. 7a)

Kuniyuzuri—section of *Utsubo Monogatari* (note 835)

295

kunō—suffering inherent in life, anguish (note 310)

kunzu—to wilt, droop, lose courage, be overpowered, bowed (by misfortune, etc.)

kurabeuma—horse-race (note 707)

Kuramadera—Kurama Temple, Shingon temple north of the capital (notes 346, 347, 777) (App. 9c, no. 1)

Kura no Kami—Director of the Palace Treasury (notes 491, 514)

kurashiwazurau—to have difficulty in living, find life difficult

kurasu—see *kakikurasu*

kurefutagaru—to be gloomy, depressed

kurehashi—log steps, staircase made of tree trunks

kuriyame—kitchen maid

Kurodo—(1) Black Door (at the north of Seiryō Palace) (App. 9g, no. 2), (2) gallery at the north of Seiryō Palace (note 332)

Kurōdo—(1) Chamberlain (notes 48, 70, 137, 156, 249, 395), (2) *see* Nyo-Kurōdo

Kurōdodokoro—(1) Emperor's Private Office (notes 48, 49, 50, 156, 249), (2) Attendants' Hall (in the household of the Regent, Chancellor, Imperial Prince, etc.)

Kurōdo no Ben—Chamberlain-Controller, a Chamberlain who served in one of the Controlling Boards

Kurōdo no Goi—Fifth-Rank Chamberlain (notes 156, 395)

Kurōdo no Tō—Chief Chamberlain, one of two officials at the head of the Emperor's Private Office (note 630)

kurogane—iron (note 719)

kuromu—to be black, dirty, filthy

kuronuri—black-lacquered (writing box) (note 877)

kuroshi—(1) black, (2) dark, (3) dirty, filthy, soiled

kurubeku—to turn round, revolve

kurukuru to—fluently, smoothly, without a hitch

kuruma—carriage (note 969)

kuruma-arasoi—'carriage dispute' (note 865)

kuruma-yadori—coach-house, building outside the main gate where carriages were kept when not in use

kurumi—(1) walnut (note 720), (2) colour combination in which the outside of the garment is yellowish-red and the lining is white (note 23)

kusezuku—to be intricate, complicated

Kusha—'The Storehouse', a Buddhist text (note 562)

kushi—hair

kushiage—see *mi-kushiage*

Kushige—*see* Mi-Kushige

kusudama—herbal ball (notes 113, 206, 918) (App. 8d, no. 3)

Kusuriko—Imperial Wine-Taster (note 729)

kusushi—laudable, praiseworthy

kusushi—doctor (note 977)

kusushigaru—to seem laudable, praiseworthy

kutai—waistband, ribbon (note 411)

kutasu—to rot, decay

kutsu—shoe (notes 270, 271, 601) (App. 8a, no. 4)

kutsuroka—loose, comfortable, informal

kutsuwamushi—long, noisy cricket, *mecopoda elongata* (note 843)

kuzuoru—to be decrepit

kuzureizu—to pour (tumble, throng) out

Kyō—Minister (note 875)

kyō—filial piety

kyō ari—to be delightful

kyōge—service of instruction and guidance (note 574)

Kyōgoku Dono—detached palace to the east of the Imperial Palace (note 378) (App. 9d, no. 7)

Kyō Kuyō—Dedication of Sutras (notes 159, 944)

kyōsan—book-mark

kyōyō su—to entertain, treat, regale

kyō zu—to be charmed, delighted

kyū—final movement (in music)

laced (threaded) trousers—*sashinuki*

lacquered cap—*eboshi*

Lady Chamberlain—Nyo-Kurōdo

Lady Chūnagon—Chūnagon no Kimi

lady-in-waiting—*nyōbo*

Lady of the Escort—Himemōchigimi

Lady of the Shigei Sha—Shigei S(h)a (2)

Lady Saishō—Saishō no Kimi

Lady Shigeisha—*see* Lady of the Shigei Sha

Lady Ukon—Ukon no Naishi

latticed shutter—*shitomi*
Leader—Dōshi
Left Guards—*see* Outer Palace Guards, Left Division
lesser attendant—*shimozukae*
lid—*futa*
Lieutenant—*Jō*
Lieutenant of the Audience Chamber—Ue no Hōgan
Lieutenant of the Guards or of the Imperial Police—Jō, Zō
Lieutenant of the Imperial Police—Hōgan
'lion'—*shishi*
Lion Dance—*Shishi Mai*
long corridor—*hosodono*
long robe—*hosonaga*
loose coat—*kazami*
loose trousers—*sashinuki*
Lotus Sutra—*Hoke Kyō*

ma—unit of measurement, *t.* 3·3 yards (note 455)
mabayushi—embarrassed, ill at ease
machikōzu—to grow tired (be weary) of waiting
machitsuku—(1) to reach (attain) something after waiting, (2) to last (continue) until
madarazuku—to be piebald, dappled
madashi—(1) already, so soon; still not yet (with neg.), (2) inexpert, untrained, inexperienced
madou—to run (bustle) about frantically, be hurried, flustered
maebarai—attendant who clears the way, etc. (for a person of high rank)
magamagashi—(1) unlucky, inauspicious, (2) disastrous, (3) ominous, sinister, (4) abominable, infernal
magau—to imitate, copy, counterfeit
mahirogu—(1) to be open (of robes, etc.) in a slovenly way, (2) to be in disorder, untidy
maibito—dancer
maid-of-honour—*nyōbo*
mairu—(1) to give (to a superior), (2) to serve, (3) to come, go, (4) to manipulate, handle, (5) to close (a lattice, etc.), (6) to eat, drink (see also *Dictionary of Selected Forms in Classical Japanese Literature*)
maite—even (still) more
majikashi—familiar, used to seeing (being seen)

majirai—(1) association, company, (2) service (at Court)
majirau—to mix, mingle
Major Captain of the Inner Palace Guards—Taishō
Major Controller—Daiben
Major Controller of the Left—Sadaiben
Major Controller of the Right—Udaiben
Major Counsellor—Dainagon
makanai—lady-in-waiting who served the Empress her meals
makanau—(1) to prepare, put in order, manage, arrange, deal with, (2) to serve, attend, look after
makanzu—see *makazu*
makarimōshi—leave-taking
makazu—to leave, retire from (= *makari-izu*)
makime—fold (crease) in paper, etc., where it has been rolled or folded
makizome—rolled dyeing (note 27)
makotoshi—plausible, seeming
makuragami—close to the pillow, by the bedside
makura (*no soshi*)—pillow book (note 1156)
Mama—a common name (*tsūshō*) for nurses (note 1100)
mama ni—(1) while, (2) since, (3) as soon as (see also *Dictionary of Selected Forms in Classical Japanese Literature*)
mamebito—sober-sides, grave (serious) person
mamedatsu—to be serious, solemn
mamegoto—serious matter
mameyaka—serious, earnest, sincere, true
mami—expression of the eyes
mamorau—to gaze, stare, watch intently
mamoru—see *mamorau*
manu—Chinese character, *kanji*
manakoi—look (expression) in the eyes
manebu—(1) to transmit exactly, (2) to learn from, imitate
manna—see *mana*
Manyō Shū—'Collection of Myriad Leaves', famous 8th-century anthology of Japanese verse (notes 62, 79, 186, 194, 199, 219, 229, 259, 274, 295, 422, 537, 782, 827, 879, 1022, 1048)
mao—complete, full, true
maro—see *maroshi*
marobasu—see *marobu*

marobu—to tumble
marōdo—guest, visitor
marōdo-i—guest room
marogasu—to turn round and round, whirl
marokosuge—bulrush, *scirpus lacustris*
maroshi—round
maroya—hut entirely covered with thatch
Masahiro—*see* Minamoto no Masahiro
masana—naughty, ill-behaved
masarite—more
masaru—to improve
mase—bamboo fence (hedge)
masegoshi—(1) across the fence, (2) outside (note 871)
Master—Daibu
Master of Asceticism—Rishi
Master of Divination—Onyōji
Master of the Buddhist Law—Hōshi
Master of the (Empress's) Household—Daibu
mata—(1) more, further, (2) specially, in particular, (3) next, following
matabisashi—annex to *hisashi*, being the portion of a room between the *hisashi* and the open veranda
matashi—complete, satisfactory
match—*awase*
matsu—(1) pine (note 1071), (2) pine torch, firebrand, (3) same as *shinobugusa*
matsu—to wait (note 1071)
Matsugimi—*see* Fujiwara no Matsugimi
matsu no ha—colour combination in which the outside of the garment is greenish-yellow and the lining is violet-purple (note 23)
Matsuri—*see* Kamo Matsuri
Matsuri no Kaesa—Return Procession of the High Priestess from the Upper Kamo Shrine on the day after the Kamo Festival (note 850)
mau—to turn round, revolve
mayu—eyebrows (notes 367, 1069)
mayumi—(great) bow
mayumi—spindle tree (note 212)
mazu—(1) at once, without any further ado, (2) first of all, above all
me—wife
me—type of edible seaweed (*laminaria japonica*) (note 358)
me aya—bewildered, not believing one's own eyes

medemayou—to be dazzled, overcome with admiration
medetashi—(1) splendid, superb (note 1157), (2) interesting, agreeable
medium—*yorimashi*
medō—bridle path (note 913) (App. 9g, no. 1)
me (ga) tatsu—to catch the eye, attract notice
meiboku—splendid, glorious
mejikashi—close, near at hand
me kuru—to be dizzy
me mo aya ni—see *me aya*
Meng-ch'ang—Chinese lord who figures in the *Shih chi* (notes 637, 638)
menoto—nurse, wet-nurse
meoya—mother
meshiagu—to summon, call
meshiiru—to call in, summon
me tatezama—turned-up eyes (note 260)
me tomaru—to be noticed, arouse attention
me wa sora ni—with one's attention (mind) on something else, absent-mindedly
me wo kuwasu—to glance meaningfully, wink (note 363)
meyari—look, glance
meyasushi—worth seeing, acceptable, passable, agreeable, pleasant
mezu—to admire, be impressed, praise
mezurashi—(1) impressive, superb, (2) rare, uncommon (note 641)
Mi—*see* Mi no Toki
mi-agamono—substitute figure (note 725)
mi-akashi jōtō—lamp kept burning permanently in front of a sacred image
Miare no Senji—High Priestess's Envoy (note 801)
mi-ariki—procession, cortège
mi-asobi—see *asobi*
mibome—self-praise, self-adulation
Mibu no Tadamine—(868-*c.* 930) distinguished poet and one of the compilers of the *Kokin Shū* (note 856)
michi—honey
Michinaga—*see* Fujiwara no Michinaga
Michinoku(ni)—(1) distant northern provinces of the main island of Japan, (2) thick white paper (note 148)
Michitaka—*see* Fujiwara no Michitaka
Michizane—*see* Sugawara no Michizane
mi-chō(dai)—see *chōdai*

298

mi-chōzu mairu—to perform one's ablutions

Middle Captain (of the Inner Palace Guards)—Chūjō

Middle Controller—Chūben

Middle Palace Guards—Hyōe

Middle Palace Guards, Left Division—Sahyōe

Mi-Dō—Buddhist hall or temple

midokoro—charm, flavour

Mi-Dokyō—Sacred Readings, a bi-annual Buddhist ceremony (notes 357, 360, 371, 726) (App. 1)

miegasane—three layers, three folds

Migi no Otodo—Minister of the Right (note 168) (App. 7a)

migurushi—disagreeable, ugly, painful

mi-gushi—hair

mi-gushiage—Palace hairdresser

mi-hashi—steps, stairs

Mihetsui—Imperial Cauldron (note 401)

miidasu—(1) to look at, glance; gaze, (2) to gaze after (a person), follow (a person) with one's eyes as (he) leaves

miiru—(1) to (take) notice, pay attention, (2) to look after, help

mijikashi—(1) low, (2) short

mijikuru—to fidget, move about

mijirogu—to move back, withdraw

mika—jug, jar, pitcher

mi-kado—gate (note 72)

Mikasa—(1) mountain in Yamato Province (note 62), (2) Inner Palace Guards (note 867)

mikawayōto—cleaner of the Palace privies, Imperial latrine cleaner

mikodori—starling, *sturnus cineraceus*

Mikomori—shrine in Yamato Province (notes 1015, 1021)

mi-koshi—(1) palanquin (note 852), (2) portable shrine (note 1019) (App. 8c, no. 1)

mikoshiyado—place where a *mi-koshi* (q.v.) was kept

mikuri—(1) water-bur, *sparganium longifolium*, (2) shrine in Echigo Province (note 879)

mikusa—water plant

Mi-Kushige—Office of the Imperial Wardrobe (notes 348, 954, 1100)

Mi-Kushige no Bettō—Mistress of the Robes

mimagau—to mistake (someone for)

mimagusa—fodder, forage

Mimana—family name (note 615)

mime—aspect, countenance

miminagusa—myosotis (notes 609, 610)

Mimitogawa—Mimito River, a stream in the capital (notes 274, 279)

mimi todomu—to strain one's ears, listen attentively

mimi toshi—quick of hearing

mimi wo katabuku—see *mimi todomu*

mimi wo tonaete—intently, with strained ears

mi-moi—water (note 783)

Mimoro no Yama—Mt. Mimoro, sacred Shintō mountain in Yamato (note 79)

minahito—everyone

Minami no In—Southern Palace (note 445, 945)

Minamoto famous warrior family descended from Emperor Seiwa in the 9th century (notes 60, 1038) (App. 6a)

Minamoto no Hideakira—(d. 940) poet (notes 319, 761)

Minamoto no Kanesuke—Governor of Iyo Province; one of his daughters was a wife of Fujiwara no Korechika, the other of Fujiwara no Kaneie (note 1037)

Minamoto no Kanezumi—(died c. 985) Governor of Kaga Province and a poet (note 956)

Minamoto no Masahiro—Chamberlain and, later, Governor of Awa Province (notes 270, 515, 532, 533, 534) (App. 2, no. 10)

Minamoto no Masanobu—(920-93) Minister of the Right 977-8, Minister of the Left 978-93 (note 168) (App. 6a, no. 4)

Minamoto no Michikata—(968-1044) government official and harpist (note 327) (App. 6a, no. 8)

Minamoto no Muneyuki—(d. 939) one of the 36 Japanese Poets (note 179)

Minamoto no Narimasa—minor government official (note 327) (App. 6a, no. 16)

Minamoto no Narinobu—(979-c. 1002) grandson of Emperor Murakami, adopted by Michinaga; officer of the Imperial Guards and later a priest (notes 60, 873, 876, 1037, 1041) (App. 2, no. 11, and App. 6a, no. 20)

Minamoto no Nobukata (1)—(969-98) son of the Minister of the Left, Shigenobu; served in the Imperial Guards and was known as the 'Captain of the Minamoto family' (notes 552, 759, 762, 764, 769) (App. 2, no. 12, and App. 6a, no. 7)

Minamoto no Nobukata (2)—officer of the Imperial Guards (note 552)

Minamoto no Norimasa—(b. 975) Secretary in the Ministry of Ceremonial and later a provincial governor (note 1000) (App. 6a, no. 17)

Minamoto no Shigenobu—(922-95) Minister of the Left 994-5 (App. 6a, no. 3)

Minamoto no Shitagau—(912-84) provincial governor and author (notes 62, 352)

Minamoto no Suzushi—character in *Utsubo Monogatari* (notes 352, 369)

Minamoto no Tadataka—Chamberlain and, later, Governor of Suruga (note 48) (App. 6a, no. 15)

Minamoto no Takaakira—(914-82) son of Emperor Daigo; Minister of the Right 966-8 and Left 968-9; he was disgraced but returned to favour (note 528) (App. 6a, no. 6)

Minamoto no Tokiakira—Director of the Bureau of Imperial Stables; later became Governor of Izumi (notes 515, 603)

Minamoto no Toshikata—(960-1027) poet and government official (notes 331, 528) (App. 6a, no. 13)

Minamoto no Tsunefusa—(968-1023) successful government official and close friend of Shōnagon (notes 327, 528, 644, 679, 1154) (App. 2, no. 13, and App. 6a, no. 14)

Minamoto no Yorisada—(b. 976) son of Prince Tamehira; Guards officer (notes 424, 644, 1112) (App. 6a, no. 19)

Minamoto no Yoriyoshi—(b. 951) Major Controller of the Left (note 256)

minarai su—to imitate (what one sees)

minarau—to be familiar with, accustomed to

Minazuki—Watery (Sixth) Month (note 3)

Minister—Daijin, Otodo, Kyō

Minister of the Left—Hidari no Otodo

Minister of the Right—Migi no Otodo

Ministers' Banquet—Daikyō

Ministry of Central Affairs—Nakazukasa Shō

Ministry of Ceremonial—Shikibu Shō

mino—straw coat (note 502)

minomushi—basket worm (notes 239, 658)

Minor Captain (of the Inner Palace Guards)—Shōshō

Minor Counsellor—Shōnagon

Mi no Toki—Hour of the Snake, about 10 a.m. (note 417) (App. 3)

miokosu—to look, glance

miru—(1) to have a love affair with, (2) to look after, attend to; examine, check

misasu—to glance, have a quick look at

miscanthus—*susuki*

Mi-Seku—*see* Sechie

mishiru—(1) to be used to seeing, familiar, (2) to be quick-witted

miso—see *mi-zo*

misohime—see *hime*

misoji—30 years (old)

mi-sōji—see *sōjin*

misoka—furtive, stealthy, secret

mi-sōzoku—see *sōzoku*

Mistress of the Robes—Mi-Kushige no Bettō

mi-su—see *sudare*

Mitake—another name for Mt. Kimbu (notes 32, 550, 554) (App. 9b, no. 8)

mitatsu—(1) to stand and look, (2) to select, single out, (3) to care for, look after, coddle, pamper

mi-tegura—see *tegura*

mitonogomoru—to retire to his room (of the Emperor)

mitsuku—to see, meet

Mi-tsuna no Suke—Assistant Director (of the Bureau of Imperial Attendants) who held the cords of the Imperial palanquin during processions, etc. (note 849)

mi-ubuya—see *ubuya*

Miwa—mountain and shrine in Yamato Province (notes 62, 883, 1008)

mi wo kau—to be reborn, reincarnated

Miya—(1) Empress, (2) Imperial Palace, Court, (3) Imperial Prince(ss)

miyabara—offspring of the Crown Prince

miyabi(ya)ka—refined, elegant, distinguished

miyahajime—installation of the Empress (note 401)

Miya no Daibu—Master of the Office of the Empress's Household (note 986)

Miya no Me—*see,* Ōmiya no Me

Miya no Omae—Her Majesty the Empress

Miya no Shiki—*see* Shiki In

Miya no Tsukasa—Great Council of State

Miyasu(n)dokoro—consort of the Crown Prince (note 415)

miyasushi—decent, seemly, becoming

miyazukaebito—person serving in the Palace

miyazukaedokoro—place of employment in the Palace

miyazukae su—to serve in the Palace

Miyazukasa—(1) *See* Chūgū Shiki, (2) employée of the Chūgū Shiki

miyazukau—to serve at Court

mi-yu—(1) hot water, (2) rice water, water gruel

Mi-Yudono—Imperial Bathing Room (note 913) (App. 9g, no. 4)

mizame—boredom with something that one has seen too often

mi-zo—garment, clothes, dress, robe

mi-zōshi—see *zōshi*

mizubuki—prickly water lily, gordon plant, *euryale ferox* (note 720)

mi-zuhō—see *zuho*

mi-zukyō—see *zukyo*

Mizunashi no Ike—Mizunashi Pond in Yamato Province (notes 199, 201)

mizura—man's hairstyle in which the topknot was parted and fastened on both sides

mizushi—servant attached to the Emperor's Dining Room (including *toji* and *tokusen*)

Mizushi(dokoro)—Emperor's Dining Room

Mizuumi—the Lake (i.e. Lake Biwa) (note 71)

mo—open or divided skirt with a long train, worn on formal occasions (notes 676, 1110) (App. 8a, nos. 18, 24)

mochigayu—special type of gruel (notes 5, 16) (App. 1)

mochinasu—see *motenasu*

mochinohi—15th day of the month (being full moon according to the lunar calendar)

modokashi—fault-finding, captious, censorious

modoku—to criticize, oppose, run counter to

modorokasu—to speckle, dapple

moe—a sprout

moji—Chinese character

mokō (no su)—head-blind (notes 126, 409)

moku—grain (of wood)

Moku Ryō—Bureau of Carpentry (note 137)

Momo no Sekku—Peach Festival (note 21) (App. 1)

monjaku—muster of the Imperial Guards (note 268)

Monjō Hakase—Doctor of Literature (notes 398, 720)

Monjū—see *Bunjū*

mono—(1) thing, (2) person (notes 102, 529, 722), (3) ceremony, festival, spectacle, (4) place, (5) book, (6) musical instrument

mono aware nari—to be moving, impressive (see *mono no aware*)

monoawase—object-match (note 936)

monoenzu—see *en zu*

monofuru—to be old (ancient)

monogatari—tale, romance, story, work of prose fiction (notes 835, 933)

monogatari su—(1) to talk, converse, chat, (2) to babble (of a child)

monogurui—fool, madman

monogur(uh)oshi—mad, crazy, harebrained (note 854)

monoimi (no fuda)—abstinence (sign) (note 157)

monoimi no hi—day of abstinence or seclusion (notes 90, 103, 157, 656, 659)

mono iu—to speak, converse

monokashikoshi—clever, knowing

monomi—festival, procession

mono mishiru—to be experienced, knowing

monomōde su—to visit a temple or shrine

mono no aware—pathos of things, *lacrimae rerum* (notes 366, 627)

mono no eyō—see *eyō*

mono no futa—see *futa*

mono no gu—implement, utensil

mono no ke—evil spirit (notes 1141, 1143)

mono no ne—sound of a musical instrument

mono no ori—(1) whenever something happens, on every occasion, (2) on a certain occasion

301

mono no rei—established custom, old practice

mono oboezu—(1) to lose consciousness, (2) to be useless, trivial

mononozomi su—to offer a prayer or request (at a temple, etc.)

monooboegao—knowing look, pedantic air

monoosu—see *osu*

monoshi—disagreeable, unpleasant; displeased, dissatisfied, ill-humoured

mono su—(1) to be (in attendance), (2) to place (see also *Dictionary of Selected Forms in Classical Japanese Literature*)

mono tsuku—see *tsuku*

mono ugaru—to be bored, find things tiresome (tedious)

mono ushi—(1) listless, languid, (2) tiresome, wearisome, irksome, hard to do

mono yukashi—curious, fanciful, inquisitive

monozokonau—to injure, damage, spoil

months, names of—note 3

Montoku—(827-58) 55th Emperor, reg. 850-8 (notes 72, 81) (App. 6b, no. 27)

Monzen—see *Wen hsüan*

morimono—offerings (presented at Buddhist ceremonies, etc.)

Morokoshi—China (note 888)

mōshibumi—request for promotion (note 20)

mōshimadou—to insist, clamour

mōshinaosu—to say (something) in order to put a good face on (smooth over, gloss over) a matter

mōshiuketamawaru—to have a conversation, exchange views

Mōsōkun—the Lord of Meng-ch'ang

motagu—to raise, lift

motari—(1) to have, possess, carry, (2) to take as one's wife

motekashizuku—see *kashizuku*

motenasu—to treat, deal with, handle; accept, use; behave

motenoku—to put out of the way, avert

motesawagu—to bustle about, busy oneself

motetsuku—to handle, deal, use

motewataru—to bring

moteyuku—(1) to become *or* do (something) gradually, (2) to go

moto—(1) place, house, (2) origin, (3) first part of a Japanese poem (notes 340, 470, 686), (4) side, edge

moto no kokoro ushinau—to lose one's mind, fall into a trance, swoon away

Motosuke—see Kiyowara no Motosuke

motoyui—cord for tying the hair (note 708)

moya—central apartment, main part of house or room (note 38)

moyōsu—to spur, accelerate, quicken, press on

mōzu—to go (to a temple)

mubemubeshi—plausible, convincing

muge ni—(1) (with neg.) not at all, not in the slightest, (2) completely, entirely, extremely

mugo—unfixed, undetermined (of time, etc.)

mujin—unsympathetic, inconsiderate; indiscreet

mukashi oboyu—to be old-fashioned

muko—adopted son-in-law, husband (notes 17, 114, 925)

mukurogome—whole body (note 535)

mukutsukeshi—frightening, formidable

mumago—grandchild

mumazoi—see *umazoe*

mumon—having no design (pattern, ornamentation)

Mumyō—name of a famous lute (notes 433, 434, 438)

munaguruma—(1) baggage cart (carriage), (2) empty carriage

mune—(1) chest, breast, (2) stomach (note 1114)

Munehira, Prince—(951-1041) son of Emperor Murakami; served as Minister of Military Affairs (note 1036) (App. 6a, no. 12)

mune hashiru—to feel uneasy (restless) (note 1109)

mune tsuburu—to be agitated, anxious, overcome with emotion

muragiyu—to melt in patches

murago—uneven shading (notes 27, 209, 404)

Murakami—(926-67) 62nd Emperor, reg. 947-67 (Apps. 6a, no. 5, and 6b, nos. 38 and 52)

muramura ni—in patches (speckles)

murasaki—(1) purple, violet, (2) chestnut colour (of horses)

Murasaki (No)—famous plain north of the capital (notes 193, 235) (App. 9c, no. 3)

Murasaki Shikibu—(? *c.* 975-*c.* 1025) lady-in-waiting to Empress Akiko (Jōtōmon In) and author of *The Tale of Genji* (note 803) (App. 6b, no. 39)

muredatsu—to leave in a crowd

mushirobari no kuruma—straw-mat carriage (note 704)

musoji—sixty years (old)

musubibumi—knotted letter, formal letter folded lengthwise into a narrow strip and knotted (note 104) (App. 8d, no. 1)

musubitōdai—oil-lamp set on a tripod

mutoku—not worth seeing, useless, of no consequence, having no power or virtue (note 591)

mutsukaru—to be angry, annoyed

mutsukashi—(1) annoying, troublesome, worrying, (2) noisy, (3) filthy, squalid, dirty

Mutsuki—Social (First) Month (note 3)

mutsumashi—intimate, on close terms (note 551)

muyuka—sixth day (of the month)

myōbu—lady of high rank (note 44)

mystic incantation—*darani*

nabesuu—to be in a row, sit side by side

nabete—(1) in general, everything, (2) regular, ordinary

Nachi no Taki—Nachi Waterfall in Kii Province (note 276)

nadaimen—roll-call (note 268)

nagagoto su—to converse lengthily, have a long conversation

nagame—(1) contemplation, gazing, (2) rainy season, long rains (notes 274, 287, 444, 559)

nagamekurasu—to spend the day in contemplation (note 559)

nagamu—see *uchinagamu*

nagara—throughout, completely (see also *Dictionary of Selected Forms in Classical Japanese Literature*)

nagasubitsu—long, rectangular fire-place or brazier surrounded by straw mats

Nagatsuki—Long-Night (Ninth) Month (notes 3, 1128)

nagayaka—long, lengthy

nagazama ni—sideways

nage—see *nage no kotoba*

nagekashi—sad, wretched

nage no kotoba—casual (unintentional) remark

nageshi—beams at the top and bottom of a threshold (between the *hisashi* and the *moya*) (note 78) (App. 8b, nos. 10, 27)

nagi no hana—onion-flower, onion-shaped decoration (notes 979, 1017) (App. 8c, no. 1)

nagoshi—calm, soft, subdued

Naidaijin—*see* Uchi no Ōidono

naige—inside and outside

Naigu(bu)—*see* Gubu

Nairiso no Fuchi—Nairiso Pool in Kawachi Province (notes 62, 69)

Naishi—Palace Attendant, lady on duty in the Palace Attendants' Office (note 95)

Naishi no Kami—Chief Attendant in the Palace Attendants' Office (note 95)

Naishi no Suke—Assistant Attendant in the Palace Attendants' Office (notes 95, 732)

Naishi no Tsukasa—Palace Attendants' Office (notes 52, 95, 724)

Naizen (Shi)—Table Office, under the Ministry of the Imperial Household, in charge of the Emperor's meals (note 401) (App. 7a and App. 9e, no. 7)

najō—see *nanjō*

nakunaku—(1) contrary to what one might expect, actually (cf. modern *kaette*), (2) imperfect, incomplete, unsatisfactory (cf. modern *namajikka*)

Naka no Mikado—Inner Gate (*see* Taiken Mon)

nakara—(1) half, middle, (2) partly

Nakatada—*see* Fujiwara no Nakatada

Nakazukasa Sho—Ministry of Central Affairs (notes 208, 255, 745) (App. 7a and App. 9e, no. 14)

namafusegashige—giving the impression that one finds (someone, something) a nuisance

namaitawaru—to be lacking in proper feeling, too casual

namakeshikarazu—to have a certain vulgarity, give a somehow vulgar impression

namamekashi—elegant, graceful, urbane, gracious, refined; charming, fascinating, captivating

namameku—to be elegant, gracious

namanetashi—vaguely odious, somehow hateful

namaoboe—hazy recollection, faint memory

names (of Court ladies)—notes 996, 1039

nameshi—discourteous, rude

namiiru—to sit next to

Naming of the Buddhas—Butsumyō

namioru—see *namiiru*

nanakusa—the seven herbs (notes 5, 609, 670)

nanasoji—70 years (old)

nani bakari narazu—to be of no importance, count for nothing

nanigashi—something or other, what with one thing and another

nani mo—everywhere, all over (see also *Dictionary of Selected Forms in Classical Japanese Literature*)

Naniwa—old name for Ōsaka (note 80)

Naniwazu—famous poem used by children for writing-practice (notes 80, 739)

nanjō—what sort of? why? (see also *Dictionary of Selected Forms in Classical Japanese Literature*)

Nanoka no Wakana—*see* Wakana no Sekku

nanome—imperfect, unsatisfactory

nanome ni su—to show no respect for, disregard, treat in an offhand fashion

Nanoriso no Kawa—unknown river (notes 272, 282)

nan to ka ya—somehow

nan to mo sezu—to think nothing of

nao—(1) also, after all, the same, even (cf. modern *yahari*), (2) usual, commonplace, ordinary

naoshi—'ordinary' Court cloak, a voluminous, wide-sleeved gown worn by men (App. 8a, no. 7)

naoshi—smooth, level

Nara—capital of Japan from 710 to 784, situated about 20 miles south of Heian Kyō (App. 9b, no. 5)

narashiba—lawn (patch) of grass

narau—to be familiar, intimate: accustomed

narebamu—see *uchinarebamu*

nari—clothes, costume, dress

Narihira—*see* Ariwara no Narihira

nariizu—to advance, be promoted

Narimasa—*see* Taira no Narimasa

Narinobu—*see* Minamoto no Narinobu

Nariyasu—an unidentified poetry-hater (note 621)

naru—to be appointed, promoted

nashie—pear-skin lacquer (a type of aventurine)

nasu—to appoint, promote

Natori—(1) river in Rikuzen Province (notes 274, 283), (2) notoriety

natsukashi—attractive, fascinating

na tsuku—to be famous

natsumushi—tiger-moth

nau—see *nayu*

nayamashi—indisposed, ill

nayamu—to be ill, indisposed

nayoraka—(1) withered, drooping, (2) soft, flexible, supple

nayu—to be worn out, faded, wrinkled, shabby

nazonazo-awase—game of riddles (note 688)

nazurau—to liken, compare

ne—tune, tone, key

nebutashi—sleepy

negi—assistant Shintō priest

negome—roots and all (see *-gome*)

neharu—to be swollen with sleep (of the face)

nekutare—disordered (dishevelled) by sleep

nekutaru—to lie with one's hair in a dishevelled (unkempt) condition

nemadou—to oversleep and wake with a start

Nembutsu—invoking the Sacred Name (note 1006)

nemogorogaru—to affect kindness, make a show of friendliness

nemu—to sleep

nen zu—(1) to forbear, restrain (control) oneself; persevere, (2) to pray

neobiru—(1) to be startled while asleep, be awakened with a start, (2) to be dazed with sleep, not properly awake

neoku—to wake (get) up

neriawaseguri—entwining two strands of thread

neriiro—glossy colour

neru—to walk slowly (solemnly)

netagaru—to look cross (vexed)

netage—(1) envious- (enviable-) seeming, (2) regretful, dismayed, (3) vexing- (mortifying-) seeming

netashi—annoyed, vexed; annoying, vexing

New Year's Day—Chōga, Kochōhai

next-morning letter—*kinuginu no fumi*
nezumochi—privet
nezunaki—mouse's squeak (note 712)
Nieno no Ike—Nieno Pond in Yamashiro Province (notes 199, 200)
nige nashi—unsuitable, ill-matched
Nijō no Miya (Nijō In)—Palace of the 2nd Ward (notes 72, 945) (App. 9d, no. 12)
Nijō no Ōji—Second Avenue, one of the 9 great avenues in the capital (note 598) (App. 9d, no. 16)
nikusage—malicious- (spiteful-) looking
nikushi—(1) ugly, (2) vulgar, common, low-class, (3) unpleasant, disagreeable; uninteresting
Nimmyō—(810-50) 54th Emperor, reg. 833-50 (note 650)
Nine-Fold Enclosure—Kokonoe
ninjō—director of dancers and singers (in *kagura*) (notes 322, 673)
Ninna Ji—Ninna Temple, a Shingon temple east of Kyōto (note 654) (App. 9c, no. 5)
Nintoku—(died *c*. 430) 16th Emperor, reg. *c*. 393-427
nioi—(1) colour, tint, shade, (2) lustre, brightness
nioau—to match, suit, go well (with)
nioiyaka—(1) glossy, highly polished, (2) beautiful, elegant
niou—to be beautifully coloured (tinted)
nioyaka—see *nioiyaka*
Nishi no Kyō—West City, the part of Heian Kyō west of Suzaku Ōji (App. 9d) (notes 351, 355)
nitchū—noon
niwabi—bonfire in a garden
Niwa Ji—*see* Ninna Ji
nō—patchwork
Nobukata—*see* Minamoto no Nobukata
nochi—descendant
nochi no ashita—morning after (usually refers to the morning after a night spent together by lovers)
nochi no koto—afterbirth, placenta
nokekubi su—to wear a piece of clothing with the collar pulled back
nonoshiru—to exclaim (laugh) loudly; make a noise, clamour
Norimitsu—*see* Tachibana no Norimitsu
noriyumi—archery contest (note 451) (App. 1)

north-east—*ushitora*
nōshi—see *naoshi*
noshihitoe—unlined robe of scarlet material
nugitaru—to remove (a cloak) from one shoulder, letting the sleeve hang down; wear loosely (negligently)
Nuidono Ryō—Bureau of the Wardrobe (note 208) (App. 9e, no. 3)
nuimono—embroidery
nuka—prostration, obeisance
nuka tsuku—to prostrate oneself, worship
nukazuki—winter cherry, strawberry tomato, *physalis alkekengi* (note 861)
nukazukimushi—snap-beetle (note 240)
nunobyōbu—screen covered with material
nunosōji—sliding door covered with material
nureginu—(1) wet clothes, (2) unjust accusation, undeservedly bad reputation (especially for sexual promiscuity) (note 867)
nurigome—store-room (note 455)
nurihone—lacquered frame (of a fan, etc.)
nushi—gentleman, man
nusubito—(1) thief, (2) unusual (original) person, rogue, rascal (note 339)
nyōbō—(1) lady-in-waiting, maid-of-honour, (2) servant
Nyōgo—Imperial Lady (note 88)
Nyōin—Empress Dowager (note 416)
Nyoiri(n Kannon)—the Bounteous One (note 833)
nyoju—see *joju*
nyōkan—woman employee (in the Office of Grounds, etc.), low-ranking woman employed in the Palace (note 896)
Nyo-Kurōdo—Lady Chamberlain (notes 348, 410, 725)

obana—see *susuki*
Obasute Yama—Mt. Obasute (lit. 'Abandoned Aunt') in Shinano Province (notes 62, 939)
oboe—see *yo no oboe*
oboe aru hito—man of note (distinction)
oboenashi—unexpected, unanticipated
oboezu—see *mono oboezu*
obomekashi—vague, hazy, indistinct
obomeku—to be vague, indistinct, unclear, uncertain
oboroge—perfunctory, general, common, ordinary

305

oboroge nashi—special, uncommon, rare

oboshi—seeming to think, being thought, apparent

oboshioku—to commit to one's memory, remember

oboshiwaku—to discriminate

obosu—(1) to think, (2) to think fondly, love, esteem

obotsuka nashi—(1) worrying, precarious, unsure, (2) vague, dubious, unclear, (3) impatient, anxious

oboyu—(1) to feel, think, consider, notice, (2) to resemble, (3) to know, remember

O-Butsumyō—*see* Butsumyō

Ochikubo Monogatari—romance in 4 books, written towards the end of the 10th century (note 1047)

ochimarobu—to fall (tumble) down

ōdoka—calm, dignified

odoriku—to dance up, spring forward

odorokashi—see *odoro(shi)*

odoro(shi)—shaggy, bushy, tangled (note 215)

odoroku—to awaken, arouse

odoroodoroshi—(1) pompous, ostentatious; exaggerated, (2) gorgeous, resplendent, (3) loud

ōdoru—(1) to be unreserved; slovenly; (2) to be vague, hazy, muddled, (3) to be senile, doting

Ōe no Asatsuna—(886–957) scholar and Imperial Adviser (note 760)

Office of Grounds—Tonomorizukasa

Office of the Crown Prince's Household—Tōgū

Office of the Empress's Household—Chūgū Shiki, Miyazukasa, Kōgōgū

Office of the Imperial Stables—Umazukasa

Office of the Imperial Wardrobe—Mi-Kushige

ōgi—fan (note 444) (App. 8a, nos. 12, 20)

Ōgisai—Great Empress (note 486)

ōguchi—wide trouser-skirt (note 623)

Ōharai—Great Purification (notes 725, 742) (App. 1)

ōharadatsu—to be very angry, furious

Ōhire—(1) mountain in Settsu Province (note 66), (2) song sung during the 'special festivals' (note 66)

oibamu—to seem old

Ōidono—(Great) Minister

oigoe—old (hoarse) voice

oikazuku—to cover, surround, throng after

oikoru—to be rampant, rank, grow luxuriantly

oinoku—to drive (chase) away

oiraka—magnanimous, generous

oisaki—prospect, outlook

oitsugu—to run after

ojimadou—to be overwhelmed with reverence (awe)

ojisawagu—to be in a state of fear and trembling

ōkami—wolf (note 719)

okashi—charming, delightful, interesting, fascinating, amusing (notes 580, 1157)

ōkenashi—unsuitable, inappropriate

okikuchi—edge (of box, robe, etc.) decorated with gold or silver foil

oko—foolish, stupid

okotaru—to recover (from an illness, etc.)

oku—(1) to settle (of dew) (notes 163, 166), (2) see *sashioku*

oku—to get up (note 166)

oku—(1) back (of a room, house, etc.), (2) end of a letter

ōkuchi—see *ōguchi*

Ōkura Kyō—Minister of the Treasury (note 875)

Ōkura Shō—Ministry of the Treasury (notes 665, 875) (App. 7a and App. 9e, no. 2)

okuru—to fall short of, be inferior

Omae—(1) His (Her) Majesty, (2) member of the Imperial family, (3) the Imperial presence, (4) the Divine presence, (5) master, Sir

Omae no Ike—Pond of the Divine Presence (notes 199, 203)

Omi—Lesser Abstinence (note 411) (App. 1)

Ōmi—great province (*taikoku*) directly west of the capital (App. 9a, no. 33)

omina—woman, female (note 372)

Omi no Kindachi—Young Nobleman of the Lesser Abstinence (notes 411, 418)

Ōmiya no Me—Shintō goddess (note 899)

Ommyōji—*see* Onyōji

omodaka—(1) water plantain, (2) pompous, haughty (note 290)

omogakusu—to cover the surface

omoiguma—deep thought, profound meaning

omoihanatsu—to banish from one's thoughts, forsake, abandon, turn one's back on

omoikakarazu—not to think of (consider, dream of)

omoikakaru—to be anxious (worried) about, think constantly about

omoikaku—(1) to notice, (2) to worry, be anxious about, (3) to love, adore, (4) to wish for, covet

omoikawasu—to (be in) love (with) each other

omoikunzu—to be disheartened, gloomy

omoimōku—to prepare, expect

omoiotosu—to look down on

omoishimu—to be convinced, obsessed, imbued (with an idea)

omoishiru—to be discerning, sensible

omoisutsu—to forsake, turn one's back on

omoitayu—to abandon, give up, put out of one's head

omoitoku—to resolve a doubt, perceive the truth

omoiunzu—to be displeased; feel hurt, disappointed

omoiwasuru—to forget

omoiyaru—to imagine, fancy

omoiyoru—to think of, occur to one

omonaru—to lose one's shyness by becoming accustomed (to something)

omo nashi—not much to see, insignificant

omonikushi—offensive, hateful

omono—(1) Emperor's (Empress's) meal, (2) rice

omonodana—shelf (board) where the Imperial meal was placed (note 270)

o-monoyadori—buttery, part of the Table Room where trays, tables, etc. were kept

omoshiroshi—(1) elegant, charming, delightful, (2) interesting, pleasant, amusing

omotadashi—honourable, glorious, creditable

omote—face, look, appearance

omote akamu—to blush

omotebuse—shame, discredit, disgrace

omote wo fusu—to cause to lose face, dishonour (note 1069)

omote—Court lady, general term for high-ranking ladies-in-waiting (note 44)

omou—(1) to think, (2) to imagine, suppose, (3) to think kindly, (4) to love, (5) to worry, grieve

omowashi—likable, lovable

ōmu—parrot (note 223)

omuna—old woman

onaji kokoro nari—to be congenial, of like mind

On-Butsumyō—*see* Butsumyō

ōne—radish, *raphanus sativus* (note 723)

on-fumi no shi—Imperial tutor, lecturer in the Imperial Palace

on-hara—child

On-Harae—*see* Ōharai

onidokoro—devil's yam, *dioscorea tokoro*

oniwarabi—devil's fern, *asplenium japonicum*

on-katagata—imperial consorts

On-mae—*see* Omae

On-Menoto — Imperial Nurse (note 651)

On-Monoimi—Imperial Abstinence (note 333)

onnae—(? erotic) picture of a woman (note 146)

onna no hōshi—nun

Onodono—(1) the Lord of Ono (note 1091), (2) Ono Palace (notes 1091, 1092)

ōnuka—ample, heavy, large, generous

onoko—(1) man, (2) courtier, Gentleman-in-Waiting, (3) servant, attendant, lackey, fellow

onokogo—(little) boy

onomatopoeias—notes 575, 716

Ono no Miya—Ono Palace, residence in the western foothills of Hieizan (note 72) (App. 9d, no. 10)

onowarawa—boy

Onyōji—Master of Divination (notes 90, 103, 1150)

Onyō Ryō—Bureau of Divination (note 745) (App. 7a and App. 9e, no. 15)

open veranda—*sunoko*

ōri—mud-shield (part of a horse's harness) (note 1139)

oribitsu box with curved corners, chip-basket (note 390)

orieda—(broken) branch

oriku—to descend

orimono—(1) figured fabric, cloth, (2) (unlined) robe of figured cloth

oroshi—scraps, leavings

oru—(1) to withdraw (from the presence of a superior), (2) to resign, retire (of Chamberlains), (3) to move forward (of a piece in backgammon) (note 660)

Ōsaka no Seki—Ōsaka Barrier, an ancient barrier on the border of Yamashiro and Ōmi Provinces (notes 537, 540, 639, 640, 780, 781, 935, 1109) (App. 9c, no. 7)

ōsaki—prolonged cry of 'Make way!' (note 318)

Osako, Princess—(d. 1049) daughter of Emperor Ichijō (note 40) (App. 6a, no. 24)

osame—housekeeper

osamedono—storehouse, warehouse

osaosashi—reserved, well-behaved, demure

ōsegaki—letter written (by a lady-in-waiting, etc.) for (her mistress, etc.)

ōse(goto)—(1) letter, message (from a superior), (2) command, order, instruction

oshi—make way!

oshiagu—(1) to help ahead, push up (in rank, etc.), (2) to open, pull up

oshidashi—women's custom of letting their clothes protrude outside the curtain of state (notes 75, 314)

oshi(dori)—mandarin duck (note 227)

oshihakarigoto—(1) speculation, conjecture, surmise, (2) unfair surmise, unjust suspicion

oshihesu—to press, squeeze

oshihishigu—to treat cruelly, oppress

oshikasanu—to pile up, lay one on top of another

oshiki—platter, tray

oshikobotsu—to separate the pieces (in *go*) (note 758)

oshikoru—to be pressed together, be in a tight group •

oshimomu—to rub

oshinabu—to be uniform (equal)

oshinogou—to wipe

Ō Shitsu—Japanese name of Wang Chih

oshitsutsumu—to wrap up

osoi—cover, hood, bonnet

osu—to say, speak (honorific)

ōsu—to impute, charge, accuse

ōsu—to say (honorific)

oto—sign, indication

Otodo—Minister

otoko—(1) husband, (2) servant, attendant (see *onoko*), (3) man (note 373)

otokoshu—master

Otoko Yama—Mt. Otoko south of the capital (note 373) (App. 9c, no. 9)

otona—old person, senior member (among ladies-in-waiting, etc.)

otonabu—to come of age, be grown up

ōton(o)abura—(1) lamp in the Emperor's bedroom (Yon no Otodo), (2) lamp

otonadatsu—(1) to be advanced in years, old, (2) to be raised, promoted

Otonashigawa—Otonashi River in Kii Province (notes 274, 280)

Otonashi no Taki—Otonashi Waterfall in Kii Province (note 274)

Ōtoneri Ryō—Bureau of Imperial Attendants (note 849) (App. 7a and App. 9e, no. 20)

ōtonogomoru—to lie down, go to bed (sleep) (honorific)

otōto—(1) younger brother, (2) younger sister

ou—flax field

ou—(1) to grow, (2) to age

Outer Palace Guards—Emon

Outer Palace Guards, Left Division—Saemon

over-robe—*ue no kinu, ao, ō*

Owari—superior province (*jōkoku*) in eastern Japan (note 138) (App. 9a, no. 29)

Ōyake—(1) Emperor, His Majesty, (2) the Court, the Imperial authorities

ōyakebara—anger over something that does not personally concern one

ōyakebito—underservant (in the Palace)

ōyakedokoro—Imperial Palace

ōyakeshi—formal, ceremonial

ōyō—see *ōyō yoshi*

oyobi—finger

oyobu—to reach (lean) forward, bend one's back

ōyō yoshi—to be good-looking, attractive

ozu—to fear, be frightened (disconcerted)

page-boy—*kodoneri(warawa)*

Palace—*see* Imperial Palace

Palace Attendant—Naishi •

Palace Attendants' Office—Naishi no Tsukasa

Palace Chaplain—Gubu

Palace Girl—Uneme

Palace of the First Ward—Ichijō In
Palace of Today—Ima Dairi
palm-leaf carriage—*birōge no kuruma*
period of official appointments—*jimoku*
Perpetual Sacred Readings—Fudan no Mi-Dokyō
P'i p'a hsing—'Song of the Lute', a poem by Po Chü-i, its Japanese name being *Biwa Kō* (notes 329, 440, 476)
Po Chü-i—(772-846) famous T'ang poet, known in Japan as Hakurakuten (notes 196, 304, 329, 337, 355, 440, 476, 643, 750, 799, 964, 1065)
pocket-paper—*futokorogami*
Prime Minister—Dajō Daijin
Princess Imperial—Himemiya no On-kata
principal consort—*kita no kata*
provisional—*gon*
Provisional Governor—Gon no Kami
Provisional Major Counsellor—Gon Dainagon
Provisional Middle Captain—Gon Chujo
Provisional Middle Counsellor—Gon Chūnagon
purgation—*harae*
purification—*see* service of purification

Quiver-Bearer—Yugei

raiban—platform of worship (note 567)
raisō to—completely, fully (?) (note 794)
ramon—hedge made of criss-crossing branches or bamboo
Ranks—I
ranks (Court)—notes 11, 907, App. 7b
Ran Shō—Great Council of State, Council Chamber (Chinese)
Regent—Sesshō
rehearsal—*shigaku, chōgaku*
rei—common, usual; frequented
reitan—cool, cold, indifferent (note 620)
reizama—usual appearance
Reizei In—palace used by abdicated emperors (note 72) (App. 9d, no. 11)
Reken—the Examination (of officials with a view to possible promotion) (notes 611, 613, 618) (App. 1)
request for promotion—*mōshibumi*
return poem—*kaeshi(uta)*
Return Procession—Matsuri no Kaesa

Rinji no Matsuri—Special Festivals (notes 66, 315, 666, 845) (App. 1)
Ris(s)hi—Master of Asceticism, member of the Buddhist hierarchy, coming below Sōjō and Sōzu and holding the 5th Rank
rite of incantation—*zuhō*
river bamboo—*kawatake*
Rōei Shū—see *Wakan Rōei Shū*
roku—reward, compensation (note 112)
Rokui (no Kurōdo)—Chamberlains of the 6th Rank, lowest rank (note 772)
Rokujō—see *Kokin Rokujō*
Roku Kannon—the Six Representations of Kannon (note 833)
rolled dyeing—*makizome*
romance—*monogatari*
Rongo—*Analects* of Confucius (note 262)
rōrōji—(1) skilled, adroit, glib, adept, (2) precocious
rōrōshi—see *rōrōji*
rōsō—short green robe worn by men of the 6th Rank (note 1049)
rōtagaru—to make much of, pet, hold dear, cajole
rōtage—pretty (charming, sweet)-seeming
rōtashi charming, delightful, dear, sweet, precious
round brazier—*hioke*
ryō—consideration, sake, advantage, benefit (*no ryō ni* = for the sake of)
Ryūen—(979-1016) brother of Empress Sadako; an Assistant High Priest of Buddhism (notes 436, 997, 1100) (App. 1, no. 14, and App. 6b, no. 83)
ryūmon — material with embroidered design

sa—that, thus (see also *Dictionary of Selected Forms in Classical Japanese Literature*)
saba—in that case (see also *Dictionary of Selected Forms in Classical Japanese Literature*)
sabaku—to scatter
sabare—(1) so be it, never mind, it cannot be helped, (2) nevertheless, all the same
saburai—(1) household retainer, servant (note 576), (2) abbreviation of Saburai-dokoro
Sachūjō—Middle Captain of the Inner Palace Guards, Left Division
sacred (Shintō) dance—*kagura*

Sacred Readings—Mi-Dokyō
Sadaiben—Major Controller of the Left (notes 11, 256, 618) (App. 7a)
Sadaijin—see Hidari no Otodo
Sadako, Empress—see Fujiwara no Sadako
sadame nashi—unfixed, flighty (note 759)
sadamu—to evaluate, rate, judge
sadasugu—to have seen one's best years, to have left one's youth behind
saekōru—to be extremely cold, frozen
Saemo—see Saemon Fu
Saemon Fu—Headquarters of the Outer Palace Guards, Left Division (notes 11, 359) (App. 9e, no. 10)
Sagano—Saga Plain in Yamashiro Province (notes 827, 829)
sagariba—locks of (women's) hair, falling over their shoulders
sage-brush—yomogi
Sahodono—Saho Palace, a building in Nara (note 1018)
Sahyō (Efu)—(Headquarters of the) Middle Palace Guards, Left Division (App. 9e, no. 11)
saibara—type of ancient song (notes 62, 217, 274, 281, 671, 783, 827, 1011)
saidatsu—to go in advance, go ahead of
saide—piece of material, strip of cloth
Saie—see Go-Saie
saihate—last
Saiin—High Priestess of the Kamo Shrines (notes 382, 908)
saimakuru—to show off (how clever one is)
sainamu—to punish, penalize
saishi—silver or gold hair ornament used by women on ceremonial occasions (App. 8a, no. 21)
Saishō—see Sangi
Saishō no Kimi—Lady Saishō, one of two ladies-in-waiting to Empress Sadako: (1) see Fujiwara no Saishō, (2) note 468
saiso—first
saitsugoro—the other day, recently
sajiki—gallery, grandstand (note 597)
sakaki—sacred tree of Shintō, cleyera ochnacea (note 214)
sakan—Clerk, 4th of the 4 classes of government officials (note 763) (App. 7b)
sakashi—(1) clever, intelligent, (2) knowing, officious, meddlesome
sakashigaru—to be conceited (knowing), consider oneself clever

sakashira—(1) smattering of knowledge, imperfect learning, (2) conceited, knowing, pretentious, presumptuous, impertinent
saki—outrider, attendant, outrunner, postillion
sakiou—to run in front, clear the way
sakkuzakku—thoroughly, earnestly, attentively
Sakon (Efu)—(Headquarters of the) Inner Palace Guards, Left Division (note 72) (App. 9e, no. 4)
saku—unit of measurement (c. 1 ft.)
sakura—(1) cherry tree (note 946), (2) pink, (3) colour combination in which the outside of the garment is white and the lining is red or violet (notes 23, 579)
Sakyō—lady-in-waiting to Fujiwara no Yoshiko (Lady Kokiden) (notes 769, 770)
Sakyō no Kimi—Lady Sakyō, lady-in-waiting to Empress Sadako and a friend of Sei Shōnagon
samakatachi—form, appearance
samakoto—peculiar, queer, odd
sama su—to look like, give the appearance of
sama yoshi—graceful, agreeable, of attractive appearance
Sambō—the Three (Buddhist) Treasures (note 159)
same(ushi)—white-eyed cow (note 719)
Sammaidō—Chapel of Meditation
Sammi—Third Rank
Samuraidokoro—see Saburaidokoro
sanae—rice sprout (note 921)
sa nagara ari—to remain in one's existing condition
Sanekata—see Fujiwara no Sanekata
Sangi—Imperial Adviser, one of 8 members of the Great Council of State ranking below the Middle Counsellors (notes 96, 630)
Sanjō—(976-1017) 67th Emperor, reg. 1011-16 (note 378) (App. 6a, no. 21, and App. 6b, nos. 44 and 75)
sa nomi—in such an indiscriminate (reckless, rash) way (note 884)
sanzaku—three feet
saoshika—stag, hart (note 302)
sara nari—it goes without saying, of course

sara ni—(1) completely, entirely, (2) (with neg.) on no account, by no means, (3) again

sara ni mo iwazu—see *sara nari*

Sarashina Nikki—'The Sarashina Diary', diary or autobiography of a Heian lady, covering the years 1008-58 (note 200)

sareba—thus, therefore

sarekawasu—to play (frolic) together

sari—relic, bone, *sarira*

Śāriputra—a disciple of Buddha (note 178)

saritomo—(1) nevertheless, after all, (2) certainly not, on no account (see also *Dictionary of Selected Forms in Classical Japanese Literature*)

saru—it (see also *Dictionary of Selected Forms in Classical Japanese Literature*)

saru—(1) to leave, (2) to be distant (away) from

saru beshi—(1) convenient, appropriate, due, proper, right, reasonable, (2) showy, pompous, (3) powerful, influential, important

sarugau—to jest, make jokes, be witty

sarugaugoto—joke, witticism

sarugau su—see *sarugau*

sarugō—see *sarugau*

saru kata nari—to let something pass, overlook, let it go (at that)

saru maji—unreasonable, inappropriate

Sarusawa no Ike—Sarusawa Pond in Yamato Province (notes 199, 202)

sasabune—toy boat made out of a bamboo leaf (note 1083)

sasameku—to whisper, murmur

sasemogusa—moxa, sage-brush, *artemisia indica*

sashiabura su—to put (feed) oil into a lamp

sashiayumu—to walk off

sashigushi—(decorative) comb

sashiirae—(1) reply, (2) greeting, salutation

sashiizu—to appear, put in an appearance

sashimajirigokoro—pushing (forward, obtrusive) character

sashimazu—to mix, intertwine

sashinuki—loose laced (or threaded) silk trousers, divided silk skirt (notes 623, 1012) (App. 8a, no. 8)

sashioku—(1) to deliver, (2) to ignore, disregard, leave

sashite—indicating (someone) by name

sashitsudou—to be gathered together, be assembled

sashitsuku—to knock (bump) into

sashiyoru—to approach, come near

sashiyosu—to bring close to, draw near

sasu—(1) to hold (an umbrella, etc.) over (someone), (2) to close, shut

sate—(1) really, (2) then, presently, by and by, (3) thus, (4) (and) further, (5) however that may be, still (see also *Dictionary of Selected Forms in Classical Japanese Literature*)

sa to—thus, in that way

sato—suddenly, abruptly

sato—one's own home (native place) (notes 356, 389)

satobigokochi—countrified (unsophisticated) feelings (see *satobu*) (note 805)

satobito—(1) high-ranking people who lived outside the Palace (notes 7, 389, 948), (2) country folk, rustics

satobu—to be countrified (provincial, unused to elegant Court life)

satoi—staying at home, remaining (at home) away from the Palace

Satsuki—Rice-Sprouting (Fifth) Month (notes 3, 454, 918)

Satsuki no Mi-Sōji—the Abstinence of the Fifth Month (note 454)

Satsuki no Sechi—see Ayame no Sekku

sau—verdict, decision

sau—to stop, block, interrupt

sa wa—(so) then, well now, in that case

Sawadagawa—Sawada River in Yamashiro Province (note 281)

sawagashi—(1) confused, disordered, (2) see *yo no naka sawagashi* (note 894)

sawamizu—marsh (swamp) water

sawaraka—light, gentle

sawaru—to be obstructed, blocked

Sayama no Ike—Sayama Pond in Musashi Province (note 204)

Scribe—Shi

se—(1) elder brother, (2) woman's lover (note 365)

Seasonal Change—Sechibun

seasons—notes 3, 4, 747, 750, App. 3

sebagariizu—to squeeze one's way out

sebashi—narrow, cramped

sechi—feast, festival

sechi ni—(1) constantly, (2) eagerly, fervently, (3) immoderately, unduly

Sechibun—Seasonal Change (note 103)

Sechie—Palace Festival (note 732)
Second Empress—Chūgū
Secretary—Jō, Zō
sedge hat—*kasa*
sedōka—ancient type of 6-line poem (notes 229, 259)
Sei—name of the Kiyowara family (to which Shōnagon belonged)
Seihan—(962-99) eminent Buddhist priest (note 177)
Seiryō Den—Seiryō Palace, the Emperor's principal residential palace (notes 45, 59, 73, 268) (App. 9f, no. 9)
Sei Shōnagon—(*c*. 965-*c*. 1025) author of *The Pillow Book*, lady-in-waiting to Empress Sadako (App. 6c, no. 92)
sei su—(1) to reproach, reprimand, (2) to be careful, look out, (3) to control, prevent
Sekai—residence of Yoshifusa's daughter, Fujiwara no Akiko (note 72) (App. 9d, no. 5)
sekai—province, region
seki—barrier (note 537)
sekkyō—preaching, sermon (note 155)
sekkyōshi—preacher
Seku—*see* Sechie
sekumairi—gift, offering, etc. made during a festival
sememadowasu—to urge (someone) importunately
semete—(1) forcibly, against a person's will, (2) deliberately, (3) very, extremely
semigoe—forced (unnatural) voice
sendan—'one thousand platforms' (note 568)
Senior Assistant Governor-General—Daini
senior courtier—*tenjōbito, uebito*
Senior Courtiers' Chamber—Tenjō no Ma, Ue
Senior Secretary—Daijō
Senior Steward—Daijin
Senji—Envoy (note 801)
Senju Darani—the Magic Incantation of the Thousand Hands (notes 831, 1140)
Senshi—*see* Fujiwara no Akiko (1)
Senshi, Princess — (963-1035), High Priestess of Kamo from 976 to 1031 (notes 382, 908) (App. 6a, no. 9, and App. 6b, no. 62)
sentō—one thousand lights (note 568)

Senyō Den—Senyō Palace, residence for Imperial Concubines (notes 88, 499) (App. 9f, no. 4)
senzoku—(1) wiping one's feet, (2) cushion (note 485)
Senzu—*see* Senju
seri tsumu—to grieve, suffer unhappiness (note 136)
service of purification—*harae*
Sesshō—Regent (note 83)
Setsubun—*see* Sechibun
seven herbs—*nanakusa*
seven-string zither—*kin*
shaded material—*susogo*
shaku—baton (notes 57, 622) (App. 8a, no. 5)
shaku—see *taifu*
Shakuten—Worship of Confucius (note 612) (App. 1)
Shakuzen Ji—Shakuzen Temple in Kyōto (notes 494, 944) (App. 9d, no. 15)
Sharihotsu—Japanese for Śāriputra
Sheep, Hour of the—Hitsuji no Toki
Shen—region in China (known in Japanese as Jin) that produced a type of aromatic wood used in Japan (note 808)
Shi—Scribe (note 787)
shi—(1) Chinese poem, (2) prose preface to such a poem (note 646)
shiau—see *shiou*
shibomu—to be wet, damp
shidaru—to hang down
shidekaku—to hang, suspend
shigaku—rehearsal (note 315)
Shigei S(h)a—(1) building in the Imperial Palace (notes 415, 416, 499) (App. 9f, no. 5), (2) name used for Fujiwara no Genshi
shigeshi—(1) profuse, dense, massed, (2) frequent
shigyō—frequently, often
Shih chi—history of China by Ssu-ma Ch'ien (*c*. 145-80 B.C.) (notes 258, 1155)
shii—forcibly, against (someone's) will
Shii—Fourth Rank (note 653)
shii(shiba)—(1) pasania, type of oak (*quercus cuspidata*) used to produce a dark dye (note 653), (2) acorn of this tree
shiji—trestle
shijikamu—to be shrunk, shrivelled, crisped

312

shijimu—to shorten
Shijōkō—the Flourishing and Shining Spirit (note 1060)
shikasuga—nevertheless, yet, however
Shiki—demon invoked by magicians (note 814)
Shiki—*see* Shiki In
Shiki—Japanese reading of *Shih chi*
Shikibu Kyō—Minister of Ceremonial
Shikibu no Omoto—lady-in-waiting to Empress Sadako (note 264)
Shikibu no Taifu—5th-Rank Secretary in the Ministry of Ceremonial (notes 123, 703)
Shikibu no Zō—*see* Shikibu no Taifu
Shikibu Shō—Ministry of Ceremonial (note 123) (Apps. 7a and 9e, no. 19)
shikigami—see *shikishi*
Shiki (In)—*see* Shiki no Mi-zōshi
shikimi—anise (note 570)
shikinami—billowing (piled-up) waves
Shiki no Kami—God of Shiki (note 814)
Shiki no Mi-zōshi—Empress's Office, building in the Greater Imperial Palace (notes 255, 622) (App. 9e, no. 9)
shimikaeru—to permeate, soak into
shimo—(1) one's own room, (2) room of a messenger, lady-in-waiting, etc., (3) lower part, bottom, (4) lower part of a latticed shutter
shimobe—servant, retainer
shimoonna—(1) woman of low (social) standing, (2) underservant, chambermaid
shimoto—(1) twig, stick, small branch, (2) baton
Shimotsuke superior province (*jōkoku*) north of present-day Tokyo (notes 786, 1107) (App. 9a, no. 10)
shimotsuke no hana—spiraea, meadow-sweet, *spiraea palmata*
Shimotsuki—Frost (Eleventh) Month (note 3)
shimozama—coarse, vulgar
shomozukae—lesser attendant, low-ranking servant (note 486)
shinai—hanging (drooping) corolla of wistaria, etc.
shinameku—to seem elegant, be refined (choice)
shina nashi—inelegant, undistinguished, vulgar
shina okuru—to be of low (inferior) rank

Shin Chūnagon—lady-in-waiting to Empress Sadako
shinden—(1) style of architecture current among the upper class in Heian Kyō (note 121), (2) main building of a Heian house (App. 8b, no. 1)
Shingon (1) 'true word', esoteric incantation, magic formula (note 596), (2) 9th-century Japanese Buddhist sect introduced by Kūkai (Kōbō Daishi) (notes 67, 586, 596, 1057, 1140, 1141)
Shinji—Bachelor of Literature (note 37)
Shin Kokin Shū—abbreviation of *Shin Kokin Waka Shū*, 'New Collection of Old and New Japanese Poems', 8th official anthology of verse, in 20 books, compiled by Fujiwara no Teika and others (note 62)
shinobiyaka—(1) discreet, circumspect, (2) quiet, hushed
shinobugusa—wall-fern, *polypodium lineare* (note 294)
Shi no Taifu—Senior Scribe (of the 5th Rank) (note 787)
shintai su—to manage, behave, acquit oneself
shion (1) aster, *aster tartaricus*, (2) purple colour, (3) colour combination in which the outside of the garment is purple and the lining is dark red or green (notes 23, 680)
shiotaru—(1) to drip with salt water, (2) to be sorrowful, weep (note 1088)
shiou—to finish, complete
shirahu—to make clear
shiragasane—white under-robe
-*shiragau*—intensifying verbal suffix with the sense of 'deliberately', etc.
shirajirashi—uninteresting, prosaic
Shirayama no Kannon—the Goddess of Mercy of White Mountain (note 377)
shirejire to—foolishly, idiotically
shiremono—fool
shiri—(1) train (note 254), (2) end of a thread, (3) back, behind, rear
shiribito—friend, acquaintance
shirikuchi—rear opening
shirinaga—robe with a long train (note 623)
shiriugoto—see *shiryūgoto*
shiromu—to whiten, clean
shiroshi—(1) white, fair, (2) bright, clear, pure, (3) new, clean, fresh

313

shiru—(1) to know, (2) to experience, (3) to have a love affair with, (4) to reign, rule, govern, (5) to deal with, manage, (6) to care, be concerned

shiru—to be stupid, foolish

shirushi—efficacy, virtue, effect, benefit (note 883)

shirushi—conspicuous, clear

shiru suji—relation, connexion, acquaintance

shiryūgoto—malicious gossip, speaking ill of someone behind his (her) back

shishi — 'lion' (note 401) (App. 8b, no. 9)

Shishi Mai—Lion Dance (note 595)

Shishin Den—Shishin Palace, the main palace where ceremonies and festivals were celebrated (App. 9f, no. 13)

Shishōkō—*see* Shijōkō

shitagasane—under-robe (part of men's formal attire) (notes 118, 623, 1014)

shitakusa—weeds, sprouts, etc. growing under trees

shitasudare—inner (inside) blinds (of a house, carriage, etc.)

shitataka—sturdy, stalwart, robust

shitatsu—(1) to make, manufacture, (2) to prepare, arrange, (3) to decorate, make (get) oneself up

shitauzu—sole (of shoe, sock, etc.)

shitawarabi—fern shoot, *pteris aquilina*

shitodo—very damp, moist

shitomi—latticed shutters or gratings whose top could be hooked up to the roof and whose bottom was removable (note 38) (App. 8b, no. 22)

shitone—cushion (App. 8b, no. 5)

shitsurau—to arrange, place, decorate, prepare

shiu—to impose one's will, force someone against his (her) will

shiyō—lower official (secretary) in the Great Council of State

shōbi—rose (note 304)

shoe—*kutsu*

Shōji—*see* Naishi

shōji—stool, bench

shōjin—see *sōjin*

Shōkyo Den—Shōkyō Palace, a building in the Imperial Palace compound (App. 9f, no. 10)

Shōmu—(701-56) 45th Emperor, reg. 724-49

Shōnagon—(1) Minor Counsellor (App. 7a), (2) *see* Sei Shōnagon.

Shōnagon no Myōbu—lady-in-waiting to Empress Sadako

shō no fue—see *sō no fue*

short-sleeved jacket—*hampi*

Shōshō—Minor Captain of the Inner Palace Guards (App. 7b)

Shōshō no Kimi—Lady Shōshō, lady-in-waiting to Fujiwara no Genshi (note 501)

Shōsō—Assistant Lieutenant (note 763) (App. 7b)

shōsoko—message, letter

shōto—(1) elder brother (notes 22, 341), (2) husband (note 341) .

shoulder sash—*hire*

shū—anthology of Japanese poetry

Shu Baishin—*see* Chu Mai-ch'en

shuhō—see *zuhō*

Shūi Shū—abbreviation of *Shūi Waka Shū*, 3rd official anthology of Japanese verse, in 20 books, compiled at some time between 995 and 1008 (notes 62, 233, 274, 295, 674, 796, 810, 827, 955, 958, 1084, 1128)

shūneshi—implacable, vindictive, tenacious

shutter—*shitomi*

six-string zither—*wagon*

sliding-door—*yarido*

Smaller Shirakawa—Ko Shirakawa Dono

Snake, Hour of the—Mi no Toki

sneezing—*hana hiru*

sō—see *sō no fue*, *sō no koto*

Sō—family name (notes 1038, 1039)

soba no ki—Chinese hawthorn (note 211)

sobau—to romp, frolic, play

sobayosu—to approach, draw close, come up to

sobotsu—to be very moist (wet)

sōbu—iris, sweet rush, *acorus spurius*

Sō Chū—Japanese name of Hsiang Chung

sodegichō—hiding one's face behind one's sleeve (note 343)

soegoto—suggestive remark, allusion, quip

sōgana—cursive script (grass writing) used to write the phonetic syllabary (*hiragana*)

sogisue—(ends of the) hair that has been evenly cut

sōgō—high-ranking ecclesiastic

soitatsu—to look after, assist

soitsuku—to draw close, snuggle against

sōji—sliding paper door, sliding screen (App. 8b, nos. 14, 26)

sōji—see sōjin

sōjimono—fasting, maigre diet (notes 31, 119)

sōjin—fasting, abstinence, meditation and avoidance of defilement (notes 117, 454)

Sōjō — Archbishop, High Priest, top ecclesiastic in the Buddhist hierarchy (notes 60, 654)

Sōkan—see Sakan

sokohaka to naku—indefinably, vaguely, without knowing where

sokoi—depth

soko(moto)—there(abouts) (see also Dictionary of Selected Forms in Classical Japanese Literature)

sokusai no inori—prayer for warding off evil (note 939)

Somedono no Miya— palace of Fujiwara no Yoshifusa (notes 72, 424) (App. 9d, no. 4)

Sōmei—Offerings of Wisdom (note 612)

somukizama upside down, the wrong way round

son-in-law (adopted)—muko

sō no fue—13-pipe flute, kind of Pan-pipe, a set of reeds with 13 pipes (notes 328, 841) (App. 8d, no. 11)

sō no koto—13-string zither (note 89) (App. 8d, no. 10)

Sonshō Darani—the Magic Incantation of the Holy and Virtuous (notes 831, 1059)

sora—(1) sky, (2) see soragoto

soradakimono—incense used to perfume screens, blinds, etc. in such a way that it was not clear (to the visitor) where the incense-burner was placed (note 251)

soragoto—falsehood, lie (notes 773, 811, 813, 960)

sora ni—(1) at random, at a venture, without preparation, (2) from memory

sorihashi—arched bridge (note 428)

sorikutsugaeru—to fall (tumble) over backwards

Sosei—(d. 909) Buddhist priest and one of the 36 Poets (note 956)

sōshi—(1) notebook, (2) collection of notes, impressions, etc. (notes 942, 1156)

sosomeku—to make a noise (din)

sō su—(1) to report (say) to the Emperor, (2) to announce

soto—quietly, lightly, gently

sotozama—different direction

sou—(1) to draw together, gather, (2) to be married

south-east—tatsumi

Southern Palace—Minami no In

Soya—First Service, first of the 3 services in the Naming of the Buddhas, lasting from 11 p.m. to 12.30 a.m.

soyomeku—to rustle, murmur

soyori—rustling sound

soyoro to—softly, gently

soyosoyo to—with a rustling (of silk, etc.) (note 575)

sōzokitatsu—to be dressed in ceremonial (Court) costume

sōzoku—(1) (ceremonial) clothes, dress, costume, (2) decoration, ornament, (3) see sōzoku su

sōzoku su—(1) to be decorated, elegant, in full dress, (2) to dress, adorn oneself

sozoro—(1) desultory, vague, incoherent, (2) absurd, silly, foolish

sōzōshi—dreary, lonely, sad

Sōzu—Bishop, Assistant High Priest of Buddhism (notes 60, 996)

span—ma

special attendant—uezōshi

Special Festivals—Rinji no Matsuri

square brazier—subitsu

su—see sudare

subae—long, slender, straight stick or twig

Subaru—Altair (the star)

subete—(1) generally, in general, (2) (with neg.) never, none (not) at all

subitsu—square fire-place or brazier surrounded by straw mats

Subordinate Official (of the Emperor's Private Office)—Zōshiki

sudare—blinds of reed or split bamboo which were raised and lowered by strings (notes 53, 797) (App. 8b, nos. 15, 24)

sudare (wo) (uchi)kazuku— to enter (leave) a room (note 267)

sue—last part (continuation) of a poem

sugaru—to be sour

sugata—clothing

Sugawara no Fumitoki—(899–981) government official and poet (note 628)

Sugawara no In—residence of the Sugawara family (note 72) (App. 9d, no. 9)

Sugawara no Koreyoshi—(812–80) father of Michizane (note 72)

Sugawara no Michizane—(845–903) famous poet, statesman, calligrapher (notes 72, 468, 501, 628, 754, 1065)

Sugawara no Sukemasa—(925–1009) distinguished scholar and official (notes 468, 501)

sugi—Japanese cedar, cryptomeria (note 883)

sugoroku—type of backgammon (note 660) (App. 8d, no. 6)

sugu—to thread (a needle)

sugusu—(1) to ignore, pass over, (2) to be advanced in years, have grown old

sugyōza—travelling priest (monk)

suhōgasane—glossy white robe lined with dark red material

suiga(k)i—bamboo fence with interstices,' openwork board fence

suihan—watered rice (i.e. rice that has been boiled and dried, and that has to be mixed with water before being eaten)

suikanbakama—type of long trouser-skirt (*hakama*) worn with a long robe (*suikan*)

suisō—(rock) crystal

Sujaku—*see* Suzaku

suji—(1) letter, note, (2) meaning, purport, (3) see *shiru suji*, (4) context, line of thought, (5) hair (of the head)

suji nashi—(1) cannot be helped, (2) lawless, unmannerly

sukasu—to deceive, delude, impose upon

Suke—Assistant Captain (of the Outer or Middle Palace Guards) (App. 7b)

Suke—Assistant Director (of a government bureau) (note 849) (App. 7b)

Suke—Assistant Master (of a government office) (App. 7b)

Suke—Assistant Governor (of a province) (App. 7b)

sukikage—light (or shadow) seen through (or in) something

sukiokashi—having a taste for art and elegance

sukizukishi — (1) fanciful, whimsical; curious, inquisitive, (2) sensual, licentious, (3) enthusiastic

suku—to be elegant, fashionable, have fanciful (original) taste

sukun—master, lord, mistress

sukuse—karma (notes 469, 506, 604, 1004)

sukusukushi—vigorous, quick, hasty, with dispatch

sukuyoka—hard-hearted, heartless

sumai—sumō wrestling (notes 592, 900) (App. 1)

sumashi—bathroom servant (in the Imperial Palace)

sumō—see *sumai*

sumu—to spend the night (with one's wife, mistress, etc.), visit and have conjugal relations

sunago—sand (note 789)

sunawachi—as soon as, promptly

Sung Yū—(*fl.* 290–223 B.C.) Chinese poet (note 892)

sunoko—open veranda going all the way round a Heian building (App. 8b, nos. 16, 19)

sunoto—outside the blinds (*sudare*)

suō—(1) dark red, (2) colour combination in which the outside of the garment is white or light brown and the lining is dark red (note 23)

suōgasane—glossy white robe with dark red lining

suriginu—costume made of printed material

surimodorokasu—to print with a scattered design or with scattered patches of colour

Suri (Shiki)—Office of Palace Repairs (note 341)

suri su—to repair, refit

suro no ki—hemp palm

suru—to wring (clasp) one's hands

suru—to make, manufacture

Suruga—superior province (*jōkoku*) near present-day Tokyo (note 123) (App. 9a, no. 26)

susa—cinnabar

susamaji — disheartening, depressing, dreary, uninteresting, prosaic

Susanoo no Mikoto—Storm God (notes 219, 323)

susogo—shaded material (notes 27, 272)

suso no harae—purification service to ward off bad luck (note 151)

susousu—becoming thinner (finer, more delicate) at the edges (of colours, brush-strokes, etc.)

susubana—snivel, snot, mucus

susubana su—to sniffle, sniff, snivel

susuki—Japanese pampas grass (notes 301, 448)
susuku—to be dirty, sooty
Sutra of Supreme Wisdom—*Dai Hannya Kyō*
Suzaku In—Suzaku Palace (note 72) (App. 9d, no. 21)
Suzaku Ōji—great central avenue of Heian Kyō (notes 72, 351, 598) (App. 9d, no. 17)
suzuro—(1) indiscriminate, arbitrary, reckless, heedless, imprudent, indiscreet, thoughtless, (2) harmless, innocent, trivial, trifling, (3) despite oneself, for some reason or other, involuntarily, without being aware (*nan to naku*), (4) casual, vague
suzushi—stiff (raw) silk cloth

tabidatsu—to leave home, abscond
tabishi—pebble
tabisho—intermediate lodging used to avoid unlucky directions (note 103)
table—*daihan*
Table Office—Naizen (Shi)
Table Room—Daihandokoro
taboo—*monoimi*
taboo tag—*monoimi no fuda*
tachi—face, features, looks
tachi ni—vertically, lengthwise
Tachibana no Norimitsu—(b. 965) government official who was an admirer (and possibly the husband) of Sei Shōnagon (notes 170, 341, 359, 361, 364, 621) (App. 2, no. 16)
tachiizu—to emerge, come out, embark on
tachikaeri—in an immediate reply, by return
tachikasanu—to stand close (be squeezed) together
tachinamu—to stand (be) in a row
tachiokuru—to stand (step) back
tachisou—to stand (nestle) near
tachitsuzuku—to follow
tada—(1) intently, fervently, earnestly, (2) quickly, rapidly, easily, without restraint, (3) soon, directly, (4) gratuitously, empty-handed, for nothing, (5) only, simply, (6) ordinary, uneventful, usual, commonplace
tadabito—commoner, ordinary person
tada katawara—directly next to
tadakoto—simple remark (note 962)

tadana—real (true) name
tada narazu—to be meaningful, have special significance
tada nari—to come to naught, be in vain
Tadanobu—*see* Fujiwara no Tadanobu
tada no hito—see *tadabito*
tadasama ni—directly
Tadasu no Kami—a Shintō deity (note 813)
Tadataka—*see* Minamoto no Tadataka
tadotadoshi—uncertain, dubious, inaccurate, halting
tadōto—contraction of *tadabito*
tagae—see *katatagae*
tagoshi—palanquin carried by hand (as opposed to the *mi-koshi*, which was carried on the shoulders) (note 852)
taguu—to accompany, go with
tai—see *tai no ya*
taidaishi—negligent, heedless, careless
taifu—(1) gentleman of the 5th Rank, (2) the 5th Rank (notes 44, 123)
Taiheiraku—the Dance of Peace (notes 838, 839)
Taiken Mon—one of the 2 main gates of the Greater Imperial Palace (note 9) (App. 9e, no. 16)
taikoku—great province (note 324)
tai no ya—wing (of a house) (App. 8h, no. 2)
Taira—famous warrior family descended from Emperor Kammu (d. 806); they succeeded the Fujiwaras as the leading political power in the 12th century (note 1038)
Taira no Kanemori—(d. 990) Governor of Suruga Province and one of the 36 Poets (note 796)
Taira no Korenaka—(*c*. 944-1006) government official (notes 43, 618, 651)
Taira no Narimasa—(b. *c*. 950) provincial official and Chinese scholar (notes 33, 42, 43, 868) (App. 2, no. 17)
Taira no Yukiyoshi—flautist and Guards officer (note 328)
Taishō—Major Captain of the Inner Palace Guards (App. 7b)
takahizamazuki—'high kneeling', a ceremonial position adopted by courtiers
Takasago—name of a well-known folksong (note 135)

317

Takase no Yodo—(1) Takase Pool, part of Yodo River (note 544), (2) name of an ancient song (note 544)

Takashina no Akinobu—maternal uncle of Empress Sadako (note 460) (App. 6d, no. 95)

Takashina no Naritō—provincial governor who rose to the 4th Rank (note 1130) (App. 6d, no. 93)

Takashina no Sanenobu—younger brother of Akinobu; Chamberlain and Minor Controller (note 1001) (App. 6d, no. 94)

Takashina no Takako—(d. 996) principal wife of Fujiwara no Michitaka and mother of Empress Sadako (notes 460, 493, 506) (App. 6e, no. 96)

takatsuki—tray on a stand (App. 8b, no. 17)

Takiguchi—Imperial Guards (notes 49, 268)

takimono—incense

takishimu—to scent, apply incense

taku—to be full, at its height (of the sun, moon, etc.)

takumidori—kinglet, *troglodytes fumigatus*

takunawa—rope of mulberry bark

tale—*monogatari*

Tama Matsuri—Festival of the Spirits (note 220) (App. 1)

tamawari—favour, recompense, reward

Tamehira, Prince—(952-1010) son of Emperor Murakami (notes 424, 644) (App. 6a, no. 11)

Tanabata Matsuri—Weaver Festival (notes 54, 55, 284, 456, 748, 754) (App. 1)

Tanabatatsume—the Weaver Maiden (note 284)

Tango—*see* Ayame no Sekku

tanjaku—record-slip, narrow strip of paper used for writing poems, etc. (note 1103)

tanomoshibito no shi—priest responsible for looking after pilgrims in a temple

taomekashi—supple, flexible, pliant

taoyaka—elegant, graceful

tasukikage—holding up (sleeves, etc.) with a sash

tatami—straw mat (note 180) (App. 8b, nos. 6, 13)

tatanawaru—to lie on top of, tumble over (in cascades)

tatazama ni—(1) lengthwise, vertically, (2) in a straight line, straight across

tatebumi—twisted letter, formal letter folded lengthwise and twisted (notes 104, 573) (App. 8d, no. 2)

tatejitomi—garden (outer) fence (note 12) (App. 8b, no. 18)

tatōgami—folded Michinoku paper (*see* Michinoku)

tatoshie—comparison

tatsu—to close, fix (of shutters, etc.)

-tatsu—to begin to (e.g. *shitatsu* = to begin to do)

Tatsu no Hi—Day of the Dragon, 5th of the 12 days in the traditional cycle (note 417) (App. 3)

tatsumi—south-east (App. 3)

taurefusu—to fall on (its, one's) side

tauru—to collapse, fall over

tawabure—amusement, pastime

tawaburegoto—joke, pleasantry

tayumu—to neglect, relax one's attention, be remiss, negligent, off one's guard

tayushi—tired, dull, heavy

tazuneariku—to go and see, pay a visit

te—T-shaped frame (lit. 'hand') of a curtain of state (note 39)

tegura—offering to the gods (note 300)

Teikoku—Japanese name of Ting Kuo

temasaguru—to fumble, toy, play with

Temmu—(630-86) 40th Emperor, reg. 672-86 (note 99)

Tenji—*see* Naishi no Suke

Tenjō—(1) *see* Tenjō no Ma, (2) Imperial Palace, (3) palace, residence, (4) *see* *tenjōbito*

tenjōbito—senior courtier (note 11)

Tenjō no Ma—Senior Courtiers' Chamber, room in the south of Seiryō Palace used only by courtiers who were permitted to wait in attendance on the Emperor (notes 11, 395, 398) (App. 9g, no. 11)

Tenjōwarawa—young Palace page (usually a son of the Regent or Chancellor)

Tenyaku Ryō—Bureau of Medicine (note 977) (App. 7a and App. 9e, no. 13)

teragomori—retreat in a temple

tetsugai—archery practice

te uku—to keep one's hand (in *go*) (note 758)

te yurusu—to yield one's hand (in *go*) (notes 758, 759)

318

thirteen-pipe flute—*sō no fue*
thirteen-string zither—*sō no koto*
threshold—*tojikomi*
time—notes 1032, 1033, App. 3
time-keeping—notes 745, 1032, 1033, 1097, and App. 3
time-post—*toki no kui*
Ting Kuo—figure in Han history, known in Japan as Teikoku (note 36)
to—outside
to—a while, moment
Tō—First Secretary of the Emperor's Private Office (note 50)
tō—retort, repartee
tō—early, soon, quickly, at once
to aredo kakaredo onaji koto—it makes no difference which way things are done
tobiariku—to fly (flutter) about
toburau—to call on, visit, see how someone is, visit an ill person
tōdai—lamp-stand
Todoroki no Taki—Todoroki Waterfall in Rikuzen Province (note 277)
Tōgū—(1) Eastern Palace (note 378), (2) Crown Prince, (3) Office of the Crown Prince's Household
Tō In—residence of ex-Emperor Uda (note 72) (App. 9d, no. 25)
toji—low-ranking female servant employed in the Palace kitchens and pantries (attached to the Emperor's Dining Room)
tojikimi — (1) wooden cross-beam, threshold (note 9), (2) the forward frame of a carriage
tojime—tying the final knot (when completing a job of sewing)
Tōka Den—Tōka Palace, the Empress's residential palace (notes 491, 499, 500) (App. 9f, no. 2)
tokaku—in one way or another, somehow
tokaku mo . . . (neg.)—not at all, not in the slightest, nothing
toki—watch, one of the 12 periods of 2 hours into which the day was divided (note 107) (App. 3)
tokimekashi — flourishing, popular, fashionable
toki narazu—unseasonal
toki ni au—to be highly reputed, popular, à la mode, successful
toki no (hito)—outstanding, remarkable (man)

toki no kui—time-post (note 745)
toki nomi (koso)—time is of the essence, the important thing is to be quick
toki no saba—rice offerings made to the gods by Buddhist priests before their noonday meal
Tokizukasa—Time Office (note 745)
toko—mace (note 1142)
tokoro—personage, dignitary
tokorodokoro—(1) here and there, (2) officials of the various government offices, (3) ladies and gentlemen, dignitaries
tokoroe(gao)—proud, self-satisfied (look)
Tokoro no Shū—Assistant Official of the Emperor's Private Office, one of 20 officials charged with minor duties in the Palace, attendance during processions, etc.
Tokoro no Zōshiki—*see* Zōshiki (2)
tokoro saru—to leave home
tokoro seshi—(1) not to know what to do with oneself, feel embarrassed, (2) crowded, narrow
tokorotagae—mistake about the place (address, etc.)
tokoro u—to lord it over, assert one's importance
tokoro wo oku—to keep one's distance
toku—(1) quickly, promptly, (2) early
toku—favour, grace, patronage
tokui—(1) popular person, favourite, (2) acquaintance, friendship
toku miru—to be indebted to, owe (something) to (someone)
tokusen—low-ranking female servant employed mainly to serve at table in the Palace (attached to the Emperor's Dining Room) (note 967)
tomi—urgent, sudden
tomigusa—rice plant (flower)
Tomi no Kōji no Udaijin—*see* Fujiwara no Akitada
tomi no o—end of a carriage shaft (note 926)
. . . *tomo arinu beshi*—it is all right even if . . ., it is not necessary to . . .
to mo kaku mo . . . (neg.)—nothing at all
tomon—city gate
tomo ni ariku—to be in (someone's) retinue
Tomo Oka—Tomo Hill in Yamashiro Province (note 881)

toneri—(1) escort, attendant, retainer, (2) Imperial Attendant (note 727)

tono—His Excellency

tonobara—(young) gentleman (note 97)

Tō no Ben—Controller First Secretary, 1st Secretary of the Emperor's Private Office chosen from the Controlling Board (notes 50, 254, 333)

Tō no Chūjō—Captain First Secretary, 1st Secretary of the Emperor's Private Office chosen from the Inner Palace Guards (note 50)

tonoidokoro—night duty room

tonoiginu—costume worn during the night watch (note 1123)

tonoimono—(1) night clothes, night dress, night things, bedclothes, (2) see *tonoiginu*

tonoisugata—see *tonoiginu*

Tonomo(ri)(zukasa)—(1) Office of Grounds (App. 7a), (2) a man or woman of this office (note 13)

tooth-blackening—*hagurome*

tooth-hardening—*hagatame*

torau—see *torou*

toribami—gathering of remains (note 667)

torihanachite—particularly, in particular

torihanatsu—see *torihanachite*

torihayasu—to entertain, be hospitable

toriko—see *muko*

torimotsu—to treat well, welcome

torinasu—(1) to misjudge, misunderstand, miscalculate; misrepresent, (2) to intervene, mediate (note 648)

toriorosu—to take off (down)

toriwaki—especially

toriwaku—(1) to distinguish, characterize, mark, (2) to be special, distinguished, superior

toriwatasu—to bring, take

toriyaru—to put (clear) away, remove

torou—to hold, grasp

toru—to feed on, eat

Tōsanjō In—residence of Fujiwara no Yoshifusa (note 72) (App. 9d, no. 19)

toshi—see *mimi toshi*

toshi ou—to be old

toshi (uchi)sugusu—to be old, aged

tōtogaru—to be overcome with respect (awe)

Tōtōmi—superior province (*jōkoku*) in central Honshū (App. 9a, no. 27)

totose—ten years

toyomu—to echo, reverberate

tōzai (wo) sasezu—willy-nilly, forcibly (lit. 'not letting the body move in any direction')

Tōzammi—*see* Fujiwara no Shigeko

travelling costume (for women)—*tsubo-sōzoku*

trouser-skirt—*hakama*

tsuba—camellia

tsubana—bulrush, reed-mace, *imperata arundinacea*

tsubo—(1) small garden, (2) chink, crevice, space

tsubone—lady-in-waiting's apartment or quarters

tsubone-aruji—lady in charge of other ladies-in-waiting (note 806)

tsubo-sōzoku—travelling costume for women (note 161)

tsubosumire—round-leaved violet, *viola verecunda*

tsuboyanagui—long, narrow quiver

tsuburu—see *mono tsuburu*

Tsuchi Mikado—another name for Jōtō Mon

tsue—c. 10 ft. (in length)

tsugitsugi—(1) step by step, one by one, (2) those who are next in line, younger brothers, etc.

tsui—see *tsuki*

tsuide mo 'naku—suddenly, unexpectedly

tsuigasane—tray on a stand

tsuiji—embankment of mud or pounded earth with a wooden framework and a tiled top

tsuisasu—to thrust

tsuitate-sōji—sliding screen on stands

tsukai—envoy, messenger (notes 66, 846)

tsukaibito—messenger, servant (note 273)

tsukaikatamu—to be well used, to have improved by usage

tsukasa—(1) official, (2) official post, (3) office, building

tsukasameshi—(1) official in the capital (as opposed to provincial official), (2) period when such officials are appointed

tsukibito—person (patient) possessed by an evil spirit

tsukihana—see *susubana*

Tsukinami—the Succeeding Months (note 1063)

tsukinamu—to sit in a row

tsuki nashi—inappropriate, unfitting
tsukiugatsu—to pierce
tsukizukishi—appropriate, fitting, suitable
tsuku—to give a name to, designate
tsuku—to vomit, be sick
Tsukumo(n)dokoro—Office of Palace Works (note 490) (App. 9f, no. 15)
tsukuribito—writer, author
tsukurihotoke—statue of Buddha
tsukurou—(1) to dress up, smarten oneself up, (2) to prepare carefully, (3) to adjust, alter
tsuma—tip, extremity, limit
tsumado—side door (App. 8b, no. 21)
tsumahajiki—snapping the fingers (a scornful gesture) (note 421)
tsumi saru—to acknowledge one's fault by paying an indemnity (forfeit)
tsumi ushinau—to clear (absolve) oneself of (from) sin
tsumu—to pinch, pluck (note 610)
Tsunefusa—see Minamoto no Tsunefusa
tsura—edge (of water, river, etc.)
Tsurayuki—see Ki no Tsurayuki
tsurenashi—calm, composed, unconcerned, indifferent, casual
tsurezure—(1) tedious, boring (notes 143, 306), (2) sad, lonely
tsuru—crane (note 941)
tsuru utsu—to strum a bowstring
tsurubami—kind of oak, quercus gilva (note 695)
tsuto—fixedly, intently, steadfastly
tsutomete—(1) early morning, (2) next morning
tsutsuji—(1) azalea, (2) colour combination in which the outside of the garment is dark red and the lining is scarlet or green (note 23)
tsutsumashi—awkward, nervous, embarrassed
tsutsumi—care, vigilance, discretion
tsutsumu—to be respectful, awed, afraid; reserved, modest, shy, diffident
tsuyameku—to be bright (glossy, shining)
tsuyayaka—polished, glossy
tsuyu bakari—only a little
tsuyugusa—dew-plant, wild hare's-ear, commelina vulgaris (note 720)
twisted letter—tatebumi
two-span room—see ma (span)
Tzu-yu—a Chinese bamboo-lover (note 643)

u—to select, choose
u—see u no hana
ubara—thorn, bramble
ube—(1) to be sure, truly, indeed, (2) right, reasonable
ubeubeshi—right, appropriate
ubuya—birth (delivery, parturition) chamber (note 400)
ubuyashinai—birth present (note 112)
uchi—see uchiginu
Uchi—(1) Imperial Palace, (2) Emperor
uchiaogu—to be proud, triumphant
uchiawasu—to arrange (adjust) carefully
Uchifushi—mother of Lady Sakyō (note 768)
uchifusu—to lie down (note 769)
uchigi—(1) long, flowing robe (worn over the hitoegasane and below the hakama (App. 8a, no. 15), (2) formal Court robe
uchigiki—note, notebook
uchiginu—beaten silk
uchihae—continuously, for a long time
uchihashi—provisional bridge (note 517)
uchihayasu—to spur on, incite
uchihazusu—to miss, fail, lose
uchikaesu—to overturn, upset
uchikasume—with a trace of; oblique, implicit
uchikatarau—see katarau
uchikunzu—see kunzu
uchime—gloss of beaten silk
uchimijiroku—to move (one's body)
uchinagamu—(1) to yawn, (2) to think, be sunk in thought
uchinarebamu—to wear for a long time, wear out
uchi no ko—temple attendant, acolyte
Uchi no Kura—Imperial Storehouse (notes 491, 514)
Uchi no Ōidono—Minister of the Centre (note 472) (App. 7a)
Uchi no Otodo—see Uchi no Ōidono
uchi su—to do, say
uchisutsu—(1) to overlook, let pass, (2) to neglect, pay no attention to
uchitokegoto (iu)—(to speak) without reserve
uchitoku—(1) to be off one's guard, relax one's attention, be at ease (unconcerned), (2) to be intimate, friendly
uchiwa su—to fan
uchiwatari—in (about) the Palace
uchizōzoku—see sōzoku su

321

Uda—(867–931) 59th Emperor, reg. 887–97 (notes 72, 275) (App. 6a, no. 1)

Udaiben—Major Controller of the Right (note 256) (App. 7a)

Udaijin—see Migi no Otodo

Udo Hama—Udo Beach, a folk-song (note 670)

ue—(1) Palace, (2) same as Tenjō no Ma (note 249), (3) the (Imperial) Presence, (4) His (Her) Majesty, (5) Madam (used of the principal consort), (6) wife, principal consort, (7) roof, (8) senior courtier (note 11)

uebito—see tenjōbito

Uemo(n)—lady-in-waiting to Empress Sadako (note 970)

ue no hakama—over-trousers (note 623)

Ue no Hōgan—Lieutenant of the Audience Chamber (note 249)

ue no kinu—over-robe of Court costume (notes 265, 623) (App. 8a, no. 1)

Ue no On-mae—His Majesty the Emperor; (rarely) Her Majesty the Empress

ueya—room in Seiryō Palace used by the Empress's ladies-in-waiting

uezōshi—special attendant who served in the Palace on occasions like the Gosechi Festival

ugaru—see kokorougaru

ugemberi (no tatami)—elegant straw mat with floral design (App. 8b, no. 6)

uguisu—Japanese bird usually translated as 'nightingale' (note 230)

ukabu—to memorize, learn by heart

ukebaru—to be arrogant, proud, fearless

ukehiku—to accept, agree

ukimon—material with a lightly embroidered design

Ukon (Efu)—(Headquarters of the) Inner Palace Guards, Right Division (App. 9e, no. 6)

Ukon no Naishi—Lady Ukon, daughter of Fujiwara no Suetsuna; served as lady-in-waiting to the Emperor (note 52)

Ukyō—lady-in-waiting to Empress Sadako

Uma—used in names, titles, etc., to refer to the Imperial Stables (note 45)

uma—piece (in backgammon)

umaba—horse-racing track

umago—grandchild

uma no hanamuke—farewell present (note 112)

Uma no Hi—Day of the Horse, 7th of the 12 days in the traditional cycle (App. 3)

Uma no Kami—Director of the Bureau of Imperial Stables

Uma no Myōbu—lady-in-waiting in charge of the Emperor's cat (note 45)

Uma no Naishi no Suke—lady in the Palace Attendants' Office (note 515)

Uma (no toki)—Hour of the Horse, about noon (App. 3)

Umaosa—Master of the Horse

umasae—see umazoe

umazoe, umazoi—mounted escort, attendant on horseback (note 988)

Umazukasa—Office of the Imperial Stables

ume—(1) plum, (2) colour combination in which the outside of the garment is white and the lining is dark red (notes 23, 386)

Umetsubo—building in the Imperial Palace compound (note 345) (App. 9f, no. 1)

Ummei Den—Ummei Palace, building in the Imperial Palace compound (note 12) (App. 9f, no. 12)

unai—(1) style of fastening a child's hair at the back of the neck, (2) child

under-robe—shitagasane

underservant—ōyakebito

Uneme—Palace Girl (note 202)

uneven shading—murago

unlucky direction—katafusagari

u no hana—deutzia scabra (notes 3, 192, 194, 853)

Urabon—Festival of the Dead (notes 662, 1090) (App. 1)

ura nashi—frank, open, candid

uraue—reverse, contrary (note 636)

uraura—clear, bright, glorious, serene, splendid

Urin In—Urin Temple near the Kamo Shrines (note 235)

urusashi—clever, ingenious

uruwashi—(1) beautiful, elegant, (2) splendid, superb, (3) correct, decorous, exact, proper, neat, tidy

uryōu—to appeal, complain, entreat

usekakuru—to disappear, abscond

ushi—see mono ushi

ushikai—driver (attendant) of an ox-carriage, ox-driver

ushikaiwarawa—see *ushikai*

ushin—searching for effect, pretentiousness, affected elegance

ushinau—(1) to kill, put to death, (2) to omit, leave out

ushioni—the cow-headed devil (note 719)

ushiro—train, tail (of a robe)

ushirode—(a person's) retreating figure, appearance from the back

ushirometashi—(1) uneasy, unsure, dubious, worrying, (2) shady, suspicious, underhand

ushiromu—to take trouble for someone, look after, advise

ushitora—north-east, the unlucky direction (note 73) (App. 3)

usu—(1) to disappear, (2) to leave, withdraw, retire, (3) to die, (4) to lose (its) charm, pall

usuiro—light violet

usuraka—light, thin

usuyō—fine, smooth Japanese paper, vellum

uta—Japanese poem, song (notes 86, 1007, 1065)

utate—terribly, odiously, confoundedly, devilishly, unfeelingly, cruelly, outrageously

utateshi—charmless, dull, dreary, unpleasant, hateful

utayomigamashi—giving oneself the air of being a poet, posing as a poet

utena—throne, platform (note 338)

utomashi—distant, estranged

utsu—(1) to beat (full) silk, etc., (2) to play (strum) (a zither)

Utsubo Monogatari—lengthy romance in 20 books written towards the end of the 10th century (notes 352, 369, 827, 835)

utsukushi—(1) adorable, lovable, charming, lovely, sweet, (2) beautiful

utsukushigaru—see *utsukushimu*

utsukushimu—to pet, fondle, spoil

utsuru—to fade

uwagumoru—to be dull, hazy, cloudy

uwaosoi—overgarment, overwear

u zu—to worry, be troubled, vexed

uzuchi—hare-stick (notes 113, 321) (App. 8d, no. 4)

uzue—hare-wand (notes 321, 385) (App. 1)

Uzuki—(1) see *u no hana*, (2) U no Hana (Fourth) Month (note 3)

Uzumasa—site of Kōryū Temple (note 920) (App. 9c, no. 6)

uzumoru—to be heaped (in a pile)

wabishi—(1) troublesome, difficult, (2) anxious, nervous, (3) wretched, lamentable, sad, pitiful

wabu—(1) to be perplexed, embarrassed, worried, nonplussed, (2) to be sad, sorry, miserable

wagashirigao—expression (on one's face) suggesting that the idea (plan, etc.) which one has derived from someone else is in fact one's own

wagon—6-string zither (note 89) (App. 8d, no. 9)

waistband ribbon—*kutai*

waistcoat—*akome*

wakadatsu—to be youthful, young-looking

Wakana no Sekku—Festival of Young Herbs (notes 5, 608) (App. 1)

Wakan Rōei Shū—anthology of Chinese and Japanese verse compiled *c.* 1010 by Fujiwara no Kintō (notes 291, 319, 363, 510, 628, 643, 798, 1079, 1098, 1099)

wakayagidatsu—to make (oneself) look young, rejuvenate

wakeme—parting (of the hair)

wakiake—garment (worn by officers) open from the sleeves down to the hem (note 252)

makite—especially, above all

wananaku—to be frizzled, curled, wrinkled

Wang Chih—hero of a Chinese story (notes 309, 1092)

Wani—(d. *c.* 450) scholar who is traditionally believed to have introduced Chinese writing and classics into Japan (note 80)

warafuda—round straw cushion

wara(wa)(be)—(1) child (boy or girl), (2) page, (3) girl attendant in the Palace (note 431)

warawamai—attendants' dance (note 432) (App. 1)

warawame—young girl

warawaoi—childhood, early years

ward—*jō*
Wardrobe—Nui Dono, Mi-Kushige
ware—himself (see also *Dictionary of Selected Forms in Classical Japanese Literature*)
warekara—shrimp-insect (note 238)
ware wa to omou—to be conceited, proud, pleased with oneself
wari nashi—(1) worried, perplexed, bewildered, distressed, puzzled, at one's wits' end, dismayed, (2) reckless, forcible, (3) immoderate, terrible, (4) unreasonable, absurd, indiscriminate, undue, (5) unavoidable, necessary
waroshi—(1) common, vulgar, of low birth, (2) trifling, valueless, despicable, (3) coarse, crude, plain, simple, (4) bad, wrong, hopeless, (5) unskilful, awkward, clumsy, (6) ugly
wasuru—to forsake, abandon
wata—band, curvature
watadono—corridor, passage, gallery (App. 8b, no. 3)
wataginu—padded (wadded) garment (note 823)
watari—ferry
watari—neighbourhood, environment
wataru—(1) to go, come, proceed, arrive, visit, (2) to pass, go by, walk past, (3) to stretch out, extend
watatsumi—(1) sea god, (2) sea, (3) conventional epithet for woman diver (notes 380, 800)
watch—*toki*
watered rice—*suihan*
waza—thing, fact
waza to—particularly, especially
wazurau—(1) to fall ill, (2) to grieve, (3) to have difficulty in
Weaver Festival—Tanabata Matsuri
weeping—note 994
Wen hsüan—famous Chinese anthology, known in Japan as *Monzen* (notes 832, 892)
West City—Nishi no Kyō
willow-green—*aoyagi*

yadori—coach house
yadori no tsukasa—temporary office or official
yagate—(1) at once, directly, (2) as they are, without any change (cf. *sono mama*, *sunawachi*), (3) soon, presently

yakata—(1) compartment, interior (of a carriage), (2) roofed boat, boat without a cabin, barge
yakata naki kuruma—uncovered carriage or wagon used to transport goods and having no compartment for passengers (note 245)
yakō—night patrol
Yakugai—cup made of Yaku shell, a green conch-shell with black spots; manufactured in Yakushima, an island off S. Kyūshū
Yaku shell—Yakugai
yamaai—mountain sedge, *polygonum tinctorium* (note 420)
yamabuki—(1) yellow (mountain) rose, *kerria japonica* (note 684), (2) colour combination in which the outside of the garment is light yellowish brown and the lining is yellow or red (note 23)
yamadori—copper pheasant (note 224)
yamagomori—mountain retreat (note 305)
yamai—see *yamaai*
yamamomo—red myrtle (note 720)
Yama no Eki—Yama (Mountain) Posting-Station (note 880)
Yamanoi (no) Dainagon—*see* Fujiwara no Michiyori
Yamashinadera—Yamashina Temple in Nara, usually known as Kōfuku Ji (note 61)
yamasuge—snake's grass, *ophiopogon japonicus*
Yamasuge no Hashi—Yamasuge Bridge in Shimotsuke (note 286)
yamatachibana—wild orange tree
Yamato Monogatari—10th-century collection of stories, centred on Japanese poems and often concerned with actual happenings during the previous century (notes 62, 202, 221, 274)
yamu—to cure (an illness, etc.)
yamu—to take offence, be angry
yamu koto (or *goto*) *nashi*—(1) dignified, impressive, of high rank (quality), (2) valuable, precious, dear
yanagi—(1) willow, (2) colour combination in which the outside of the garment is white and the lining is green (note 23)
yanaibako—wicker (osier) basket

Yang Kuei-fei—beautiful concubine of the T'ang Emperor described in a famous poem of Po Chü-i (her Japanese name being Yōkihi) (note 196)

yangoto nashi—see *yamu koto nashi*

ya osoki to—no sooner than, as soon as

yarau—to drive away, force to leave

yarido—sliding-door (App. 8b, no. 23)

yarisugusu—to let (someone) pass

yarisutsu—to tear up and throw away

yariyosu—to draw near, approach

yasashigaru—(1) to be embarrassed, ashamed, confused, (2) to be amiable, soft, gentle

yasoji—80 years old

yasukarazu iu—to criticize, find fault with

yasurau—to stand still for a while, stop

yatsuru—to be shabby, worn out

Yawata—site of Iwashimizu no Hachiman Shrine (note 597)

yaya—well well, oh, good heavens!

Yayoi—Ever-Growing (Third) Month (note 3)

yo—(1) world, (2) period, time, (3) relations (intercourse) between a man and a woman

yō—lustre, gloss

yobai—(1) shooting star (in *yobaiboshi*), (2) a man's clandestine visit to his mistress at night (note 891)

yobe—last night (evening)

yobimotsu—to call out, ask to come along

Yodo(gawa)—Yodo River, large river south of the capital, emptying into Ōsaka Bay (App. 9b, no. 4)

yodono—(1) bedroom, (2) Yodo Plain (note 1102)

Yodo no Watari—Yodo Ferry (note 542)

yo fukashi—towards dawn, towards the end of the night

yogaru—to spend the night away (from one's wife, etc.), to stop visiting (someone) at night

yo hitoyo—all night long

yoi no sō—priest on night duty (notes 588, 625)

yoki—axe (note 385)

yōki—tray, platter

Yōkihi—Japanese name of Yang Kuei-fei

yoki tokoro—good rank, high social standing

Yōmei Mon—gate at the east of the Greater Imperial Palace (note 72) (App. 9e, no. 12)

yomihesu—to overwhelm (daunt) someone by one's poetic skill

yomogi—sage-brush, *artemisia indica* (note 789)

yo ni—exceedingly

yo ni shirazu—unheard of, unspeakable

yo no naka—(1) the world, society, (2) relations between a man and a woman

yo no naka (nado) sawagashi—an epidemic rages, there is an epidemic

yo no oboe—fame, reputation

yoori—breaking the knots (in preparation for the Great Purification) (note 725)

yoriku—to go up to, approach

yorimashi—medium (note 106)

yorobou—to totter, stagger

yorokobu—(1) to express one's thanks (gratitude), (2) congratulate

yoroshi—(1) well-bred (note 123), (2) fair, moderate; commonplace, ordinary, tolerable, average, passable

yoroshū omou—to disregard, take scant interest in

yoru no otodo—bedchamber

yosari—(in) the evening

yoshi—connexion, acquaintance

yoshi—(1) well-born, of high rank, (2) pretty, beautiful

yōshi—girl

yoshi nashi—useless, futile, meaningless, pointless

Yoshino—mountainous area some 60 miles south of the capital (notes 32, 365) (App. 9b, no. 7)

yoshiyoshi—never mind! I don't care

yosōshi—majestic, imposing, impressively attired

yosou—to compare, liken to

yō su—to polish

yosuga—affinity, relation, companion, spouse, mate

young gentleman—*tonobara*

young nobleman—*kindachi*

yowainobu—to promote longevity, extend one's life span

yo (wo) komete—before daybreak, while it is still night

yōyō—gradually, slowly

yu—hot spring (note 546)

yuamu—to take a bath

yudake—wide sleeve (of a robe), fashion of making one sleeve or both sleeves especially wide (note 1111)

yūdasuki—mulberry sash worn by Shintō priests (note 847)

yuedatsu—to give oneself airs, strike an attitude

yūgao—moonflower, bottle gourd, *lagenaria vulgaris* (note 299)

Yugei—Quiver-Bearer (note 248)

yui—roll (of silk, etc.)

yukari—affinity (note 194)

yukashi—(1) see *mono yukashi*, (2) interesting, delightful

yukashigaru—to be curious, intrigued

Yukinari—*see* Fujiwara no Yukinari

yukiyama—snow mountain (note 376)

yumeawase—dream interpretation (note 935)

yuminarashi—twanging the bow-string (note 268)

yu no ha—leaf of a citron tree

yuraraka—loose

yurubu—to become less cold, wear off (of cold); melt, thaw (note 422)

yurugasu—(1) to exert oneself, be at pains, cudgel (one's brains), (2) to jog, totter, move unsteadily, (3) to shake

yurugiariku—to walk (1) proudly, (2) restlessly, uneasily

yururaka—slow, gentle, easy

yūsari—evening, night

yūshi—traveller

yusuru—to bustle, fuss, stir

yuu—mulberry

yuyushi—(1) grave, ominous, terrible, fearful, (2) disgusting, disagreeable, repulsive, detestable, (3) brave, bold

yuzuke—see *suihan*

yuzuriha—*daphniphyllum* (note 220)

zae—learning, scholarship

zae no onoko—Kagura singer

-zama—(1) (in the) direction (of), (2) appearance, seeming; likelihood

zenji—former governor

zither—*koto, kin*

Zō—*see* Jō (Lieutenant)

Zō—*see* Jō (Secretary in a Ministry)

Zodiac (Chinese), signs of—note 73 and App. 3

zōgan—'elephant eyes', a type of material (note 985)

Zoku Gosen Shū—12th-century anthology of poems (note 1002)

zōshi—maid of all work, general servant

zōshi—(1) sleeping quarters assigned to ladies-in-waiting, officials, etc. in the Palace, (2) room, hall

zōshiki—(1) servant, attendant, lackey, (2) Subordinate. Official in the Emperor's Private Office, one of 8 young men who served in a lowly capacity in this Office, but who were usually promoted to be Chamberlains (note 911)

zuhō—(Buddhist) rite of incantation (note 586)

zuijin—after-runner, escort

zukyō—recitation of the Sutras, reading of the Scriptures

zumon su—to say a prayer, recite a spell (charm)

zunsa—see *zusa*

zun zu—see *zu su*

zuryō—provincial governor, deputy governor, or other high provincial official (note 846)

zusa—attendant, servant

zushi—small cupboard (note 657)

zu su—to recite, chant (note 746)

zuzu—rosary